INTRANETS VS. LOTUS NOTES

INTRANETS VS. LOTUS NOTES

Joseph T. Sinclair
David B. Hale

AP Professional

AP Professional is a Division of Academic Press, Inc.

Boston San Diego New York
London Sydney Tokyo Toronto

AP PROFESSIONAL

An Imprint of ACADEMIC PRESS, INC.
A Division of HARCOURT BRACE & COMPANY

ORDERS (USA and Canada): 1-800-3131-APP or APP@ACAD.COM
AP Professional Orders: 6277 Sea Harbor Dr., Orlando, FL 32821-9816

Europe/Middle East/Africa: 0-11-44 (0) 181-300-3322
Orders: AP Professional 24-28 Oval Rd., London NW1 7DX

Japan/Korea: 03-3234-3911-5
Orders: Harcourt Brace Japan, Inc., Ichibancho Central Building 22-1, Ichibancho Chiyoda-Ku, Tokyo 102

Australia: 02-517-8999
Orders: Harcourt Brace & Co. Australia, Locked Bag 16, Marrickville, NSW 2204 Australia

Other International: (407) 345-3800
AP Professional Orders: 6277 Sea Harbor Dr., Orlando FL 32821-9816

Editorial: 1300 Boylston St., Chestnut Hill, MA 02167 (617)232-0500

Web: http://www.apnet.com/approfessional

This book is printed on acid-free paper. ∞

United Kingdom Edition published by
ACADEMIC PRESS LIMITED
24–28 Oval Road, London NW1 7DX

ISBN 0-12-645540-6

Printed in the United States of America
96 97 98 99 IP 9 8 7 6 5 4 3 2 1

Contents

Chapter 20: Cross-Platform Document Standardization 361

Chapter 21: TCP/IP Groupware Briefs 379

Acknowledgements

This book came at a transition time just as many software vendors were introducing new TCP/IP groupware or porting their existing groupware to work on intranets and the Internet. What started out as a simple project ended up as a project overwhelmed with a fast growing body of competent groupware to consider. And there's more to come. Thus, I must acknowledge that we couldn't cover it all, and there's lots of good groupware now available that's not covered or is covered too lightly. My thanks to my co-author David Hale, network administrator, Knoxville, Tennessee, who worked hard on the book and to David Smith, network consultant, Dripping Springs, Texas, with whom I discussed over the phone many topics in the book. Especially valuable in my research was *Introduction to Groupware, Workflow, and Workgroup Computing* by Setrag Khoshafian and Marek Buckiewicz, a valuable book for those responsible for managing the use of groupware. A special thanks to Carole McClendon, Waterside Productions, Lafayette, California, who did a great job as an agent.

As always, my thanks to my spouse Lani Wallin Sinclair and my daughter Brook for their support and endurance through the arduous process of writing the book and to my in-laws Jack and Mary Wallin for their support during prolonged visits.

Joseph T. Sinclair

Chapter 1

INTRODUCTION

This book presents the various aspects of collaborative work on PC network systems and shows how you can use existing Internet programs to handle such collaboration. Is this a Notes bashing book? No. On the contrary, Lotus Notes is the archetypal groupware program with which all groupware programming must be compared. This book reviews the features of Lotus Notes as well as those of a variety of Internet programs. Lotus Notes emerges as today's leader in integration and functionality. But maximum integration and functionality may not be for everyone, and you can make other intelligent choices.

At the one extreme is the Wall Street financial firm where most of the work is analytic and intellectual. Most of the executives graduated from top universities, many with MBAs, JDs, or Ph.Ds. The support staff is well educated. Everyone uses a PC extensively. Learning another computer program is just one of many tasks on the list of things to do today. Lotus Notes is the choice for collaborative work via the office PC network.

At the other extreme is the firm in which much of the work is clerical. Most of the executives are supervisors. Few of the employees have college degrees. Learning new computer programs without requisite training is not part of the job description. In this business environment one or two simple Internet programs used via an internal TCP/IP network may suffice nicely.

Take a closer look. Notes has a lot of functionality built in. That's great if you need it all, but it comes at a cost: the cost of training. If you don't have employees who can learn it on their own, which most businesses do not, training becomes a major concern. On the other hand, if you don't need all the functionality, a World Wide Web (Web) browser and an Internet e-mail program may cover many collaboration tasks for you. A Web browser is easy to learn: a half hour with a fellow employee is all it takes. An e-mail program takes a little longer, but not much.

But the Internet? Yes, Internet programs are being used on internal networks (e.g., LANs and WANs) that use TCP/IP as a network protocol. Transmission Control Protocol (TCP) and Internet Protocol (IP) together make up the network protocol for the Internet (i.e., the invisible programs that make the Internet work). TCP/IP can run on an internal network, too, and coexist with other network protocols. Thus, the same programs you use on the Internet can be used on an internal network. In fact, many business organizations, from large corporations to small firms, are using Internet programs on internal TCP/IP networks (now called *intranets*). Such intranets can be as useful to a three-person firm as they can to a thirty-thousand-person corporation.

GROUPWARE DEFINITION

If you approach the idea of groupware from the point of view of seeking a definitive description, you may find one that's plausible. Unfortunately, that might be more of a setback to your understanding than a step forward. In fact, there seem to be many definitions of groupware, none of which measures up to the task of encompassing all the human collaborative activity that takes place online now or that will take place online in the future. This book uses an approach that offers an open-ended definition of groupware. Below you will see the book's definition outlined with group software ideas, some actual and a few speculative. The book covers each of the software ideas more thoroughly in later chapters. Any categorization is arbitrary, and you will see below that in each section the book provides two blank lines for you to add your own ideas for new groupware or for existing software that might be converted into a new type of groupware. Use more lines if you need to. Groupware is still an infant, and perhaps one of your ideas will help it grow.

Communications

- E-mail
- Phone
- Video-Phone
- ____________________
- ____________________

A clever computer user can use a good e-mail program to perform the functions of many of the groupware ideas below. E-mail has recently gained new capability and is now an even more powerful groupware program than it was prior to 1996. The idea of using a telephone online or using videoconferencing are not earthshaking by themselves, but when you combine them with some of the other groupware ideas, they can create new capability for productive collaborative efforts.

Work Management

- To-do list
- Scheduling
- Work flow
- Task management
- Project management
- ____________________
- ____________________

Work management software comes in various configurations to suit various work tasks, work systems, and work styles. Although there are already some well-known labels for such software, there are likely to be new variations of such software in the future together with new labels.

Conferencing

- Real time (text, audio, video)
- Convenient time (e-mail lists, forums)
- White board
- Story board
- ____________________
- ____________________

Online conferencing can be easy, convenient, efficient, and inexpensive. It already has a productive history, but the story is just beginning.

Publishing

- Image management (documents images)
- Document management (ASCII documents)
- Interactive multimedia document management
- File sharing
- Information sharing (via databases)
- Collaboration
- ____________________
- ____________________

Publishing is essential for many collaborative efforts. In a sense, publishing is simply making specific information available to a group that requires it. Although most publishing is currently text, that will change as digital multimedia technology pervades the business world. For the people who work to create a published product or whose work is creating documents, collaboration software provides a productive way to work on documents together.

Training

- Seminar
- ____________________
- ____________________

Computer Based Training (CBT) is not necessarily thought of as a collaborative activity. Nonetheless, it can be, and training is becoming an increasingly important business activity.

COMBINATIONS

Although the above definition of groupware may seem clearly and neatly outlined with individual software ideas, most group software combines a number of the ideas above. You might even think of such software ideas as components or building blocks. Additionally, you can use some types of groupware, even if they seem singular in purpose, to perform other functions (i.e., emulate other groupware). For instance, you can use collaboration software, which is document centric, as task management software.

OTHER CONSIDERATIONS

Infrastructure

- Networks
- Administration
- Security
- Databases
- Replication
- Routing
- Development platform
- Server software
- Client software

Some of the software technologies used with groupware do not seem significant by themselves. When you use them with group software, however, they provide the essential infrastructure to support collaborative online work. The book therefore provides background information on them.

Dedicated Groupware

Groupware by definition is software with a *generic* quality that allows you to develop applications dedicated to a wide variety of specific tasks with a minimum of programming. An increasing amount of client/server software that looks like groupware is *dedicated* to specific uses. The Great Plains client/server accounting software provides a good example. It consists of a participatory online accounting system and offers more than just number crunching. Such dedicated groupware, however, is beyond the scope of this book. Although this book advocates the broadest possible definition of groupware to facilitate new ideas and new uses, software dedicated to one business activity is perhaps better evaluated with similar software rather than with groupware.

TCP/IP

Groupware has been around for a few years. Most groupware runs on Local Area Networks (LANs) or Wide Area Networks (WANs), which until recently were unlikely to be TCP/IP networks. Because TCP/IP can coexist with other network protocols, many organizations convert their LANs and WANs to TCP/IP specifically to use Internet programs. This is an easy and inexpensive means of being able to use Internet technology internally. This book limits its coverage to considering traditional and new TCP/IP client/server programs that offer groupware functions. The book also discusses some traditional groupware that has been converted to TCP/IP compatibility. In other words, the book does not cover groupware that won't run on a TCP/IP network.

Keep in mind that individual PCs must have TCP/IP compatibility as well as server computers. You enable a single PC with TCP/IP by using a TCP/IP protocol program. Some operating systems such as Windows 95 have the protocol built in.

INTRANETS

An *intranet* is an internal TCP/IP network situated in an organization. Because TCP/IP works the same whether for an intranet or for the Internet, you can use Internet programs such as Web browsers and Web servers on an intranet. Although the operating system of choice for the Internet has been Unix, the TCP/IP protocol is completely cross-platform and will run on any operating system. Windows NT seems to be growing quickly in popularity for intranets and includes software to fully enable Internet technology. In this book, a great deal of the discussion implies the use of groupware on intranets simply because a great many people working together are employees of the same organization.

Intranet Access to the Internet

All organizations will want to connect their intranets to the Internet for at least three important reasons. First, the connection gives employees e-mail access to the entire world and the entire world e-mail access to employees. E-mail has already carved out a substantial niche in business communications at the expense of the telephone (including fax), the U.S. Postal Service, and even Federal Express; and that niche will grow much larger. Second, the connection gives employees access to the Web, an important information resource growing more important each day. Third, the same programs you use on an intranet you can use on the Internet (e.g., Web browser). No additional software training is required.

An outside connection naturally gives rise to concerns about security. Competent security is a well-established feature of the TCP/IP protocol, and that security capability grows more competent with the current boom in TCP/IP software. A chapter in this book covers network security. For the moment, however, suffice it to say that a connection to the Internet can be made without jeopardizing an organization's security.

The Internet

Although a discussion of groupware seems to imply an intranet, many people who work together are not employees of the same organization. Because TCP/IP groupware can be used over the Internet as easily as over an intranet, the ideas and discussions presented in this book apply to the Internet as well to intranets.

When Is an Intranet More Than an Intranet?

Organizations will find intranets very valuable for a variety of work tasks. Sometimes an intranet is not enough, however, and an Internet connection proves to be a valuable part of the intranet system. The Internet provides a convenient means of enabling employees in the field to remotely access an intranet. Rather than phone in via long distance to a special bulletin-board-like system, employees in the field can get local access to the Internet and thereby connect to their organization's intranet. Remote computing via the Internet is potentially more powerful and less expensive than alternatives.

Home workers use a special type of remote computing. With a dial-up Internet account, an employee working at home can connect to the organization's intranet via the Internet for long periods at a low cost. This capability effectively integrates the home office into the organization and potentially reduces overhead.

Most organizations find a growing need to be in close communication with more and more of their vendors. As outsourcing grows, more vendors will be service or information providers that require convenient and easy communication with the organization. The

Internet furnishes an ideal means of linking organizations with their vendors. The Internet extends an intranet to include an organization's vendors at a low cost.

When Is the Internet an Intranet?

Do you have a small organization? Two people? Ten people? You might find it more cost-effective to use the Internet as your intranet rather than to get an LAN up and running with a server computer and server software. All you need are a few dial-up accounts with an Internet Service Provider (ISP). ISPs usually have special rates for groups. You can rent space on your ISP's hard disk and use the Web server to create your own intranet Web site too. The practicality of this approach depends on your network requirements, but don't overlook this possibility.

If you use the Internet as your intranet, you will probably need plenty of hard disk space. Most ISPs charge a lot for extra megabytes of storage. One possible way to get around that is to have your ISP co-host a hard disk drive for you. You provide the SCSI-2 hard disk, your ISP installs it, and you work out a fair additional monthly charge. This way you may be able to have 500MB on the Internet very inexpensively. A 500MB SCSI-2 hard disk costs a nominal amount today.

One can magically convert a twisted pair (normal physical telephone line) for one analog telephone line into two digital telephone lines (two B channels) by converting the twisted pair to an ISDN line. Each of the two digital lines runs twice as fast as an analog phone line, and they can even be bound together for a faster line yet. The process of dialing up is much faster on a digital line, too. ISDN is already inexpensive in many states and getting less expensive in others. Thus, you may be able to add faster telephone lines with a quicker dial-up at a reasonable cost without adding physical telephone lines into your office. This technology enables the Internet to be a better intranet.

Beyond ISDN is cable access to the Internet via your cable TV provider. The convenient feature about cable access to the Internet is that it runs full time. It's always on; it's very fast; and presumably it will be cost-effective for you as well. Don't sign the lease for that new office unless the building has cable TV service throughout.

INTERNET, INTRANET

The unfortunate choice of the term *intranet* as a name for internal TCP/IP networks was a result of the audio deficiencies of digital journalists. These people spend most of their time writing—many of them at home now—and seldom talk with anyone. The term intranet with a lowercase *i* is easily distinguishable from Internet with an uppercase *I*; that is until you pronounce it. In conversation, of course, Internet and intranet are indistinguishable, thereby condemning the Net literati to a sentence of prolonged confusion. To end this topic on a more optimistic note, however, it is becoming clear that people will talk less and less and e-mail more in the future; thus, the problem will resolve itself.

WHAT THIS BOOK OFFERS

Groupware is a complex topic. This book extracts a derivative outline of the various groupware functions from relevant group software and shows how you can perform groupware functions using specific Internet programs. The choice of programs used as examples does not constitute an endorsement of such programs. Any such an endorsement without a complete and careful analysis of all programs available would be an affront to the energetic North American software industry that generates this superb technology. The book instead uses each program featured as an example of its particular genre.

An endorsement of any particular Internet program would not make sense for another reason. The number of new Internet programs, especially Web programs, makes TCP/IP networks an increasingly robust environment for which to create software. Any preference for a program presented by this book might be obsolete as soon as the next great new program rolled off the software assembly line, which could be before the book even reaches the shelves in the bookstores.

Clearly, the Internet and the Web will grow more robust more quickly than the other groupware development environments such as Lotus Notes. (On the other hand, Lotus Notes is well connected to the Internet and is itself part of the Internet environment. Presumably, Lotus Notes will be able to take advantage of anything the Internet has to offer.) The reality is that each business activity has its particular set of requirements. Out of the richness of the TCP/IP groupware offerings, each business will make choices that address its needs.

Businesses will make such choices on the basis of cost, training requirements, scalability, ease of conversion, maintenance requirements, and the other usual considerations. The choices will not be the same for everyone. There is no one-size-fits-all solution, and the choices will expand for a while before they start to consolidate. Thus, when this book offers you examples of how your collaborative work requirements may be met by the various TCP/IP programs presented, it is not to provide you with answers but to give you a basis on which to make better choices.

The approach of the book emphasizes how to use TCP/IP programs to get group work done rather than how to set up and run TCP/IP systems and software. Therefore, it is a nonprogrammer's book, although programmers may find some useful ideas within. Additionally, the book does not pretend or attempt to cover expensive enterprise systems; therefore, network operators and managers may find more information elsewhere that pertains to their activities and concerns. On the other hand, small businesses can't afford full-time network managers, and personnel can't take the time to develop the expertise that would enable them to read and understand books written for network managers. This fact provides another reason the coverage of programs is generally limited to shrink-wrapped (retail) software rather than enterprise software. Much shrink-wrapped software is usable by nonprogrammers.

There is another reason shrink-wrapped software is favored over enterprise software. Most groups or teams to function well must be relatively small. The larger the group, the more complex the group's structure must be to guide the group's activities successfully and the more complex the groupware must be, too. Much groupware is developed with small groups in mind rather as a means to bring wholesale increased efficiency to large organizations.

WHAT THIS BOOK DOESN'T OFFER

This book does not compare prices of the various groupware alternatives. That task is better left to the magazines, which are more current. Although Lotus Notes often appears to be the most expensive of the groupware alternatives, a first-rate suite of Internet programs may be just as expensive or even more expensive. In addition, this book makes no attempt to catalog all of the Internet programs, or other programs, that you might use to provide groupware functionality. The widespread innovations made by software publishers in this niche of the market today are astounding. Using Internet programs to match the functionality of Lotus Notes is a grass roots phenomenon. Businesses do it, and software publishers are responding vigorously to this new market. In 1996 and beyond, hundreds and then thousands of new TCP/IP programs will become available that address the various aspects of groupware functionality. Any attempt to catalog them all in a book now would be instantly obsolete.

CLIENT/SERVER

Groupware is a client/server idea. Do not confuse the groupware client/server software concept with the physical existence of the client and server. For a LAN, the server is a dedicated computer, often a high-powered PC; that is, it is a computer dedicated to the task of serving files off its hard disk to other PCs on the network. A LAN server usually has a large hard disk and often does not even have a monitor or keyboard. The other computers on the LAN, which do something, are client computers (see Figure 1.1). Because this book is not about hardware, however, the terms client, client/server, and server will not mean hardware. For the purposes of this book, the hardware is irrelevant.

TCP/IP is the magic network background software that enables you to run Internet programs on your operating system on your PC yet connect and communicate via a network with other computers using other operating systems. Thus, the computers, the network, and the TCP/IP protocol make up only the infrastructure. What matters to understand this book, however, is client/server *software*. For the purposes of this book, a server is a *program* that runs on one computer but is available across a TCP/IP network that may include variety of computers and operating systems. Similarly, a client is a *program* running on one computer but able to communicate with server programs on other computers via a TCP/IP network. For instance, a Web server provides HTML documents upon request to clients. The client in this case is a Web browser (see Figure 1.2). Keep in mind also that one computer can run multiple servers. For example, a typical Internet service provider (ISP) runs at least four servers on one computer: a File Transfer Protocol (FTP) server, a Gopher server, a Web server, and a

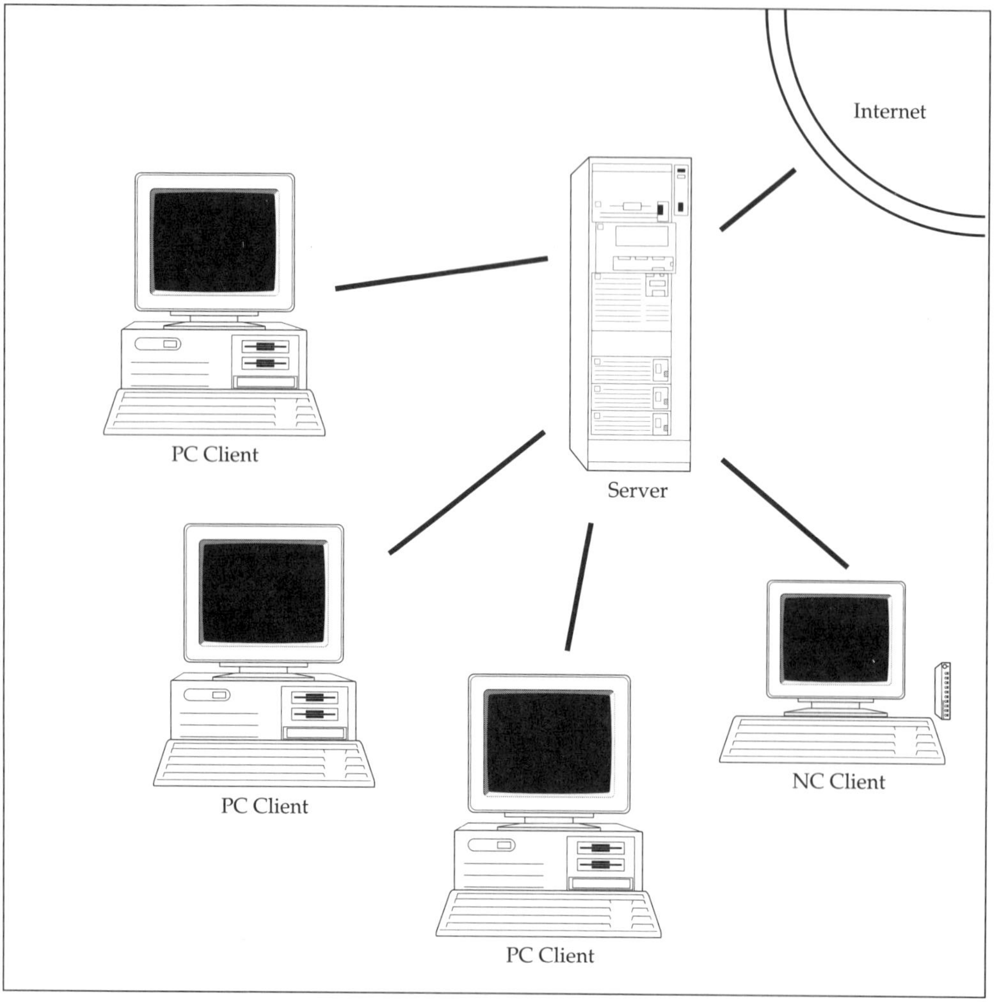

Figure 1.1: A client/server hardware system.

mail server. All these servers are software programs and all run simultaneously.

Every Internet program uses a client/server protocol or *is* a client/server protocol. As long as the client and server use the same protocol, they are compatible and can function together even if they are created by different software publishers. Thus, a Netscape Web browser (Navigator) works with an O'Reilly & Associates Web server (WebSite), because the two are based on the Web protocol (Hypertext Transfer Protocol, HTTP). The Netscape browser, however, will not

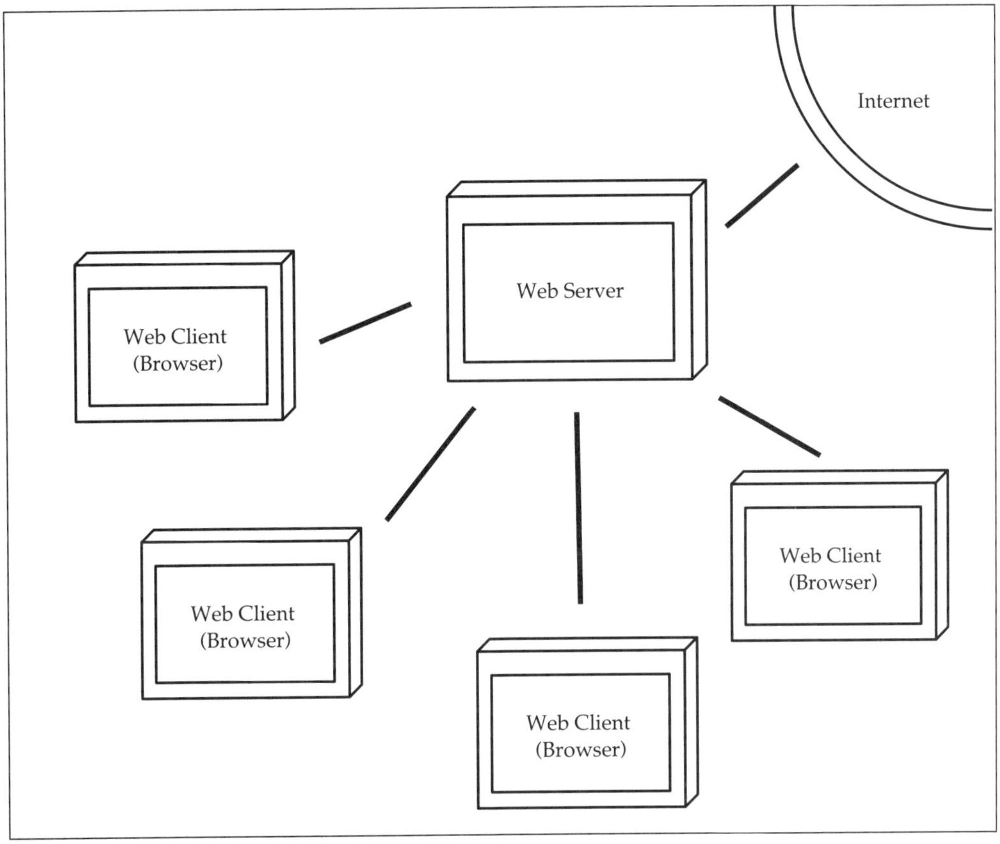

Figure 1.2: For this book, envision a client/server software system. A Web server serves Web clients (browsers).

work with the Real Audio server, which provides sound files unless Netscape incorporates the Real Audio protocol into its browser or provides an Application Programming Interface (API) for Real Audio. (In this particular case that has been done. Netscape uses a generic API that provides for third-party plug-in modules that a Netscape user can easily install. Thus, you can incorporate the Real Audio plug-in into the Netscape browser. Then, the Netscape browser becomes, in effect, a dual client.)

To understand groupware or any other network programs, you must clearly perceive which is the server and which is the client. Sometimes this is not so apparent. For instance, when you use your e-mail program to send a message to a colleague, it appears that you have made a direct communication from you to that person. In fact, e-mail programs (clients) work through a mail server that provides e-mail services. Thus, the communication is not as direct as it seems. Look for the client and look for the server, and you will understand Internet programs better.

The *server* is a program at the Internet site that serves up whatever it is that needs serving. For instance, a Web server serves up HTML documents (ASCII files known as Web pages) to visitors to the Web site who have requested such a document by clicking on a hyperlink using their Web browser. Other types of servers serve up other types of files (text, audio, video, executables). Some servers may have multiple capabilities. For example, the GNNserver (a Web server) can serve up not only Web documents, but also replies to SQL queries made to a database application; it has an Illustra multimedia database engine built in.

How do Internet site *visitors* handle these served-up files? They use a *client*. The other half of the client/server paradigm, the client is simply a program that runs on the visitor's computer, receives the served-up files, and makes some sense out of them. Thus, a Web *browser* is actually a Web client. Who knows why people don't call it a client. The server and the client work together. The server serves up the files, and the client receives them, interprets them, and displays or plays them.

What's confusing is that sometimes servers go by different names such as *daemons* or *databases*. What's more confusing is that often clients go by different names too, such as *browsers*, *players*, *viewers*, or *readers*. But make no mistake, the Internet is a robust network environment replete with client/server systems. To understand what's going on, you must keep the client/server software paradigm in mind. Where there's a client, there's a server somewhere too. If you are a Net surfer, you need to understand only the clients. But when you decide to use groupware on the Internet, you must understand the servers too.

VANs

For business use, the typical ISP provides a FTP server, a Gopher server, a Web server, a mail server, and perhaps a mailing list server (e.g., Listserv or Majordomo). Many of these servers can be obtained at little or no cost from sources on the Internet, which has traditionally been a sharing environment rather than a commercial environment.

These servers are ubiquitous on the Internet, and businesses also use them on intranets. Internet technology, however, is exploding, and the explosion has created a huge new commercial environment on the Internet. Software developers have invented hundreds of new client/server programs for the Internet, particularly for the Web. Naturally, these new servers have a price. Many have a substantial price. The question is, who will make these new servers available to you?

For intranets, you can answer the question quite easily. If you see that new client/server software can provide you with the functionality you seek, you simply buy it, install it, and use it. Using an intranet, you spread the cost of the software over multiple users (i.e., employees in your organization).

Individual computer users (e.g., home workers) as well as small and medium-size firms, however, may use an ISP as their source of network services for business. ISPs typically have many consumer customers and offer business services only as a sideline. The ISPs will be reluctant to spend money for new client/server software systems for small numbers of business customers. Even if they do buy new servers, they will not offer a great variety of servers. Thus, ISPs may not be the answer to the question for those without intranets. (Remember, the question is, who will supply the new server software becoming available.)

A Value Added Network (VAN) is a relatively new concept in network services. VANs are commercial network services that provide specialized servers. Individuals and firms may not be able to afford the high cost of some of the new server software. They will turn to VANs to get specialized network services. VANs offer the new servers, albeit at a higher cost than standard ISP service. Different VANs will offer different combinations of the new servers. CompuServe, for example, offers a Lotus Notes network. Anyone or any business can connect to it (for a fee over and above the normal CompuServe fee) and use Lotus Notes. Although the CompuServe Notes network is not specifically a TCP/IP network yet, it is a high-profile example of a VAN. It offers a specialized server, a Notes server. If you are not on an intranet, there will be many different TCP/IP VANs in the future to provide you with the combination of server services you need. Remember, the ISP or VAN that provides your Internet service can be anywhere (e.g., Hobart, Tasmania). It does not necessarily have to be close to home.

COMPUTERS

Because most computers used in business are PCs, this book discusses primarily PCs and Windows. Mac and Unix computer users should not be scared off, however. Think of the PC as a metaphor for a Mac or for a Unix workstation (as painful as that may be) and of Windows as a metaphor for Mac or X Windows. Much groupware is written for all major computing platforms. As long as the client is written for the operating system you use and the groupware is TCP/IP compatible, you can use the groupware via a TCP/IP network.

GROUPWARE

People have worked together electronically via PC networks or in mainframe/dumb terminal systems for a long time. What is different about groupware?

First, most shared systems generally have been highly structured and have used structured information. A structured system is one that is cast in concrete and provides an individual user little capability to change the system or create diverse subsystems within it. Structured information is information limited to a few formats, usually text and numbers. For instance, from a relational database you typically get text and numbers but nothing else. With digital multimedia technology, people are beginning to routinely use a variety of information forms such as graphic files, audio files, video files, and executables as well as text and numbers. Shared systems either do not handle such media at all or do not handle it well.

Second, most shared systems have not had communications or ad hoc publishing capability built in. You can share the work with others via the computer, but you cannot communicate directly or conveniently with other users within the shared system. Even in systems where communication is provided, you cannot publish selectively or flexibly within the shared system.

On the other hand, groupware has provided a flexible digital environment in which to create diverse collaborative work systems that may be adapted to changing business realities on an ongoing basis with a minimum of additional programming. Groupware also easily accommodates diverse media and provides the capability to handle a specific medium (e.g., digital photographs) as well as an opportunity for multimedia enhancement of traditional information. Groupware usually has communication capability built in and in many cases is itself a type of communications program. Groupware often features selective and flexible multimedia publishing capability, too.

A different way to explain groupware is to say that shared systems require users to conform to a predesignated structure which often models the hierarchical structure of business organization and which dictates the media to be used. The emphasis in such systems is to provide easy interaction *between a user and the system* (see Figure 1.3). In contrast, groupware allows users to make the power of the computer adapt to the way the users desire to work in a wide variety of situations and provides the platform to easily use any digital media required to get the work done. The emphasis in groupware is to provide easy interaction *between users* via the communications and publishing capability of the programs (see Figure 1.4).

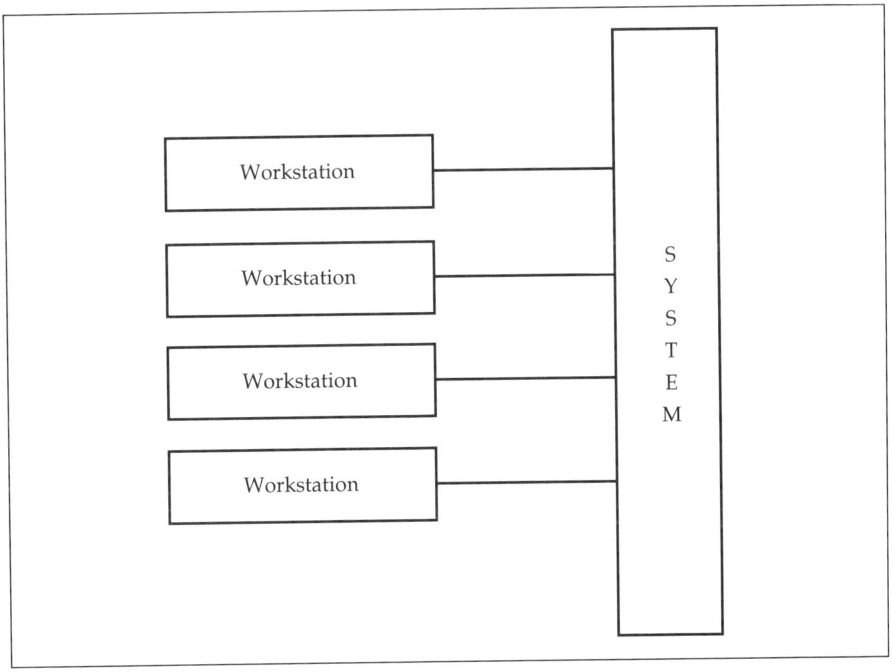

Figure 1.3: A hierarchical shared system.

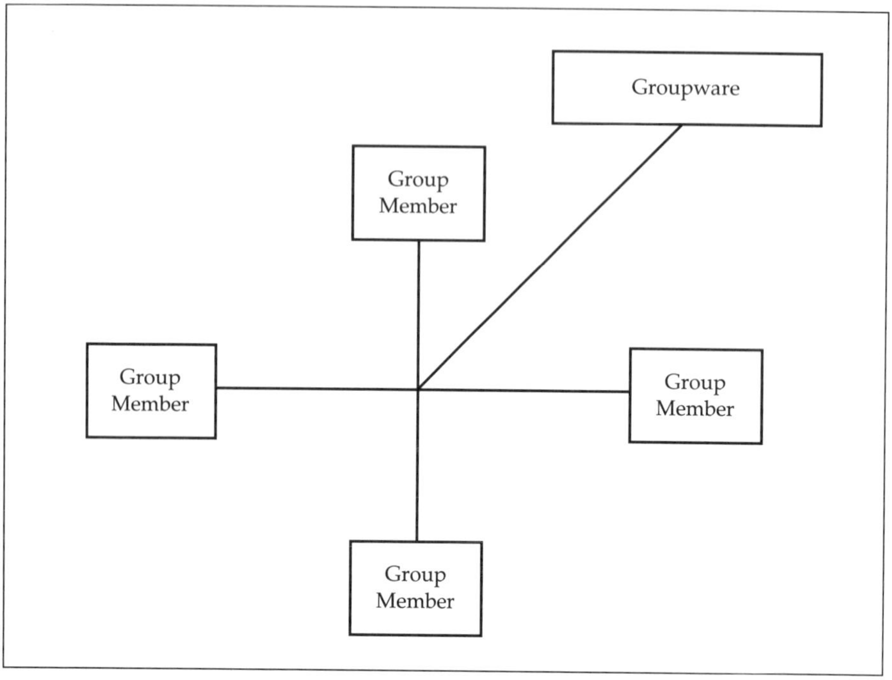

Figure 1.4: Groupware.

Just as shared systems have reflected the traditional hierarchical structure of business organizations, groupware reflects the currently fashionable team approach to getting things done. The real potential of groupware is in empowering people to work together in self-directed groups or teams to achieve a high level of creativity, effectiveness, and efficiency. Shared systems serving hierarchical business structures still have their place, but groupware enabling team work has become a popular new work medium. Often they exist side by side in the same business organization. And they are not so clearly delineated in practice as they are by writers in print. Nonetheless, if you want to take full advantage of groupware, you have to move away from the psychology of hierarchy toward the psychology of team work.

CLASSIFICATION OF GROUPWARE

The classification of groupware that follows is based on time and location and will be helpful to keep in mind for the remainder of the book. It is presented to generate ideas about using groupware rather than as a definitive way to analyze the current digital groupware technologies (see Figure 1.5). Undoubtedly, it will leave out groupware ideas unknown to the authors that will be in shrink-wrap by the time you read this book.

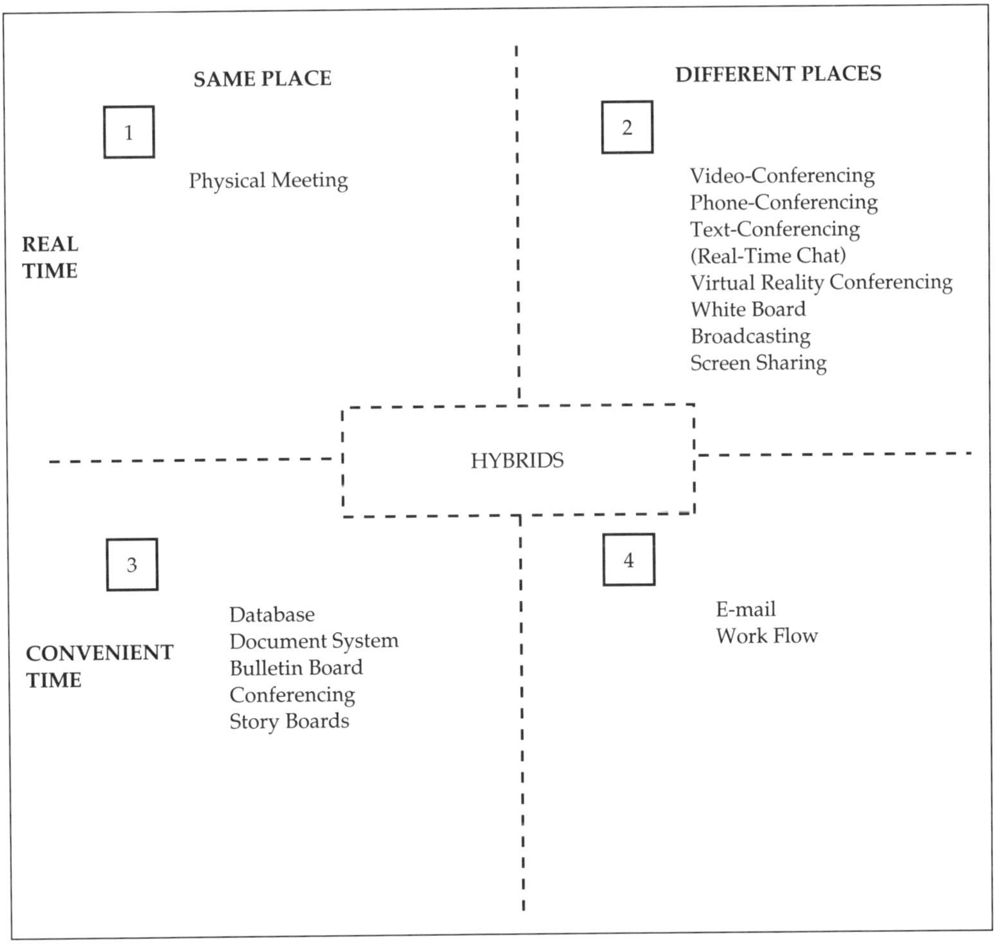

Figure 1.5: Classification of groupware by time and location.

Real Time, Convenient Time

It's important to distinguish between real time and *not-in-real-time,* which this book refers to as *convenient time.* Real time is now. It's live action. It's the way people interact most of the time. It's talking to one another. It's a live television broadcast. It's live videoconferencing. It's typing text back and forth on the Internet Relay Channel (IRC) instead of talking.

Convenient time is history. It's an archive. It has already happened. It's like a letter you get out of the mailbox and read when it's convenient, but it was written a few days ago. It's like a collection of letters; you read them to see what was going on. Unfortunately, things are not so clear cut. Convenient time, although not live, can be up to date. For instance, when you exchange e-mail messages with others in a convenient-time conference, you may carry on a conversation that would have taken 15 minutes in real time. Because of the delay inherent in convenient-time online activities, the same conversation might take place over an a half day, a whole day, or even a week. For most purposes, such a conversation is up to date. It's not really history yet, but it's not live either.

The idea is that real time is often inconvenient to some or even all the group members. For instance, how many times have you attended a meeting at a time when no one in the group wanted to meet, but it was the only time everyone could be present? For matters that do not have to be taken care of right now, groupware offers an alternative. It offers conferences that can be held over a longer period enabling group members to participate at their convenience. In this case, *convenience* means as soon as they can reasonably fit it into their schedule.

Quadrant 1: Real Time, Same Place

The *real-time-same-place* quadrant (1) shows a physical meeting in which people show up in person to interact with other group members. Certainly there are plenty of computer aids for physical meetings. Such software, however, is beyond the scope of this book. It is worth noting, however, that when such computer aids are used, the potential exists to connect them online to integrate them into the digital techniques represented in the remaining quadrants.

Quadrant 2: Real Time, Different Places

The *real-time-different-places* quadrant (2) shows real-time digital conferencing in which people are online at the same time (real time) but are in different places. Phone conferences, videoconferences, and real-time chats (text conferences) are well-known examples. Virtual reality conferencing is now available too. A real-time white board that is used in conjunction with real-time chat or another real-time conferencing technique falls into this category (e.g., Netscape Navigator 3.0 Cool Talk). A broadcast such as from a satellite down-link or a Real Audio stream on the Web is properly placed in this quadrant too. Finally, screen sharing (like a white board) in which all group members can see a screen or window is a workhorse technique for this quadrant. For instance, using any real-time conferencing technique and being able to see a document, a spread sheet, an image, or something else in a separate window can be very useful.

Quadrant 3: Convenient Time, Same Place

The *convenient-time-same-place quadrant* (3) shows a digital location where employees come in at their convenience (convenient time) to obtain information (data) in one place online. The online contact is between a person and the data source. The place in this case is not physical. It is a software application somewhere on the network that stores information. Databases by themselves contain information that employees must access to do their work. Some may be legacy databases (preexisting databases). Others may be databases created recently to accommodate group work. (In addition, database technology is used in other systems that hold information.) Document systems enable employees to access, at their convenience, the documents they need to do their work. Story boards are brainstorms that take place at the convenience of employees. Kiosks are for employees who do not have access to a computer. Bulletin boards and convenient-time conferences store e-mail messages that represent past and current discussions of various topics. Group members can read the e-mail and then participate by adding additional e-mail messages. Convenient-time conferencing can also be a repository of a-mail (audio files) or v-mail (video files) as well as e-mail (text).

Quadrant 4: Convenient Time, Different Places

The *convenient-time-different-places quadrant* (4) shows processes that enable online communications to take place between group members rather than between a group member and a data resource. E-mail goes from one group member to another or to multiple group members. Only when it goes to *all* group members (e.g., Listserv) or into a repository (e.g., a threaded conference) should you view it as appropriate for another quadrant. In the case of work flow, the work gets passed on from workstation to workstation (person to person) until it is finished.

Hybrid

Hybrid digital activities include group efforts that use digital techniques from the different quadrants. For example:

- A physical meeting (1) in which someone uses a computer accessing a groupware database (3) to project the data onto a screen for all to see.
- An electronic white board (like the type used to print copies of what was written on the board) at a physical meeting (1) that broadcasts (2) what is written on the board to meeting participants in different locations (e.g., a physical meeting incorporating distance online participants).
- A physical meeting (1) broadcast (2) to participants in different locations who are enabled with e-mail (4) to provide their input into the meeting. See a CNN talk show on your television and think how you might adapt this idea to your own intranet use using a similar mixture of online techniques.
- A real-time text conference (2) archived in a document or database system (3) that group members can access at their convenience.

As you can see from the few hybrid examples, no quadrant is the best answer. Rather, the techniques from the various quadrants should be applied as appropriate to the group work situation. Hybrid techniques are also valid for appropriate situations.

Although the authors don't know of a story board program that's available for purchase, all the other techniques mentioned above represent TCP/IP software that's available today. Certainly, there are enough building blocks for you to build a system that meets your needs. With such a generous assortment of building blocks available, it makes little sense for this book to attempt a precise definition of groupware.

SUMMARY

Although it has been a long time since Lotus introduced Notes, groupware is still in its infancy. Now is the beginning, not the end. Thus, an open-ended definition of groupware is offered by this book. The software considered by the book is widely available commercial software, with an occasional shareware or public domain program mentioned. Experimental software and academic software not yet converted to commercial products is not considered. Thus, the book focuses on what is possible to do with programs you can obtain today. Even though the book includes occasional speculation about groupware that might appear in the future and about combinations of today's software that perhaps have not been tried yet, it is well grounded in what is possible now. The intranet movement started at the grassroots because ordinary white-collar workers and their self-employed colleagues found TCP/IP programs easy to use, inexpensive, useful, and efficient in getting work done. This book informally surveys the software market to give you some ideas about software you can use to get your work done and then introduces you to some of that software with step-by-step instruction.

This book is about software, software that you can use to get things done, not about group behavior. Human behavior is infinitely complex, and the more people in the group, the more complexity seems to materialize. How will groups best use software to get things done more efficiently? The authors leave that question to those who study it at the universities and in the research units of large organizations. The truth is that not a lot is known yet. Meanwhile, you are going to invent the future as you take the software tools at hand and apply them to your daily work activities. Inevitably, you will need to work with others, and working together online is now a reasonable alternative to the old ways. It is hoped that this book will help you find productive ways to collaborate with others in this new digital environment.

Chapter 2

EVOLUTION OF GROUPWARE

This chapter provides an evolutionary perspective on groupware to give you a better understanding of how using groupware compares with using a traditional PC.

GROUPWHAT?

The term *groupware* is fairly new. The concept behind the word, however, is not. In fact, it could be argued that the first widespread use of groupware occurred as early as the 1970s during the infancy of the Internet. It is fairly easy to figure out what groupware is generally by looking at the word: *group* refers to two or more people with a common goal, and *ware* is a shortened form of the word software. Therefore, groupware at its simplest level is computer software designed to help two or more people achieve their common goals. Unfortunately, the simplicity ends there.

Philosophies about the best way to define and design groupware are as varied as the number of companies that are trying to sell groupware-related products. Chapter 1 introduced you to some of the ideas about the software tools that might make up a groupware system. This chapter describes the other core components of a usable groupware system such as networking requirements, hardware independence, and cultural considerations.

Requirements for the Ideal Groupware

Groupware creates a shared virtual environment optimized for getting work done. Ideally, groupware takes the key resources of your company's physical office building and makes them easier to use. The offices, the conference rooms, the filing cabinets, the record books, the data, the mail room, the telephones, the copier, the library—almost everything—is collected into one place: your computer. All these infrastructure assets are integrated and available at people's fingertips in computers, freeing people to focus on the most valuable and irreplaceable asset any organization has: association with other people. No matter where people are, with good groupware they can participate in and add value to the organization's business. For example, when you need to have a conference, you can start a virtual conference rather than trying to find an opening on everyone's schedule and reserving a conference room. People who need to participate in the conference are able to join the conference, regardless of their schedules, adding their ideas and thoughts.

Foundations of Good Groupware

There are key features that every groupware alternative must include. The computers that use the groupware must be able to pass data to and from one another; that is, they must be networked. Groupware should also be able to run on whatever hardware is already in place in the organization.

Networked Architecture It is generally accepted that for a groupware application to be effective, it must be built on a networked environment. All the members of a group can't be in the same place at the same time. Some people may be in different buildings. Some may be in different cities. When groupware is built to work over a wide area network, these geographical boundaries are no longer an issue. In the ideal groupware scenario, if you are able to access the network at least periodically (e.g., by modem, satellite uplink, or ethernet), you can be *at work* wherever you happen to be.

Ease of Use People won't use a new tool if it is harder than doing things the old way. The best way to bring people on board to use a new groupware system is to make sure that using the system is intuitive. In other words, using groupware should be no more difficult than using other normal computer programs such as word processors. Of course the more complicated features may prove to be fairly difficult to use, but overall, the user's interaction with the software should be friendly.

Hardware Independence A good groupware system must be usable by everyone in an organization regardless of hardware. The ideal groupware system will be accessible not only by the people in your own organization, but also by those people in other organizations with whom you need to work from time to time. (Naturally, you want to be able to control precisely which people outside the organization can access your system.) A groupware system therefore must

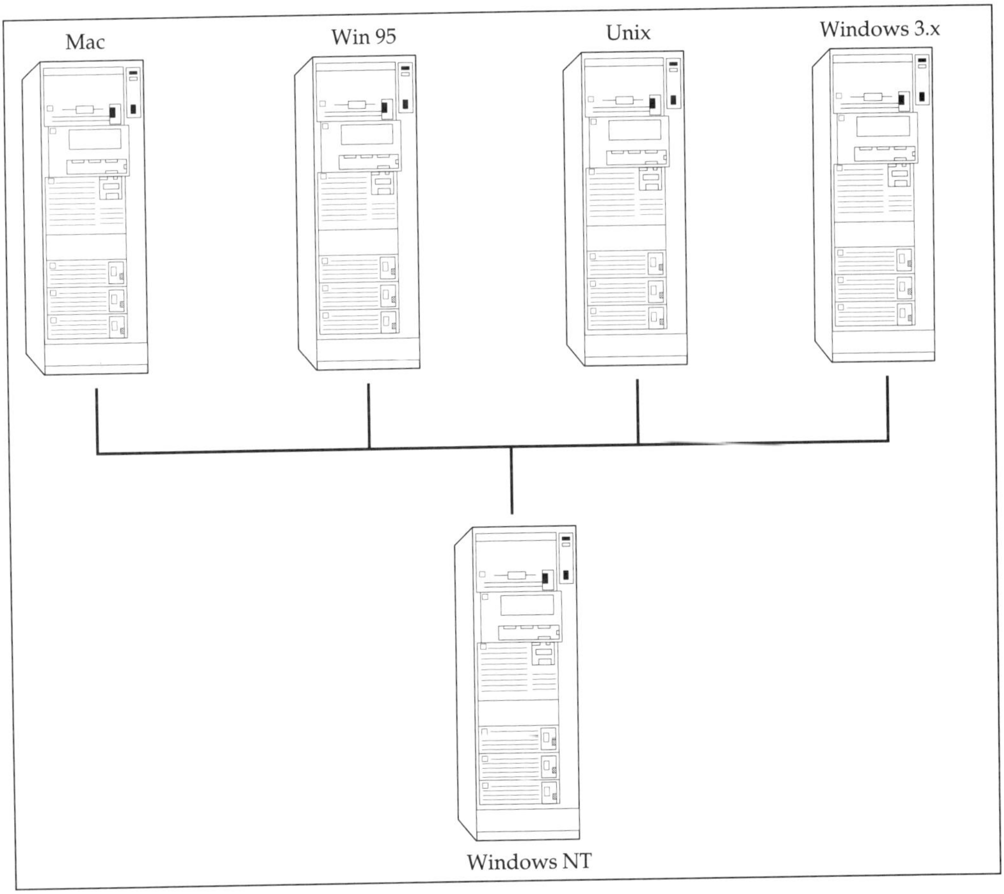

Figure 2.1: A groupware system must be capable of supporting all types of hardware, including PCs, Macs, and Unix workstations.

run on as wide a variety of computing platforms as possible. In other words, just because your company uses Macs shouldn't mean that you are unable to access a supplier's groupware system that is running on a Windows 95 system.

Groupware Culture Groupware will never replace face-to-face human interaction. It will never replace people. That's not what it is supposed to do. A corporation that focuses solely on creating a perfect hardware and software infrastructure for its groupware system while neglecting to get its people involved will ultimately end up with a deficient system. If the culture of an organization has not evolved to the new standard in business of knowledge-sharing and openness, all the computing infrastructure in the world won't make groupware work well for that organization.

The wisdom that is collected in the stores of a groupware library, the ideas for great new products in a conferencing database, the solutions to seemingly impossible problems—these are what groupware can free people to focus on. But if the company has people or departments who don't trust one another, groupware won't work as well.

People have to learn how to be good groupware users. At first, it may take incentives for people to participate. One Memphis company was featured in a magazine article for offering cash awards to the most prolific contributors of useful knowledge to its groupware system. Whatever it takes, a company or department must proactively encourage participation in a groupware system.

In practice, it seems that part of what determines the quality of a groupware system is often how invisible it is to the people who use it. Most of the tasks should be second nature to someone familiar with using a personal computer. The system should allow for individual differences in the way people create, think, and organize.

Grassroots Groupware The corporate groupware culture often exists before management realizes it. In fact, many employee groups and departments have taken it upon themselves to initiate the use of groupware in their organizations. The use of intranets and Internet programs as groupware has been a grassroots phenomenon, not a top-down directive. Management should not hamper the efforts of such groups. The innovating employees should instead receive the necessary resources to extend and improve their groupware system.

Where's the Ideal? If this is the outline of the ideal groupware, how close is it at hand? To answer this question, the remainder of the chapter gives groupware some historical perspective.

GROUPWARE AND THE INTERNET

Even though the Internet got its start as a military project, one of the more popular windfalls is that it opened new communication channels. Researchers at universities quickly adopted the Internet as a way to collaborate on research projects and share information. E-mail and electronic file transfer gave them lightning-fast access to the work of their colleagues around the world. They quickly devised a way to share information among whole groups of people with similar research interests in the form of e-mail mailing lists (Listservs). Later, with discussion newsgroups (Usenets), they enhanced mailing lists by making the handling of e-mail messages more convenient. Both Listservs and discussion groups are types of convenient-time conferencing. These pioneering computer users were simply making use of the new technology in the ways that seemed natural to them. They needed to collaborate on work, share information, and discuss ideas in a widely dispersed group, so they dreamed up electronic mailing lists, newsgroups, and (eventually) the Web. Though they may not have realized it at the time, they were inventing groupware.

Where Did the Internet Come From?

The Internet is more than a multitude of computers hooked together; it's more than just a network. Perhaps at one time, that's all that it was, but not any longer. The word Internet has come to describe an entire subculture, or perhaps a super-culture, of world society. This special group includes millions of computers, many millions of people, and billions of documents, all held together by hundreds of thousands of miles of wire, a handful of software tools, and a culture that is unique to modern times.

If the Internet were just a network, there would be nothing special about it at all. In fact, many businesses have been connecting their computers across distances for a long time, as has the government. Networks that pass information over long distances have been around for decades in the form of telegraphs, radio transmitters, and long distance telephone lines. Computer networks are significantly newer than the telegraph, but the idea of electronically transmitting information over vast distances is an old one. The specific networking technology used in the Internet took shape in the late 1960s and 1970s as part of a U.S. military initiative to create a network that could remain operational after a nuclear strike. Once the technology stabilized, the Internet began to grow and grow. Today, it is the largest computer network that has ever existed.

Clearly the sensation surrounding the Internet goes beyond the technology (though the technology is remarkable). The synergy created by the convergence of some key factors has given the world a unique new technological tool. These factors include the following:

- Access—virtually unrestricted global access to an enormous network
- Hardware independence—the ability to use it from almost any type of computer platform (Macintosh, Windows 95, Unix)
- Simplicity—improvements in ease of use of the networking programs
- Culture—a culture of human cooperation and information sharing

More and more, the Internet affects the way we do business with each other and how we get our work done. In fact, from this perspective, the Internet looks a lot like the ultimate groupware!

Internet Evolution

Before there were computer networks (and a long time before there was groupware), scientists, engineers, and statisticians used computers to solve tough problems quickly. They would input numbers into mainframe computers, and later they got back answers. Everybody was satisfied. Soon, though, people realized that if one computer could help them answer these tough problems, then multiple computers hooked together could help them even more. The concept of networking was born.

One other group that was particularly interested in computers that could connect to one another was the U.S. government. Especially interested was the branch of the government that had computers all over the world, a service vitally important to the well-being of millions of people: the military. The military needed a way of hooking its computers together so that if any one part of the network was destroyed by an enemy, the computers wouldn't be prevented from communicating with one another.

There were two ways to approach this problem. First, the military could have fortified all the parts of the network so well that none of it would be vulnerable to enemy attack. When you are dealing with a network, that covers thousands and thousands of miles, however, so this approach is just about impossible. The other answer, the one that the military chose to develop and the one on which the Internet that you know today is based, was to design the network system as a matrix of networks. This idea gives data many different paths through which it can flow to get to its destination—many individual networks interconnected to form a web.

ARPAnet, Internet The military organization that sponsored the initial research on these networks was the Advanced Research Projects Agency (ARPA), hence the name of the Internet's predecessor, ARPAnet. ARPAnet took form in the 1970s. ARPA sponsored the development until the 1980s. The very earliest version of ARPAnet connected four universities in the western United States. It eventually included computers at additional universities. During the mid-1980s more and more networks were joined using the technology initially researched and developed for ARPAnet. The Internet was born. ARPAnet was eventually superseded and phased out as a result of the Internet's success.

TCP/IP—Internet Glue The key to making this web-like network operate well lies in the communications software layer known as the protocol that runs on all the computers on the network. All networks use a protocol for communication. The protocol (actually a group of protocols) used by the Internet is known as TCP/IP (Transmission Control Protocol/Internet Protocol). TCP/IP breaks up the data to be sent over the network into manageable chunks called packets (the TCP part). It also wraps special encoding information, including the final destination, around the packets before transmission (the IP part). The packets are then sent into the Internet to find their way (or actually, to be forwarded by one network after another) to their destination along the path of least resistance in the Internet. When the packets arrive, they are reassembled into something that is intelligible to the destination computer. All computers that are on the Internet are running

TCP/IP in one form or another. TCP/IP is the glue that holds the Net together.

Groupware's Arrival Another primary goal, beyond defense, of creating this reliable network was to allow for the shared usage of computing resources. Professor X at Small State University could log in to a supercomputer at Giant State Tech and use the big machine's computing power to perform intensive computational tasks.

There was, however, a practical additional benefit to the network. It was only a matter of time before the people who used these networked computers developed ways of using the communications link to talk to each other. Researchers at universities that had computers connected to the big network discussed and collaborated electronically on research projects and exchanged resources, ideas, files, and information using new tools like e-mail, file transfer, newsgroups, and remote log-in (Telnet). They also used it to discuss other areas of common interest, such as science fiction, bicycling, and humor. Out of the murky depths of this evolving networking technology crept a new creature. Groupware, though still unnamed, was born!

Academia's Secret For years, the Internet remained a secret of the consortium of academicians and government agencies. Part of what kept it a secret was that one had to be familiar with what amounted to a secret code to use it. One needed to understand cryptic words like Telnet and FTP, to know Unix or some mainframe operating system, and to remember what commands to type when.

Of course, no one was *trying* to keep the Net a secret. In fact, most people using the Net realized that the more people who contributed to and participated in the Internet, the more valuable a resource it might become.

Why Did the Internet Catch On?

People (i.e., intelligent people) saw the value of the stores of information and knowledge resources to which the Internet gave them access. This led them to continue refining the way the Internet worked. The Internet continued to grow in spite of its arcane interface, in large part because of the four factors discussed below.

Unrestricted Access Who can be a part of the Internet? Almost anybody who wants to be. The biggest barrier to an individual who wishes to get on the Internet today is perhaps financial. You must be able to afford a basic $800 used computer with a modem and $10 per month for an Internet service provider (ISP). Nor is the Internet limited to people. Many businesses can afford an intranet (an internal Internet) as a direct communications link between employees within the company and to customers who are on the Internet.

In 1994, several of the national online services (e.g., America Online and CompuServe) added the capability to send e-mail to Internet addresses. Suddenly, almost overnight, just about anybody with a computer and a modem could send mail to anyone else with a computer and a modem. The Internet seemed to catch fire with billions of words pouring across the network every day. Businesses now use the Internet for daily communications that used to take place by phone, fax, and the Postal Service.

The Net is rapidly becoming omnipresent in our society as well as in others around the world. This phenomenon is providing new levels of interaction between people who need each other's skills and knowledge.

Open Standards and Hardware Independence It doesn't matter if the $800 computer mentioned above is a Mac or a PC running Windows. It can still access the Internet. By design, Internet software must follow a set of standards that have been made available to the public (i.e., *open standards*). Any software developer can create innovative new Internet communications software as long as it follows the standards. Most new operating systems such as Windows 95 have TCP/IP built in. It is the TCP/IP software layer that enables your computer to make use of Internet programs like Web browsers and e-mail clients.

With the commercial growth of the online world has come the development of a new type of computer known as the *network computer* or *NC* for short. The NC is designed to be inexpensive and easy to operate. It gets most of its digital resources from the network. It will give new capabilities to groups of employees who have never used computers before. Some NCs, such as WebTV set-top units, are even designed to fit into a household just like any other appliance (e.g.,

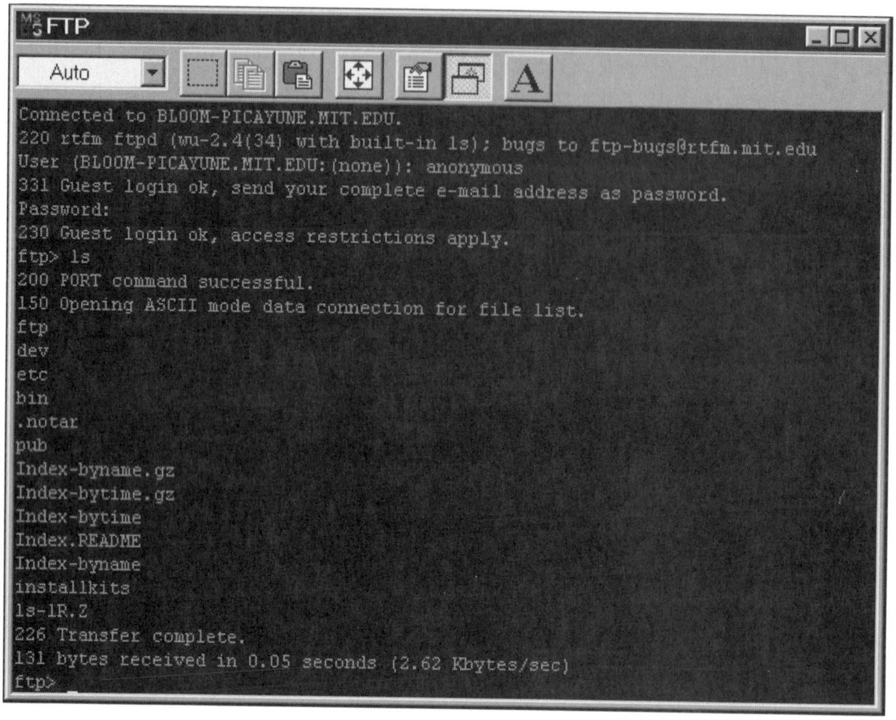

Figure 2.2: Cryptic line mode interfaces like this one made the Internet difficult for most people to use during the early years of network development.

VCR, stereo, TV) and provide affordable, easy-to-use access to the Internet.

Improvements in Ease of Use The Internet is getting easier to use. In the early days of the Net, you had to understand how to type in the correct text commands to navigate (see Figure 2.2).

Later, the University of Minnesota developed Gopher, a better way for novices to burrow through all the information to find what they needed. (Gopher is the mascot for the University of Minnesota athletic teams.) Today, on the Web, you can point with a mouse and click to get where you want to go (see Figure 2.3).

A Culture of Cooperation The Internet has been built through the cooperation of people all over the world. For instance, the Web was invented in Switzerland. There is no organization that *owns* the

Figure 2.3: The advent of the Web has given the Internet an easy-to-use, point-and-click interface.

Internet. Instead, people have agreed to abide by a set of common technical and cultural standards to create something extraordinarily useful.

"Give something back to the Net" is the cardinal rule of the Internet. This goes back to the time when the Internet was a fairly small community of university and military sites that recognized the need to keep expanding the resources available on the network. When a new presence is established on the Internet—for example when a company sets up a Web site—it will usually provide something that is of benefit to the Internet. It might be free software, useful information, entertainment, a service, or something else. There is no official rule that says a new presence must to do this; it is just expected as a common courtesy. The benefits to the Internet community are obvious, and the company benefits from having a useful or popular resource associated with its name.

OTHER FACTORS IN THE EVOLUTION OF GROUPWARE

The Internet is not the only infrastructure for groupware. There were other important trends concurrent with the evolution of the Internet.

Mainframe Groupware?

Groupware-like software made an appearance in mainframe computing. Many mainframes include bulletin board facilities for discussion, messaging systems, and even text-based real-time conversation software. One such conferencing system that runs on Digital Equipment's OpenVMS mainframe operating system is called VAXNotes. VAXNotes works like other convenient-time conferencing systems such as Usenet or a Lotus Notes discussion database. The effectiveness of such mainframe-based communications software is minimal, though, because of the way such systems are rigidly structured and because they require a user to be familiar with cryptic commands and conventions. The same can be said of many mainframe-based transaction processing applications. They are not as flexible and user friendly as PC based client/server solutions.

The Rise of the PC

About the time the Internet was getting started, another recent arrival in the computing field had just begun to take hold. In the mid-1970s hobbyists around the world began to experiment with new kits that enabled them to do something remarkable: build a microcomputer of their own. The hobbyist days of the personal computing industry were short lived. In the late 1970s, Apple Computer started selling its first personal computers. In the early 1980s IBM began selling its version of personal computers. With its usable operating system (purchased from Microsoft) and reasonable cost, the IBM PC sold well as business and home users began integrating the personal computer into their daily affairs. In 1984 Apple gave the world the Macintosh, revolutionizing user interfaces for personal computers.

Networking PCs on LANs and WANs

As the popularity of PCs grew, business users soon demanded ways to share files with one another. PCs were networked within offices to form Local Area Networks (LANs). But just being on a LAN does not constitute groupware in and of itself. File server computers were placed on the LANs to provide a place to *hang* files so that others on the network could access them. This is a useful function of a LAN, but it's crude groupware.

Essentially, file sharing on a file server, although supporting group work, is not a convenient or good means of communications. It takes programs with convenient file management and communications capability built in to support efficient collaboration. Software is needed to organize and present information and files in a way that makes sense. Some form of interactivity between users is needed. A lone file server to which everyone in a group is connected is a good start, but it is not a good solution.

WHAT'S A LAN? A WAN?

A network consists of two or more computers connected to share electronic resources. Usually, there are at least several computers on a network. The Internet has several million computers connected to it. Networks have two major categories, local area networks (LANs) and wide area networks (WANs). The Internet is an example of a WAN. The network that connects computers within a department or group in an organization (typically within the same building) is a LAN. LANs in turn are connected to one another to form a WAN. This description is an oversimplification but gives you the general idea.

The important thing to remember about a network is that it allows computers to communicate with each other. For the different machines on a network to talk to each other successfully, they must all be speaking with a common communications language. The technical word for this language is *protocol.*

Appearance of Lotus and Other Groupware Vendors

Lotus Development Corporation was seeking to fill the need for more advanced collaboration software when it introduced Notes in the late 1980s. Eventually Notes was adopted by several large companies, making it easy for employees to work together over an internal company network. Over the years Notes has been refined in several ways so that it is the standard by which all other groupware applications are measured. There are millions of registered Notes users around the globe in thousands of organizations.

Novell's GroupWise is centered on a proprietary messaging system that excels at messaging, file sharing, and scheduling. Another groupware competitor, Collabra, received a high-octane injection to its development efforts when it was purchased by Netscape in 1995. Netscape has begun to integrate much of Collabra's group work functionality into its product line of servers and clients.

Grassroots Intranets

In early 1995, corporate employee groups and corporate departments began realizing that the technologies introduced by the Internet could be easily transferred to a private network. In other words, if your internal network adds TCP/IP capability, you can grab a Web server off the Internet, install it on your PC, and start publishing information for the rest of your organization in a matter of hours. Best of all, you can often do it for less money than implementing a vendor-specific solution such as Notes or GroupWise. Personnel in many companies jumped at the chance to provide on all employees' desktops a single client that could be used to access information instantly and interact with other employees and customers. The stage was set for the rise of the intranet.

The intranet, which started as a grassroots movement, has been discovered and embraced by upper management so that it appears in late 1996 to have turned into a top-down movement in many organizations rather than a bottom-up movement. Business organizations form a microcosm of society, and intranets have become popular for many of the same reasons that the Internet has become popular. For instance, hardware diversity is an important issue for most organizations. A network system that is hardware independent provides the infrastructure for conveniently connecting all the computers, rather than just a portion, within an organization.

It is important to understand that a TCP/IP network works the same whether it's an intranet or the Internet. If your computer has the TCP/IP protocol, you can access an intranet (and all the networked resources of the organization) or the Internet (and all the world-wide network resources) with exactly the same Internet software, no adjustments required (e.g., Web browser).

SUMMARY

The Internet, intranets, and groupware are, in many respects, birds of a feather. They have evolved as a result of people's desire to communicate in order to get their work done. For groupware to be effective in any organization, it must do the following:

- Run on any hardware in the organization
- Be reasonably easy to use
- Be accepted within the organization's culture

The Internet led the way by connecting diverse computers and providing communication capability. The advent of PCs and LANs in the 1980s led to the development of commercial groupware products such as Lotus Notes. In the mid-1990s, grassroots PC users discovered the capabilities and advantages of using traditional Internet programs on internal TCP/IP networks (i.e., intranets). As a result, organizations as well as individuals began to use groupware.

Chapter 3

NETWORK MULTIMEDIA

As the Internet shows quite dramatically, multimedia communication is popular. It is the difference between a typewritten page and a full-color magazine. Yet even the full-color magazine is not a good analogy because multimedia can do so much more than a printed page. This chapter provides you with the multimedia building blocks you need to look at communication and group work with a more digitally robust imagination.

Text has been the common electronic medium for a long time. Because the book covers it thoroughly in another chapter, it is not covered here. Nonetheless, text remains fundamentally important to multimedia communication.

INTERACTIVITY

Interactivity is an important part of multimedia publishing. It gives users a choice. Instead of linear progression through a multimedia document, they can choose to branch off in another direction. Hyperlinks enable this capability. Hypertext consists of links from text to text. Hypermedia consists of links from text to other media (e.g., graphics) or from media to media. Both are available in Web documents. HTML forms collect input for processing and provide a user the opportunity to communicate by entering input.

Don't get carried away using hyperlinks and interactivity in your Web publishing. Years of experimenting in education indicate that a shallow level of interactivity is best. You don't want someone to get lost in a maze. Therefore, keep your hyperlinks to a minimum when using them for navigation. When using them for reference where users are likely to ignore them until they are finished reading, it makes sense that you can use them that way more generously.

AUDIO

Although not all PCs have a sound board, an increasing percentage of them do, and most PCs sold now include them. The day is approaching when sound will be considered standard fare in multimedia communications of all kinds. Even on the Web, audio is making deep inroads.

Sound files used on the Web are AU and AIFF for Unix, WAV for the PC, and SND for the Mac. A visitor uses these files by downloading them and playing them in a player program. This is a little awkward and requires action on the part of the visitor. If the visitor doesn't have the proper player, there will be no sound. Download times are long for audio files because they tend to be quite large. These factors do not facilitate the seamless use of sound in Web presentations. There are some relatively new audio protocols for the Web, however, such as True Speech and Real Audio that make the integration of audio more transparent. The sound files do not have to be completely downloaded to work. They produce sound immediately by streaming.

Streaming audio is real-time audio in the sense that you hear it as it downloads into your browser rather than waiting until the download is complete and then playing it in a audio player. Nonetheless, most streamed audio is recorded sound, so to say that you hear it in real time means that you hear the recording in real time. Streaming audio will handle a live broadcast, too, and Real Audio has done many live broadcasts at its Web site. For example, the first broadcast of a football game on the Web was done by Real Audio in the fall of 1995.

Voice and Music

The sampling rate determines the quality of the sound. Music requires a higher sampling rate than voice. The Multimedia PC Marketing

Council (MPC) recommends that a 44.1kHz rate be used for 16-bit digital audio for music and a 22.05kHz rate be used for voice (see Table 3.1).

The storage space required for sound is large and is currently an impediment to widespread Web usage. New compression technology and streaming, though, reduce storage requirements.

Recording and Editing

Although you can record with a relatively inexpensive analog tape recorder, the sound quality may not be suitable. You will do better to record with a digital tape recorder, which is about three times as expensive but will ensure satisfactory sound. You can also record digitally directly onto your hard disk using only a microphone and your audio board. Although this may be convenient for many uses, it is not optimal for recording in the field unless you have a laptop with a large hard disk.

Audio editing software is inexpensive to obtain and comes bundled with many audio boards. Such software is the equivalent of thousands of dollars in studio equipment (see Figure 3.1). Efficient editing requires a large amount of space on your hard disk reserved specifically for such use. As much as 200MB is not too much and will prove too little if you do a lot of audio editing.

Stock Audio

You can purchase music and sound effects for use in multimedia presentations. Such multimedia assets are sometimes royalty free. You pay for the CD. Others require a royalty payment in addition to whatever you pay for the CD. There is plenty of good stock music available,

Table 3.1 Audio File Sizes

Sound	*Sampling Rate*	*MB/Minute*	*MB/Hour*
Music	44.1kHz	5.25	315
Voice	22.05kHz	1.3	78

Note: The files sizes are for monaural; double the rates for stereo.

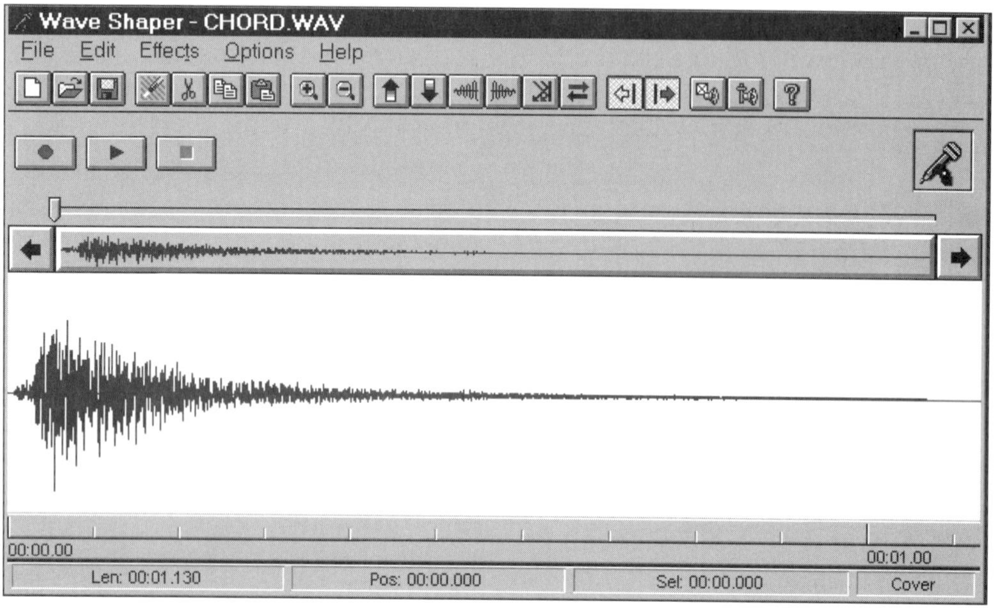

Figure 3.1: Audio editor.

and it can be an inexpensive source of music. The alternative is to hire an orchestra or a rock band.

MIDI

Musical Instrument Digital Interface (MIDI) music is synthetic. A digital synthesizer synthesizes it from computer instructions written by a composer (person) using a program that emulates writing real music. The synthesizer imitates various instruments in the orchestra. Today, the best synthesizers can imitate a large number of instruments, and MIDI music can sound very real. The synthesizer plays the MIDI music through the PC sound system.

As new instruments in past centuries have come into widespread use to become well established, MIDI music has become a well-established medium that will continue to grow in capability and stature. Composers have more control and more efficient control over MIDI music than over normal music. The synthesizer is the director and the orchestra (or rock band or jazz combo). Because no orchestra is involved in the performance of the music, MIDI offers the potential for lower costs. Additionally, MIDI music takes about 1,000 times less space (on a hard disk, the Web, or a CD) than digital recordings of traditional music. Although MIDI is strictly for music and sound effects, it seems odd that there is not an Internet protocol for it.

DIGITAL GRAPHICS

Digital graphics have made the Web. The attractiveness of adding color, art, graphic design, photographs, and other color graphics to digital documents has made the Web a compelling medium. It is almost unthinkable to show plain pages, even for mundane documents, without some color accent, if not a more substantial color treatment. This is just as true on an intranet as on the Internet, which means that you must be concerned with graphics as well as text.

Color Basics

Color quality directly relates to file size. The more quality, the more bits per pixel and the larger the file size, as shown in Table 3.2.

Web browsers can generally show two types of graphic files: *.GIF* and *.JPG*. The first, Graphics Interchange Format (GIF), uses 8-bit color and compresses at about 2:1 without loss. The second, Joint Photographic Experts Group (JPEG), can be compressed to various ratios but with loss of quality. About 10:1 compression can be achieved with JPEG without noticeable loss in quality, except for the most demanding situations. Greater compression means shorter download times and less waiting by visitors to Web sites.

Resolution indicates image size rather than color density for color monitors. People use three different sizes, as shown on the following page.

Table 3.2 Digital Color

Bits	*Number of Colors*	*Size for 300 x 200*
4-bit	16	30 K
8-bit	256	60 K
16-bit	65,000+	120 K
24-bit	16,000,000+	180 K

640 x 480	For small monitors
800 x 600	Standard
1024 x 768	For large monitors

When you make a graphic for the Web and its dimensions are greater than 640 x 480, people with their monitors set on 640 x 480 will have to scroll to see the entire image. The density of good color monitors today is about 72 dpi (dots per inch). New color monitors introduced in 1996 (Active Matrix Liquid Crystal Display — flat panel) can achieve densities of up to 600 dpi in black and white and up to 150 dpi in color. They are expensive now but will undoubtedly decline in price to consumer price levels. The higher density will support easier reading and sharper images, which will eventually be a real breakthrough for Web publishing. Meanwhile, for Web images, 8-bit color is widely used at resolutions under 640 x 480.

Stock Images

As with audio, stock images are available. Clip art, photographs, illustrations, design elements, and backgrounds are readily accessible on royalty-free CDs or out of catalogs. There are also image catalogs on line with thousands of images from which to choose.

Kodak Photo CD

Color photographs make great additions to Web documents. One inexpensive and easy way to digitize color photographs is to use Photo CD (see Figure 3.2). You simply take photographs as you normally do, then take your film into a photo finisher and have your roll of 36 put on a Photo CD. It will cost about $30. One CD can hold up to three rolls. The price includes developing, thumbnail prints, and each photograph placed on the CD in five different sizes. You will be interested in the three smallest sizes: wallet, snapshot, and standard. If you have your monitor set at 800 x 600, the wallet will be about one-twentieth of the screen, the snapshot about one-fifth, and the standard about two-thirds. The snapshots are about the right size for attractive placement in a Web document. It is easy to copy the images from the CD and save them in GIF or JPG format for use on the Web.

Photo CD is wonderful technology. It's easy, inexpensive, and high quality. If you can get the photographs, you can get them on the Web. Try this today.

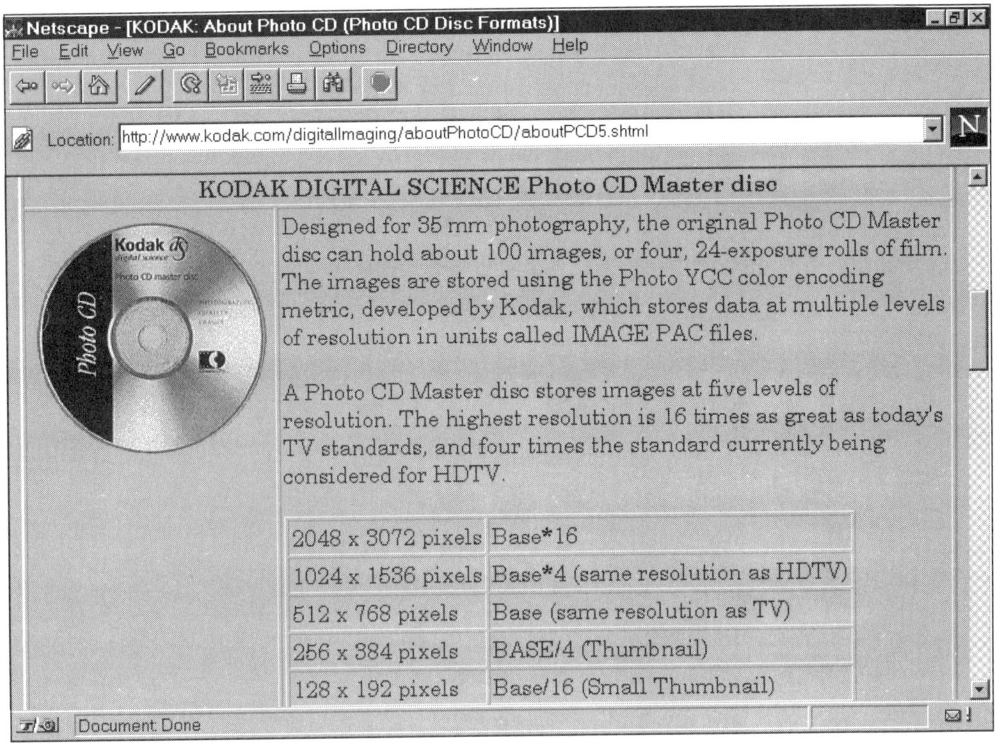

Figure 3.2: Kodak Photo CD.

Digital Cameras

Digital cameras are an alternative to Photo CD. Good ones cost over $3,000, but you can get workable digital cameras for $300 to $800. Unless you will be doing a great deal of digital photography, you are probably better off using a good 35mm camera and Photo CD. It will be less expensive and higher quality.

Art

Good art and graphic design make a substantial difference. The plain look is out, and the designed look is in, so don't cut corners here. Find a good digital artist, and put that person to work. Art doesn't have to be comprehensive or voluminous. It can be simple with reusable elements. But don't do without. It is particularly important to present an attractive look in anything you publish on the Web for the public, but even in a small office, graphic design can add life to your publications. Even if you don't hire a digital artist, there are plenty of techniques you can use to brighten up your documents, such as the templates (which include graphic design elements) provided in HTML authoring programs.

Imagers

You can use paint or draw programs to create or manipulate color images. Paint programs work with bitmaps; draw programs work with vectors and curves. The files for one program are incompatible with those of the other. Draw images may be converted to bitmaps but not vice versa. Before you put a any color image on the Web, it must be converted to a GIF or JPG bitmap. (See Figure 3.3.)

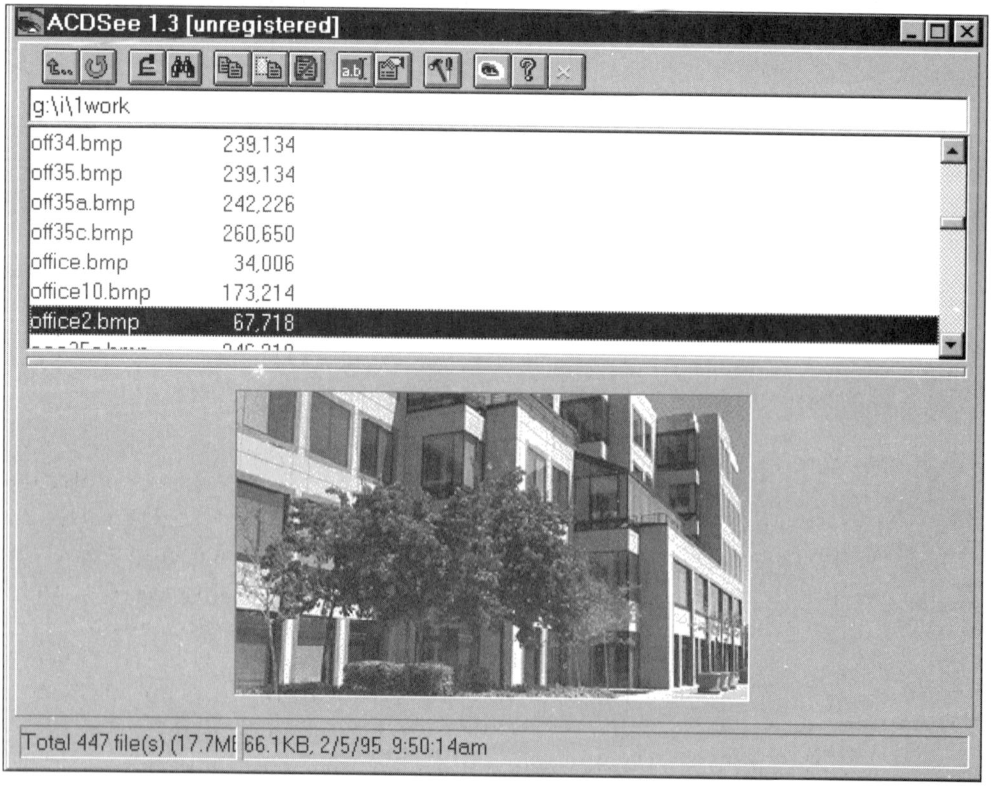

Figure 3.3: ACDcee is a handy image utility that helps you keep your images well organized.

Most image programs have an abundance of capability, much of which is difficult to understand unless you are a digital artist. Nonetheless, you can do basic work with these programs that will help you prepare images for your Web site. Changing the contrast and brightness are quite easy and can turn a poor photo into a usable one. Don't be afraid to experiment with these programs. See *http://sun1.bham.ac.uk/s.m.williams.bcm/images/viewers.html.*

Some image programs will make transparent GIFs. One color is indexed to be replaced by the background over which the graphic is placed in a Web document. Thus, you can make one color transparent. Used correctly, an image gives the appearance of floating on the page. See *http://melmac.corp.harris.com/transparent_images.html.*

Animation

Although animation is very useful for illustrating a wide variety of published information, it is labor intensive and expensive. If you have a budget for it, use it. If not, use other publishing techniques.

One type of animation, sprite animation, can be done by anyone. A sprite is a small fixed graphic that moves along a predetermined path over a fixed background after being launched. Sprite animation programs are easy to use and useful. For instance, suppose you want to make a page title graphic more lively. Turn it into a sprite and have it move on the page. Although easy to do with a sprite animation program, it is more difficult to do it on the Web. Difficult or not, it is a useful design technique that can be used by most publishers.

Motion Video

Motion video is still emerging in normal computing environments, but it is not a full-functioning multimedia element yet. It will probably take another generation of computers (the 686?) and color cards to enable full-motion video to play effortlessly on your screen without an add-in video board. Nonetheless, video is usable today on fast computers. If you have an intranet with a wide bandwidth, you may be able to use video successfully—even if it isn't perfect yet—but not via the TCP/IP protocol. A packet network, TCP/IP does not carry the steady stream necessary to show the 30 frames per second required to meet the national TV standard. Thus, even with adequate bandwidth, video is not yet reasonably functional on an intranet or on the Internet.

You can have Web site visitors download video files and play them in a viewer. The files are huge, the download times long, and many visitors become impatient. Just as this is not a satisfactory process for audio, it is not a satisfactory process for video. But like audio, video can be streamed. That means that the video begins to play as soon as it starts downloading. With video streaming, a fast computer, and a modem connection, you may be able to get a rate as high as 12 to 15 frames per second. This is a long way from the national TV standard of 30 frames per second, but it's a start. Presumably, as TCP/IP research evolves, faster video transfers will become feasible.

Xing and VDO are two streaming video vendors. Streaming video requires compression before it is presentable. It also requires a special server. Both the compression and the server are expensive. How well they work is a matter of opinion, but it will be a few years before this technology is completely viable. Meanwhile, it is something with which you can experiment. (See Figure 3.4.)

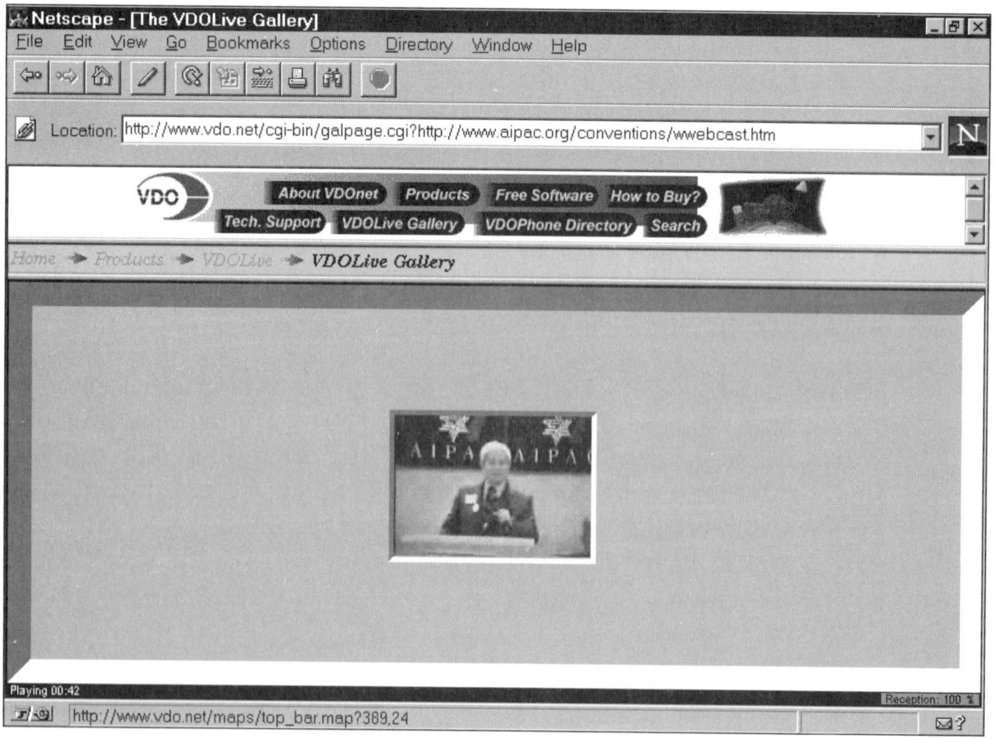

Figure 3.4: VDO streaming video.

Video technology is complex, with a variety of competing systems, and it is beyond the scope of this book to show the download sizes of video files for the various systems. ISDN provides a guideline, however. It is generally acknowledged that ISDN is *almost* enough bandwidth to carry videoconferencing (in windows less than full screen) at a normal rate of 30 frames per second. ISDN runs at 128Kb per second or about 12.8KB per second.

Videoconferencing

Intel's Pro Share enables videoconferencing at a high frame rate over an ISDN line. It does not work over a TCP/IP network, however. Videoconferencing software for TCP/IP networks is becoming generally available, but it works at a low frame rate. Even the inexpensive cams work at low frame rates. This is not a technology that is ready for business yet, but it will provide you with experience and build your confidence if you experiment with it. Before too long, videoconferencing will undoubtedly become usable for business, and videoconferencing software will become more popular.

CU-SeeMe is the standard videoconferencing used on the Web, and White Pine Software markets an enhanced version of it. If you have a cam, it's easy and fun to work with.

Virtual Reality Markup Language

Virtual Reality Markup Language (VRML) is 3-D for the Web (see Figure 3.5). Like animation, it's probably not something you will use without a large budget, but it may provide specific uses for your personnel. For instance, engineering departments can use it for CAD drawings, and scientists can use it for 3-D modeling. VRML will also be incorporated into normal programming where appropriate. For instance, OZ Interactive offers a business conferencing program, OZ Virtual, that uses VRML to create cyberspace for meetings. How effectively this will work compared with normal conferencing programs remains to be seen, but it is certainly worth a look (`http://www.oz-inc.com`).

Multimedia

Macromedia's Director is a popular multimedia authoring program used to make multimedia titles for CDs and to make other sophisticated

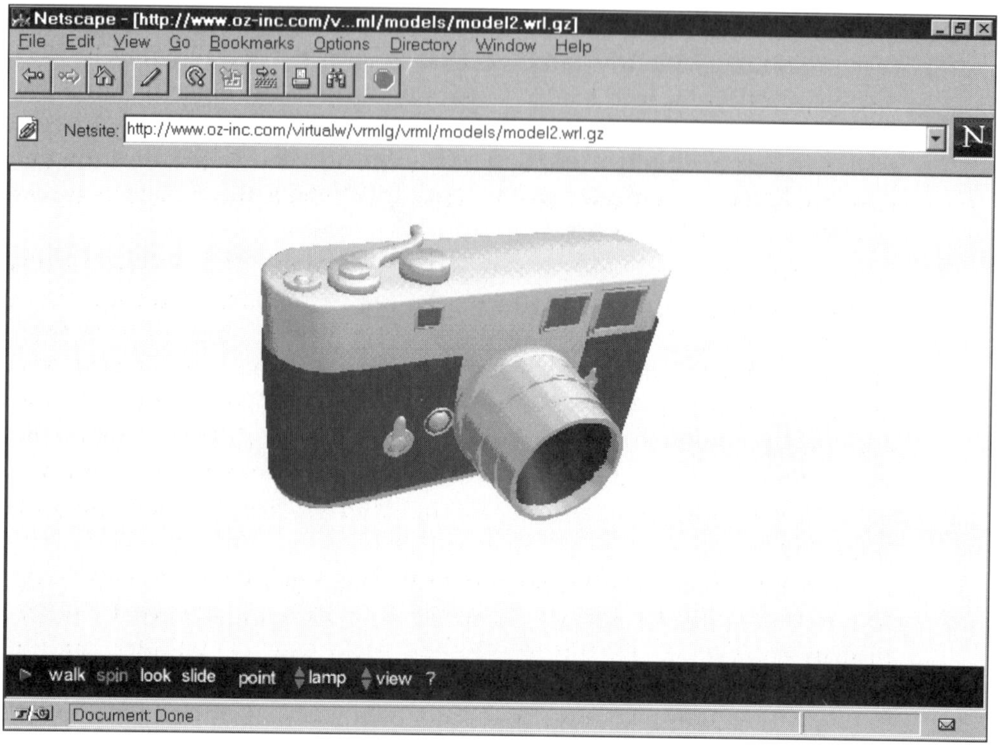

Figure 3.5: A camera in 3-D in a browser using VRML.

presentations. Macromedia also offers the Shockwave plug-in for the Netscape browser and other browsers. The plug-in plays Director *movies* via the Internet. If you have existing Director multimedia presentations, you may be able to port them to the Internet using Shockwave. If you have highly sophisticated multimedia presentations that you desire to offer on the Web, using Director and Shockwave may provide the means. Other multimedia authoring systems also offer plug-ins. Shockwave is not the only one available.

Animation, Audio, Multimedia Movies, Video, and VRML

What do animation, audio, multimedia movies, video, and VRML have in common besides being more of that digital folderol? They all may require huge files to work effectively, and they're all megabyte hogs. They may work well on an intranet that offers the bandwidth to carry them. For the Internet, however, they are delivered slowly over normal modem connections. This is an important consideration for planning your use of groupware if you have personnel who will access your intranet remotely via the Internet. If you are using the Internet as your intranet, the narrow bandwidth with which most people access the Internet is a fact of life you cannot ignore.

An additional fact of life is important, too. Many of these techniques require plug-ins for a browser. If you are using these internally and can ensure that all employees will use the proper plug-ins with their browsers, there is no problem. If not, there may be a significant portion of your organization that cannot effectively use these techniques because personnel do not have the proper plug-in, do not know where to get it, do not understand how to install it, or have no motivation to go to the trouble. Of course, on the Internet this problem is compounded manyfold.

Although these techniques have much appeal, until the capability to use them is built into the browser, they may be ignored by a significant portion of the Internet public. How much capability can the browser include? Clearly, it cannot hold the code for every plug-in that anyone wants to develop. Thus, the ultimate plug-in is for the Java programming language, and that is built in to the most recent versions of the Netscape and other browsers. In other words, Java is incorporated into the browser, so you don't need a plug-in and can use any Java program.

Embedded Programs

One of the compelling features of multimedia is that it places programming right in the page of a multimedia document. For instance, suppose you create a document regarding travel in India. It will be handy to give your readers the exchange rate for rupees. It can be updated daily (or hourly) automatically from another Internet source with a little programming. Why not go a step further and give your visitors a calculator to calculate how many rupees they will get in exchange for the amount they input into the calculator? How do you embed such programs into Web documents? Use CGI scripts or Java. Much useful programming is inexpensive and quick to develop. It's a powerful capability of the Web multimedia publishing system.

DOWNLOADING

For the Internet particularly, but also for intranets, download times are significant. Most transfer rates are specified in *kilobits* (Kb) per second. Files sizes are measured in *kilobytes* (KB). There are eight bits in a byte, but when you send a byte across the network, it takes about two bits of overhead. Therefore, a rough rule of thumb is that it takes about 10 bits to produce a byte on the network. Ten also just happens to be a easy number to use for division.

Using this rule of thumb, you can calculate how many kilobytes per second a 28.8 modem will deliver. A 28.8 modem has a transfer rate of 28,800 bits per second (or 28.8 kilobits per second). Divide 28.8Kb by 10 to estimate that a 28.8 modem will deliver about 2.88KB (kilobytes) per second if it is working at its maximum. In other words, it will take about six minutes to download a 1MB file under optimal conditions using a 28.8 modem.

AUTHORING PROGRAMS

Think of a word processor as a text authoring program. Other authoring programs are similar; they just manipulate different media. There are authoring programs for multimedia presentations, animation, and VRML that you may be able to use without being a programmer. And there are authoring programs for the Web that create HTML documents. For some, you don't even have to know HTML. Already a variety of available Java authoring programs, such as Aimtech's Jamba, do not require you to be a programmer.

Authoring programs come in three varieties. The first is for programmers only. These authoring programs are touted as a *visual* programming tools. Visual Basic is an example. A second type of authoring program requires *scripting* in order to be used effectively. Scripting to programmers is easy programming, but to nonprogrammers it is still programming. Director is an example of this type of authoring program. A third type enables nonprogrammers to create a wide range of useful products without requiring programming capability. Attachmate's Emissary and Netscape Gold are HTML authoring programs that fit in this category.

Perhaps more so than for other programs, for nonprogrammers hands-on evaluation is the best way to judge an authoring program.

Try it before you buy it. If it doesn't do what you want it to do as easily as you would like to get it done, try something else. Unfortunately, an authoring program for nonprogrammers always sets a limitation on what you can do. It is always possible to do more if you can write the programming rather than use the authoring program. Nonetheless, authoring programs provide nonprogrammers with a reasonable means of getting many things done without hiring a programmer.

Fortunately, the easiest-to-use authoring programs are text-based multimedia authoring programs. The Web fits neatly into that category, and you will find that the Web variety of text-based multimedia authoring is easy to do even if you have to learn HTML.

SUMMARY

Text-based multimedia is a great publishing medium for public publishing. The success of the Web shows that clearly. It is also great for publishing privately (internally) on your intranet. It produces rich information easily distributed via a network, and it's reasonably easy to author. It's inexpensive and saves the agonies of dealing with paper.

Chapter 4

COMMUNICATIONS

Regardless of whether your definition of groupware is software enabling two people to collaborate or software giving a larger group the capability to collaborate, *person-to-person* communications software is important. This chapter focuses on this limited perspective of group communication.

E-MAIL

The Internet was an e-mail medium long before it took on other characteristics such as those provided by Gopher and the Web. E-mail on the Internet was the original groupware. It facilitated sharing of information by researchers at universities with the military industry and sustained the collaborative efforts of talented people separated by long distances. If it was a little crude by today's standards, it nonetheless worked well. Unfortunately, only a small portion of society had access to the Internet until the 1990s, and for most people electronic collaboration was a dream rather than a reality.

Many have overlooked e-mail as being groupware for two major reasons. First, until late 1993 the national online services and other major e-mail providers were not connected to the Internet. E-mail was available but was not in widespread use. It was fragmented. E-mail between online service providers for the most part did not exist. For instance, if you were on CompuServe, you could not send e-mail to someone using America Online. At the end of 1993 and during 1994 virtually every national online service and many other BBSs finally connected to the Internet, establishing total national interconnection. The only holdouts were some corporate networks.

Second, e-mail was not totally compatible across systems and was sometimes difficult to use. Until 1996 the capability of e-mail systems varied. Some were limited to messages of 32KB or 64KB. Some could transmit attached files internally but not on the Internet. It was difficult to remember to whom you could send what. For some systems, you had to encode binary files. However, with the widespread adoption of Multimedia Internet Mail Extensions (MIME) finally realized about mid-1996, everyone can now enjoy full e-mail capability. If an online service or BBS does not offer MIME in late 1996, it will not be competitive. Thus, 1997 will be the first full year you can send an e-mail message, attach a file of any kind, and send it to anyone anywhere who has an Internet e-mail address. Although there are still corporate holdouts, the national system for fully-functioning e-mail is in place.

The Meaning of MIME

Prior thought patterns can blind one to some obvious facts. In 1996 e-mail is very powerful groupware. For the remainder of the decade people will find just how powerful it can be. Of course, for the many people who have used e-mail productively as groupware already, this is not hot news. Nonetheless, even those who have been using e-mail intensely may be surprised by how fully functioning e-mail in the hands of everyone will accelerate the pace of business.

E-mail messages are text files. Binary files such as color graphics, formatted text, and executables (programs) didn't quite fit into the e-mail system. The original attempt at accommodation was to encode the binary files; that is, convert the binary file to text files so that they could be sent as e-mail messages. The recipient decoded them. This was, and is, a rather awkward process. This method of sending binary files is not convenient to either sender or recipient.

With MIME, sending a binary file(s) along with your e-mail message is as easy as executing a menu command and specifying the file(s) to be attached to the message (see Figure 4.1). The recipient receives both the message and the binary file(s) in their normal form; that is, neither the sender nor the recipient must take any additional

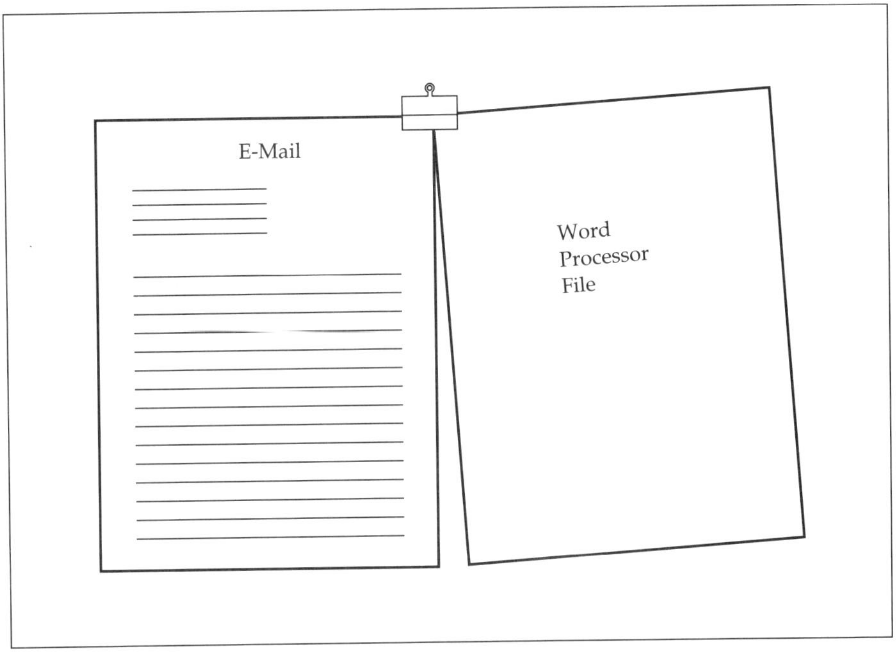

Figure 4.1: Attach files to your e-mail.

steps to make the MIME system work. Both, however, must have e-mail systems with MIME capability. There's no reason you can't send a text file along with an e-mail message either; that will work just fine. For instance, you can send a WordPerfect word processor file along with your e-mail message.

If you can send text files or binary files of any size attached to an e-mail message to anyone who has Internet e-mail or anyone on your intranet, what else do you need to collaborate with people in getting some work done? E-mail plus MIME is very powerful groupware technology. It is multimedia technology. It is easy-to-use technology. And by the end of 1996 virtually everyone who has e-mail (except in some corporations) will be able to use it.

The Future of MIME

The protocol committees of the Internet upgrade protocols regularly. MIME will be expanded by its protocol committee to include features that facilitate collaborative efforts according to Nathaniel Borenstein, one of the creators of MIME. Thus, those setting the protocols envision that just attaching binaries to e-mail messages is not enough. Functionality will be added in the future that helps people work more easily with each other.

On another front, HTML and e-mail will begin to converge. Although protocol committee work is just beginning now, by the end of 1997 e-mail software will include the capability to send information packages according to Dr. Edward Levinson, president of Xison and co-chair of the Internet Engineering Task Force (IETF) MIME-SGML working group. For instance, suppose you want to send a multimedia Web document that consists of an HTML document and two digital graphics (an HTML file and two GIF files). You can currently attach these three files to an e-mail message and send them to someone. The recipient must detach (save) them from the e-mail message into a directory (folder). Then the recipient can view the multimedia Web document with a Web browser. With the anticipated new MIME packaging capability, the three files can be packaged as one file instead of three files and attached to an e-mail message. Then the recipient can activate a Web browser that will automatically view the package of files. There is no need to detach (save) the package (files) into a directory (folder). This method is much more convenient for recipients.

The practical result is convenient universal multimedia e-mail (Web e-mail). This multimedia e-mail can take on any type of configuration. It might be a short message with color photos or a full-fledged multimedia Web production many megabytes large.

This ability to deliver multimedia Web presentations via e-mail will be a significant step forward. Although it is possible today with MIME, it is not completely convenient to recipients. With the convergence of HTML and e-mail, sending multimedia e-mail messages or Web presentations will become easy and natural for both senders and recipients. With the extension of the MIME protocol to include collaboration-enabling capability, working together with multimedia information will become easier also. *Multimedia information will be delivered seamlessly by the ordinary e-mail of 1998.*

Legacy Corporate Networks

The only caveat regarding MIME is that there are archaic corporate systems that do not have MIME e-mail yet. These legacy systems create four disadvantages for those using such systems. First, users cannot send binary files via e-mail to others on the Internet. They are restricted to sending bare e-mail messages. Second, users are restricted to receiving only e-mail messages; no files can be attached. This second disadvantage may seem to be the same as the first, but it has a different wrinkle. By being on the Internet, you create certain expectations about your communications capability. When people send you e-mail with attached binary files that you cannot receive, confusion as well as miscommunication and mistakes can occur, some of which may have legal implications.

Third, for corporate networks that do not have MIME, the disadvantage is that the users may not have multimedia capability in-house where it may do the most good. For many corporations, most of the work collaboration occurs in-house, and without MIME or another convenient file transfer capability, the collaboration is limited to text information. Of course, for a LAN or a WAN there may be other methods of sharing binary files, but such methods may not be as convenient and therefore may not be as easily or as widely used. Fourth, you can argue that your corporation does not need multimedia communications capability, and perhaps it doesn't today. Having limited e-mail capability, however, keeps that small percentage of employees who might otherwise experiment with multimedia communications from experimenting. Someday when your corporation needs more robust communications, there will be no corporate knowledge or experience regarding the practicalities of using multimedia communication for your particular business.

Some enterprise e-mail systems handle MIME ineptly. Everyone who uses e-mail regularly realizes that MIME doesn't always work perfectly with enterprise systems. Unfortunately, there is an apparent propensity for software developers to cut corners when designing enterprise e-mail systems, presumably because a high value was not placed on Internet compatibility until recently. Einar Stefferud, president of Network Management Associates, indicates that many providers do not enable MIME according to the specifications of the protocol, which are clear and precise. The resulting incompatibility problems make the use of the MIME protocol a little rough around the edges. Nonetheless, within a few years all providers are expected to be in strict compliance.

E-mail Features

Although e-mail programs can be complex and offer a smorgasbord of features, simple e-mail capability is convenient and powerful by itself.

If you add a capable method of sorting and storing messages received and a system that provides multiple address books and multiple groups of addresses for mass mailings, you have a basic groupware system that will make collaborating with others easy.

There's not much to be said about basic e-mail. There are places to put the addressee(s), the subject, and the body of the message. Additionally you can copy an addressee(s), blind copy an addressee(s), or attach a file. Where e-mail programs differ is in regard to additional features.

Message Storage Typically, e-mail programs include a storage system for received e-mail that provides for creating a folder tree (multiple folders) as shown in Figure 4.2. You file incoming e-mail as it arrives. Such a system provides much flexibility. For instance, if you are working on five projects, you can have a folder for each project in which you store all e-mail relating to each project. Unfortunately, heavy e-mail traffic can eventually overwhelm such a system, particularly if you permanently store all e-mail for legal purposes, business purposes, or just to keep good records. As everyone in business begins to use e-mail routinely, the volume of e-mail traffic to be stored will soar. For many, it has already. An awareness will settle upon people that they need to keep e-mail records just as much as they keep written correspondence records. More sophisticated storage systems—robust database systems—will be required to handle routine e-mail correspondence.

Address Books Just as Rolodexes are handy for telephones, address books are handy for e-mail. One huge address book may be too unwieldy, however, and the capability to create multiple address books is essential. Thus, you may want to have an address book for each one of your five projects. You need to have quick convenient access to the e-mail addresses of people involved in a project, and when appropriate, it's easy to send one e-mail message addressed to everyone involved in the project.

The ability to create groups is important, too. For instance, suppose one of your projects (one address book) involves people in three cities: Orlando, Tampa, and Miami. You decide you want to send one e-mail message to only the 17 people in Orlando and no one else. You can create an Orlando group within that project's address book. With one e-mail message you reach everyone in Orlando. The ideal address book will have a structure much like a folder tree in Windows 95,

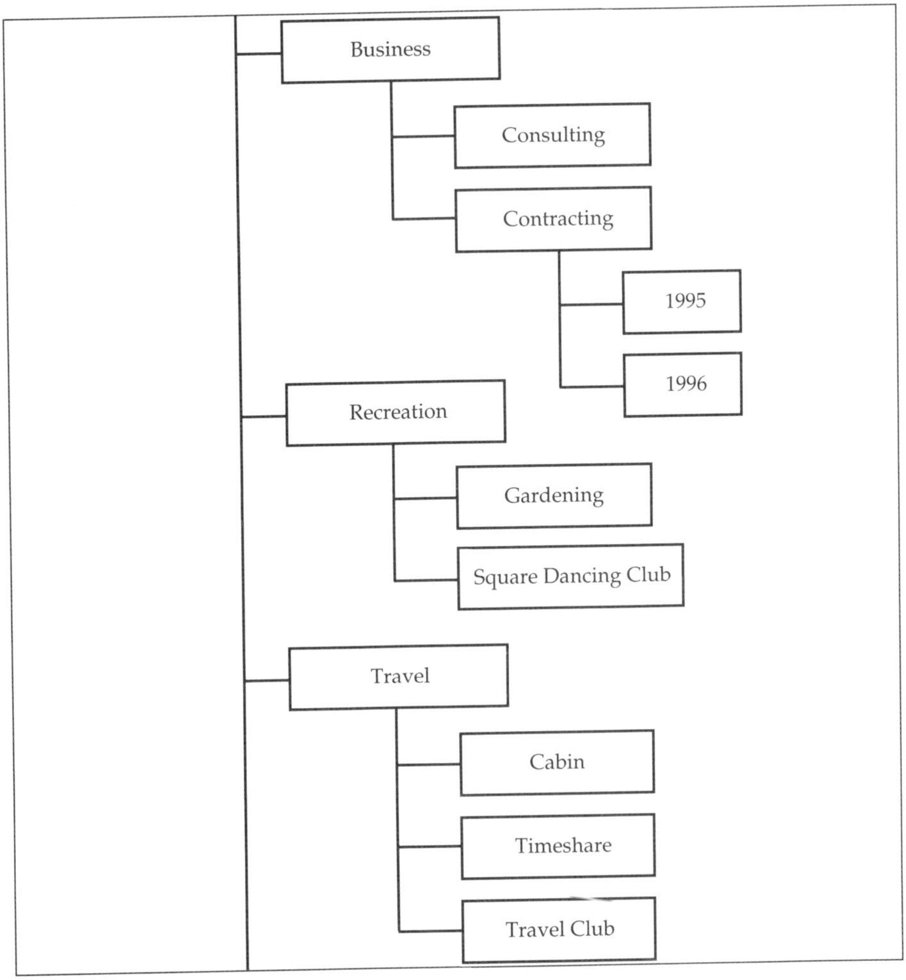

Figure 4.2: Storage folder tree in an e-mail client.

within which you can copy or move files anywhere to any folder (see Figure 4.3). Similarly, you will be able to copy or move a person's address to any group (up the tree) or any subgroup (down the tree).

It seems clear, however, that for many people structured address books will be an incomplete system. A database system in which *groups* and *subgroups* can be created on the fly by queries will make more sense. In fact, it is inevitable that e-mail address book programming and Personal Information Managers (PIMs) will completely merge in the future. Considering the high competency of

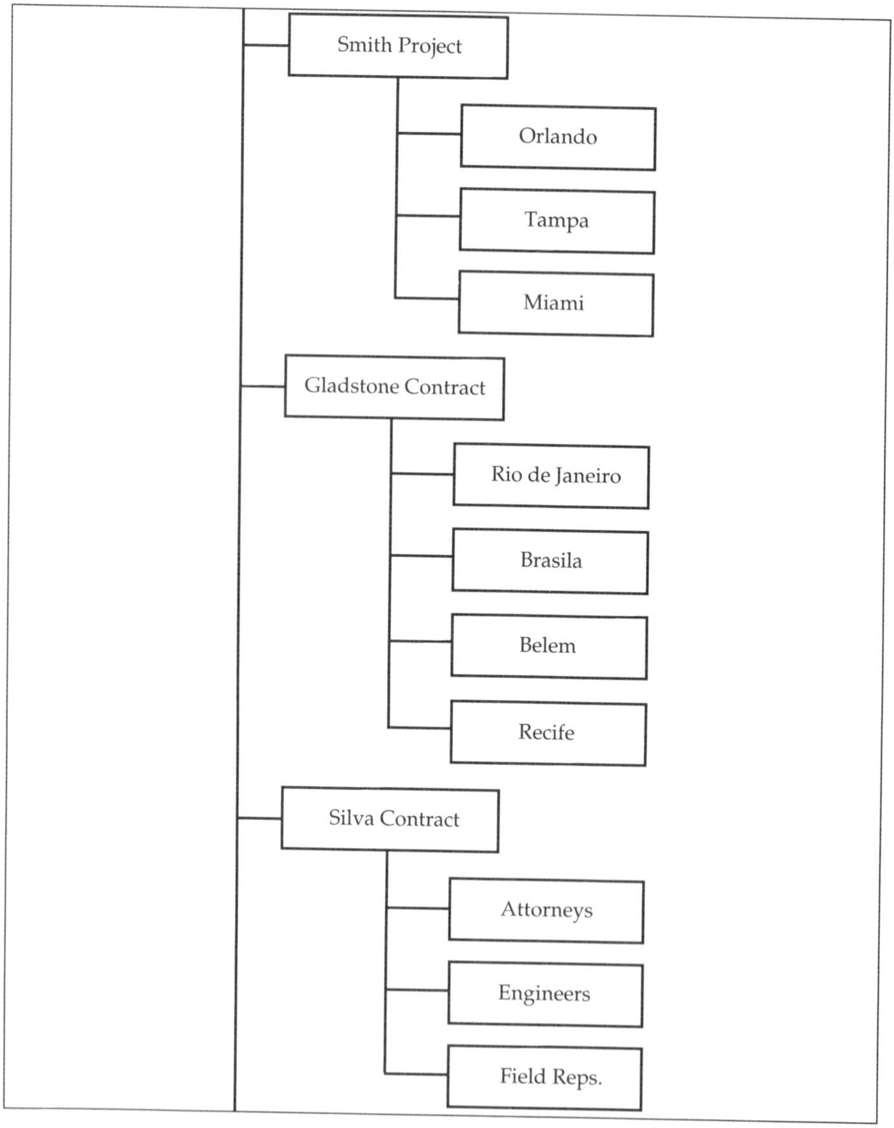

Figure 4.3: Address books and groups.

digital technology currently, it is surprising that PIMs and e-mail address books have not yet completely merged. Having total convenient control over your e-mail addressing is an important feature for using e-mail as groupware.

Directories An e-mail program (client) should have the capability to use a network address directory established by your intranet, if you are on one. This gives you the names and e-mail addresses for your organization, which can be very handy. Likewise, an e-mail program should have the capability to use the address directory of a dial-up online service to which you subscribe. In this case, you can have direct access via your online connection to hundreds or thousands of names and e-mail addresses for fellow subscribers to your online service.

Groups E-mail is groupware that can be used for permanent groups of employees working together for one employer, for temporary groups of people working together on projects, for ad hoc groups of people who may collaborate for only a day or a week, or for small informal groups of people whose work consists of a task or small number of tasks rather than a project. The groups can be employees in the same building, employees spread out over numerous corporate locations, employees and vendors, employees and customers, or employees and contractors and subcontractors. Each of these situations, and the hundreds of situations not mentioned, will have its own communication and collaboration requirements. In other words, groupware is not just for structured groups; it's for all collaborate efforts and for any group of people who collaborate to get something done. MIME-enhanced e-mail with competent message storing and addressing capability is flexible enough to handle a wide range of these group work situations.

Windows 95

Microsoft has stated it is committed "to making a reality of [the] vision of electronic messaging as the central nervous system for organized communication." With that in mind Microsoft has created Mail Application Programming Interface (MAPI) and Telephony Applications Programming Interface (TAPI). MAPI and TAPI are 32-bit protocols introduced by Windows 95 to allow programs to work together easily for the purpose of integrating e-mail and other communications functions. These protocols are available only for 32-bit Windows programs. One noncompliant Windows 3.1 communications program being used, for example, may render TAPI inoperable. Another feature of Windows 95 is the built-in TCP/IP protocol. This means that any TCP/IP communications program that works in

Windows will also be able to connect to the Internet or an intranet without any additional software.

Is MIME Enough? MIME facilitates multimedia communication and collaboration with other computer users across the Internet or across your corporate network, but it does little to integrate e-mail into your overall computing environment. Besides e-mail, people communicate by fax and phone, and more and more, by teleconferencing. The new MAPI and TAPI software protocols facilitate sharing the capability of communication programs with noncommunications programs as well as sharing telephone connectivity between programs.

MAPI MAPI enables communication by fax or e-mail out of any program that uses the MAPI protocol. It provides a protocol whereby programmers can save time, effort, and money by writing a single messaging application that will work without modification on multiple messaging systems. This also means that users of different messaging systems can use one program to use them all. Additionally, it means that people or organizations can choose their e-mail system and their programs (e.g., spreadsheet) separately without worrying about whether the software is compatible.

For instance, if you are working with a spreadsheet program and want to e-mail a report to someone, you can do so right in your spreadsheet program if it incorporates the MAPI protocol. The spreadsheet program does so by calling up your MAPI-compliant e-mail program and conveniently attaching the spreadsheet report file to a blank e-mail message. All that's left for you to do is address the message, write whatever communication is appropriate, and send the message.

You can see how this capability enhances the groupware potential of the spreadsheet program as well as the groupware capability of the e-mail program. For MAPI to work, both the e-mail program and the spreadsheet program have to be MAPI compliant.

TAPI TAPI allows a variety of programs to use the same modem, some at the same time, without each program providing its own separate modem set-up and driver. While your Web browser is waiting for a Web document, you can send e-mail from a separate e-mail program, all on the same phone line. This is important for using e-mail communication as groupware. Anything that makes using e-mail more convenient encourages the use of e-mail for a greater variety of routine situations.

Exchange Windows 95 includes an Exchange client, an electronic messaging program in that it handles both e-mail and fax in the same place. When you receive a fax, the fax goes into your incoming messages log along with your incoming e-mail messages. When you want to send a fax, Exchange calls up your fax program to enable you to do so. Exchange is also an e-mail client and handles both incoming and outgoing e-mail messages. Exchange is the precursor of the new messaging clients that will proliferate soon. After all, there's no reason to handle your fax and e-mail messages in different programs.

Being MAPI and TAPI compliant, Exchange will work with other programs that are MAPI and TAPI compliant. For instance, you can use Word for Windows 7.0 to write an e-mail message and send the message right from Word via Exchange. The other programs in the Microsoft Office Suite and competing office suites work the same way. This is great groupware.

Although Exchange has an elaborate address book system, it lacks the ideal features mentioned above. For whatever reason, the version of Exchange in Windows 95 seems to load lethargically and appears to use an undue amount of system resources. It is a good idea inadequately executed and will give third-party developers a great opportunity. Still, it is a step in the right direction. Microsoft's Office Suite competitors have similar MAPI and TAPI capability. With a lean and mean but robust messaging client, groupware can take a significant step forward in its evolution soon.

Copy and Paste You can use a simple, easy-to-use, traditional technique for e-mail, one that transfers information between programs manually (see Figure 4.4). Incredibly, many Windows users do not seem to be aware of this technique or are not aware of its full potential.

Suppose you're working in your word processor. You highlight what you want to send, copy it to the clipboard, switch to your e-mail program, and paste it into a blank e-mail message. For instance, you can highlight an entire document in your word processor with one keystroke, copy it to the clipboard with another click or keystroke, switch programs with yet another keystroke, and paste it into your e-mail client with a final click or keystroke. In other words, you can draft

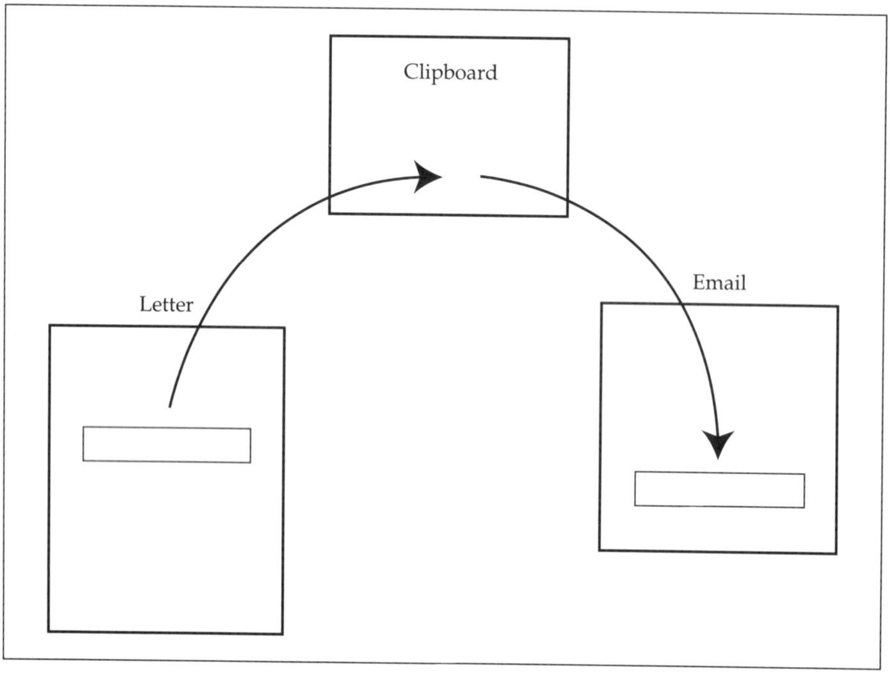

Figure 4.4: Copy and paste—an underused groupware technique.

an e-mail message in your word processor where it may be more comfortable for you to write, and with four easy keystrokes you are ready to send it out of your e-mail client. For shorter blocks of text you can use your mouse to highlight. The only limit on the size of the text block is your available internal memory (RAM).

This method is quick, easy, and dependable. It relies upon no protocol except the clipboard. It works with any program that uses text, and it doesn't take a three-hour training session to learn. And you can do it without Windows 95. The ability to easily transfer characters and numbers out of any program and put them into an e-mail message is a powerful groupware feature that has been around for a long time.

Inline Graphics Although you can send a color graphic file along with a MIME e-mail message, you cannot embed the graphic in the page. An embedded graphic is an *inline* graphic (see Figure 4.5). Because Hypertext Markup Language (HTML) supports inline graphics, however, you can send an HTML document instead. You can attach an HTML document and the graphic file to an e-mail message

Figure 4.5: Documents with and without inline graphics.

and send it. The recipient will have to use a Web browser to see it. It seems reasonable that the next step forward for MIME e-mail will be to support inline graphics and other multimedia elements for e-mail. On the other hand, the incorporation of e-mail clients into Web browsers, which seems to be a current trend, encourages the transfer of HTML documents attached to e-mail today. Multimedia e-mail (i.e., e-mail with inline multimedia elements) is even more powerful groupware than today's MIME e-mail, because it allows you a little more convenience and creates a more attractive message.

Hyperlinks It is useful to have the text of any Web address in an e-mail message actually be a hyperlink to that address. The Netscape browser/e-mail client finds the Web addresses and automatically enables them as hyperlinks. This is an important groupware technique, because it adds a measure of convenience to the recipients of e-mail messages. This capability, in essence, turns an e-mail message into a quasi-Web document.

Work Flow The essence of work flow is that it is passed from person to person along a prearranged path until the work is complete. In an electronic system, the work is passed along electronically; that is, transmitted over a network to the next person or workstation in the flow. It is easy to see that a program dedicated to work flow might offer some advantages to collaboration work that requires structured activities (see Chapter 16). Moreover, it is also easy to see that you can put together a usable work flow system just using e-mail, particularly e-mail with MIME. You may have to establish and enforce your work flow procedures nonelectronically, but you can still pass along the work instantly and conveniently.

Forms One device that makes work flow go smoothly is a form. Some estimates indicate that as much as one-third of all paper work is processing forms. Thus, it makes sense to adapt e-mail to provide forms-handling capability, and it makes sense to use such capability to enable work flow processes using e-mail.

E-mail as an Information Repository

Your E-mail Is there wisdom in the collection of your paper correspondence going back over the years? Sure there is. Can you access it easily? Probably not. Do you use this repository much? Probably not as much as you would like. For e-mail, past electronic correspondence becomes a repository of information that can be used easily with text search engines and other electronic techniques. Thus, today's e-mail is tomorrow's database, but not just a database with an odd collection of dead letters. Envision e-mail, as well as other electronic documents, as corporate wisdom (or individual wisdom) that does the following:

- Has a continuing value
- Is easily accessible (searchable and well organized)
- Is easily integrated into contemporary text (copy and paste, conversion)

Why reinvent the wheel? If you did it well in 1996, you can do it well again in 2003. In 2003, just do a quick text search that brings up the old e-mail correspondence, skim through it, refresh your memory, get some ideas, and while you're at it, steal some of the old text *without retyping it*.

What about a word processing electronic document repository? In the future, e-mail will begin to look more like word processing, and word processing will evolve into a more agile multimedia medium.

Each will adopt the best qualities of the other, and the distinction between these two will disappear. Meanwhile, don't treat your e-mail lightly. Treat it as a valuable database for the future.

The Usenet discussion groups illustrate the idea of e-mail as an information repository well. The e-mail of the discussion group members makes up a vast database of information on thousands of topics. The information is easily accessible with a news reader. It's categorized by topics. Subtopics are arranged in threads. And you can use it today. There's no reason you can't treat your e-mail or your company's e-mail the way Usenet treats the e-mail of its discussion groups.

Other People's E-mail If you were a biotech scientist, wouldn't you like to have a database with all the past e-mail for the Usenet Enzyme discussion group or the DNA discussion group? When you treat your own e-mail as a database of information, you can start thinking of treating the e-mail of others as a database of information too.

Such databases are beyond the scope of a chapter on person-to-person communications. If you want to make such databases materialize, however, you must take action today. You need to develop an archive system for your own e-mail, and you need to start systematically collecting other people's e-mail resources that are valuable to you now or that will be valuable to you in the future.

The Future of E-mail

E-mail started as a simple tool that's easy for almost anyone to use. Typically, new users first see it as a memo. Then they see it as a letter. Finally, they come to think they can use it for anything. It can be a report, a database, or any other form of text. You can copy and paste a 40-page report into an e-mail message with just a few clicks and keystrokes. As was discussed under MIME, however, e-mail will go even further (see Figure 4.6).

In 1996, *Digital Signatures* and everything below it on the chart became routine for those who needed such features. By 1998, or certainly by the end of the decade, the remaining capabilities will be in place.

E-mail traffic becomes a burden to most active business people just as much as snail mail does. With snail mail, you open your mail by the waste basket and toss as much as you can with as little scanning as possible. With e-mail, you can scan the *Subject* lines easily today and

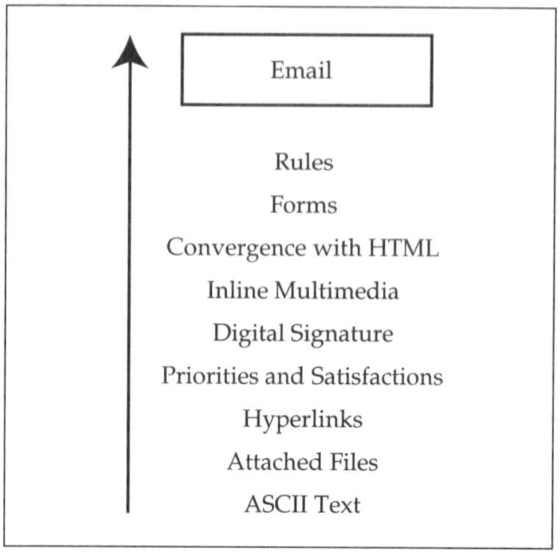

Figure 4.6: E-mail will evolve quickly into a more flexible and more capable medium.

eliminate some messages you don't care to read, but it remains burdensome. In the future, you will be able to use rules for filtering that will sort, route, and process your e-mail for you. This takes a portion of the burden off you, something that's possible with snail mail only by employing a secretary.

It's easy to see that e-mail will not remain the simple device it is today. To be sure, it needs to retain its essential simple character so that people will continue to find it easy to use. Nonetheless, e-mail software will grow in capability, thus making such enhanced capability available to the people who need it and will use it.

FAX

A fax is a graphic image of a sheet of paper. When generated from a word processor and a fax program, where it is never printed on a piece of paper, it is a digital image. As a digital image, it is a large file and one that is cast in concrete, so to speak. It seems likely that fax will eventually decline as an electronic medium for most businesses as e-mail becomes more widely used. E-mail is faster, more convenient, smaller (file), and less expensive, and you can send multimedia files with e-mail, too. But fax has one advantage: it is difficult to alter. An e-mail message, unless encrypted, is easy to alter. If you are sending something that you do not want the other party to alter, fax may be your best bet. When you want to digitize and transmit a paper document, of course, fax is the most convenient way to do so. Thus, fax will continue to have its uses (see Figure 4.7).

Presumably, a fax file can be attached to an e-mail message and transmitted via a MIME e-mail system. That would work if the parties at both ends of the transmission had the same fax program. Another way to send an image of a piece of paper via e-mail is to scan it and send the scan file along with an e-mail message. This may prove a useful technique for those who want to get away from the use of fax machines. It seems likely, however, that people will continue to use fax when they need the unique capability that fax offers. Fax programs can be useful groupware, particularly when they have capable message-storing and addressing functionality built in or when fax messages can be stored and retrieved in the same place as e-mail messages.

PHONE

Phone programs are a relatively new way to communicate over a TCP/IP network. In contrast to other Internet audio protocols, phone programs are two-way real-time transmissions. The sound quality is not as good as that on a telephone yet, and each computer must have audio capability and a microphone, but it works. It is yet another way

	E-mail	Fax
File Size	Small	Large
Changeable	Yes	No
Attach Binary	Yes	No
Hyperlink	Yes	No
Security (Encryption)	Yes	No

Figure 4.7: Fax and e-mail compared.

to communicate in a digital environment. Is it groupware? It will not replace your phone any time soon for business, but it has potential. It can be particularly effective when combined with other group work software. Look for the use of TCP/IP phone programs to grow as software developers incorporate them into other groupware, and look for the conferencing capabilities of phone programs to grow, too. The Netscape 3.0 browser with Cool Talk has a phone built in.

Video-Phone

Motion video with sound is similar to the phone programs. Videophone quality over a TCP/IP network has a long way to go. This is teleconferencing software, and there is no reason you cannot use teleconferencing software between just two people. As with a phone program, teleconferencing requires a computer with sound capability and a microphone. Additionally, a video camera (cam) is required. Simple, minimal-quality, black and white cams that plug into a serial port are now available for less than $90.

The Trouble with Phone and Teleconferencing

By their nature, both phone and teleconferencing programs are used in real time, which creates a problem for a TCP/IP network. A TCP/IP network is a packet network, meaning that the network software breaks up digital information into packets and sends them. The packets make their way through the network, and the network reassembles them at the other end of the transmission. Along the way, the packets stand in line (in queues) along with packets from other sources waiting to be handled by the network. Only when every packet reaches the other end can the network reassemble them. As long as the network is not strained, this technology can support real-time transmissions. As the network approaches its capacity during times of heavy use, however, there may be delays for the packets moving through the network.

Bandwidth (carrying capacity) presents a problem for teleconferencing. For minimally acceptable teleconferencing, ISDN capacity is required. This is about eight times the speed of a 14.4 modem or four times the speed of a 28.8 modem. Phone quality also improves with higher bandwidth. Until higher bandwidth is universally used, phone use may be limited and teleconferencing may not catch on. If you are on an intranet and are not working with people who have a dial-up connection to the Internet, bandwidth may not be a problem for you depending on the carrying capacity of your network.

The packet nature of the network that was not designed for real-time transmissions and the limited bandwidth show that phone and teleconferencing are not mature software technologies yet. Neither of these problems is insurmountable, and solutions will come. Although these shortcomings should not deter you from experimenting with phone and teleconferencing, the practical use of these programs for business may be a few years away.

USE YOUR PHONE LINE

Teleconferencing is a reality today for those with ISDN or other high-speed phone lines. You can do it effectively with reasonably inexpensive equipment and software using your phone line. This capability, however, is not related to the Internet and therefore is not covered in this book.

E-MAIL REVISITED

Building Block

If you want to disagree with the authors that e-mail is groupware, at least look at e-mail as a building block for groupware. In fact, the prime feature of network computing is that it enables communication, and e-mail is the easiest, most straightforward means of electronic communications, except perhaps for your telephone. So, think of e-mail as a building block for use with other Internet protocols and programs to facilitate people working together; that is, as a building block for groupware.

Authoring

If you think of e-mail as a building block, you have a powerful easy-to-use authoring package right at your fingertips now (see Figure 4.8).

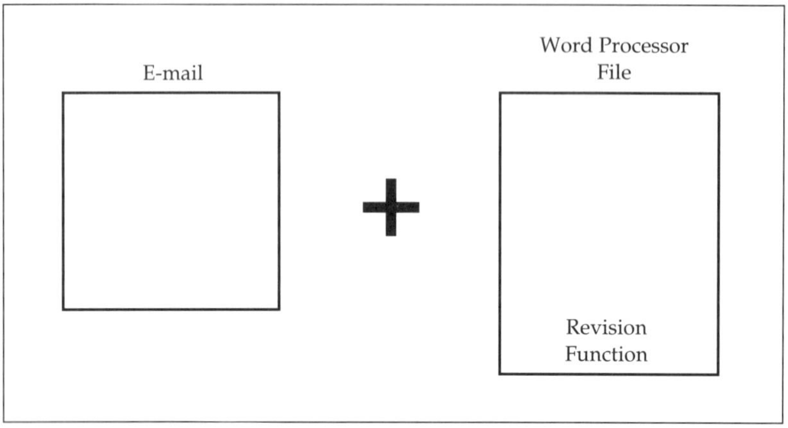

Figure 4.8: Powerful groupware.

Most up-to-date word processors include *revision capability*. This allows you to send out a document to be edited or otherwise revised by another person, or even other people. It provides controls, visual queues (colored text, strikeouts), and management features. How do you learn to use it? Read the manual that comes with your word processor. It's as easy as it is handy. Now, with MIME e-mail, you can pass around a word processor document by attaching it to an e-mail message you send to co-workers and others for review or for co-authoring. What could be more productive? What could be easier? *This is very powerful digital technology.* Combine revision capability with the use of document templates, and the document on which you collaborate will be automatically typeset (by the template) at the time of printing on a laser printer. Thus, with the use of two relatively simple computer programs, a word processor and an e-mail client, you have put together an effective authoring package that will satisfy perhaps half of all your groupware needs for years and will do desktop publishing in addition. This package is widely available and inexpensive. In fact, most computer users have it already. Try it today, if you haven't tried it yet, and collaborate on authoring with someone.

O-MAIL

Is there any reason e-mail has to be text? Why can't it be a-mail or v-mail? The e-mail client of the future will show your incoming messages. Until you click on a message, you won't know whether it is text, audio, or video. If it is text, it will pop up as a text message as it does now. If it is audio (a-mail), it will start playing, and you will listen to it. If it's video (v-mail), it will pop up and start playing, and you will watch it. Thus, the e-mail client of the future will not be an e-mail client at all. It will be an omni-mail client handling o-mail.

Although o-mail is possible today, video technology is still difficult to use, and it will be another two or three years before computer users begin to feel comfortable with it. But a-mail is a different matter. A-mail is not only possible today but is already being used (covered in a later chapter). A-mail is simply a personal convenient-time audio communication. Envision a-mail as e-mail in a slightly different form, creating additional possibilities for group work. A-mail is to the computer what voice-mail is to the telephone.

In some e-mail programs, an attached file is shown in the e-mail client as an icon (in Windows 95) representing a certain file type. Suppose the attached file is a Real Audio file. If you click on the icon representing the file, the Real Audio plug-in (player) automatically starts to stream that file. This is effective a-mail today. There is one additional step beyond e-mail to play the Real Audio file (you have to open the e-mail message and then additionally click on the icon), but it's convenient. From the sender's point of view it is less convenient. You must record your voice message and compress it into a Real Audio file using the Real Audio's encoder. Nonetheless, it's just a matter of time before the sending process becomes easier to use. Clearly a-mail has much potential even today, and you might want to try it soon. Certainly leaving a message on a phone answering machine achieves much the same purpose as sending a-mail, but not everyone has a phone answering machine.

COMMUNICATIONS SUMMARY

The communications software covered in this chapter is person-to person communication. Person-to-group communication is covered in the chapter on conferencing. Nonetheless, these technologies and their software overlap. Communications is the cornerstone of groupware, and perhaps no aspect of groupware is as easy to understand and use as e-mail used person to person.

Chapter 5

WORK MANAGEMENT

The operative word in the definition of groupware is *work*. Collaborative software comes in the form of games or other frivolous activities, but groupware is designed to help people collaborate in getting work done. Therefore, managing the work to be done takes on major importance in the groupware scheme of things. A variety of established groupware functions regarding work now exists, and new ones are certain to be invented soon. This is an important software field that that will experience considerable growth in the next few years.

Always keep in mind that work management software need not be limited to your organization. You may want to include your vendors, consultants, contractors, subcontractors, and even customers in your work management systems.

TO-DO LIST

A simple to-do list can be valuable to both employees and managers. Personal Information Managers (PIMs) usually contain a to-do list, and such lists have proven popular features. To-do lists in PIMs are strictly for the use of one person, however, and do not constitute groupware. When they become part of an online to-do system, they begin to look like group software. For instance, ECCO Pro is a sophisticated PIM that includes to-do lists and can enable communications with co-workers on a LAN. When combined with ECCO Share, a TCP/IP intranet-enabling program, ECCO Pro becomes TCP/IP groupware.

For instance, if your boss can add a task to your to-do list via the intranet, the two of you are, in a sense, a group collaborating to get the task done. Suppose you come in the morning and find on your to-do list that you are to call the *Daily News* to arrange a full-page ad for next Friday, and you are to do it by the end of the day. You make a five-minute phone call to make the arrangements at the *Daily News* and you're done. You check off the task on your to-do list (online). Now your boss can check back to find that you've taken care of that task. Lotus Notes and FTP's GroupWorks allow you to do this. Lotus Notes includes a to-do list template that can be customized to send you e-mail notification of impending appointments or overdue tasks.

Suppose instead that your boss had instructed you to drive to the *Daily News* to negotiate next year's advertising contract and to finish by today's 3:00 PM staff meeting. Your experience indicates that it takes at least two meetings and about a week to negotiate the annual advertising contract with the *Daily News.* Additionally, you're working on a top-priority project that won't be finished for two more days. The to-do list should provide a means for you to report these considerations back to your boss, who will have to make a decision regarding priorities.

You should be able to add tasks (online) to the to-do list of your boss, also. This is best done tactfully. For instance, you might *assign* your boss the task of renewing the casualty insurance for the main warehouse building at the 4:30 PM meeting today with Eastside Risk Management Associates, which you are unable to attend. Likewise, you should be able to assign tasks to fellow employees, and they to you. Naturally, to-do list groupware must be used with all the consideration, courtesy, and attention to the chain of command that would have to be used without the software, but simple to-do lists in an online system can constitute productive groupware.

SCHEDULING

Like the to-do lists, a calendar is part of every PIM. It is only when the scheduling program is part of an online system, however, that it is groupware. It allows people to work together by dynamically coordinating their activities via their calendars. The simple features mentioned below are rudimentary, and most scheduling software includes additional features.

Scheduling online can take on a number of different configurations, depending on the work styles of the managers and employees. For instance, suppose you want to schedule a meeting for next Thursday that will have to include your boss and the company financial officer. One method would be for you to look at their schedules online to see when they have time available to meet with you, and then set the time for the meeting. This works fine as long as all the schedules are published openly and not many people are invited to the meeting. If the schedules are unpublished, however, the scheduling software—not you—will have to determine when the meeting can be held. The scheduling program will poll all the calendars and determine a time. The program might even offer some alternate times for the meeting. Finally, if many people are to be invited to the meeting, it is probably easier to let the software decide when the meeting can be held than to try to figure it out yourself. Once the time for the meeting is decided, the scheduling software should mark the meeting on all the participants' calendars. For instance, Novell GroupWise has advanced scheduling and calendaring functions built in to the program. To search for a free time among a group of people, you just select their names in the address book and click a busy search button. Resources, such as meeting rooms, can also be included in the busy search. When a time is found, the click of another button sends e-mail to all members of the group, asking them to attend. If a member responds affirmatively, the meeting is automatically placed on his or her personal calendar.

WORK FLOW

Some might question whether work flow software is really groupware. It is an automated document production process analogous to an assembly line. It is structured and does not necessarily accommodate communication up and down the chain of command. In fact, the chain of command may be irrelevant. The production process—the assembly line—is everything. This software idea is good for a standardized process involving standardized information where the tasks are repetitive. This software is good for paper factories that routinely process a high volume of documents.

A good example is residential mortgage loan processing. A family desires to buy a home but needs a loan. They go to a financial institution and meet with a loan officer who collects pertinent information from them. Based on the information in hand, the loan officer makes a decision to either discourage the family or accept the loan application. Once the application is accepted, it enters *loan processing*. Loan processing is simply the accumulation of documents. The documents accumulated are the same for each loan. The documents represent things such as employment verification, property value (appraisal), and credit check. Thirty to 40 separate documents or more are normally required. The people who request and receive these documents are loan processors. Decisions made within the loan processing activities are usually in regard to sufficiency, authentication, and proper format. If there is a problem, it is typically handled outside the work flow system. For instance, if the property appraisal comes back too low to support the loan sought, the loan officer, not the loan processing personnel, discusses the situation with the appraiser. Other such problems that arise fall to the loan officer to handle on an ad hoc basis. The loan process itself concerns only collecting the proper documents, authenticating them, and making sure that they are in proper form and showing the requisite supporting information. When all the documents have been collected they constitute a loan package that is then sent to an inside loan committee or to an outside underwriter. The loan committee or the underwriter decides whether to grant the loan based solely on the documents in the loan package.

Loan processing involves much detail, but the details are expressed in documents, in the authentication of the documents, in the format of the documents, and in the requisite supporting information that the documents show. Compiling a loan package is essentially a document assembly line. A work flow program that accounts for the documents as they are assigned, requested, and received accommodates what is a collaborative effort. Within a true work flow program, the documents are all in digital form, and many routine communication tasks such as passing documents on to their next destination can be done automatically by the program rather than by loan processing personnel. The loan processing normally includes outside contractors such as credit bureaus and appraisers. If they can be brought into the online work flow, the loan processing can achieve even greater speed and efficiency. Remember in 1995 when it took 45 days to get a residential loan? It shouldn't take more than a week now.

Keep in mind that loan processing is a rigid system. Although decision points may be built into the system, anything nonconforming, any problem, is immediately bounced out of the system to be handled outside on an ad hoc basis (i.e., handled by the loan officer). Another way of looking at this is that any problem is immediately sent to a special station in the work flow where it is handled by a problem-solver (i.e., the loan officer) on an ad hoc basis. Although the system used may be collaborative software, it is dedicated to one process that is repetitive. Work flow software deals with routes (paths along which documents move—see Figure 5.1), rules (what information is routed where), and roles (what job is performed at what workstation). The logic for work flow can be complex. Work flow software replicates the work processes of the real world into a digital environment.

Lotus Notes is especially useful for creating work flow applications. Notes' application development feature makes it easy to design a custom work flow database. At any point in the process Notes can notify key members of the work flow team with e-mail notifications and

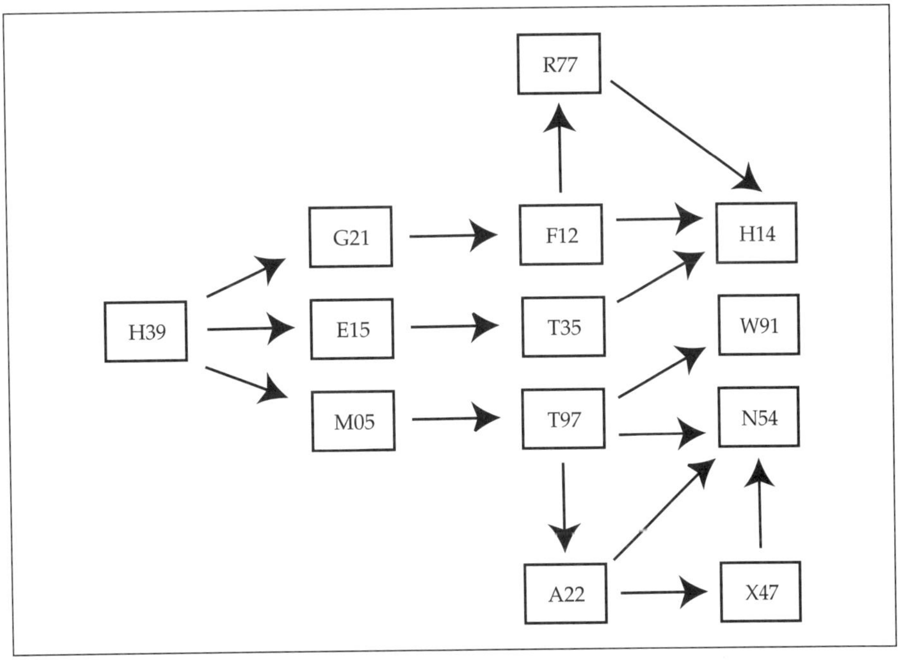

Figure 5.1: Work flow diagram.

reminders. The Notes scripting language enables you to quickly customize your application's interface, logic, and functionality. For example you can easily stick a button at the bottom of a loan application form that sends the form to the loan officer's e-mail box. Another pair of buttons (that only the loan officer can see) can be placed further down on the form for approval or denial. The approve button forwards the form to the disbursement department; the deny button sends it back to the representative who is assisting the applicant.

TASK MANAGEMENT

Task management is like to-do list software but with more functionality. It is not as structured as work flow software, and it is not as comprehensive as project management software. It should be as easy to use for an ad hoc mini project lasting three hours as for a planned project lasting three weeks.

For instance, suppose Mr. Townsend is the general manager of the Tremble Motors dealership and has been away on a business trip for two weeks. He returns on October 15 to find that there are 135 Lightning Bolt XGLs on the lot. On November 1 another 60 are scheduled to arrive from the factory. He had expected to find about only about 70 on the lot. He immediately uses the task management program to create an ad hoc workgroup (task force?) to plan and conduct an open house over the next weekend with a blow-out sale on Lightning Bolt XGLs. He directs the company financial officer to calculate the lowest price they can charge for a Lightning Bolt XGL and still make a 2% profit. He directs the sales manager to prepare an immediate marketing campaign that will include a weekend open house at the dealership the coming weekend. He asks the sales manager to assign Patty Hendricks, a salesperson, to manage the open house because she did a good job on previous occasions. He directs the account manager at Bayview Advertising to prepare newspaper advertising for Friday's paper and requests that Lem Stevenson be assigned to get the job done quickly because he did a good job on previous open houses. Within minutes he has created a mini project with the task management software and assigned people their tasks, which they receive via the Internet or the intranet, along with the beginning outline of the project. They in turn assign additional tasks to subordinates. Some of the subordinates assign additional tasks to their subordinates and to select vendors. Because Mr. Townsend gives the project priority and because he does it online, the entire process happens very quickly. Now everyone involved can look at the outline of the entire project and see what needs to be done and what has already been done. The status can be checked at any time. The task management software provides for easy revision, for informal communication up, down, and across the chain of command, and for the convenient delivery of information as soon as it is available. ECCO Pro together with ECCO Share enables this type of task management through the use of ECCO Pro's unique note pad outlining and columns combination.

Beyond a simple to-do list, a task management program might provide a project view of the tasks assigned, timing alarms, better feedback and communications, and the capability to publish multimedia information. It might be used for an ad hoc project like the Tremble Motors example or for a long-term project. It is essentially unstructured. The person engineering the project creates the structure, and the structure tends to be informal and malleable. Certainly, this is practical groupware. It supports a wide variety of collaborative efforts across a wide spectrum of situations and does not presuppose any particular structure. Task management software is not necessarily simplistic. It might have a full range of advanced capabilities to handle a long series of complex tasks. But it should be easy to use for small or short-term projects too.

PROJECT MANAGEMENT

Project management programs have been around for a long time, but many have not completed the transition to being groupware programs yet in the sense of enabling full communication among work participants in every phase of the project. Project management programming has great potential as groupware, however, and you should see it as a comprehensive task management program. Project management is more structured, more formal, and more comprehensive than task management. It is for complex projects and long-term projects. It supposes careful planning and perhaps even a prolonged planning period. That is not to say it is not flexible. A project management plan should be easily revisable to adapt to the inevitable changes required to manage complex projects, particularly long-term projects.

The Gantt chart is the typical format for project management software. It displays each task on a time line, showing its duration and its relationship to other tasks. Traditionally, project management software has been used by project managers and their staffs to organize and administer a project. Although the project manager's other employees may use the program, they use it more as a task assignment program than as a collaborative program. A project management program as groupware not only is a collaborative program for those within an organization, but can also include those outside the organization who work on the project. This is important because often the bigger the project, the more likely it is that outside contractors and vendors will be used. In other words, when all staff members, employees, contractors, subcontractors, vendors, and in some cases even customers are online and plugged into the project management software, it becomes real groupware. Lotus Notes can enable such project management. For outside vendors to see your Notes database, however, they must be *cross-certified* on your Notes server (see Chapter 10 for more on Notes and certification).

As organizations downsize and outsource, collaborative project management groupware will become increasingly important because it will become the only sanity-saving way to keep track of what's going on. (Other groupware will also be needed for internal purposes to achieve the efficiency required after the downsizing.)

The development and construction of an apartment complex is a good example of a long-term project that can benefit from project management groupware. Project management software has been used productively for real estate development projects, but project management groupware has the potential for increased quality as well as increased productivity. The project starts with the real estate developer, an idea, and a rough financial feasibility analysis. It progresses to an architect and a general contractor for their input. An appraiser analyzes the project and adds to the financial analysis. The developer applies for and obtains a commitment for permanent financing and then arranges a construction loan. The developer purchases the land. The general contractor constructs the infrastructure on the land. At this point numerous subcontractors, vendors, utility companies, lenders, and government agencies are involved in this project. The general contractor constructs the buildings. The construction lender disperses the construction funds based on the percentage of work completed. When the project is completed, an interior decorator elaborately decorates the model apartments. A marketing effort is started, and a property management operation is put in place. This project typically might take place over three years or more and involve hundreds, if not thousands, of employees, consultants, professionals, vendors, contractors, and subcontractors.

What is the value of having everyone plugged into a digital groupware system for an apartment development project? With communication going up, down, and across the hierarchy, a higher level of innovation and quality is possible. Better timing is possible. Greater flexibility is possible. Early detection and faster reaction to problems are possible. Greater efficiencies are possible. Project management groupware will not automatically realize all these benefits, but with the skilled use of such groupware, the benefits are achievable.

You might note that using groupware for such a real estate project will require that virtually all participants involved be online. Drywall contractors and plumbers online? More and more, business organizations are requiring not only that outside contractors be online, but that they use specific programming too. If you are not online yet yourself, you may be forced to go online soon by one of the companies with which you do business. However, project management groupware does not necessarily have to include outside contractors; it can be used solely in-house too. For example, GroupWorks provides your team with a single virtual space to hold discussions, share documents and other files, and assign tasks to one another that relate to a single project. Tasks assigned within any project also appear on all individual's to-do list so that they have a single point of reference for their responsibilities.

The auto companies today are developing cars from start to finish digitally and online. New cars are top secret until introduced to the public both on TV and in the showrooms. Yet, Detroit has every contractor and vendor connected to proprietary project management groupware that not only spans a large number of manufacturing organizations but also includes heavy-duty engineering capability. A car has thousands of parts and thousands of suppliers involved in the development and manufacturing process. Development time for new models has been compressed from 48 months to 32 months and less. Quality is higher than ever. Secrecy has been maintained. This is the promise of project management groupware. Of course, this is not done with shrink-wrapped project management groupware, but shrink-wrapped groupware will be appropriate for a wide range of business activities.

FIVE IN ONE?

Is it possible that all five of the software ideas in this chapter can exist in one work management program? Certainly. The trade-offs are familiar. Do you use a superb program that fits your situation and is easy to learn and use but has limited functionality? Or, do you use a program that has an abundance of functionality that you can grow into but that is more complex, requires substantial training, and perhaps provides only average performance for the immediate activities at hand? In the case of groupware, Lotus Notes fits the latter description, except that it provides above-average performance.

Another consideration is that even small organizations can use all of these software ideas sooner or later for one activity or another. Most business have assembly line processes as well as long-term projects, even though the general management style might stress ad hoc team work. The question then becomes, do you use one work management program that fits all, or do you match a variety of work management programs to the appropriate departmental activities in your organization?

Chapter 6

CONFERENCING

Conferencing online is group communication in which each person in the group can participate fully. This type of communication has proven to be a very valuable online group activity not only for research, education, and business but for personal activities as well. CompuServe forums and Internet newsgroups are popular examples. Conferencing is growing in popularity for a variety of activities and is also spreading to new media as the advance of digital technology permits.

Online conferencing is a powerful type of groupware. It provides the infrastructure for members of a group to interact with each other as much as the work at hand demands. Not-in-real-time conferencing provides a measure of convenience that is not available with other modes of communication. Conferencing can be a one-time activity of limited duration or an ongoing activity that lasts indefinitely.

Do not think of conferencing as necessarily like a CompuServe forum with hundreds or thousands of members. Online conferencing can be set up for two people or for 20, as well as for a larger group. For your work you can set up one conference, one conference for each major project, one conference for each work group, or all of the above. Conferencing is flexible, inexpensive, and easy—and it works.

REAL TIME

Online conferencing via text that takes place in real time (as you do it) has not been so popular. For lack of bandwidth (transmission capacity) real-time conferencing is normally done only with text, referred to as *chat*. Because people can use the telephone to talk with other people, and even set up conference calls, networks have not been used much for voice communication. Things are changing, however, and real-time conferencing—text, voice, and video—seems likely to grow in popularity over the next few years.

Real-time conferencing via text generally has not been available for business use on networks, because the Internet Relay Channel (IRC), which is a real-time conferencing protocol, offers limited capacity for convenient private use. Real-time conferencing features are now available in Web software (*Web chat*), and such features promote the use of real-time text conferencing on both intranets and the Internet (see Figure 6.1). Because there is no convenience factor and everyone must be online at the same time, face-to-face meetings will continue to be preferred over real-time conferencing when those in the group are in close proximity geographically. When the group is geographically dispersed, real-time conferencing can save travel time and expense.

Over the next few years it's possible that voice conferencing will come into greater use. Not only does it simulate telephone conference calls inexpensively, but it facilitates radio-style broadcasts. This gives the boss an opportunity to lecture the troops or an instructor the capability to conduct a real-time seminar online. Real-time voice conferencing is on the verge of becoming useful today on the Internet, and an increase in bandwidth may accelerate its acceptance. Acceptance may come more quickly for intranets where bandwidth is not a limiting factor. Because the existing phone system is reliable and convenient, however, the use of voice conferencing via a network may enjoy only modest growth.

Teleconferencing is the ultimate real-time conferencing (see Figure 6.2). Pentiums (and their equivalent) have the capability of handling full-fledged motion video via software without add-in boards. Unfortunately, normal dial-up connections do not have

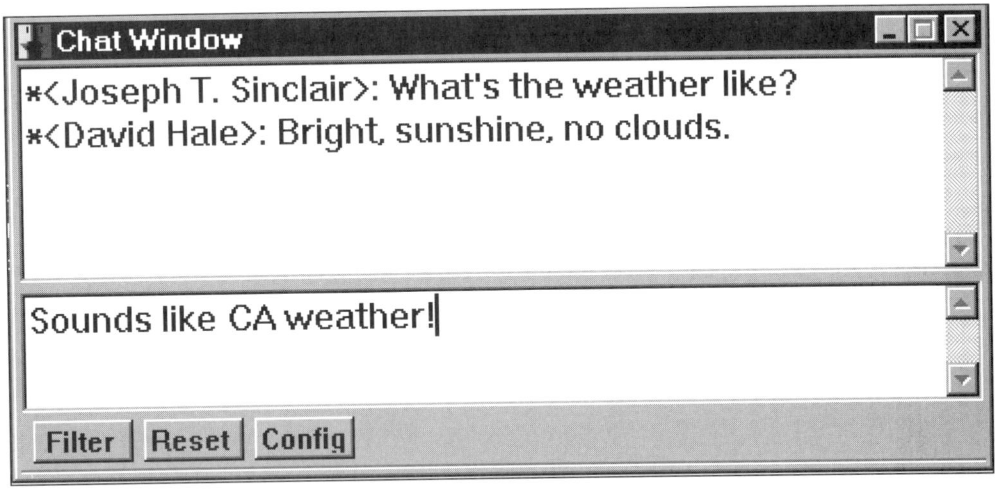

Figure 6.1: Real-time Web chat in Netscape Cool Talk.

the bandwidth to handle video well. You need ISDN, cable, or an intranet to use teleconferencing effectively. Additionally, although teleconferencing is convenient via the phone system, TCP/IP networks cannot handle full-fledged teleconferencing well yet. Thus, teleconferencing on TCP/IP networks may not grow fast until both digital video technology and network technology advance further. Nonetheless, teleconferencing has tremendous potential as groupware, and you can use it today, albeit in crude form.

FOR ONLY $80

Teleconferencing is possible over the Internet today. Try the CU SeeMe software (`http://cu-seeme.cornell.edu`) from Cornell

Figure 6.2: CU SeeMe teleconferencing.

University. It works at only a few frames per second in black and white with a 33.6 modem compared with 30 frames per second for color television. But it works. You need a video camera (cam), which you can buy for about $80 (for black and white). The cam sits on your desk and plugs into a serial port in your PC.

Simplicity

Keep in mind that one of the necessary virtues of a real-time groupware program is simplicity. People using groupware in real time cannot be distracted, interrupted, or shut down by software that is too complex to use effectively under the pressures of urgency that exist in most real-time group situations. The software must be transparent; it must work so easily that group members do not notice that they are using it. How many times have you packed your briefcase for the commute home while reading *Forbes Magazine* and talking on the phone? The phone makes high-tech communication with another person at a distance a natural and almost transparent activity. Real-time groupware must provide the same transparency.

A Full-Bodied, Real-Time Conference

This is a recipe for those on a generous budget. Set up a conference call on the phone (not cheap). Get on the Internet and run a Web server (easier than it sounds). Use your Web browser to access the Web sites of other conference participants. Netscape and some other Web browsers enable you to access multiple Web sites (multiple Web documents) in multiple windows. If your monitor is large enough, you can display the multiple Web documents simultaneously in multiple windows. If not, you can easily and quickly switch between windows to get effective conferencing capability (the phone) and multimedia presentation and viewing capability (the Web). The only new trick you have to learn is running a Web server (see the section on temporary Web sites in the chapter on publishing), and that's not difficult. Of course, if you have access to a permanent Web server for posting documents, you can use that Web server instead of running one on your own PC temporarily.

A Budget, Real-Time Conference

For a budget real-time conference, use the same setup as above. Instead of the phone, however, use a Web chat program (real-time text conferencing) on one of the temporary Web servers being used by one of the group members. In the alternative, the Web chat program might be on a permanent Web server somewhere or in Netscape Cool Talk.

An Intranet Real-Time Conference

An intranet makes things easier if you are organized before the conference. The intranet real-time conference technique is the same as the prior two real-time conferences except that all group members use the same Web server. Most group members have storage space on the intranet's server computer. The intranet Web server can provide access to group members' ASCII and Web documents. Provision should be made, however, for group members who do not have storage space on the intranet. Storage space needs to be arranged for them before the conference so that they have a chance to upload digital files that they want to share with the group during the conference.

WHITE BOARDS AND SHARED SCREENS

White Board

A white board is a blackboard, except that a blackboard is slate used with chalk, and a white board is a synthetic surface used with colored markers. A digital white board mimics a physical white board in real time. One party in the real-time online conference uses a mouse to write or draw on the white board. The other parties see immediately what has been written or drawn on their respective white boards. Netscape Cool Talk includes both a white board and a real-time chat, making real-time conferencing possible without any additional software (see Figure 6.3).

Shared Screen

The white board is one type of shared screen. In one window of your PC you can see the white board, while in another window you can be using some type of communications software to communicate with other group members. Although a white board is action-packed (you can watch the writing or drawing materialize in real time), other shared screens may be more passive. For instance, if the shared screen is a text document, a spreadsheet, or an image, it won't have much action, but it still accommodates useful information for the group to share.

Show You, Show Me

A variation on the shared screen is a conference in which all group members have their own screen to show the group. Every group

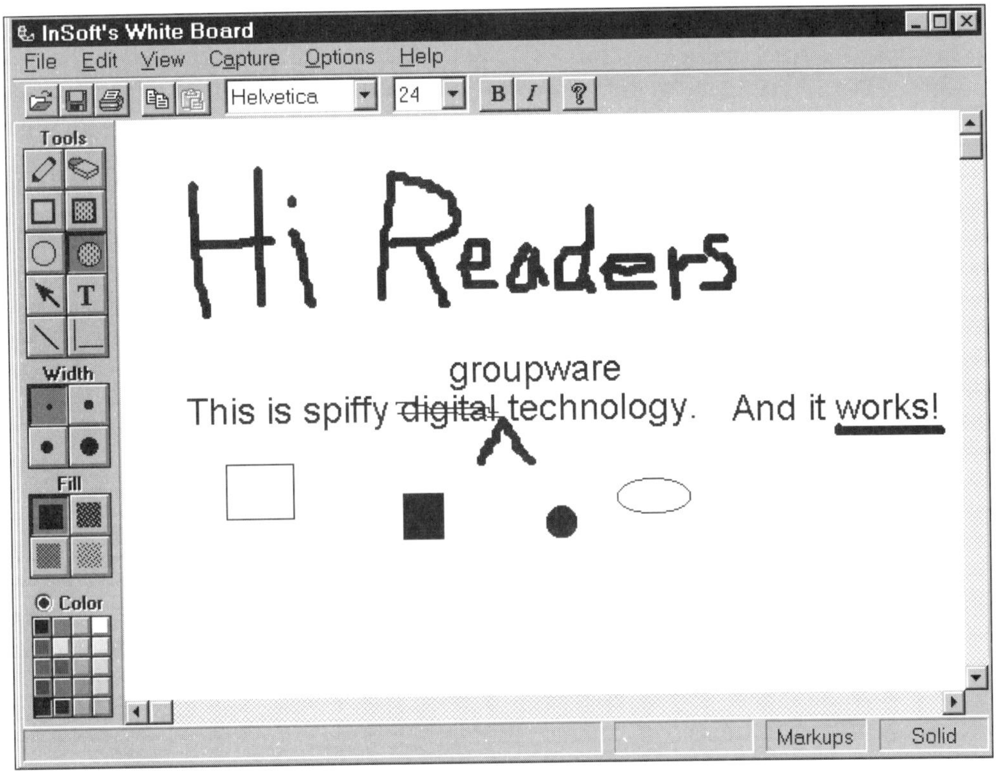

Figure 6.3: White board in Netscape Cool Talk.

member can run a Web server. Group members can access each other's Web severs with Web browsers as appropriate during the real-time conference. Thus, the shared screens can show text, images, and all the other multimedia elements of a Web presentation. (See "A Full-Bodied, Real-Time Conference" above.)

If the idea of every group member running a Web server is too overwhelming, the idea of one party (conference leader) to the real-time conference running a Web server should seem natural (e.g., like one instructor at the blackboard). Other group members can access the Web server with their Web browsers to read the text and see the images presented by the conference leader. Anything the conference participants want posted, they must send ahead of time to the conference leader.

CONVENIENT TIME

Orfali, Harkey, and Edwards in their fine book *Essential Client/Server Survival Guide* refer to *real-time* conferencing and *anytime* conferencing. "Anytime conferences allow people to participate in group discussions when and where they want." Although the term *anytime* is an appropriate way to describe *not-in-real-time* conferencing, it lacks a certain ring of responsibility in regard to group work. Perhaps it's all right for CompuServe or the Internet, but if you are involved in an online conference with your colleagues at work who are expecting your input, it's doubtful that you have the luxury of participating *anytime* you want. You are be expected to participate as soon as it is reasonably convenient for you to get online—and the sooner the better. Therefore, this book uses the less catchy but perhaps more conservative term *convenient-time* conferencing. Indeed, the operative word is *convenient*. A convenient-time conference takes place over days and weeks rather than in an hour. People participate in it when they are not involved in doing something with higher or more urgent priority. Not to participate in a timely manner, however, is not a realistic choice if you want to keep your job.

Convenient-time conferencing is superb groupware. It allows people to participate in a group discussion when they can work it into their schedules, and it has the potential for eliminating some meetings (not all meetings) or making meetings shorter. Although it can be used effectively for group work in-house, it is particularly effective where some of the group members are in different geographical locations and cannot attend meetings regularly. Convenient-time conferencing is essentially the use of e-mail in a group setting. If you look at other group software programs, many are just perpetual convenient-time conferences with special features.

Mailing List

A mailing list server such as Listserv or Majordomo provides automation for you (see Figure 6.4). To create a conference, you place the e-mail addresses of your co-workers Steve, Jennifer, McCabe, and Brook, along with your own on a mailing list and give it a name such as *happyworkers5*. You do this via an e-mail message to the mailing list server. Now, when you send a message to *happyworkers5*, it goes to the mailing list server first, which in turn automatically sends it out to

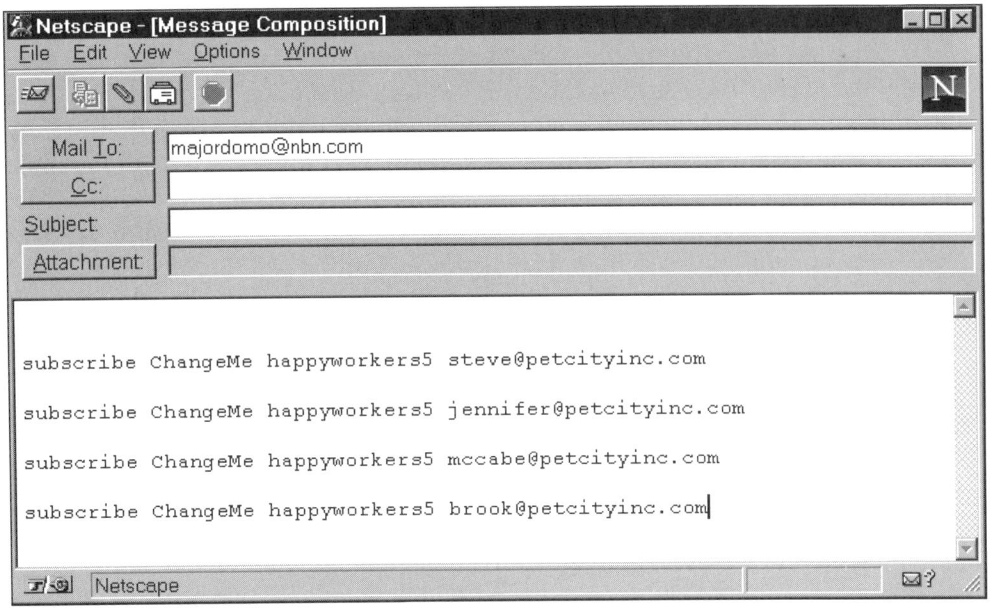

Figure 6.4: Subscribe to a Majordomo mailing list.

Steve, Jennifer, McCabe, Brook, and you. When you get a message from *happyworkers5* (including your own message), you place it in a *happyworkers5* folder you have created for the group. You have created a conference.

LISTSERVS

A mailing list program is generally referred to as a Listserv, because Listserv was one of the first mailing list programs used on the Internet. Today Majordomo seems to be a more popular mailing list program, but mailing lists are still generically called Listservs.

Conference

What is missing in conferences created with a mailing list? Mailing lists are unstructured. A more organized system is to have the messages reside on a conferencing server (database) arranged according to topic.

The topics or *threads* are determined by the *Subject* line of the message. Suppose the name of the conferencing server group is *laborlovers5*, and only Steve, Jennifer, McCabe, Brook, and you have access to it. When you send a message to *laborlovers5*, it stays there. Now you access *laborlovers5* with your mail reader (client), and it shows you all the messages that have been received neatly arranged according to their threads. Brook is working on a *Wall Street Journal* ad campaign for next year, something in which you have no immediate interest. Steve and Jennifer are working on last month's sales figures for the Midwest, which are of great interest to you because you are the sales manager for North Dakota, South Dakota, Nebraska, Minnesota, and Iowa. When you access laborlovers5, you immediately read the messages in the *Monthly Sales Report* thread. The messages in the *WSJ Ad* thread can wait until the end of the day when you have more time. This is the way bulletin boards, forums, or newsgroups work. Using a conferencing server automates the archiving and saves you the trouble (see Figure 6.5).

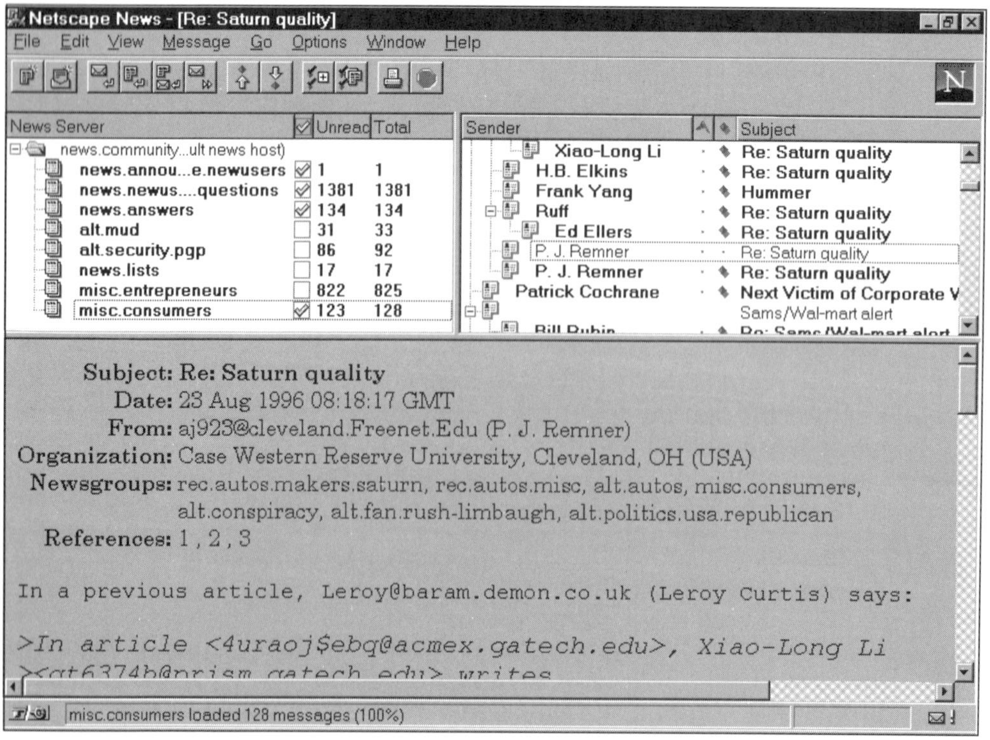

Figure 6.5: News reader in the Netscape browser.

Keep in mind that the conferences on the Internet (i.e., Usenet newsgroups or discussion groups) and forums on CompuServe were originally groupware. Many still are. Researchers, academicians, and many others use them to communicate and get work done. This fact is sometimes obscured by the large numbers of newsgroups and forums that are recreational or frivolous. Keep in mind also that the public newsgroups and forums that exist for serious work are more loosely organized than if they were smaller, dedicated to a specific project, or set up for a specific company; but they get work done nonetheless.

E-mail Conference

Convenient-time conferences can be carried on in an unstructured environment with e-mail. For instance, if your e-mail client provides for filing your messages in folders and if you can create groups in your e-mail address book, you can create a conference (see Figure 6.6). Again, suppose that Steve, Jennifer, McCabe, and Brook are in your work group. You create a group in your address book with only their e-mail addresses in it. You name the group the *fabfive-out*. When you send a message to *fabfive-out*, a copy goes to each one of them. Next you create a folder for the group. You name it *fab5-in*. Each time you get a message from any of them, you place it in the group folder. When you send a message to the group, you also place a copy of your message in the *fab5-in* folder. Finally, *you make sure that all the others are doing exactly the same*. You have effectively created a conference. If you can't read the messages immediately as they come in, place them in the *fab5-in* folder. You can read them later when you are ready to review the group work. You simply open the group folder and read the messages. You can even simulate threads in your e-mail client by creating subfolders and filing messages according to categories.

Voting

Some conferencing software includes devices to help the work group reach consensus. A device that handles voting is a good example. It allows the group to vote, tallies the vote, or may even provide for a secret ballot. A device that provides for a voting period, a displayed tally, as well as the ability to change your vote before the voting period is over, presumably encourages consensus. The fence-sitters may

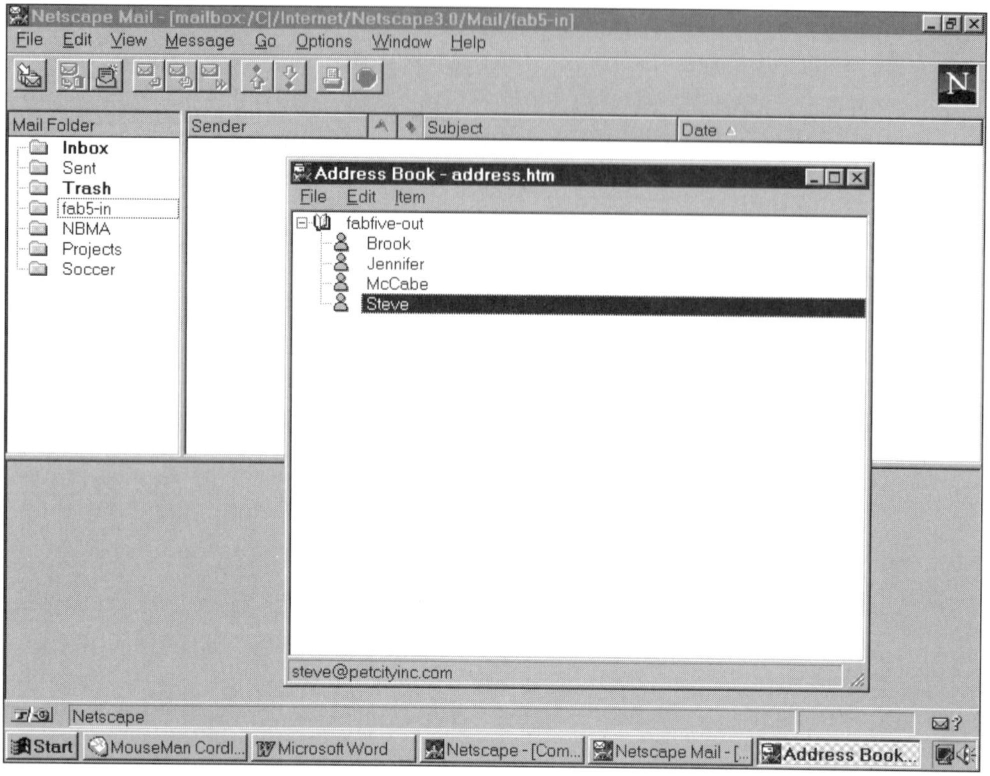

Figure 6.6: Groups and folders can create a conference.

change their votes to go with the majority before the voting period is closed. Or perhaps some politicking materializes on the side. When voting is the primary reason for the conference, more elaborate voting procedures are appropriate in the software.

Storyboard

Storyboards have been successfully used in the entertainment business for many years. They are at once a statement of a scenario or idea and a receptacle and repository of creative ideas. For instance, if you are doing a half-hour documentary for KCAT-TV in San Clemente, California, on the problem of mountain lions eating people, you might break the documentary into 10 scenarios. One will be the requisite interview with a park ranger, so you will have a storyboard labeled *Ranger Interview*. The scenario will be expressed by the following statement:

A park ranger will be interviewed in a state or federal park regarding recent problems with mountain lions.

The storyboard might be a cork bulletin board in a room along with the other storyboards for the documentary. Now, the camera operator for the documentary pins on the storyboard an advertisement torn from the newspaper for an authoritative book on mountain animals (good background information). One of the writers scribbles a note that there was a mountain lion problem in Guyamaca Rancho State Park a few weeks ago and pins the note on the storyboard. An audio technician pins up a note with the name of a forest ranger who was quoted in a mountain lion story in the *San Francisco Chronicle*. An interviewer types on an 8 x 5 card, "How about having the interview out in the field with rifles and hounds for dramatic effect." She pins the card on the storyboard. Someone from the news department pins up a note saying that there will be a regional forest rangers' convention in town next month. The janitor pins up a shopworn park map of the state park where a man was mauled by a mountain lion last year. And so it goes. The storyboard is like an ongoing brainstorm and information collection conducted in convenient time.

There are two ideas to consider here. First, storyboards don't have to be limited to the entertainment industry. Brainstorming is a widespread business activity. Second, storyboards don't have to be on cork bulletin boards. In fact, storyboards are not so different from conferences. You can think of them as special-purpose conferences. Should they be separated from the normal course of business conducted via groupware?

The answer appears to be yes. You usually carry on brainstorming in special informal and relaxed sessions in which any outrageous idea is duly noted without judgment. Spontaneity is the desired result. You brainstorm to generate creative solutions to problems or to generate innovation. Guidelines for conducting brainstorming sessions exist to ensure an environment that fosters spontaneity. Although creative ideas are not out of place in normal conferencing, they are likely to be measured and deliberate. Normal conferencing may not be the best place to conduct brainstorming. Indeed, a normal conferencing program may not even be the best software for an ongoing brainstorm session. It seems that a special conferencing program dedicated to storyboarding can not only provide special functionality for this important activity but also encourage maximum spontaneity and creativity.

Should a storyboard be anonymous? Storyboards have always been anonymous. Within a small group, however, everyone knows who contributed what to the storyboard, and anonymity is not an essential feature. Nonetheless, in large impersonal groups, particularly within highly structured organizations, anonymity may be an important ingredient for a successful storyboard.

It's worth noting here that the authors know of no TCP/IP storyboard groupware available to purchase, but it is reasonably easy for you to set up a storyboard in Notes, even one with a few special bells and whistles. Internet conferencing software can effectively be used as a storyboard as long as the use of the conference is dedicated to storyboarding.

Keep in mind that perpetual storyboarding on every project has served the various Disney enterprises well over the years. It might be worth your consideration.

Multimedia Technology

One uses e-mail for convenient-time conferencing. Today e-mail has multimedia capability (MIME e-mail covered in the chapter on communications). That means that you can use any digital multimedia element in a conference. You simply attach the multimedia file (e.g., BLOB) to an e-mail message and send it. See Figure 6.7. All recipients can use the file that you send, if they have the requisite program to use the media. This capability, relativity new to many network users, opens up many new opportunities for enhanced communication and group work.

Figure 6.7: It's a bird. It's a plane. No, it's a BLOB.

Must a convenient-time conference be carried on with e-mail? Certainly in the future there may be convenient-time conferences that consist solely of audio bites or video clips; that is, a-mail and v-mail. Instead of sending a message, you might send a voice sound bite (relatively short recording) or perhaps a harangue or a lecture (longer recording). In some conferences you might send only video clips (relatively short video recordings). Sound bites and video clips are easier to make but take longer to hear or view than text. Text messages take longer to write but can be read very quickly. Before the end of the decade, in a typical conferencing program, all three are likely to be enabled. Although today audio and video files must be attached to a text message, as audio and video come into widespread use, this anomaly will almost certainly be addressed. Messages will be easily made in any of the three media, and online conferences will seamlessly handle all.

Storyboards, those sponges for wild spontaneous ideas, make great use of multimedia technology. A picture is worth a thousand words, and the sound of music is ever so difficult to describe in text. Although there are sure to be shrink-wrapped storyboard programs dedicated to the use of the entertainment industry, the use of digital storyboards seems likely spread to other industries.

Chapter 7

PUBLISHING

Publishing in print is a special type of communication. It is a broadcast. It goes from the one to the many. It is mass distribution. Often it is impersonal. Publishing brings to mind a Stephen King novel or *Time Magazine*. On the other hand, publishing online can be intimate, selective, and customized. In a groupware setting, it is scalable. You can publish to one person, one group, several groups, the entire organization, or to outside people too. For the purposes of groupware, publishing will simply mean distributing or making available information to those who need it.

IMAGE MANAGEMENT

A traditional use of computers has been the digitization and storage of documents. Paper documents are scanned, and the images are stored. Because scanned images are huge, a huge amount of digital storage space is needed. The retrieval of such scanned documents is usually done via a document control number, although more sophisticated systems exist. This type of system is in essence a database for Binary Large Objects (BLOBs). The BLOBs are black and white digital images of paper documents. This type of system publishes the documents to an organization's personnel through wide-scale document sharing. When someone needs a document, it is easily retrieved.

Is an image management system a type of groupware? Perhaps not. After all, you can get the documents only after they have been created. It is not a system that facilitates creating the documents in the first place. Nonetheless, a system like this that effectively publishes huge amounts of information routinely needed by personnel is an important aid to doing group work. Considering whether a document retrieval system is groupware accents the value of publishing to group work. When a document retrieval system becomes part of another system that is more clearly groupware, the retrieval system often adds a crucial dimension to the other system.

DOCUMENT MANAGEMENT

Another type of document management software relates to electronic rather than paper documents. With this type of software, the documents can be stored more economically. Most such systems use ASCII documents, which take little digital storage space. These documents support more comprehensive and convenient indexing. For instance, you can even do a full text search on a word, and the software will search every word of every document quickly to help you find something. Often this software features hypertext, which provides easy navigation.

Electronic documents are easily edited. Something published on this type of system can be conveniently changed without creating a new document from scratch. In fact, these systems are popular for large maintenance manuals, governmental regulations, and other such publications periodically revised. Because the documents are easily edited, this feature alone can support group work even if convenient group work procedures are not built in to the system.

Standard formatting is sometimes a feature of these systems. The federal government has used Standard General Mark-up Language (SGML) to provide a standard instruction mechanism for formatting documents. Many corporations and other organizations have followed the federal government's lead in using SGML. Many government contractors and subcontractors have adopted SGML too. The documents can look much different from each other, but they are all formatted with the same standard set of instructions (to the computer). The documents can be rendered for viewing in a nicely typeset print-like appearance. In fact, the system is used for printing as well as online documents. The formatting is unlimited. SGML is covered more thoroughly in a subsequent chapter.

Although most document management systems are not conceived as groupware, the publishing capability and the editing capability make it easy to temporarily rig some groupware-like procedures that facilitate people working together in creating new documents or changing old ones. Additionally, like the image-retrieval systems, document management software can be an invaluable adjunct to groupware.

WHAT ABOUT PAPER?

How do you get hard-copy paper documents into a digital document management system? You scan them and use an Optical Character Recognition (OCR) program to convert them to ASCII text. Because OCR software produces results less than a 100% accurate text translation, you should run the resulting documents through a spell checker to create additional accuracy. You can buy a full-width scanner for under $300. It is likely to come bundled with OCR software. The most expensive part of using OCR software to convert paper documents is the labor, but that's less expensive than retyping.

HYBRID DOCUMENT MANAGEMENT

Cross-platform replication of electronic documents has become popular. The formatting of a document in one program or on one operating system is usually not translatable to other programs and other operating systems. A replication program translates the document into a format that preserves the appearance of the original document but can be viewed on any system with the replication viewer (client). In other words, the replication software takes the look of the document as it would appear in print (or on the screen) and replicates it in a way that other programs and other operating systems can see it exactly the same way. The Adobe Acrobat system is a leading example.

Although these hybrid systems try to be more than an image management system, their underlying nature (paper replication) limits what they can do. They are not as flexible and perhaps do not have the long-term potential of ASCII-based hypertext documents systems.

FILE SHARING

File sharing has been around since networks became popular. In fact, originally network servers were essentially file servers. File sharing is a crude sort of publishing. You put a file in a folder on a hard disk and then tell people it's there. Those who need the file can download (or open) a copy and use it. LANs and WANs became popular because they provided a way for people to share programs and files. Keep in mind, too, that file sharing is a multimedia system. File sharing is clearly a crude type of groupware, allowing people to work together via an online system. In fact, it might be said that groupware is really just a sophisticated type of file sharing.

The trouble with file sharing is that it's difficult to keep track of all the files and make them available to the appropriate personnel at the appropriate time. It is also awkward to collaborate using file sharing. You have to create your own system for keeping track of the files you are working on (and the revisions of the files you are working on) by using certain file-naming conventions and the like. File sharing allows collaboration, but makes you do all the work to facilitate the collaboration. It is a passive system in that you must retrieve a file. It is not delivered to you. Additionally, you cannot deliver a file to someone else. You can only inform others that it is stored in a certain folder and request that they get it.

In spite of its deficiencies, file sharing is a proven way to distribute and share digital assets and thereby collaborate on work. FTP enables file sharing on TCP/IP networks, and the Web HTTP protocol can use FTP too. Indeed, for particularly large files that cannot be reasonably be attached to an e-mail message, FTP is the only practical means of online distribution.

FILE SIZE

There is a file size that's too large to attach to an e-mail message. What that size might be will differ with each situation. For instance, if you send someone a 5MB file attached to an e-mail message, it will take almost a half-hour with a 33.6 modem to download the message. Who would wait that long for a message to download? Most people will think something is wrong with their connection and will terminate their online session. If you send such a file, you must warn the recipient that it is coming. Additionally, some e-mail systems may not be able to handle such large attached files. The better practice is to distribute large files by making them available in a folder for downloading via FTP.

Many people need to wean themselves from traditional thinking about FTP and uploading and downloading files. For instance, at one time not so long ago it seemed like a big project to download something from a remote source that was 1MB. It still does. Today, however, most people are on a dedicated connection to the Internet where they work or have unlimited usage from an Internet Service Provider (ISP) for $20 per month. Modems run at 33.6, and operating systems multitask. That means you can easily download a 5MB file in less than 30 minutes *in the background* while you are using your computer for something else. With a dedicated line or unlimited service, it costs nothing extra.

Multimedia technology has made inroads into document processing and other business processes and will continue to do so. Digital multimedia files grow larger and larger. Other digital resources grow in size too. People need to get away from the mentality that large file transfers are burdensome and expensive because they are neither any longer. Thus, file sharing and transfer continue to be viable means of sharing information and work. Placing files in a folder at an anonymous FTP site (easy to set up) is a reliable method of sharing for old Internet hands and will continue to be useful for everyone (see Figure 7.1). Transfers of 20MB are common today, and transfers of 100MB are not unheard of.

It is sensible that all users should have an anonymous FTP site where they can place large files for people with whom they collaborate. Although group work has moved away from file sharing to e-mail, e-mail with MIME, conferencing, and other advanced techniques, file sharing still has its place. That place is handling large files for people who need them. To be able to come to your anonymous FTP site and get the files when they need them and without having their e-mail systems clogged by long downloads is a convenience to others and to you. You don't need the site every day, but when you

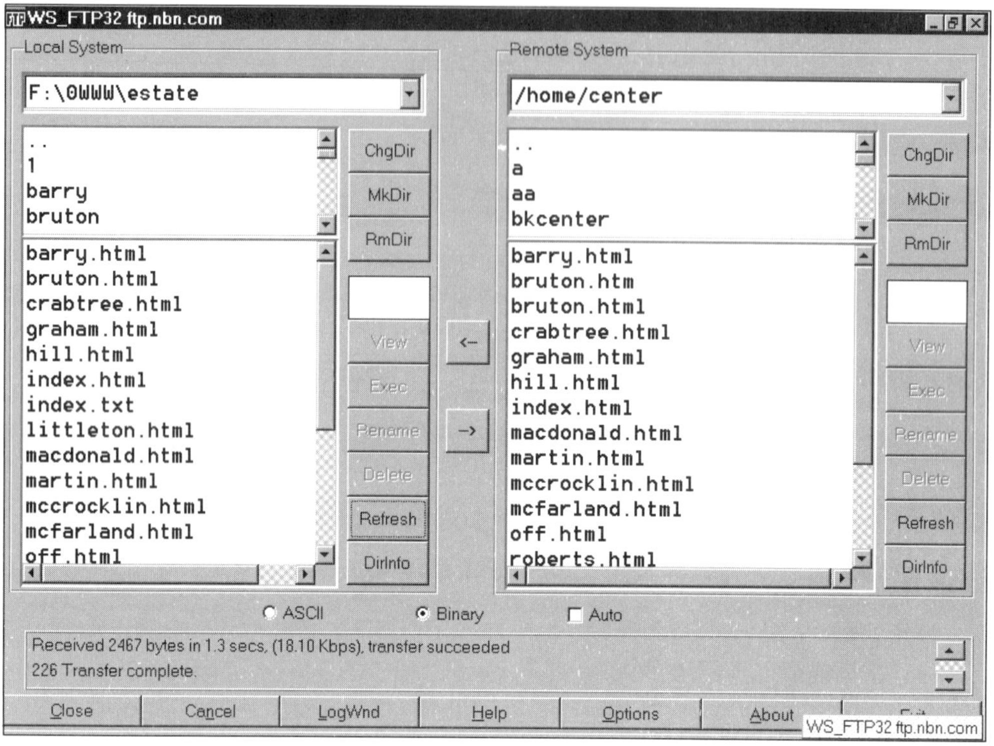

Figure 7.1: FTP folder (directory) tree.

need it, you really need it, so if you haven't set it up ahead of time, you're out of luck.

INFORMATION SHARING

Databases play an important role in sharing information. Although databases are covered in a separate chapter, it makes sense to mention them here. When you make a database available online to a group of people, you are in a sense publishing the data. This is a sophisticated type of publishing in that the database user uses only the data retrieved, which inevitably is only a small portion of the total data stored in the database. Additionally, many database applications facilitate different levels of access to the data, so you can assign different users different privileges. Normally, you expect text and numbers to make up the data in a database. Yet, a database can contain full-fledged text documents or even binary files. Thus, using a database provides unique capability and flexibility in publishing information.

AUTHORING (COLLABORATION)

Because much of the work that is done with digital technology is white collar paper work, an important capability is to publish for the purpose of collaborating on text documents. The book describes a technique for doing so with an e-mail program and a word processor in the chapter on communication. Such a technique has limitations, however, and groupware authoring programs (generally called collaboration programs) exist that offer a broad range of functions to assist two or more people to work together to create a text document. In fact, when most people think of groupware, collaborating in producing documents is the first thing that comes to mind.

Authoring Software

Authoring software publishes the document or series of documents that make up the group project to all members of the group. It offers templates for easy document creation. It includes normal word processing and desktop publishing capabilities. It facilitates edits by one or more group members acting as editors and publishes the results. It keeps track of all edits or changes and structures the control of the project, reflecting the hierarchical structure of the group. Even access can be structured, with some group members having total access and others having only limited access. In short, it facilitates practical collaboration on documents online for those in the same building or geographically dispersed (see Figure 7.2). Theoretically, there is no limit to the number of people an authoring groupware program can accommodate for a project. Nonetheless, as for identical projects done without computers, there is a limit to the number of people who can work efficiently together.

For authoring, replication becomes an important issue. For instance, if group members work on more than one network (one server), the document being created must be replicated periodically to each network's server. Since the document is likely to be stored in a database, each database must be replicated on the other database servers. The

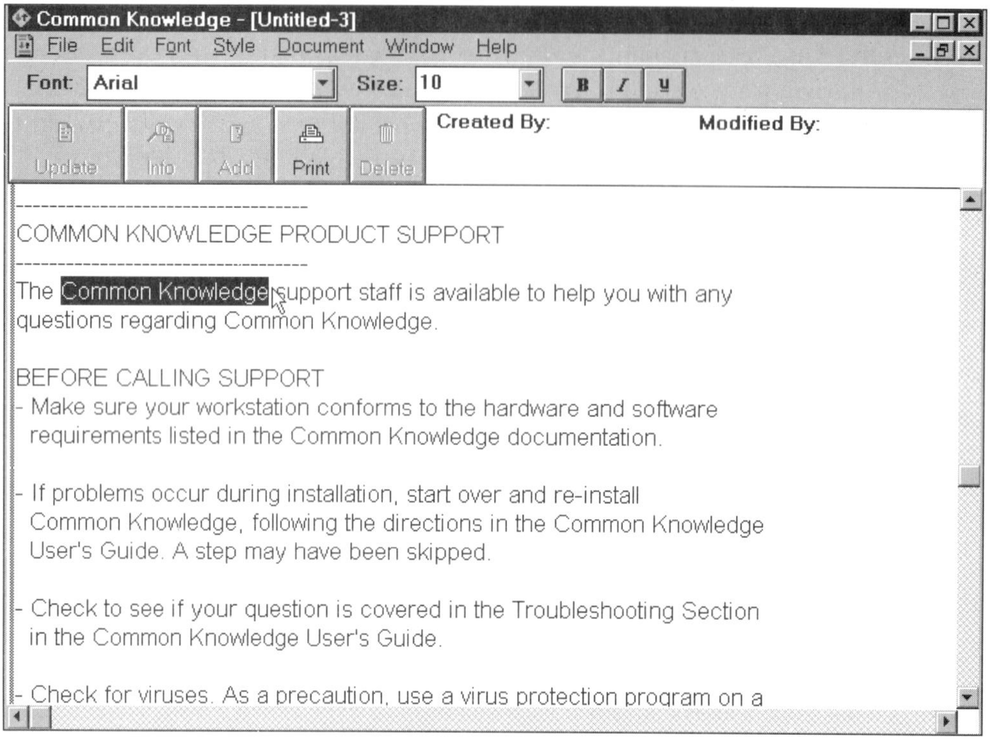

Figure 7.2: Editing documents in Common Knowledge.

replication must have rules regarding edits and changes. Only through intelligent replication can group members keep the creative process under control and always have access to the up-to-date version of the document.

Lotus Notes, covered in a later chapter, has extensive replication capability. It extends beyond collaborative documents to cover all the information stored on each Notes server, including other information that is not necessarily collaborative. This is perhaps the ideal system but not the only replication software available.

Authoring and Conferencing

What's the difference between authoring and calling a conference to draft a document? Authoring involves fewer people and is content-driven. It is primarily hands-on work as opposed to primarily discussion. Authoring software should include the ability to attach and send files (e.g., MIME e-mail), to make comments and corrections (e.g., revision mode in word processor), and to make available documents (Web server). Sometimes it is desirable to make the documents available on a check-out, check-in basis. When the document is checked out, no one else can use it. Other techniques can be used to control versions and control access to the document being drafted. Lotus Notes has this type of functionality built in, and it is available in other groupware programs. Even with these special capabilities, it is easy to see that authoring and conferencing groupware may be similar. In fact, authoring and conferencing may be two aspects of just one groupware program.

INTERACTIVE MULTIMEDIA DOCUMENT MANAGEMENT

Although "interactive multimedia document management" is an apt description of Lotus Notes covered in a later chapter, in this chapter the heading describes the publishing system known as the World Wide Web (Web).

Development Platform

E-mail and the Web are the two most important protocols on the Internet for many purposes, and groupware is no exception. Thus, the remainder of this chapter is devoted to the Web. The Web is at once a capable interactive multimedia publishing system and a front end for almost any type of computing via CGI, ODBC, and various other APIs and through the use of CGI scripts, Java, and other programming. Therefore, it provides competent infrastructure for supporting almost any type of groupware. Certainly, much groupware now under development and much yet to be developed will be Web programs or programs somehow connected to the Web. Thus, one view of the Web is as a development platform. No other program ming except Lotus Notes rises to the generic level of a popular development platform. Because there is a chapter on TCP/IP as a development platform, however, no more will be said about that here. This section of the chapter will focus on the Web as a publishing system.

Web Collaboration

The Web is a way to post documents for anyone online to view. For groupware use, you will undoubtedly want to limit access to the documents posted. Whether you are on the Internet or an intranet, there are several ways to do so. Thus, the Web can provide nicely typeset documents accessible by only members of the work group.

The documents, of course, must be marked up in HTML. Web documents can easily be cross-platform documents with proper planning and with a Web software package assembled with groupware functions in mind. For instance, most up-to-date word processing software includes a utility that converts word processing documents to HTML documents. Because there is a chapter devoted to cross-platform documents, details will not be presented here, but it is probably accurate to say that conversion (HTML < > formatted text) is not a major obstacle to collaborating in the creation of text documents. Keep in mind also that the Web will display ASCII documents *as is* in a Web browser.

Web authoring programs that enable users to compose typeset documents without viewing native HTML are handy tools to use for collaborative documents. To work effectively for groupware, however, they must work on HTML documents posted on a remote Web server; that is, the documents you work on will be from the Web server, not from your own PC. A number of such HTML authoring programs exist. Because they get the documents from the Web server, they must be Web browsers too. Thus, programs like Emissary, Oracle PowerBrowser, Netscape Gold, GNNpress, and others provide exactly the capability outlined (see Figure 7.3). These browser/authoring programs enable you to collaborate on documents using the Web as a publishing mechanism much the same as you would collaborate on a word processor document.

Web Publishing

The Web is a convenient publishing system just for publishing text. It offers easy access, easily read typeset documents, simple document creation or conversion, hyperlinking, and multimedia capability. It's hard to imagine a more ideal online system. Most groups need information resources to get work done, and the Web is a convenient place to publish resources that everyone can use conveniently. Statutes, maintenance manuals, white papers, research reports, public records, and other voluminous compilations are all easily published on the

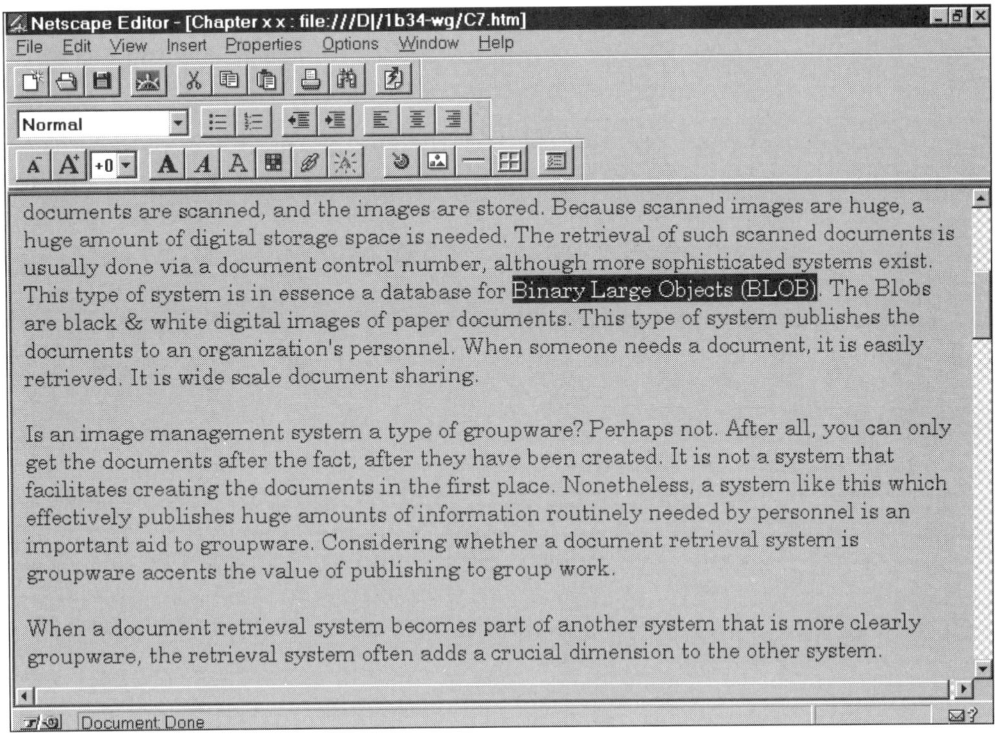

documents are scanned, and the images are stored. Because scanned images are huge, a huge amount of digital storage space is needed. The retrieval of such scanned documents is usually done via a document control number, although more sophisticated systems exist. This type of system is in essence a database for Binary Large Objects (BLOB). The Blobs are black & white digital images of paper documents. This type of system publishes the documents to an organization's personnel. When someone needs a document, it is easily retrieved. It is wide scale document sharing.

Is an image management system a type of groupware? Perhaps not. After all, you can only get the documents after the fact, after they have been created. It is not a system that facilitates creating the documents in the first place. Nonetheless, a system like this which effectively publishes huge amounts of information routinely needed by personnel is an important aid to groupware. Considering whether a document retrieval system is groupware accents the value of publishing to group work.

When a document retrieval system becomes part of another system that is more clearly groupware, the retrieval system often adds a crucial dimension to the other system.

Figure 7.3: Netscape Gold in editing mode.

Web to provide group members easy access. In many instances, these will be resources that might not have been available to all group members otherwise. Thus, the team effort is enhanced.

The multimedia capacity of the Web is almost unique in its agility for handling graphics, audio, video, and other multimedia elements. Again, it's difficult to imagine a more congenial environment in which to use such diverse digital elements. This will become more and more important as the black and white printed page standard for business turns into a multimedia document published online: a new business information standard. But aside from publishing multimedia documents, the Web is a good means of distributing multimedia elements. Is it better to send a digital photograph to five members of your work group via e-mail, put it in a folder to make it available for an FTP download, or post it at a Web site? In the first case, it's a long download that may cause some confusion without advance warning. Even when the recipient receives it, it must be displayed in the correct viewer to be seen, if the recipient has the correct viewer. In the second case, a person must make the effort to visit the FTP folder and, after downloading, again find the correct viewer with which to see the photo. In the third case, a recipient simply goes to the Web site and navigates to the photo via hyperlinks. The photo is fully displayed without further action. Recipients who need to get a copy of the photo can download it through their Web browser. Thus, for both publishing multimedia documents and distributing multimedia elements, the Web can be very handy.

Who is to say that a work group needs only text documents or multimedia documents? With full multimedia capability, the Web can deliver a richly enhanced multimedia presentation or be the front end for almost any type of digital activity. If publishing text documents is a proper function for group work, it's easy to envision that a full-fledged multimedia presentation might also be a proper function. A full-fledged presentation takes considerably more effort to create than a Web document, but in some cases it might be justified. For instance, you can make a multimedia presentation with Director (a multimedia authoring program) and have Web site visitors play it in their browsers using the Shockwave browser plug-in.

In addition, there are already plenty of multimedia titles and other multimedia presentations in existence that might be desirable resources for a work group and can be easily adapted to the Web. Don't overlook embedded programs. For instance, suppose a program written to run on Unix makes calculations that all members of your work group need to make with their Windows 95 PCs. Group members can potentially Telnet into the Unix server to use the program. To do so, however, they will have to use Unix commands, programming commands, and a command line interface. More conveniently, with CGI scripting or other minimal programming, it might be possible to use the Web as the interface for the calculation program, thereby providing easy access to the program in a familiar environment. For instance, integrating a legacy database into a Web site is very close to this idea and not difficult to do—depending on the complexity of the legacy database. Not just coincidentally, many of the browser/authoring programs can actually create some industrial-strength multimedia presentations as well as integrate programming applications into Web sites.

Web Printing

Little has been published anywhere about Web printing. Nonetheless, the Web is a wonderful printing mechanism (see Figure 7.4). At first blush, it doesn't appear to be a competent printing press. After all,

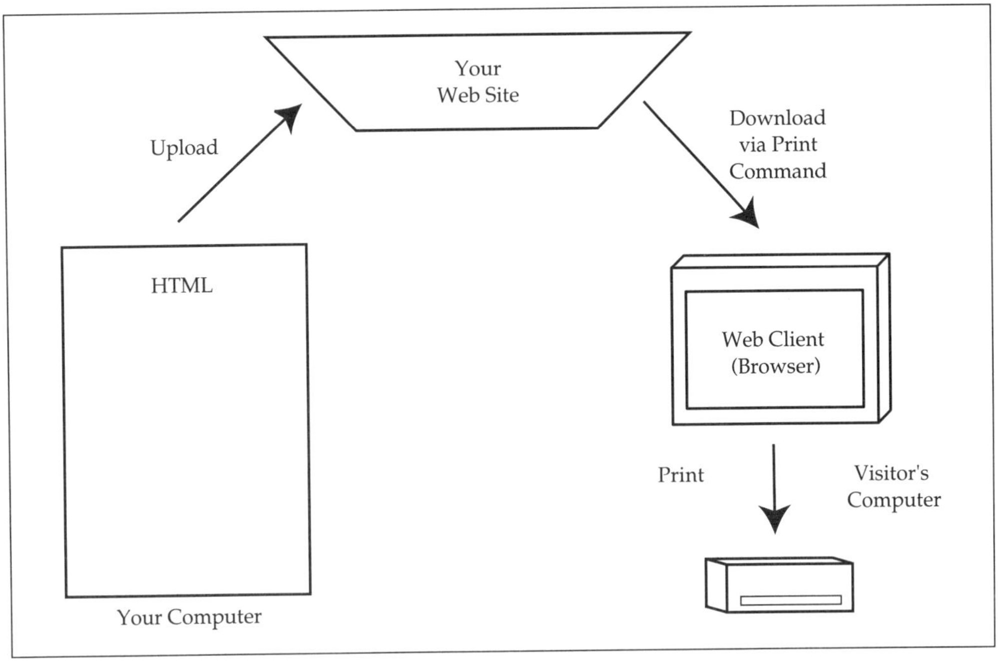

Figure 7.4: The Web can be an effective printing press.

who knows what fonts a browser user will have selected in his or her browser, what size the browser's fonts will be, and what other glitches may interfere with proper printing? On the other hand, if one carefully sets up specifications to maximize control over printing and is diligent in informing members of the work group about the settings they must make in their browsers, Web printing can be made both consistent and useful. Although the idea of groupware is to do everything in a digital environment, many employees still have old habits not easily broken. Laser-printed documents for the group delivered via the Web might be occasionally necessary and welcomed by some group members. Keep in mind that the in-line graphics of the Web document are nicely printed too.

The Temporary Web Site

When you get a SLIP or PPP account with an ISP, you usually don't get a permanent IP address. The ISP has a set of IP addresses that it uses over and over again. It assigns one dynamically to you every time you dial up to get on the Internet. Thus, it's not practical to go on the

Internet and make a server available, because no one will know your IP address ahead of time to access your server. If, however, you have a permanent IP address (you probably do if you have an ISDN line) or can get one temporarily, you can go on the Internet and make a server available for those to whom you have given your IP address ahead of time. In this case, the IP address is expressed in four sets of numbers separated by three periods (e.g., 209.43.229.10).

Why would you want to make a server available over the Internet? Normally when you think of an Internet server—whether it's a Web, a Gopher, or an FTP server, you think of a server that operates around the clock 365 days a year; but it doesn't have to work that way. Why not a temporary server?

One hour? Three hours? Twenty minutes? Does the idea of a temporary Web server have any potential? For example, WebSite will run just fine in Windows 95. It's easy to install, and you can turn it on and off as you need to use it. All you need is a specific IP address to make it available to others—an IP address that you can announce before you get online. When you review all the Web groupware that is available—groupware that works through the Web—surely there is something you can use in real time to get work done with other people. No making elaborate arrangements with ISPs. No extra ISP charges. No being forced to use an ISP's choice in software. You can do it all on your own computer. Simply use your dial-up line. Give your IP address to the other participants along with notification of the session time, and you're in business.

IF YOU DON'T KNOW YOUR IP ADDRESS

If you cannot get an IP address with which to notify people, you can get online and find out what your IP address is; that is, the IP address that has been assigned to you dynamically for that session. Then you can notify people by e-mail or telephone. It's not as handy, perhaps, as having more lead time to notify people, but it will work.

If you are doing group work, why would you want to enable one-way communication by running a temporary server? In other words, why would you want to be the publisher? Fortunately, one-way communication is not necessary. You can be online with your Web browser *at the same time and on the same line* as you are with your Web server. Consequently, you can be the host as well as a participant.

Here's one of many ways this can work. Suppose you and two other people working together have information you want to publish to the others. All of you can get on the Internet at the same time running a Web server and a browser on your computers. Each person will be able to publish as well as read the publishing of the others. The only missing link is the real-time communication. That can be supplied by either the browser (e.g., Netscape 3.0 Cool Talk, which includes real-time chat) or a Web chat program running on one of the three Web servers (see Figure 7.5). Although it seems that this might be a slow system using multiple programs simultaneously over a narrow bandwidth, it runs surprisingly fast, primarily because so much of the time spent using the Web is idle time.

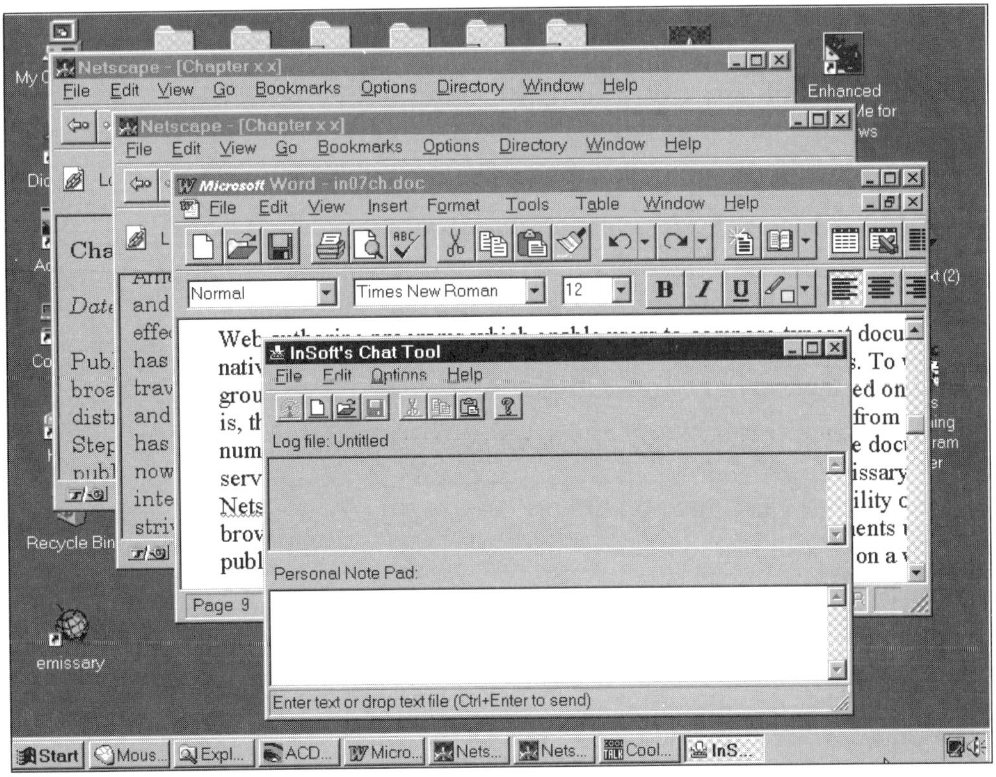

Figure 7.5: Two browsers, a word processor, and Netscape's Cool Talk Web chat opened for a group authoring session.

Suppose you and the other two people are in different locations working on a report, each doing a different section. Your word processors automatically convert text to HTML. Each time you get online, you can see each other's progress on the Web servers. You can discuss your progress via Web chat. With wide enough bandwidth, you can discuss your progress via teleconferencing or Web phone. Clearly, the temporary Web site is a powerful idea and one that's easy to execute. And if you don't like what you've read so far, you can always resort to an electronic audio communication device; that is, you can publish with your Web server and discuss it over the phone—a real phone.

COPY AND PASTE

You have all those windows open on your monitor, and you're looking at your colleagues' Web servers. Why not copy and paste a little? Can you copy something from your browser (showing the documents on a colleague's Web server) and paste it into your word processor? Sure. Highlight it in the Web browser, copy it to the clipboard, and paste it into the word processor. Can you copy something from your word processor and paste it into a document at a colleague's Web site? The answer is yes if you are using an authoring browser such as Netscape Gold and if you have been given authoring access to your colleague's Web documents. Simple to do.

MONSTER MONITOR?

How large should a monitor be? In the three-person example, each person will want to have two browsers showing two Web documents, a word processor, plus a video window, audio conferencing program, or Web chat for a total of four windows open on the screen at the same time. Clearly, the late 1990s represent the age of the 21≤ monitors.

A WORD ABOUT WEB BROWSERS

One of the promises of the Web, the Internet, intranets, and network computers is simplicity, and the Web browser is the focus of simplicity. Therefore, the browser has become the *gateway* to modern computing.

The Gateway (Browser)

Browsers are among the easiest programs to use ever devised. Point and click with some occasional typing is about all you have to do to use a browser. With hyperlinks (navigation), forms (input), and CGI (programming) capability built into HTML documents, you can perform a wide range of tasks within a narrow range of browser functions.

Hyperlinks

Hyperlinks enable you to jump from text to text, text to binaries, and binaries to binaries. You can navigate inside documents, between documents, between sources of documents, and inside databases. You can go from a block of text to a digital photograph delivered by a database application and then on to an embedded program. This capability with its limited array of control functions provides a flexible range of functions for getting things done.

Forms

The forms HTML markups enable a user to supply input into the system—in fact, directly into a Web document. A system cannot function fully on point and click alone. HTML forms can receive typed-in input to trigger a variety of additional functionality. For instance, you can make a query to a database using a form in a Web document.

CGI

CGI enables programmers to tap the power of the computer using the forms capability of HTML. Tapping the computer to run programs means that almost anything can be done through the use of CGI scripts. In addition, CGI scripts themselves are programs, and you can even write entire programs in CGI scripts. After all, CGI scripts are often written in complex computer languages such as C.

Powerful System

The browser represents not just a simple program but a fully enabled computing system that is channeled through an easy-to-use software device. The question you have to ask is, when does that easy-to-use device become something as complex as the programs of the past?

The E-mail Client

Many e-mail clients are almost as easy to use as browsers. Many browsers include e-mail clients to provide a certain convenience in online computing. But simple e-mail clients may not be adequate for heavy e-mail users, which will soon mean everyone in business, and e-mail clients will grow more robust, even the ones included in browsers.

Newsreaders

Many browsers also have news readers built in. You use the news readers for Usenet, which provides a potent resource for current information. The news readers are easy-to-use programs too. Unfortunately, you have to understand how Usenet works to understand how to use a newsreader, which makes things just a little more complicated.

Other Internet Programs

Some browsers incorporate other Internet programs such as Gopher, Telnet, FTP, and IRC. This is confusing, because the Web HTTP protocol itself will handle these Internet protocols. For instance, Web browsers handle Gopher just fine through the HTTP protocol. Most people will not need a separate Gopher program. On the other hand, although a Web browser handles uploads and downloads via FTP, you will want to use an FTP client if you do a lot of uploading and downloading for a purpose such as maintaining a Web site. A Web browser that includes a full-featured FTP client provides FTP capability well beyond what the HTTP protocol furnishes. FTP clients are not difficult to use, but as with any other program, there is something to learn.

Plug-Ins

How many Internet programs can you incorporate into a browser? As we mentioned above, once you get away from the most popular

Internet programs—which are incorporated into many browsers—the other Internet programs are not as likely to be incorporated. You must use the others as stand-alone programs. What other programs can you incorporate into a browser?

Through the magic of the Netscape browser API, you can incorporate any program into a browser. An API, together with the easy installation and connection of an external program module, creates the concept of the plug-in (or add-in). That is, you simply plug the program you want to use into the browser, figuratively speaking, and that program will work fine. Plug-in programs are typically viewers, players, or readers that add functionality by using a file downloaded from the Web. Shockwave provides a good example (see Figure 7.6). Macromedia sells a capable multimedia authoring program, Director, which is popular with multimedia developers for both business and educational use as well as for making multimedia CD titles. The browser plug-in for Director is Shockwave. If you make a multimedia presentation using Director that works on a PC, you can also make it work through a browser by employing the Shockwave plug-in. You place the presentation file at a Web site. A Web-site visitor comes in, sees that it's available, and downloads it where it plays in the browser

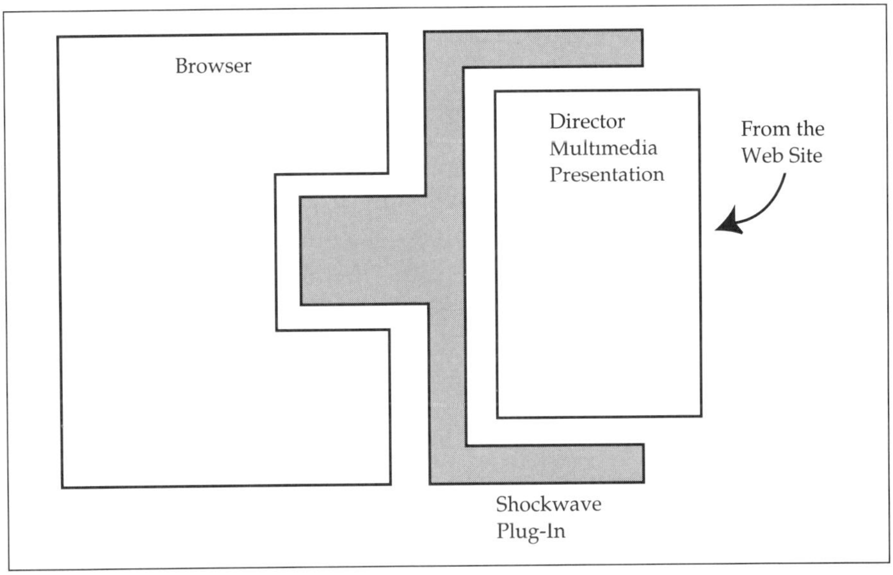

Figure 7.6: Multimedia presentation in Shockwave.

plug-in. The Shockwave plug-in is a player of Director multimedia presentations. To use Shockwave, a browser user must download it from Macromedia's Web site and *install* it. This is a relatively simple procedure. Thereafter, the browser user can play Director presentations wherever they are available at Web sites.

Many Netscape plug-ins are now available. Perhaps there will be dozens before long. Soon, some new programs will be introduced that exist only as plug-ins (i.e., they will not exist in stand-alone versions).

The Ultimate Plug-In

Why bother with individual plug-ins if you are developing new programs to be used through a Web browser? Why not have one plug-in that handles all external programs? In essence, that's what Java is. One plug-in fits all. Java is the programming language for the Web. As long as a browser is Java enabled, if you write a program in Java, it will work in the browser. Thus, Java promises unlimited programming through a Web browser. What does a Java program look like? It looks and works the way the Java programmer wants it to look and work. That is, it can look like anything and can work in any way.

Why not just use CGI scripting instead of Java? CGI scripting works fine. It can be done with easy-to-use (for programmers, not civilians) scripting languages such as Perl or complex programming languages like C. The easy-to-use scripts do not run fast and do not use computer resources efficiently. The lower-level languages like C run fast and efficiently but were not designed for network use. In contrast, Java was designed for network use and runs faster and more efficiently than most CGI scripting languages, although not as efficiently as a low-level language like C (see Figure 7.7). Java, presumably, also provides greater security for network systems.

Today the situation seems to be that old programs (legacy programs) will be adapted for use in browsers by the creation of plug-ins. Many new programs will be written in Java and thus can be used in Java-enabled browsers without a plug-in.

Swiss Army Knife

It is somehow ironic that the simple Web browser born in Switzerland should go out onto the Internet to acquire great worldly attire and thereby unfold into a Swiss army knife. And not the lean model—the

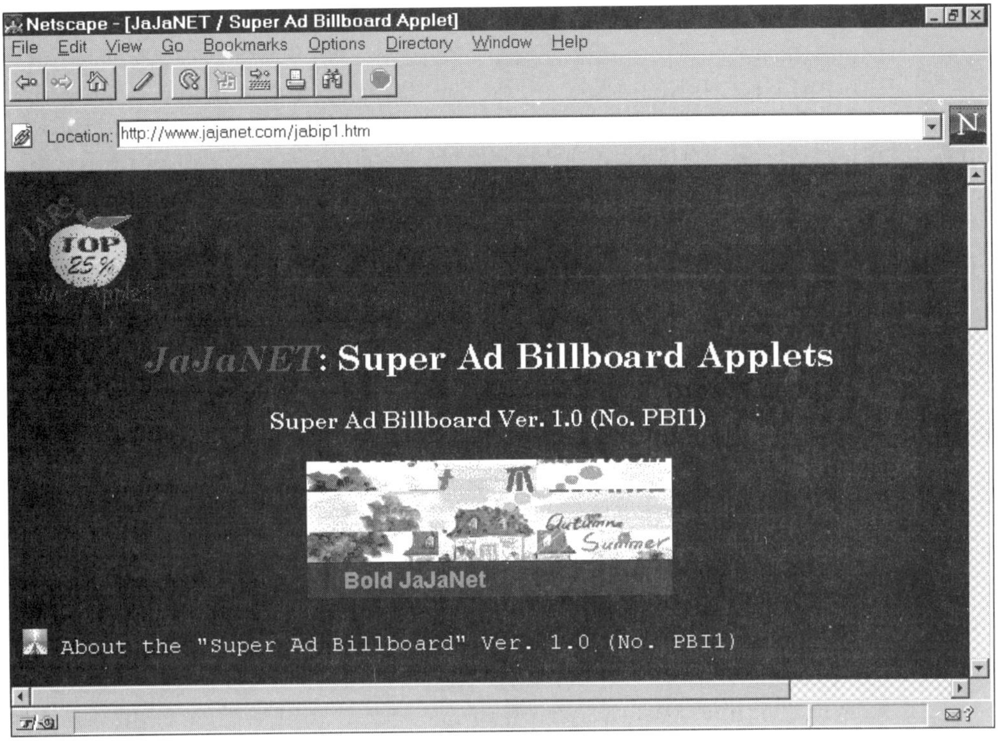

Figure 7.7: Java applet.

big fat model. With an e-mail client, a newsreader, CGI scripts, plug-ins, and Java, the browser looks like a 20-pound Swiss Army knife. Can the 30-pound version be far behind? What has happened to the browser as the focus of simplicity?

For example, try some of the Shockwave presentations on the Web. There is nothing uniform about them. They may have intuitive navigation, but they are just as likely to have obtuse navigation. Although using Shockwave may be easy, Shockwave multimedia presentations are whatever they are, and many aren't easy to use, because many multimedia titles are not easy to use.

Also try some of the Java presentations on the Web. Some are simple applets that dance around or do simple calculations. Others are full-fledged software applications (e.g., spreadsheets) that will compete with established software. Many of these full-bodied Java applications will be as complicated to use as any other software. Moreover, try the new groupware features that come with browsers. Netscape 3.0

offers a white board, real-time chat, and video capability in addition to e-mail. More collaborative features are in store apparently. Although it appears that this is good news for the readers of this book—and it probably is—such robust features come at a price. Browsers become more complicated to use. Already large, browsers become larger and perhaps less nimble. The focus on simplicity is easy to lose.

Balance

Somewhere in the process of adding clients, plug-ins, and Java to the browser, the browser acquires a vast potential to be simple no longer. To be sure, the Internet and intranets hold promise for features other than ease of use. For instance, distributed programming can mean greater efficiency in maintaining software, lower-cost computing devices, easy collaboration, and convenient access to data. But ease of use seems in danger of being lost in the shuffle. It seems important that those who build intranets to enable group work keep ease of use well in sight. The danger is, of course, that even today you can build a TCP/IP system so complex that extensive training becomes the entry ticket to use the system. There should be a balance between ease of use and comprehensive functionality. It will be different for every organization and even for individual departments in the same organization.

On the other hand, it has become clear that there are no apparent limits to the programming that can be used on the Web. For some, ease of use is not the issue. Those people will find that the Web presents a robust programming platform that offers some real advantages over traditional programming platforms, particularly in regard to groupware.

Scalability

As you can see, the Web browser (as a metaphor for the Web system) is functionally scalable software. It can be simple, or it can be complex. Because it is scalable, you need to pay some attention to where your work group should be on the scale. If one person in your work group is thinking that HTML is too complicated, and another is thinking that the group should write more CGI scripts, you may need to establish a standard of practice for the group that will keep group members working together. Because the Web system is functionally scalable, however, it is indeed a system that can serve a wide spectrum of work group aspirations.

A WORD ABOUT WEB SERVERS

You have got your browser and you've been around the block (i.e., world) a few times. Now it's time to get back to work. How can you hope to collaborate working with anyone else without a Web server on your desktop? Before you drop this book into the shredder, please note that's it quite easy to set up a Web browser in your computer and use it. Probably the most difficult task is the setup, but some software vendors have made that as easy as setting up any other software. Try the O'Reilly & Associates WebSite server. You can download it free from the company's Web site (`http://www.website.ora.com`). It practically installs itself. If you know your IP number or intranet address and start now, you can download it, install it, get online with it, and have a friend browse in to take a look at some of your HTML documents, all before an hour goes by (see Figure 7.8). Give it a try.

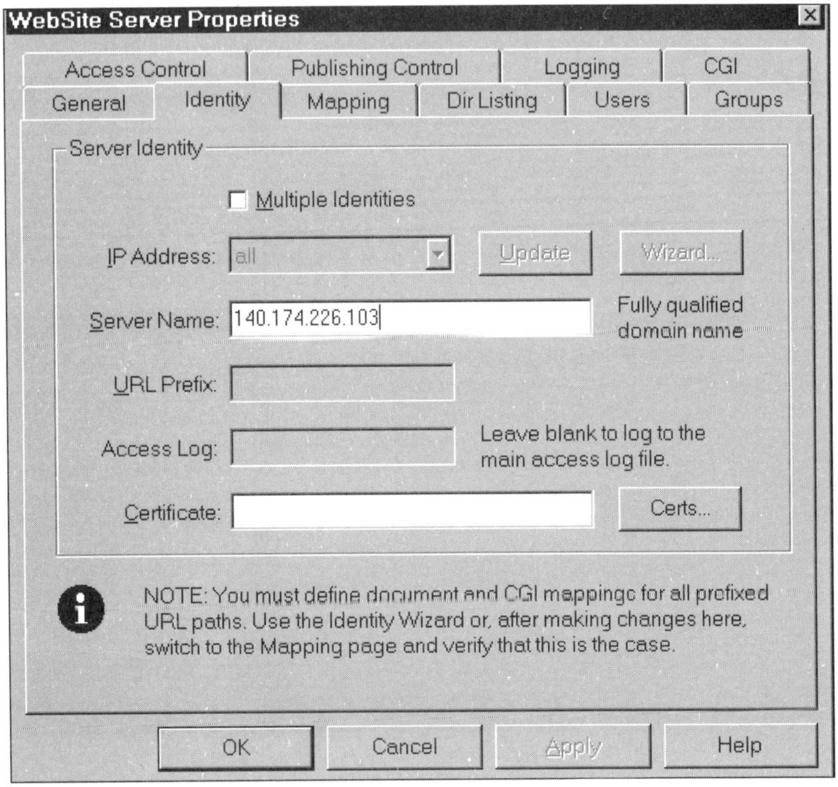

Figure 7.8: Configuration utility for WebSite. Simply enter your IP number.

Intranet

What are the practical considerations of running a server? If you're on an intranet, you can run it full time. Assuming you don't do anything to configure the server, all employees on your intranet will be able to browse in and take a look at what you're offering. What you will be offering is all information in folders on the folder tree below the folder containing the WebSite server (see Figure 7.9). Even normal documents can be seen as ASCII documents. Any HTML documents will show up as Web documents, of course.

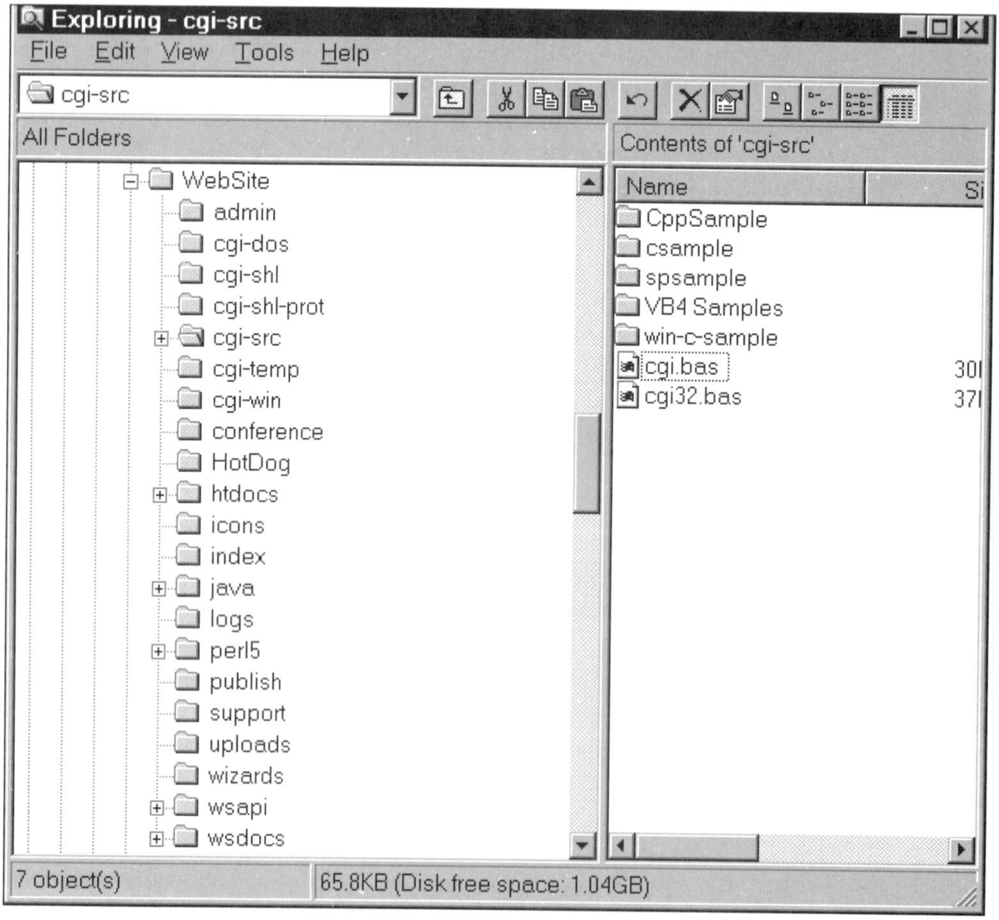

Figure 7.9: The Web server provides access to all folders below its location on the folder (directory) tree.

If you want to learn how to configure the server, you can make certain folders off limits, and you can limit access to your server to only individuals you specify. There's plenty to learn, but don't let the learning stop you from installing a Web server today. What are other ways you can control server access? First, it's easy to turn it on and off. When it's off, no one can reach your information. Second, you can control what is in the folders below the Web server folder. Don't put anything there you don't want others to see. Third, don't tell anyone about it. If people don't know the server is there, they won't come browsing around. Keep it a secret, and tell only members of your work group.

Will the server stop you from working? In a multitasking operating system like Windows 95, Windows NT, OS/2 Warp, and the Mac Power PC you can run multiple programs at the same time with little loss in performance. Thus, you can run your Web server full time and still use your normal computer programs effectively. But because you can turn it off easily, there's no need to run your Web server full time unless you have a special purpose for doing so.

Internet

Unless you are connected to the Internet full time, you will not be able to provide around-the-clock Web service with your Web server. You will have to employ the *Temporary Web Site* technique described earlier in this chapter. One use might be to look upon your Web server as a broadcasting device. Go *on the air* with it every day at 3:30 P.M. for an hour (see Figure 7.10).

Advanced Technique?

Is running your own Web server on your desktop an advanced computer technique? Many software vendors don't think so. Windows NT is packaged with the Internet Information server. Microsoft's Web authoring program, Front Page, has a Web server in it; it is apparently to be packaged with Microsoft Office in 1997. Oracle's PowerBrowser has a Web server in it. And WebSite runs on Windows 95 as well as Windows NT. If your company doesn't put a Web server on every desktop soon, you'd better get a job with the competition.

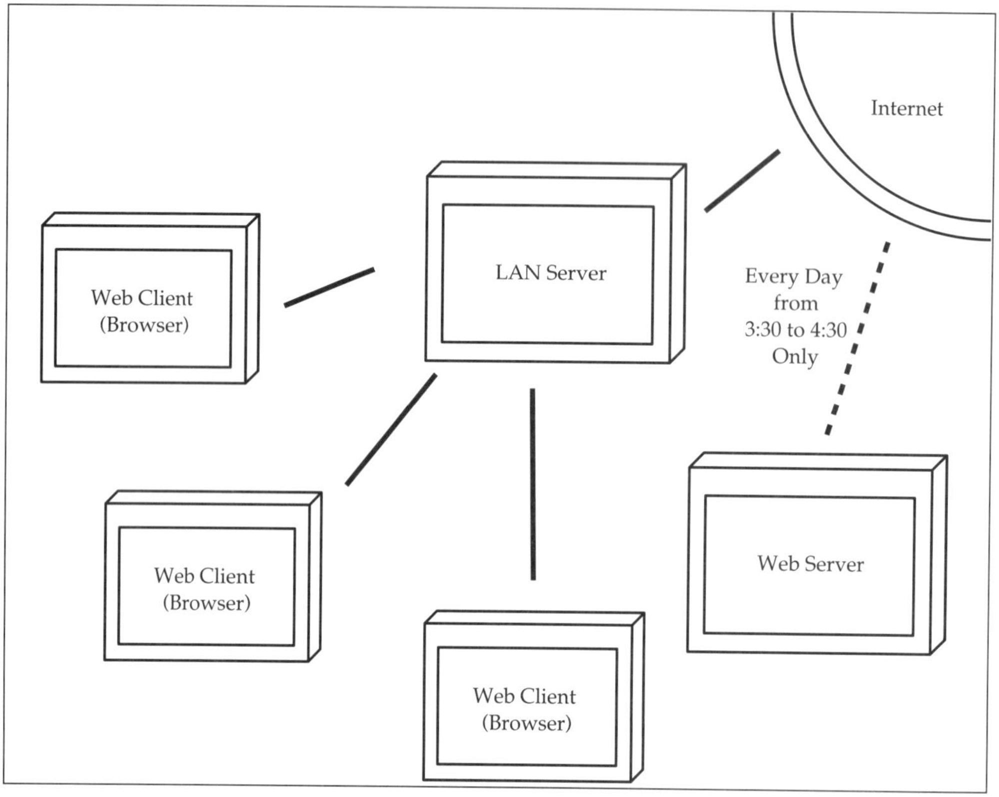

Figure 7.10: Broadcasting updates every afternoon from 3:30 to 4:30.

BEYOND THE SOFTWARE

With a quick trial of WebSite, you can put the software worries behind you. Now that you have a Web server, what will you do with it? The Web server is your personal way of publishing to others electronically. You control it. You don't have to rely on anyone else except perhaps to configure it occasionally. It's a powerful groupware tool. And there are advantages to publishing that that other groupware software doesn't offer.

For instance, suppose you have the responsibility of completing a report with input from eight other people in your work group. You can keep them apprised of your progress by e-mail. It's as easy to send each a copy of the latest version of the report as it is to send one a copy. From their point of view, however, they keep receiving updated versions of the report whether they need them or not. Cluttering their e-mailboxes is probably not particularly endearing. Why not publish the revised reports on your Web server?

Don't let the ideas in this book define the use of your Web server. Invent some uses. Look at a Web server as a prime building block for creating groupware. But to use a building block, you have to have the confidence of experience. Install a Web server on your desktop today. And remember, a plain old phone conference in which all participants can see the same Web documents on their computers is great groupware and easy to orchestrate.

PUBLIC PUBLISHING ON THE WEB

Although the focus of this book is online publishing of a private nature, there are two aspects of public Web publishing relevant to group work. The first is when part of the group's work is to provide information to or interact with the public. The public in this case might be the rest of the employees in the organization, customers, or the general public. For some types of group projects, the capability to publish online for such publics is a prime benefit. For instance, development teams in software companies have made use of the digiliterati to beta test software. The software and the information about the software (e.g., documentation, demos, white paper) are published on the Web. The public, in effect, becomes a part of the work group to test the software. There is no reason that work groups in other industries cannot integrate the public into their electronic work processes where appropriate.

The second aspect of Web publishing important to group work is the obvious one. The Web has become an important information resource. The Web enables a work group to take advantage of the vast amount of information that others have published on the Web for public access. The Web will continue to grow dramatically as an information resource to the point where it will become indispensable to almost every work group imaginable. There is no shortage of books to tout this aspect of the Web, so we will not dwell on it. Nonetheless, the capability to access the Web with a Web browser—the same programming you use as part of your groupware—makes your work online that much more convenient.

SUMMARY

Information is the fuel that powers business today. Work groups need the fuel to reach their goals. That's why online publishing is an important component of groupware. It provides a mechanism for publishing information to the group that's needed to get the work done. It also provides a way to publish to the group the group's own work in progress. Online publishing for work groups covers a wide range of activities, from image management to Web site management, as well as a wide range of technologies from enterprise systems to simple Web servers. It is difficult to imagine a groupware system without online publishing capability.

Chapter 8

TRAINING AND TRAINING

This chapter covers two distinct and perhaps unrelated topics. First, it treats training software as groupware, because training is a collaborative activity and because training is an integral part of many business activities. Second, it briefly comments on training personnel to develop proficiency in the use of groupware.

TRAINING SOFTWARE AS GROUPWARE

Good education is a collaborative process. Commercial training courses given in the lecture mode that do not keep attendees awake do not fare well in the competitive American training industry. On the other hand, instructors who involve their attendees in the learning process by asking questions, providing exercises, and using other participatory techniques help their attendees learn faster and better. Seminars, a common mode of commercial training, are often relatively small and somewhat informal groups in which participation is encouraged. Access to the instructor is direct, immediate, and informal. Attendees of commercial training seminars usually come away from a seminar feeling it was pleasant and worthwhile. Successful in-house seminars are the same. A seminar well done is often a satisfying way to learn something.

American industry spends billions of dollars each year on training and always seeks ways to make training less expensive and more effective. Seminars can be expensive and inconvenient, partly because everyone must be in the same place at the same time. This may involve travel or other unproductive inconveniences for both instructors and students. In the last decade computer-based training (CBT) has become a significant new mode for training personnel. CBT now takes on several forms, among which are programmed learning, interactive multimedia presentations, and online publishing. CBT strives to be interactive; that is, CBT takes advantage of the latest digital interactive technology by employing hypertext and hypermedia as well as multimedia. Nonetheless, the interactivity for CBT is still interactivity between a student and a computer presentation. If CBT can provide interactivity between a student and an instructor and between a student and other students, it can be more enjoyable and more effective in many situations. Such CBT is now possible on TCP/IP networks.

Seminar Groupware

Although it is possible for you to use existing TCP/IP programs to conduct a seminar online in real time or in convenient time, there are currently no inexpensive programs known to the authors to be dedicated to conducting seminars online; that is, there is no inexpensive instruction or seminar groupware. If there is to be instruction groupware or seminar groupware, then its raison d'etre will be interactivity. It will be collaborative educational software that provides the infrastructure for electronic interaction among participants—including the instructor—as they all strive toward the common goal of learning. It will be groupware.

To keep things simple, the discussion for the remainder of this section will be about seminar groupware. Still, think of seminar groupware as representing instruction groupware, course groupware, lecture groupware, or groupware for whatever your style of educational activity.

Because networks are becoming ubiquitous—it seems everyone in business is likely to be on the Internet by the end of the decade—a grand opportunity awaits those who invent seminar groupware and those instructors who are ready to take advantage of it. Groupware providing for education to be conducted online might be the next Internet killer application.

Normal Groupware

When students have collaborative projects to complete as part of their course work, they can use normal groupware to work on such projects with other students. Projects are usually more like normal work than they are like interactive educational activities, so normal groupware suffices. One major advantage groupware has over the normal situation in which students do projects off line is that the instructor is able to easily monitor student progress online without requiring periodic reports or without being overly intrusive.

Where a seminar or course consists solely of students working on projects individually or together, normal groupware is appropriate to conduct the learning process. The instructor can communicate adequately with students individually and monitor their work.

Current Building Blocks

Speculating on future Internet killer applications, while fine sport, must be limited in a serious how-to-now book. Thus, the following paragraphs survey those current Internet programs that one might incorporate into seminar groupware.

E-mail

As a basic means of communication, e-mail has a secure place in the online education scheme, even if it isn't included specifically in seminar groupware. Don't forget that the origin of the Internet was the wiring together of the research universities and the military-industrial complex to facilitate communication and information sharing.

Listserv

Mailing lists are a good convenience-time seminar vehicle. The Listservs are very easy to set up, the instructor can easily control them, they are inexpensive, and anyone with e-mail can use them. Moreover, everyone can take full advantage of the MIME capability of e-mail for dissemination of multimedia materials. In fact, an active mailing list group today is something like an ongoing seminar with multiple instructors.

Although a Listserv looks like good seminar groupware on paper, there are psychological factors to consider. An instructor may have control over the Listserv, but unlike in a classroom, he or she has little control over students on a Listserv. In a classroom, if a student does not participate, the instructor can call on the student or otherwise act to get the student involved in the educational process. In most educational settings, about 20% of the students do 80% of the participating if students are left on their own. A diligent instructor can act to make sure that every student gets involved. A Listserv is similar. About 20% of the people on a Listserv do about 80% of the participating. Unfortunately, an instructor does not have the direct control over the students on a Listserv. It is an indirect relationship in a process being conducted in convenient time.

To get a critical mass of six or eight students participating to make the Listserv interesting, you normally need to have about 40 students on the Listserv. This reality illustrates that no effective software exists in a psychological void. Psychological factors are important determinants in the success or failure of any software in its application to a specific situation. To make Listservs more applicable to seminar activities, either the instructor has to develop techniques for dealing with nonparticipating students or the software has to be changed to deal effectively with nonparticipating students.

Clearly, although the Internet technology has generated many building blocks, there is much experimentation to be done with seminars conducted online before this killer application is perfected.

Web Chat

Although the Internet relay channel (IRC) is similar, Web chat is a real-time mechanism for group communication and is a reasonable way to conduct a seminar online. You can offer it easily and inexpensively at a Web site that has a Web chat server.

Real Audio

Voice beats text for education in many situations. Real Audio has the potential to be used for both a real-time online seminar (broadcast) and a convenient-time online seminar (recordings played in real time) as shown in Figure 8.1. TrueSpeech is a similar Internet protocol.

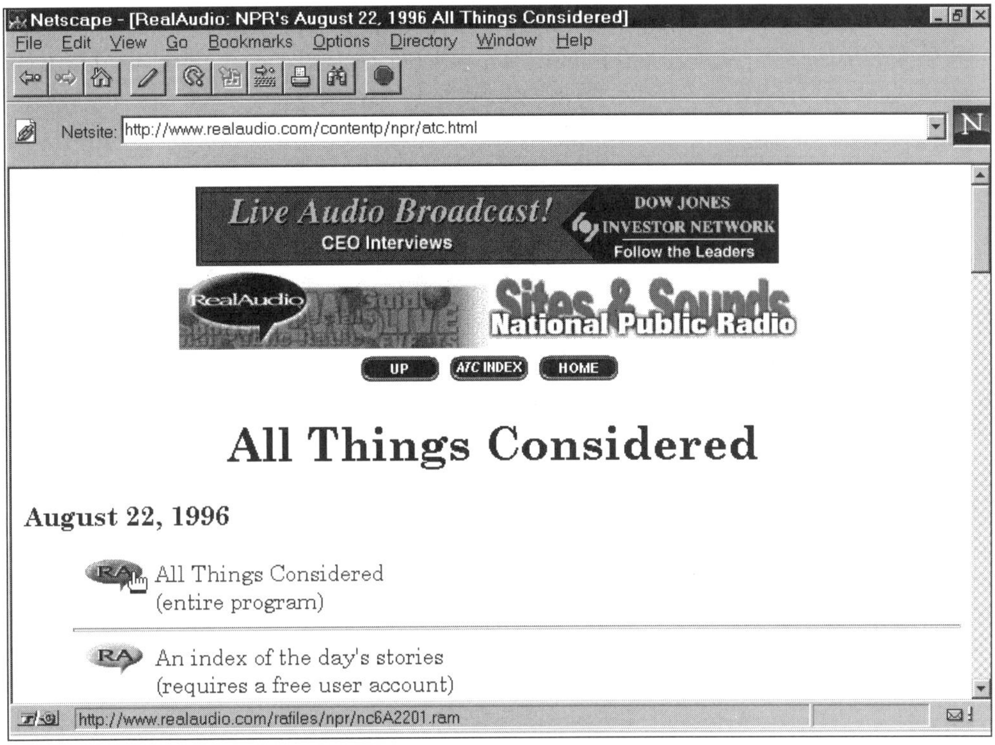

Figure 8.1: A link to a Real Audio streaming audio file.

Phone

Unlike with Real Audio, using a phone on the Internet is a two-way activity (see Figure 8.2). Phone conferencing is a realistic method for conducting small group discussions, but not many people can be accommodated with today's software. In the future, when the number of people on a phone conference can be increased, Internet phone software may prove a useful seminar technique.

Video

Seminars and courses have been conducted by video for decades. It can be a cost-saving, one-way delivery system. But a one-way system is not interactive. Two-way real-time video educational systems are very expensive and do not enjoy widespread use. The combination of the Internet and expanded bandwidth (with ISDN lines or TV cable)

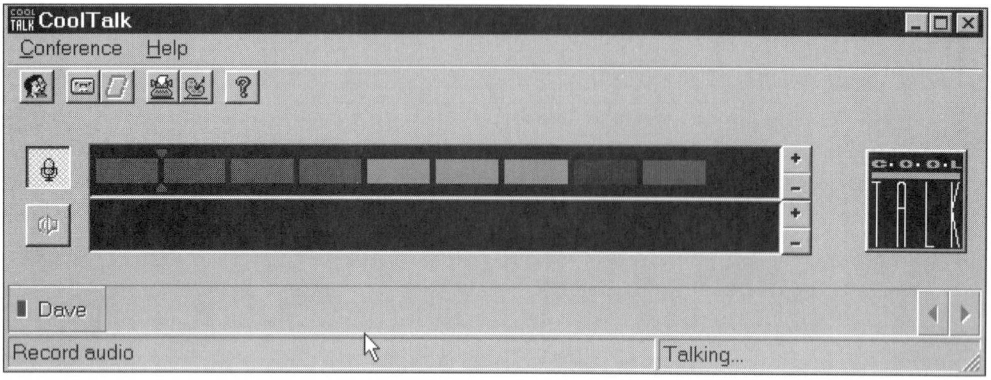

Figure 8.2: Web phone in Netscape Cool Talk.

will provide the infrastructure for cost-effective teleconferencing, which can accommodate seminars effectively. Moreover, when combined with other techniques, effective seminar groupware can be developed.

Web

The Web is a superb multimedia publishing environment. In a seminar conducted online it can act as a multimedia blackboard. With the ability of Windows 95 and other multitasking operating systems to run multiple programs at the same time, the Web potentially can be used simultaneously with other seminar groupware. The Web publishes text, color graphics, audio clips, and many other multimedia elements.

MUD/MOO

Multi-User Dimension (MUD) and MUD ObjectOriented (MOO) are interactive online games or online environments in which you can interact with many other people in real time. One of the attractions of MUDs and MOOs is that they are often based on fantasy, and you can assume an imaginary identity. You can participate through an avatar. Some of the MUDs and MOOs are very compelling online activities. It does not stretch the imagination too much to see that the adaptation of this technology to educational endeavors has the potential to generate some compelling seminar groupware.

Athena University, an online university (`http://www.athena.edu`), uses a variation of a MOO called a Virtual Education Environment (VEE). It is much like a MUD or MOO except that it hosts educational activities rather than games or game-like activities. It is text-based virtual reality—insofar as virtual reality can be text based. In addition to chatting with other people in real time, you can manipulate cyber-objects and move between environments. As MUDs, MOOs, and VEEs move from text to graphical environments, they are likely to become even more compelling.

At least one software vendor is pursuing this technology for conferencing. Oz Interactive (`http://www.oz-inc.com`) offers a Virtual Reality Markup Language (VRML) browser to access online virtual environments for conferencing as shown in Figure 8.3.

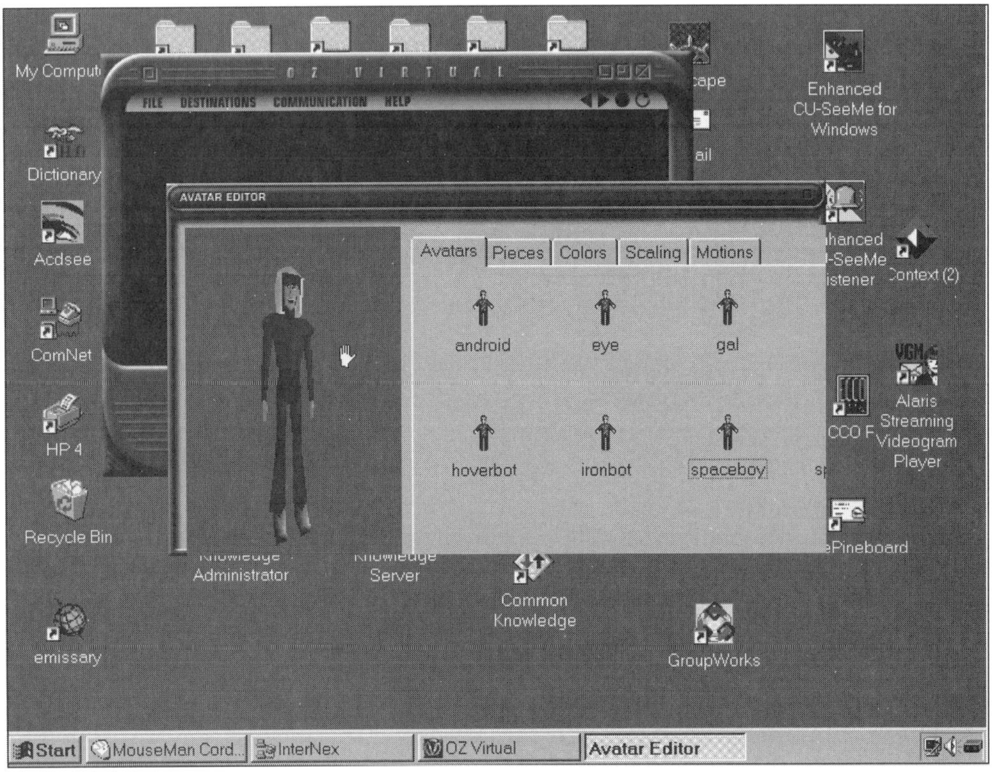

Figure 8.3: Oz Virtual conference.

Educating Your Colleagues

In the future, it seems likely that temporary groups will become common. As downsizing continues, organizational teams are more likely to include members (consultants or temporary workers) from outside the organization. When a project is finished, the team disassembles. New teams, including new outsiders, are assembled for new projects. In addition, many groups will have no organizational identity or continuity but will be groups of specialists assembled by a lead contractor to do a specific project. In such situations where people are not accustomed to working with each other and may not understand each other's specialties, education must play a role in enabling the group members to work together. In other words, group members will need to educate each other enough to be able to cooperate effectively to get the job done. Thus, both educating your colleagues and being educated by your colleagues are likely to become more important activities in project work. Seminar groupware that enables an individual group member to enlighten colleagues regarding that individual's role and expertise facilitates the smoother operation of the group's endeavors. Thus, education becomes more integrated into group work. It seems likely also that most groups with geographically dispersed members will employ online techniques to communicate and share information. Consequently, it is likely that online education for such groups will play a significant role in groupware.

GROUPWARE TRAINING FOR PEOPLE WHO USE GROUPWARE

Another aspect of education and groupware is the topic of groupware training for people who use groupware. It is a topic well beyond the scope of the book, and little space is devoted to it here. Nonetheless, training is perhaps the most important consideration in using any software for business, and groupware is no exception. In fact, training may be more important for certain types of groupware than for other types of software training. To learn to use a word processor, you don't have to interact with anyone. It's just you and the computer and the word processor program. To learn to use some groupware programs effectively, you must interact with at least one other person, and that adds a huge dimension to the requisite training.

E-mail

You can teach an employee to effectively use an e-mail client more easily and quickly than many other programs. Even advanced techniques are easily taught and learned. Unfortunately, that's only half the story. The other half of the story is training employees to use e-mail to communicate efficiently. This task compares with teaching employees to use the phone effectively. Many businesses overlook such training, and productivity suffers as a result.

The problem is that the use of e-mail tends to grow out of control. People spend too much time reading and writing e-mail messages, many of which are unnecessary or do not communicate effectively. As a result, the productivity increases you expect from new digital communications systems may not materialize. Therefore, it is important that training and use guidelines be instituted so that they realize productivity gains from the use of e-mail. Even self-employed people must develop e-mail discipline to avoid wasting time. Any consideration of e-mail training should attempt to answer the following questions:

- When should one use e-mail? What situations and what type of communications does e-mail handle well? What types of information does e-mail handle well?
- When should one use the phone? What situations and what type of communications does the phone handle better than e-mail? What types of information are better delivered over the phone?
- When is it appropriate to meet with a person rather than communicate by e-mail or the phone?
- What formats are conducive to easily written and easily read e-mail?
- Who should use e-mail and who should use the phone?
- Should employees with poor written communications skills be barred from using e-mail?

In short, it takes perhaps two hours to train someone to use an e-mail client effectively. It takes two years to train someone to communicate effectively with writing (perhaps an optimistic underestimate). Many of these issues are not new. But now there's a new medium to make things more complex.

Conferences

Conferences are meetings. There is no shortage of literature on meetings and their place in the scheme of things in the business world. Because conferences may be held in convenient time in a digital medium rather than in real time in person does not negate the fact that they are meetings. As meetings, they are susceptible to all the concerns about meetings as a means of getting things done. Here are some questions for you to consider for conferences conducted online:

- Is this meeting necessary? If so, should it be conducted online? Why?
- What is the purpose of the meeting?
- Who will run the meeting?
- Should the meeting be held in convenient time or real time? If convenient time, should there be a termination time set for the meeting? Or will it continue indefinitely?
- Who will attend the meeting? Should the meeting be published (or broadcast) publicly?

When educating people to answer the above questions, you should also address the following questions:

- When should groups use online conferencing? What types of meetings does online conferencing handle well?
- When should groups meet in person? What types of meetings are better conducted with everyone in the same room at the same time?
- When should groups use what conferencing protocols? What types of meetings are better conducted by (1) convenient-time conferencing, (2) real-time chat, or (3) teleconferencing?
- What formats are conducive to easily written and easily read e-mail messages for conferences?

As it is for e-mail, the training to enable good judgment and competent management when using conferencing is more difficult than the software training and perhaps taken less seriously.

Authoring

Training to use authoring software can be a mechanical type of training. Much authoring software focuses on collaboration for producing paperwork such as writing reports. Two people or at most just a few people are involved, and they can probably work out productive work procedures among themselves. They may need training to use authoring software, but it is primarily software training.

For authoring software that involves more people or that is used for projects besides producing paperwork, the same issues arise as for e-mail and conferencing software. Teaching people how to integrate the software into effective work practices is more difficult than teaching people how to use the software.

Work Flow

For actual work flow situations, the relationship tends to be between an employee and the software system rather than between an employee and other employees. For that reason, software training is effective. For other work flow situations such as scheduling, the difference between mechanical systems and digital systems is perhaps modest, and software training alone can be effective. It's those other techniques of to-do lists, task management, and project management—in which numerous people are involved and the software calls for cooperation and collaboration—that may require training beyond software training. Such software tends to be used for highly structured projects making training for the software important, but there's enough of a human element that training on the human side should be seriously considered too as a means to get the most mileage out of the software.

CONCLUSION

Training people to use certain types of groupware may not be effective without training in regard to human behavior and effective communication in addition to training regarding the use of the software. Browsers, e-mail clients, and other Internet software is easy to use and requires perhaps less training than almost any other software. In contrast, training in writing, communication, management, group dynamics, and teamwork is needed just as much as software training to enable employees to reach anticipated productivity increases.

SUMMARY

This chapter has covered two almost unrelated educational topics: training software as groupware and training for people who use groupware. The first topic assumes that training is as much a business and group function as other business activities and explores the use of Internet programs to facilitate such training. Because the seminar is a predominate part of corporate and professional continuing education, the discussion focuses on conducting seminars online. It seems likely that many of the groupware online techniques will be applied fruitfully to conducting seminars online but that currently, no inexpensive conferencing software known to the authors specializes specifically in enabling online seminars.

The second educational topic recognizes that there is another dimension to training people to use groupware beyond merely teaching them how to use Internet programs. That human dimension is not covered in the book but is one that you must take seriously to realize the productivity gains anticipated from the introduction of groupware into the workplace.

Chapter 9

DATABASES FOR GROUPWARE

Databases for groupware must be considered from two points of view. First, how can a database be used as part of a group work program? What functionality can it provide to make the program work better? Second, how can existing databases full of data be accessed through the use of groupware? As mentioned in the chapter on publishing, is valuable to put the information in databases at the fingertips of people who will need it to do work. The topic of databases is complex, well beyond the scope of this book, and this chapter is provided only for background information.

TYPES OF DATABASES

Flat File

A flat-file database application is a list or two-dimensional table. Each row (record) represents a specific collection of data, and each column (field) represents an individual information item. The list or table stands alone and is not related to another list or table. You can make queries against the list to obtain information and create reports, and you can create a form to input data into the database. Figure 9.1 shows an example of a flat-file database.

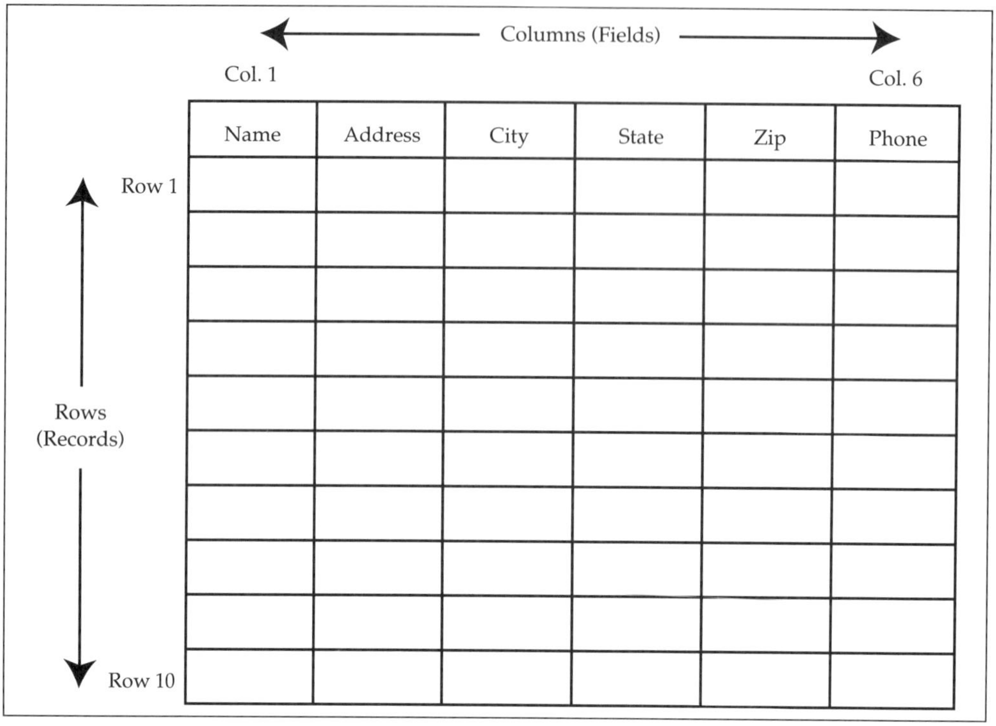

Figure 9.1: Flat-file database.

Relational

A relational database is in a sense a three-dimensional table. That is, it is two or more tables wherein each table has a column in common with another table (see Figure 9.2). The common column is the link between two tables, and the links between tables create the logical structure for the database application. In addition to making queries, creating reports, and using forms, with a relational database you can also create new tables using data from two or more tables. Making complex queries to two or more tables provides you with substantial power to manipulate data. Most of the database programs or engines (e.g., Microsoft Access, Paradox, Approach) sold in shrinkwrap today are relational databases, as are most of the scalable enterprise database engines (e.g., Oracle 7).

The real power of relational databases is in the queries that are possible. You can make a query to multiple tables, giving you considerable power to manipulate the data in the database for your purposes.

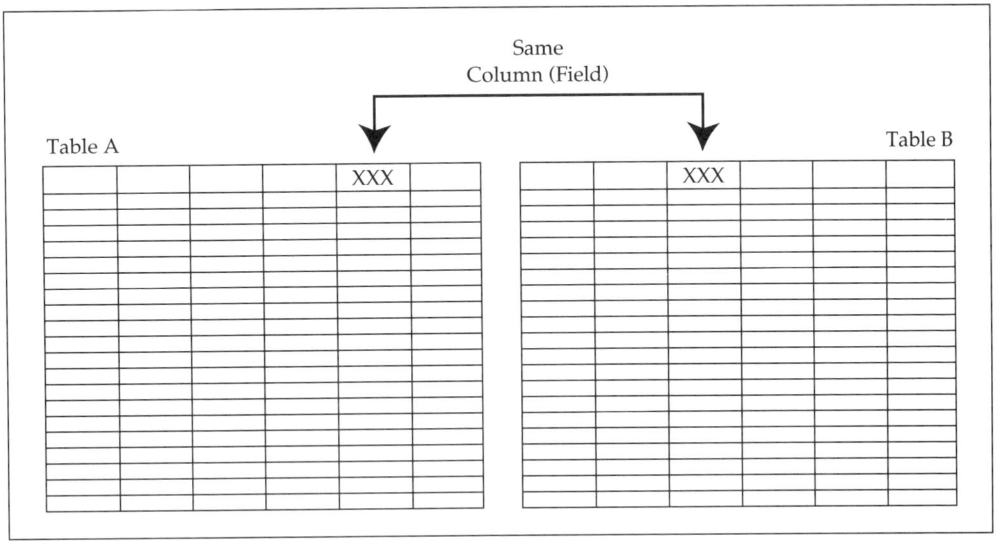

Figure 9.2: Two tables related by common column.

Relational databases can also eliminate redundancy. For instance, if marketing has a table, manufacturing has a table, and billing has a table, only one of these departments needs to keep the name, address, and phone number of a major customer. Even though this information is in only one table, because the tables are related, it can be used by each department as if it were in that department's table. This is a simplistic example, but it indicates that a relational database with multiple tables is much more than a flat-file.

IBM originally developed the Structured Query Language (SQL) that made relational databases feasible. Today, virtually every relational database program will do SQL queries and operations in addition to the proprietary database operations of the program itself.

Object-Oriented

Relational databases are great for text, numbers, and dates. But what about BLOBs (binary large objects)? A BLOB, shown in Figure 9.3, might be a digital color graphic, an executable (a computer program), or an entire digital text document (i.e., more than a word or phrase). Relational databases don't handle BLOBs very well, if at all.

An object-oriented database includes classes of objects. For instance, a relational database handles three classes of data well: text,

Figure 9.3: BLOB.

numbers, and dates. That's about it, whereas an object-oriented database handles a variety of classes of data and may include the capability to add new classes. By defining a class well, an object-oriented database can provide convenient functionality for data objects in that class. Thus, an object-oriented database handles well multimedia elements such as color graphics, audio files, and the like. The limitation of an object-oriented database is that it does not work well with queries. After all, normal queries are made with text, and data objects in an object-oriented database are not necessarily text.

Hybrid

A new type of database known as a hybrid object-oriented-relation database attempts to combine the best of both worlds: effective multimedia object handling and effective queries. These databases are starting to be known as universal databases. They hold much promise for the future. Because the Web is a multimedia publishing system, universal databases seem to be tailor-made for it.

For the Web

Any database can be accessed from a Web document. You can use CGI scripts to connect a flat-file or a database engine to a Web document. With any legacy database there may be a variety of approaches you can take to getting it connected to a Web document. If you start from scratch, however, in most cases you will want a database application that handles multimedia elements agilely while enabling useful queries. The hybrid object-oriented-relational database is the best choice for both current and future use. The Informix Illustra database, shown in Figure 9.4, is the leading example of this category of database engine, and Informix has integrated Illustra and DataBlade technology into some of its other database software too. The Illustra database is bundled with GNNserver (a prime Web server) available free at the Global Network Navigator Web site (`http://www.gnn.com`). GNNpress, a Web browser/authoring tool, is also available free. This is the groupware steal of the century; it doesn't get any better than this.

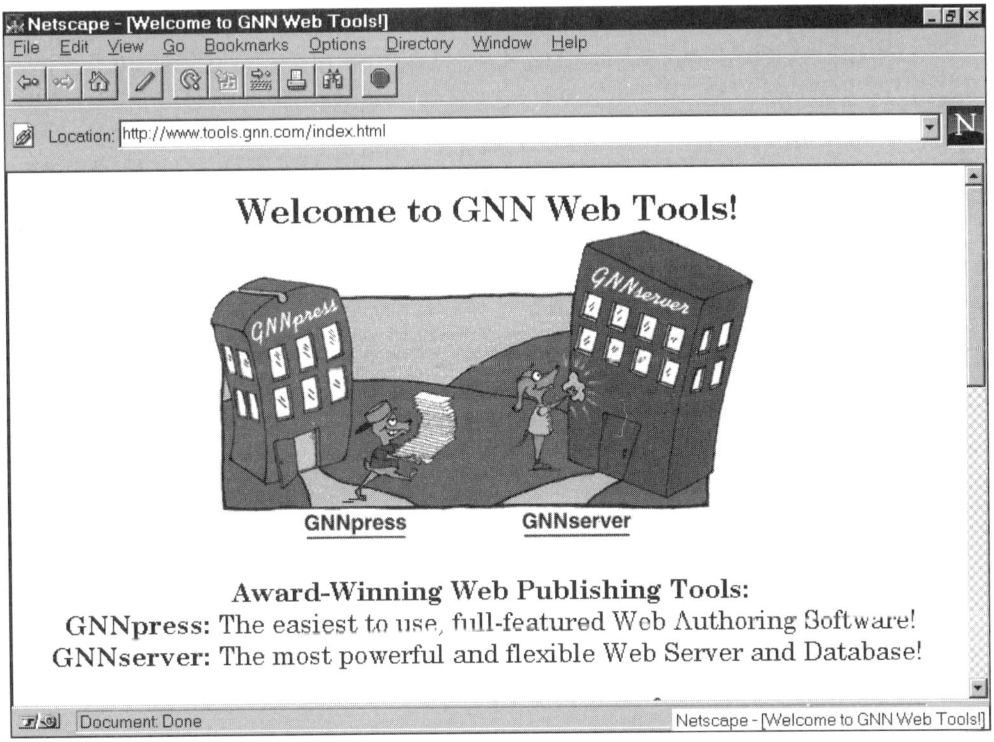

Figure 9.4: The Illustra database is included in GNNserver.

DATABASE FUNCTIONS

Groupware uses many information items including documents, data in database form, communications, and multimedia elements. Filing them in directories (folders) is no longer adequate. The volume grows too large. Only database technology can provide an efficient means of keeping track of such a volume of information. Most groupware programs that do not include a database in one form or another today are likely to do so in the future as people learn to expect more from groupware. For instance, Lotus Notes is a database, albeit a specialized one.

Replication

Because the client/server paradigm rules the online environment, any one groupware database may serve only a limited number of people. Servers are likely to be PCs, not mainframes. If a database is to be made available to a large number of people within an organization, it is likely that it will have to exist on a number of servers simultaneously. Then the problem of synchronization must be considered. How do you publish the changes made in one database to the other supposedly identical databases? You have the same problem with each instance of the database.

A replication function is necessary. Periodically, the updates made to each instance of the database must be transmitted to the other databases to bring them up to date. Whether this is done once a day or 10 times a day depends on the needs of the business, but only through replication can the overall system stay current.

Groupware Programming

Groupware generally has to do with handling information. Paper information has proliferated with the computer to the point where it is swamping everyone. As computer technology carries people into a digital world, information will proliferate more, even when the use of paper declines. In addition, information is evolving into multimedia information. For instance, a document that is simple text in today's world will be text, color graphics, and who knows what in tomorrow's world. The trouble is that tomorrow doesn't mean next year anymore. It means tomorrow morning. The only way to keep track of all this information is to store it in a database where it can be accounted for and retrieved when needed. Thus, groupware developers will turn to database technology more and more to make groupware more practical and easier to use. Indeed, much groupware is already based on database technology. For instance, Lotus Notes is like a hybrid object-oriented-relational database engine adapted to a special use.

ACCESSING DATABASES

Getting information from databases is a common activity in business and one that Web technology facilitates. The Web can provide access to one database or to an enterprise system that includes many databases, old and new. Because access is through a Web browser, it is simple and uniform for all database access activities.

Getting the Data

A huge amount of information is generally stored in databases. Making that data available (publishing it) through groupware to people who need it for their work is crucial in many organizations and at least highly desirable in others. Making the data available through a separate database application, as is widely the case, is fine. For employees, however, it is another software program to learn, and they may have to take some awkward steps to get the data into the groupware where they use it. If the data can be accessed directly from the groupware, so much the better.

A group work program with an Application Programming Interface (API) for databases makes it easy to connect a database to the groupware and provide the capability to formulate queries and otherwise access the database right from the groupware. The standard database API is Microsoft's Open Database Connectivity (ODBC). If a group work program is ODBC compliant, you can connect it to an ODBC-compliant database with minimum effort.

Because an organization is likely to have multiple databases on multiple platforms, the database issues can get very complicated. It might be simple for one group work program to get access to one database, but it becomes awkward to connect to multiple databases. An organization needs considerable middleware to draw its diverse databases into one or more enterprise systems. If the groupware is to have access to all the databases, it can do it through the middleware. In any event, groupware can put a familiar face (the groupware interface) on a complex set of databases.

Web-Database Applications

There is a method other than middleware for accessing the data in databases: do it through the Web. The HTML forms markups provide for receiving input from an HTML document (Web document) that can be used to enter data into a database, make queries to a database, and otherwise operate a database There is a flood of Web-database development tools on the market now, and it will be difficult for you to find a database engine that cannot be adapted to be accessed easily through a Web document. Many of the tools are simple enough for nonprogrammers to use, particularly for database applications that are not complex. Thus, the Web, in effect, becomes the middleware for potentially making all of an organization's databases available on an intranet or on the Internet.

Converters Some of the tools are converters; that is, they convert database tables, queries, and reports to static Web documents automatically (see Figure 9.5). In fact, before long every database engine will include an automatic converter, and utility converters will no longer be necessary. Automatic converters facilitate the easy publishing of data on the Web from virtually any database application. For many database applications, this is something you can easily do yourself if need be. Static publishing is one thing, however, and dynamic use is another.

Programming Web-Database Applications In order to use a database application dynamically on a TCP/IP network, you must convert the database application to a Web-database application. This cannot be done automatically. Moreover, different Web-database development tools may be required for different databases, depending on what mixture of legacy and recent database applications you happen to have in your organization. In other words, to convert all database applications to Web-database applications can be a substantial undertaking for an organization.

The benefits of bringing all database applications under the Web umbrella are as follows:

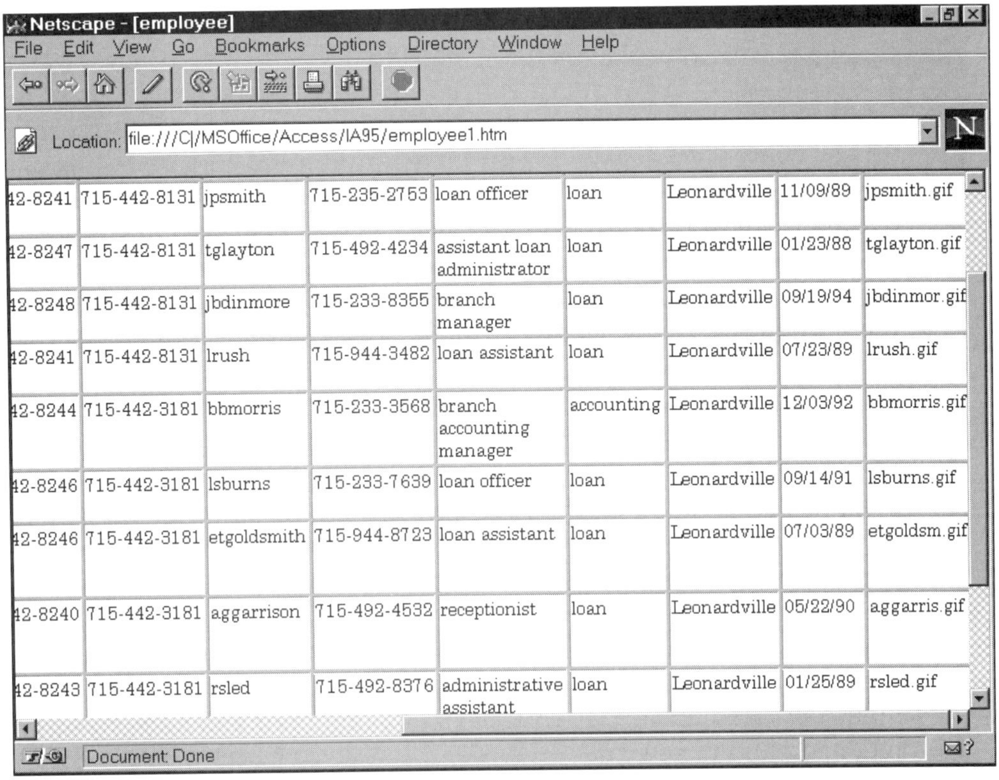

42-8241	715-442-8131	jpsmith	715-235-2753	loan officer	loan	Leonardville	11/09/89	jpsmith.gif
42-8247	715-442-8131	tglayton	715-492-4234	assistant loan administrator	loan	Leonardville	01/23/88	tglayton.gif
42-8248	715-442-8131	jbdinmore	715-233-8355	branch manager	loan	Leonardville	09/19/94	jbdinmor.gif
42-8241	715-442-8131	lrush	715-944-3482	loan assistant	loan	Leonardville	07/23/89	lrush.gif
42-8244	715-442-3181	bbmorris	715-233-3568	branch accounting manager	accounting	Leonardville	12/03/92	bbmorris.gif
42-8246	715-442-3181	lsburns	715-233-7639	loan officer	loan	Leonardville	09/14/91	lsburns.gif
42-8246	715-442-3181	etgoldsmith	715-944-8723	loan assistant	loan	Leonardville	07/03/89	etgoldsm.gif
42-8240	715-442-3181	aggarrison	715-492-4532	receptionist	loan	Leonardville	05/22/90	aggarris.gif
42-8243	715-442-3181	rsled	715-492-8376	administrative assistant	loan	Leonardville	01/25/89	rsled.gif

Figure 9.5: Small database of employees in branch loan office converted to a Web document.

- All database applications are available on your intranet or on the Internet.
- Access is through a Web browser (Web document).
- Uniform access minimizes software training.
- All data is directly available dynamically to any employee who needs it.

You need to keep the distinction clear between publishing data as is done with automatic converters and making data available dynamically. Making data available dynamically is making it available in such a way that employees can enter data, make queries against the data, and otherwise manipulate the data as they need it.

Relevance to Groupware Databases are information resources that group members use to do work. Therefore, it is important to incorporate them into your groupware system. As indicated above, that will be easy for you if all you need to do is publish database data. If you need to make data available dynamically, you will have to mount a more substantial development effort. In either case, the data can be made available to group members through the Web. From a group member's point of view, Web access to data, whether static or dynamic, makes access easy. Moreover, you can easily integrate data into Web documents along with other multimedia elements like text, color images, executables, and audio. As a result, Web access to data is a solid building block for groupware.

The Methods The way you publish data is to convert it to Web documents with an automatic converter. The result of this straightforward and easy task is a Web document(s) that you upload to your Web server to make available to personnel. You can publish tables, queries, views, and reports; consequently, you can query a database and publish the result. However, you might note that there is a difference between the publisher querying the database to publish the result and the end user of the data having the capability of querying the database.

Making a database application available through a Web document—just as it is available through its normal user interface—can work a variety of ways depending on the database application. The input and queries are done via CGI scripts or daemons (programs that run in the background with Web servers). The queries are written in SQL (universal database language) but must fit into a larger development scheme. Database engines are connected to the Web server through ODBC drivers or other APIs, but in some cases database application files are used instead of database engines, and there is no connection between the database engine and the Web server. Although easy database applications can be engineered for the Web easily enough—you may be able to do it yourself—most Web-database applications fall under the jurisdiction of database programmers.

Temporary Database Access

As was mentioned about Web servers earlier in the book, a temporary Web site may make sense for specific situations. The same is true for database access. If you need to share a database temporarily with others, why not use a Web site on your PC to do it? All you need to do, once the Web-database application is finished, is to connect to the Internet as you normally do and start your Web server. Anyone who knows your IP number and the period of availability can visit your temporary Web site to access the database. As soon as you get off line, it's no longer available.

If you want people to have access to your database application or data for a period, but you don't want them to have long-term access to it or they don't need long term access to it, the temporary Web site is a good solution. Security regarding outsiders is not necessarily the problem it normally is. Only those who have been notified of the IP number and the period you are to be online will know enough to visit your temporary Web site. On an intranet, you control the period of availability by simply starting or stopping your Web server.

For situations in which the data is sensitive, there is a risk that an unauthorized group member could obtain all the data either inadvertently or purposefully. If you publish the data, it will be in HTML document format. Anyone accessing it can easily download the Web documents and thereby get all of the data you have published. For a database application used dynamically, getting all the data in a short time depends on how the queries are written. If an end user is enabled to make a general query, that person can make a query that will extract all the data. If the queries enabled for end users by the application allow only small amounts of data to be extracted by each query, it is more difficult or impossible for an end user to extract a substantial amount of the data in a short time. If data sensitivity is an issue, the temporary database is not a viable means of ensuring security, and normal secure practices should be established.

MOVING DATA

Generally, there are two ways to move data. You can either export or import a database application with your database manager. This means the entire application including the data is exported or imported. Because the applications are created in proprietary programming, they are not freely portable between database managers (database engines). Thus, if you are importing a database application from an alien program, your database engine must have the proper filter to make a successful import. Few database engines will have so many filters that they can import any database application from any database engine.

Therefore, if you are going to distribute data, you can do it using a database application file as long as other group members have the means of using that file. If everyone is using the same database manager, there is no problem. If not, you have a compatibility problem.

If your purpose is to simply import or export data, you can use an ASCII-delimited file. Every database engine can import and export ASCII-delimited files. A delimited file is one in which the columns (fields) are separated by a comma, a tab, or some other character. Most people use comma-delimited data files. This practice presents a problem, because the columns themselves may contain commas that will interfere with the export or import. The solution is that quotation marks are used to set off the column, and the commas inside the quotation marks don't count for delimitation purposes. This is all done automatically for you in the export process. Below is a comma delimited file for a small database of employees in a fictional branch loan office.

Portion of a comma-delimited database of employees in a branch loan office.

```
"Elizabeth J.","Eller","Betty","551 Platt","Leonardville","AR",
"93381","715-442-8245","715-442-8131","ejeller","715-233-
9440","loan administrator","loan","Leonardville","05/02/81",
"ejeller.gif"
"Judy P.","Smith","Judy","79 Allen Ct.","Leonardville","AR",
"93381","715-442-8241","715-442-8131","jpsmith","715-235-
2753","loan officer","loan","Leonardville","11/09/89",
"jpsmith.gif"
"Troy G.","Layton","Troy","4735 Luff Rd.","Salamora","AR",
"93379","715-442-8247","715-442-8131","tglayton","715-492-
4234","assistant loan administrator","loan","Leonardville",
"01/23/88","tglayton.gif"
"John B.","Dinmore","John","2791
Yorkshire","Leonardville","AR","93380","715-442-8248","715-442-
8131","jbdinmore","715-233-8355","branch
manager","loan","Leonardville","09/19/94","jbdinmor.gif"
```

Notice that each column is encapsulated by quotation marks and separated from other columns by commas. Notice also that each row (record) is delimited by a blank line. This is raw data. There is no application programming here. Thus, the file is freely portable between any database engines. For a view of this database in Microsoft Access, see Figure 9.6.

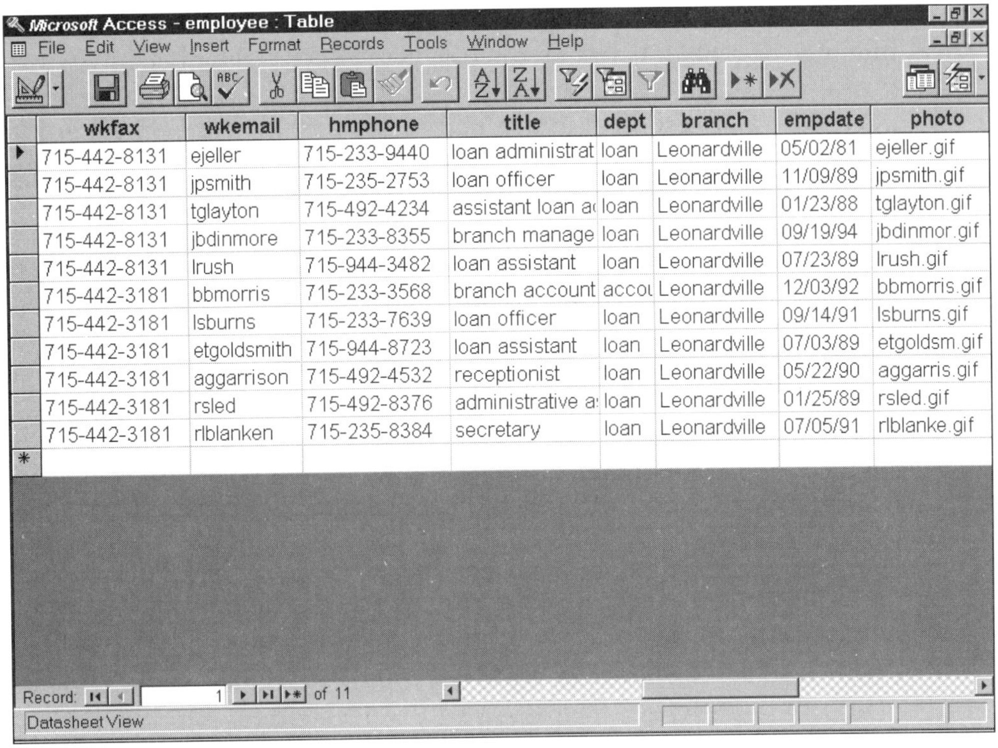

wkfax	wkemail	hmphone	title	dept	branch	empdate	photo
715-442-8131	ejeller	715-233-9440	loan administrat	loan	Leonardville	05/02/81	ejeller.gif
715-442-8131	jpsmith	715-235-2753	loan officer	loan	Leonardville	11/09/89	jpsmith.gif
715-442-8131	tglayton	715-492-4234	assistant loan a	loan	Leonardville	01/23/88	tglayton.gif
715-442-8131	jbdinmore	715-233-8355	branch manage	loan	Leonardville	09/19/94	jbdinmor.gif
715-442-8131	lrush	715-944-3482	loan assistant	loan	Leonardville	07/23/89	lrush.gif
715-442-3181	bbmorris	715-233-3568	branch account	accou	Leonardville	12/03/92	bbmorris.gif
715-442-3181	lsburns	715-233-7639	loan officer	loan	Leonardville	09/14/91	lsburns.gif
715-442-3181	etgoldsmith	715-944-8723	loan assistant	loan	Leonardville	07/03/89	etgoldsm.gif
715-442-3181	aggarrison	715-492-4532	receptionist	loan	Leonardville	05/22/90	aggarris.gif
715-442-3181	rsled	715-492-8376	administrative a	loan	Leonardville	01/25/89	rsled.gif
715-442-3181	rlblanken	715-235-8384	secretary	loan	Leonardville	07/05/91	rlblanke.gif

Figure 9.6: Database of employees in a branch loan office.

Exporting Raw Data

To export data in ASCII form is easy. You simply use the export command to put the data in a file. The file, in ASCII text, often has an extension like .txt or something similar. If you look at it in a simple text editor, you see everything. It's very straightforward.

Importing Raw Data

Importing raw data is a little trickier. If you get comma-delimited data from someone and you both have exactly the same database application with identical tables, importing is just as simple as exporting. You import the data, and it magically turns up in the table in your database application. If you get data from someone who has a different database application but you both have a table that is exactly the same, importing comma-delimited data for that table works the same way. It's very easy to do. If you get data from someone and you don't have a table that matches the data but all the data is short text columns, importing is again very easy. Your database manager will automatically construct a table to house the data. All the data will magically appear in the new table. This, also, is a very easy process. The worst problem you may have is that some of the columns in the receiving table are not wide enough to receive some of the data. To avoid truncation, you will have to use the database manager to widen those columns.

When you import data and you don't have a table that matches the data and the data is not all text, it gets tricky. In this last case, you have to analyze the data to see what it is. You can do this by looking at the data in a text editor. For instance, if you see that the third column is more than a short text phrase and seems to include a large block of text, it's probably a memo column, which is different from a text column. You must indicate to your database manager that column three is a memo column. Likewise, if column five is full of numbers, it may be a number column that is different than a text column. You will need to indicate to your database manager that column five is a numeric column. Perhaps there is a date column too. As soon as you have matched the new columns in the new table to the data, you can import the data into the new table easily. But sometimes it takes a little trial and error. A better way to approach this is to get the specifications on the table from the person from whom you get the data. Then you can set up the receiving table (new table) easily and import the data without problems.

Relevance to Groupware

Exporting, importing, and transferring raw data via comma-delimited ASCII files is very handy for work groups. It is very similar to copying and pasting and not much more complicated. In fact, there's no reason you can't copy and paste the text in a comma-delimited database file. Try exporting and importing some raw data today to get a feeling for how well it works. You'll need to know how to do this sooner or later.

TEXT SEARCHING

Another type of database is important too, but mention of it was omitted above to avoid confusion. Documents make up a database. Documents are organized in hundreds of ways, some of which are very structured; others are unstructured. With one technique, however, you can gain access to all documents easily: text searching. Text search engines have come into popularity, accelerated by the emergence of the Web as an important new medium. After all, the Web is a document system.

Text search engines first go through all the documents in a document repository and index each word in every document. This is a considerable digital process that can take a long time for large repositories. Once each word is indexed, however, a text search engine can search with blinding speed. You search for information using key words. The text search engine retrieves every document containing the key words. Naturally, some of the documents retrieved will be irrelevant to the information sought. You can use various techniques to narrow a search, but few searches will be perfect (return only the information sought). Therefore, a text search engine is designed to do sophisticated searches, after which it ranks the documents in descending order according to the statistical probability that they include the information sought (see Figures 9.7 and 9.8).

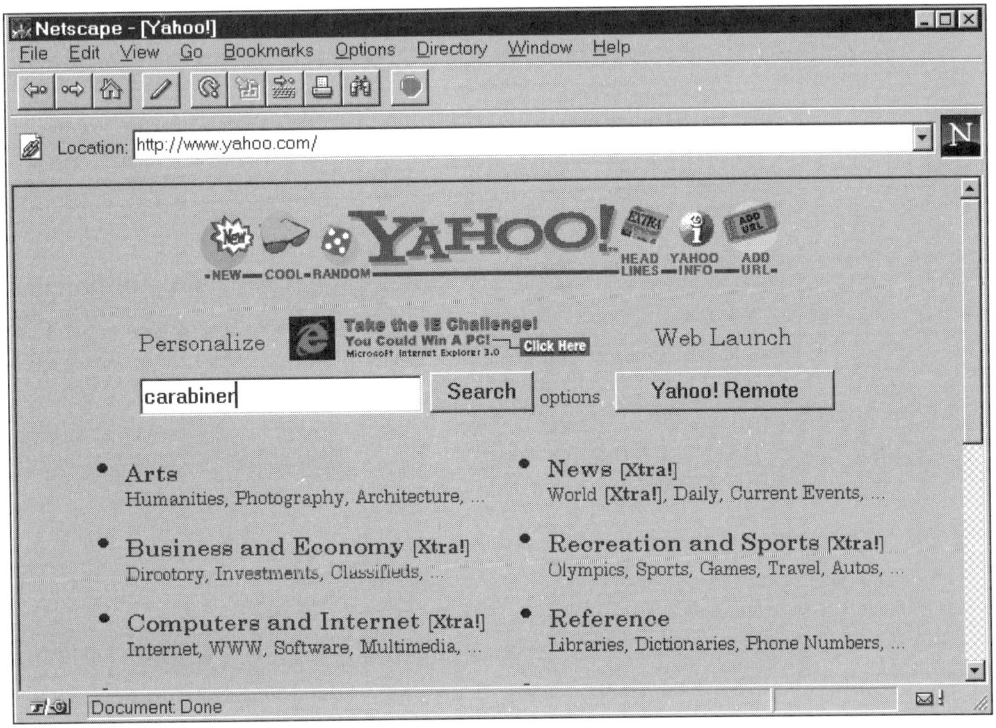

Figure 9.7: Yahoo! search engine on the Web.

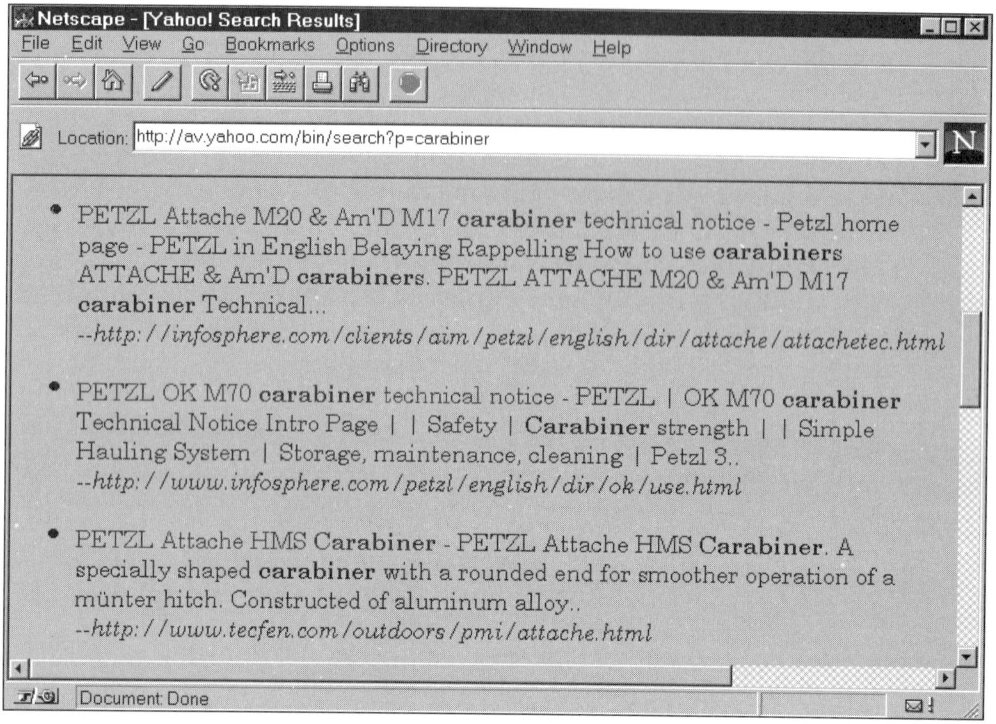

Figure 9.8: Results of search on the word carabiner.

Text search engines are very useful for finding information in document systems. In this sense, document systems include e-mail message archives, Web documents, word processor documents, and almost any kind of text files. Text search engines appropriately employed can benefit group work efforts. Every text repository you have should be covered by a text search engine. End users find them easy to use, and they are easy to operate and maintain. If you are not using text search engines yet, it may be profitable for you to consider their employment.

MEMORY

The data of an organization, whether letters, e-mail messages, document systems, databases, or whatever, constitutes the collective wisdom of that organization. They are the organization's memory. If part of that data is not accessible, for whatever reasons, that part of the organization's memory is forgotten (although some of that memory may continue to exist in the minds of certain employees). Setting up an enterprise system to access all of an organization's data keeps the organization's collective wisdom alive.

If an organization has collective wisdom, what about a work group? What about a work group's memory? It may seem silly to discuss a work group's collective wisdom and memory, but consider the following factors:

- The work of any group should go into the archives of the organization where it becomes part of the organization's memory. Every little bit helps.
- If a work group endures long enough, its archives begin to be valuable to the group itself. Information accumulates and must be organized, accounted for, and made available to group members. Over long periods it's easy for group members to forget information or forget where it is.
- Many groups are succeeded by another group that picks up where the first group left off. The first group's archives might be valuable to the second group.
- E-mail traffic can be particularly enlightening where important topics were discussed intelligently and thoroughly. Such traffic should be organized in threads and archived.

The point here is not to *get organized*, although that is always appropriate to do. Everyone recognizes the above circumstances. Rather, the point is to preserve the data (information) of the group and the organization and make it available to personnel who can use it. Digital technology can make it easily available—available to the organization's personnel and particularly available to work groups that need it. Text search engines and other techniques make useful information easy to find, and the organization doesn't *forget*. Groupware can potentially assist a work group's contribution to the organization by organizing and preserving information, at the same time making the information of the organization conveniently available to the group. For more on this short topic, see Chapter 4 (section entitled "E-mail as an Information Repository").

DATABASE TRENDS

The use of databases continues to grow with the advance of digital technology. As people use and handle more information, the management of the information becomes an issue. Databases are the most appropriate and most efficient means of managing information in many situations. As information presentations of all kinds grow larger and richer with multimedia information, databases are used more and more to keep such information well organized and accessible. Work groups need to have capabilities to handle data and databases. The Web and Web-database technology provide a sound platform on which to ground the handling of data by work group members.

Because groupware programs are often designed to handle data, using database technology even within groupware programs themselves is important for increased functionality and performance.

Chapter 10

LOTUS NOTES

This chapter introduces Lotus Notes, outlines necessary infrastructure for deploying Lotus Notes, describes features found in Notes, and presents information on how these features can best be used in a group working environment.

WHAT IS LOTUS NOTES?

Lotus Notes is software that provides a cluster of tools that allows a single person or groups of geographically separated people in an organization to communicate and organize data with detailed security capabilities. This cluster encompasses databases, e-mail, replication, complex documents, security, and application development.

Databases

A *database* is an electronic container for a collection of information. Databases are designed to make organizing and accessing large quantities of information, or data, easy. A Notes database is made up of *documents*, which consist of *fields* held together by a *form*.

E-mail

Notes e-mail (Notes Mail) works very much like any other type of e-mail, but because it is combined with the rest of Notes' features, it has some capabilities not available in other software products.

Replication

A replica is an exact copy. Notes allows you to make replicas of a database through a process called *replication*. There is a distinction, though, between a copy and a Notes replica. When you make a photocopy of a piece of paper, there is nothing that links the photocopy to the original. Changes that you make to the original do not show up in the copy, nor do changes in the copy show up in the original. Once the act of duplication is finished, it is a *fait accompli*. In marked contrast, Notes replication is an ongoing process. When you replicate a Notes database, those two copies are inextricably linked. Whenever any changes are made to the original, they automatically show up in the replica at regular intervals, as changes to the replica show up in the original. You can have several replicas of the same Notes database.

Complex Documents

Notes documents can contain a variety of types of information. Figure 10.1 shows a Notes document with graphics, embedded attachments, and formatted text.

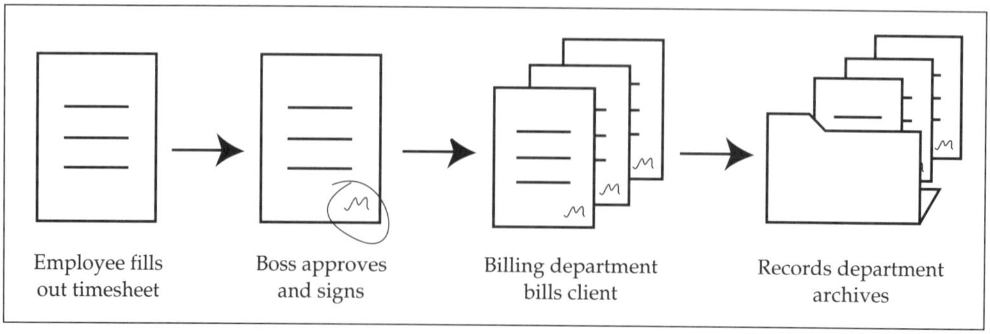

Figure 10.1: Notes automates everyday work flow tasks like the one in this diagram.

The following definitions are useful in understanding Lotus Notes:

- **Graphics**—Notes databases can contain graphics, including drawings that were created in other software, scanned photographs, clip art, and other images. If you want to have your company logo on all the documents in a database, you may.
- **Spreadsheets**—A spreadsheet is used to hold and manipulate numbers. For example, you can use a spreadsheet to balance your checkbook and automatically figure your balance based on information you enter about withdrawals and deposits.
- **Document links**—Notes can use hyperlinks. This means that a Notes document can contain a link to another document in any Notes database or to documents stored on the Web.
- **Formatted text**—Formatted text is text that has stylistic enhancements added to it. For instance, text that has **bold** and *italicized* words is formatted text.
- **Embedded attachments**—You can place links to almost any document in a Notes database. Even files created by other applications such as word processors and spreadsheets may be linked.
- **Sound**—If your computer has the necessary hardware and software, you can create and listen to audio files. This means that you can record a voice message to your boss, put it in a Notes e-mail message, and send it to him or her.
- **Video**—Creating video is not something that most computer users are currently able to do. However, with the advent of low-cost computer video cameras, such as the Connectix QuickCam, more and more people will use video as way to communicate.

Security

Notes has several features, the sole purpose of which is to make sure that the information that you and your organization keep in Notes is secure. There are three basic reasons that you need security features in any software:

- To make sure that only the people who are supposed to see data have access to it.
- To ensure that the data stored on a computer is not susceptible to alteration, deletion, or corruption by malicious individuals.

- To provide confidence that information sent over a network has not been intercepted, altered, or forged in transit.

Notes provides such security by using authentication, encryption, digital signatures, and access control. These are covered in more detail in the chapter on security.

Application Development

The jobs that people do often change. In order to be flexible enough to remain useful when work methods change, Notes provides the capability to make changes to the way its databases work. You can even make brand-new databases with custom buttons and features that you design to accomplish very specific tasks as they arrive.

It is important to remember that these features are blended together in Notes to provide a flexible environment. This flexibility translates into a software product that can be useful for many tasks within your organization. It's easy to come up with tasks to which Notes is suited. Just think of those tasks that you do at work every day that require you to interact with your co-workers. For example, you have to fill out a weekly time sheet that logs the number of hours you spent on various projects for several clients. At the end of the week, you carry it down the hall and turn it in to your manager. After reviewing the time sheet and signing it, your manager has a runner deliver the time sheet to the billing department in the building across the street. When billing employees finish collecting the information for each client, they send it to the records department, which files it neatly away in an archive.

This scenario describes millions of business processes that take place in organizations every business day. Notes enables you to take this process and make it electronic. You can actually recreate the time sheet in Notes to automate the process. The capability to automate this whole process can be very valuable to a group that needs to work more efficiently. The features in Notes allow for the creation of custom applications to meet specific needs. For example, the time sheet form in Notes can have rules embedded within it to ensure that all the necessary information is entered before the form is saved. As a result, you never send an incomplete time sheet to your manager, thus saving the time that it takes to carry the sheet back down the hall to you to have you finish the job. When you finish filling out the form, all you need to do is click a button with your mouse, and the time sheet automatically goes forward to your manager over the intranet. No more running up and down the hall with paperwork. In fact, every time the time sheet is passed on to someone new, it simply travels over the intranet. This method saves time and legwork. When your manager is satisfied with your time sheet, the built-in security features of Notes enable her to place an electronic signature on it before passing it on. Utilizing Notes' built in security features, only the people who are authorized to do so are able to perform certain actions, thereby eliminating the need for a physical signature on a paper document.

Upon receiving your manager's virtual signature, the time sheet again passes over the intranet to the billing department. When the billing department receives the electronic form, it can export the data into a Lotus 1-2-3 spreadsheet (Lotus 1-2-3 is a program that crunches numbers). The spreadsheet automatically tallies up what each client owes your firm, calculates taxes, and generates billing statements. This function saves the time that the billing department employees used to spend entering all the information from your paper time sheet into their databases. When billing is done, a mouse click on another button automatically copies the time sheet into another Notes database that serves as an electronic archive. Notes stores all the time sheets produced by your company in this database. With a proper backup schedule in place, this archive is every bit as effective, if not more so, than the old paper filing system. It also takes up less physical space than a room full of filing cabinets. From just this example, you can see that Notes can do many useful things for people who work with each other.

Definition of Notes

When somebody asks the question, "What is Lotus Notes?" a laundry list of the functions described above, such as e-mail, databases, and graphics, often follows. While Notes possesses all these capabilities, a simple listing does not begin to describe the essential nature that distinguishes it from other software. From the example above, you can see that a better way to understand Notes is by gaining an understanding of the different types of business tasks that it can help you complete. In some ways, Notes is not like any other currently existing software. Define Notes not by asking, "What is Notes?," but by asking,

"How will Notes help me do what I need to do?" If you use Notes to read, send, and manage e-mail, it is an e-mail application. If you use Notes to track Customer Support calls through to their resolution, it is tracking software. If you need to combine customer tracking with e-mail, you can do that too.

NOTES USAGE

For the last several years, Notes has been the de facto leader in what the members of software industry have dubbed groupware. Organizations typically use Notes for the following types of tasks:

- Internal document publishing and document management
- E-mail
- Database access and transaction processing
- Discussion databases
- Work flow (work management)

Internal Document Publishing and Document Management

Perhaps your company has an employee handbook with which everyone is required to be familiar. The handbook can be placed in a Lotus Notes database, then all employees can open the database from their PCs to find the information they need. The database can be searchable, making it much easier to find specific information than searching in a printed handbook by flipping pages. Also, if the information in the handbook changes frequently, it is much easier to update the electronic version in Notes than to create a new printed manual. As soon as the updates are made in the handbook database, everyone in the company has instant access to them without the lag time associated with traditional publishing methods. Changes to documents can also be managed; that is, they can require a manger's electronic signature before the changes are published electronically.

E-mail

Notes Mail takes the benefits of traditional e-mail such as instantaneous communication and enhances them. Notes Mail provides secure transmission with its encryption and signature features.

Database Access and Transaction Processing

You can combine Notes with third-party products to provide access to other databases. Suppose your company has a large database with millions of records in it on a mainframe computer. Although it is inappropriate to store those documents in a Notes database, you can use a special Lotus Notes database combined with other third-party products to access the information in those records. The advantage to doing this is that you can use the familiar environment of Notes on your PC while still gaining access to the data in your company's old (legacy) database on the mainframe.

Discussion Databases

Because Notes databases can be accessed by many people from different locations, they are especially well suited to providing a forum for holding electronic discussions (convenient-time conferencing). The way Notes discussion databases work is quite simple. A database for a particular topic is the Notes conference server. Suppose the discussions are to be about ideas for new toys that your company might consider making. One day you have an idea for a new kind of swing set. All you need to do is open the new toys discussion database and click the *New Topic* button. You enter a subject for your message such as, "How about a Yogi Bear swing set?" You then write a message describing the set, the target market, and the reasons you think it will sell. Later, some of your co-workers will open the database, read your idea, and click on the *Compose a Response* button to type a response to your Yogi Bear swing set idea. Perhaps one will note that this idea has already been tried unsuccessfully by another company. The discussion can go on and on like this. Newcomers to your team can easily come up to speed on the current topics of discussion by simply reading the old threads in the discussion database.

Work Flow (Work Management)

Notes can take established work patterns and automate them, increasing the efficiency of those patterns. A person in a business process who completes work on a document can electronically *push* it along in the chain to the next person, who is notified by an e-mail message that the document is ready. You can also design databases to proactively send reminders after a period to people regarding documents that are pending.

THE FUTURE OF NOTES

Because it provides elegant integration, quick development, and time-proven methods of achieving many of the tasks listed above, Notes has achieved a dominant position in the groupware hierarchy. As many software leaders have seen, though, the stay at the top is often short. The Internet, particularly the Web, has become a legitimate groupware tool in many computer users' desktop tool box. As a result, Lotus and its parent IBM have had to scramble to remain the leading groupware vendor. Lotus has very wisely attempted to do this by adopting an "if you can't beat 'em, join 'em," attitude and has integrated the strengths of the Internet with the superior security, development, and information management features built into Notes.

Notes' destiny in the coming years rests partly outside Lotus's control. Even though Lotus markets Notes as an extremely good fit with the Internet, many companies realize that they can achieve their intranet objectives with Internet tools. Also, there is an army of motivated software developers rapidly creating TCP/IP groupware products. Notes clearly faces a significant challenge to its reign over the groupware market.

COMPONENTS OF A NOTES SYSTEM

In spite of any threat to Notes posed by the Internet, the focus for purposes of this book is what you can achieve today. Notes remains a superior tool for implementing a richly featured groupware system. Unlike the Internet, Notes was designed from day one to be full-featured, multipurpose group software. Right out of the box, Notes provides three essential capabilities that are the core of its groupware personality. Notes is a secure shared-database structure with integrated e-mail and a development environment you can use to tailor databases to your needs.

A Notes server is a network-attached computer running the Lotus Notes server software. A Notes client is a desktop or laptop computer running the Lotus Notes client software. The Notes client interface is shown in Figure 10.2.

Notes Servers and Clients

The Notes server stores your organization's information, handles Notes e-mail, controls the access of Notes users, manages the replication of databases, and transfers information requested by an authorized client over the network to the client. Typically, a server is always available (i.e., it is never turned off except for maintenance) so that clients may request information from it at any time.

Your organization must carefully map out its strategy for deploying Notes servers. Depending on the size and geographic locations of your offices, there may be only one or two Notes servers, or there may be 100. It is beyond the scope of this chapter to describe these strategies, but keep in mind that Notes' ability to keep multiple, geographically separated Notes servers in synch is one of its greatest strengths. Also, don't forget that the day-to-day maintenance of a Notes system can quickly become a full time job, if it is used by more than a handful of users.

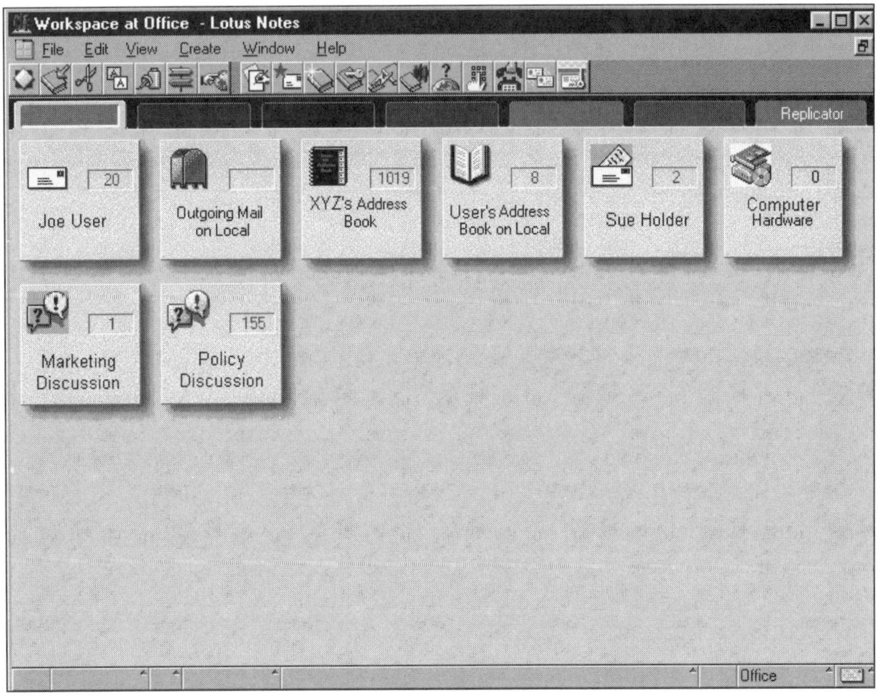

Figure 10.2: The Lotus Notes client appears almost identical on any operating system you run on your computer.

Server Administration and Server-Side Security

Once the Notes servers are in place, the Notes administrator must maintain them. Among other responsibilities, the administrator is in charge of adding, removing, and enabling user accounts to the Notes server's address book in a process known as certification. The address book holds vital information about all the authorized Notes users in an organization.

Certification All the Notes servers in an organization share common certification data so that users certified by the Notes administrator can be given access to the other Notes servers in the organization. To make use of any of the data on an organization's Notes server, you must be certified on the server by the Notes administrator. Once certified, a user receives a special file, *user.id*, which identifies the user to all the Notes servers in the organization. A Notes *user.id* created on a server that does not share your organization's common certification data cannot be used to access your Notes servers without express permission from the administrator. This means that your company's main competitor cannot create its own *user.id* file and use it to gain access to the secret information on your Notes servers.

The administrator is also largely responsible for determining which databases on a Notes server can be replicated to another server or to a user's hard drive.

Authentication To access a database on a Notes server, you must have your *user.id* file and you must know your password (see Figure 10.3). Any time that you try to access a database on a Notes server, you are prompted for your password before you can see the database on your screen. This is one way to validate that you are in fact who you claim to be. Of course, someone who steals your *user.id* file and finds out your password can pretend to be you and access all the databases that you can. Your password is created when your Notes account is created.

Access Control Access to any Notes server is controlled by a special list that contains the names and *user.id* information of all users who are allowed to open databases on the server. The administrator is in charge of setting up this list for each Notes server in an organization. This is the first level of security in a Notes system.

Figure 10.3: Notes requires you to enter a password whenever you open a Notes database for the first time.

Secure, Shared Database Structure

Notes Database Basics Notes organizes and stores information in databases, which are simply collections of information. (Chapter 9 gives more background information about databases.) Notes databases do not conform to the traditional relational structure for databases. Lotus Notes databases consist of documents, views, forms, and fields. The following scenario introduces these database components.

To form a picture of a Notes database, imagine that you are going to list everything in your top desk drawer on index cards, one item per index card (see Figure 10.4). The fill-in blank that contains the item name is labeled *item.* You then categorize each item according to purpose (e.g., office supplies, personal effects, currency) in a second fill-in blank labeled *category.* Finally, you put the number of each item that you have on hand in the third fill-in blank labeled *inventory.* The contents of these cards make up a database.

Each of the individual cards is equivalent to what is known as a Lotus Notes *document*. The individual pieces of information (item, category, and inventory) that make up the content of the cards are *fields*.

You will probably want all index cards (documents) to look the same so that you know exactly where to look for a particular piece of information on any given card. To do this, you might follow a template for each card, putting item at the top, category in the middle, and inventory at the bottom. This template provides you with a consistent, organized way of looking at and adding to the information on the cards. Your template is equivalent to a *form* in Lotus Notes.

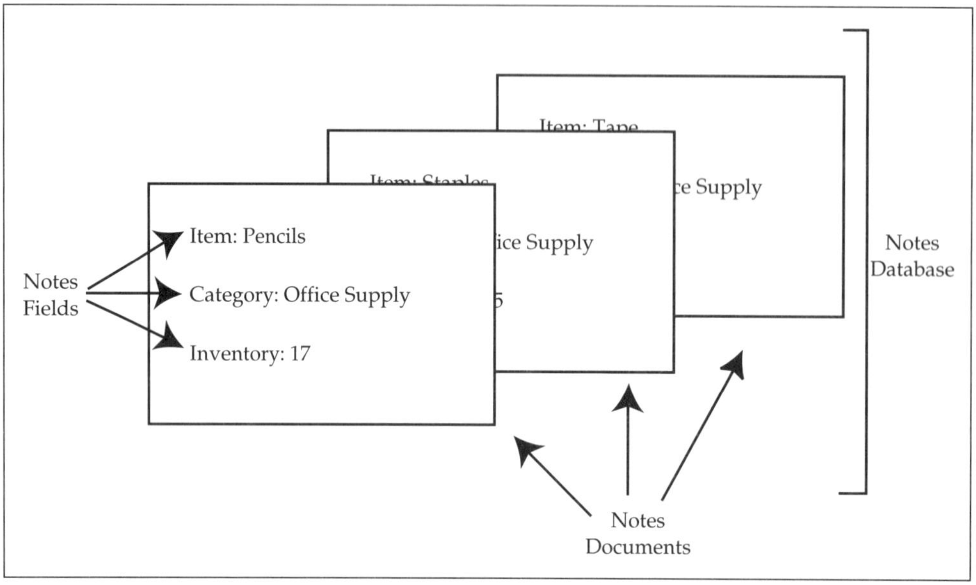

Figure 10.4: The contents of these index cards constitute a simple database.

If your drawer is full of stuff, you might end up with several hundred cards. It will be difficult to find anything in your database, if you have to thumb through all those cards. Making a list that shows you the contents and locations of each document in your database will be a good way to help you find the information. Notes does this for you by providing *views* with each database (see Figure 10.5).

Of course, creating all these cards and views will take a long time, but with Notes doing the work for you, the whole process takes seconds. With Notes, you can easily create different kinds of views to look at your database in different ways. You can make a *View by Category* view that shows you all the documents that are in the same category grouped together. This ability to create your own views can be a big help when you are trying to look at information in a way that the database's designer did not think of.

Notes can use many different kinds of databases for different purposes. Some specially designed databases hold publications (e.g., company policies and procedures), others facilitate conversations (e.g., conferencing), and still others automate work flow.

Notes databases are hybrid databases, because they are more flexible regarding types of content they can hold. Fields in a Notes data-

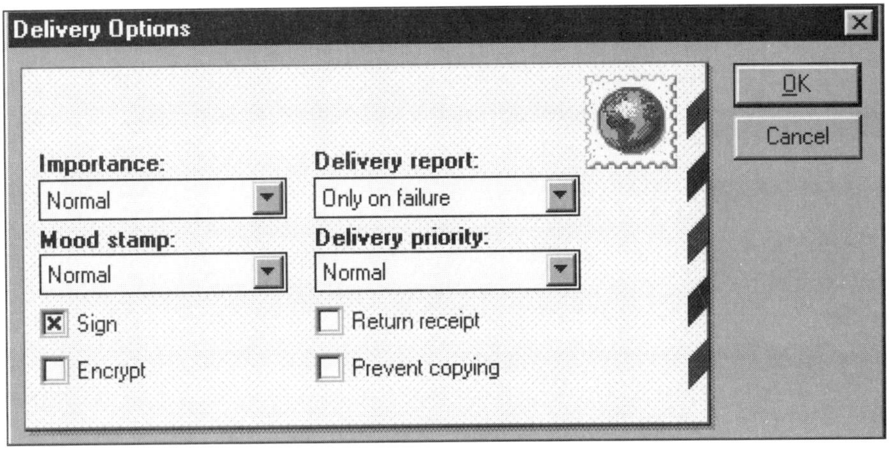

Figure 10.5: Notes presents the information in a database using views like this one.

base support multiple data types. You can include within a database field formatted text, graphics, audio files, spreadsheets, and even files created in other applications (in the form of attachments).

Shared, Secure Databases Groupware's raison d'etre, above and beyond any other, is to share information. Notes is the leading groupware because it excels in sharing. With Notes, you can copy a Notes database that you have created on your PC onto a Notes server. Anyone who has access to that Notes server can see your database, but only if you allow it.

If you want only the marketing department to see your database, you simply give only those individuals in marketing access to your database on the Notes server. This type of control is managed from within the database's Access Control List (ACL).

The ACL consists of a list of people (or other Notes servers) who may access the database. Within the ACL, you can assign seven access levels:

- No Access—Just as it sounds, *No Access* allows no access to the database.
- Depositor—People with *Depositor* access may deposit data to the database only through interactive forms that you, as the database's creator, specify.

- Reader—Those who have *Reader* access can read the documents in a database but cannot create, edit, or delete documents.
- Author—Individuals with *Author* access may not only read the documents, but may create and edit their own documents (but not documents created by other members of the database).
- Editors—*Editors* may create their own documents, as well as edit and delete documents created by others.
- Designers—*Designers* have all the abilities of *Editors*, and they can create new views and forms in a database.
- Manager—The database *Manager* is in charge of specifying which access level is assigned to each member of the ACL, who may access the database, and the maintenance of the database.

All these access levels may also be assigned to groups that have been created by the Notes administrator (e.g., Marketing).

This type of security is superior to that currently available for the Web. (Lotus's new combined Notes/Web server product, Domino, claims to provide this level of security to Web clients. (See the end of this chapter for more information on Notes and the Internet.) The best security you can provide with most Web servers is password protection at the folder level. For example, say you create a folder called *personnel* on your Web server that contains one file for every employee in your organization. These files contain confidential data like salaries and benefits for each employee as well as nonsensitive data such as office location and office phone number. You do not want unauthorized people to lay eyes on these documents.

With a regular Web server, you can specify that people who ask to view any document in the *personnel* folder must enter a preassigned user ID and password first. You then assign all the authorized people (e.g., the personnel in your Human Resources department) user IDs and passwords. But what if another group of people who are not authorized to view the classified information, like co-workers, need access to the nonclassified information in these documents? Using a Web server to distribute this information requires a separate set of documents without the sensitive data be maintained. Notes, however, by providing its security on several levels, allows anybody to see all the publicly available information contained in documents but requires a user ID and password to view confidential parts (fields) of the document. This way, only one document (or record) needs to be maintained for each individual. Some people will see all the fields in a document, while others see just the name and office location information (see Figure 10.6). This granularity of security combines with the application development environment described later in this chapter to make Notes a powerful work flow tool.

Notes users can also encrypt the contents of fields, documents (including e-mail documents), and databases. Encryption is a process of making a document unreadable. This means that only individuals who have the encryption key can see the information. One situation in which you might want to use encryption arises when you replicate to a laptop a database with important company information. If someone steals your laptop, you'll be glad your data is encrypted. Notes

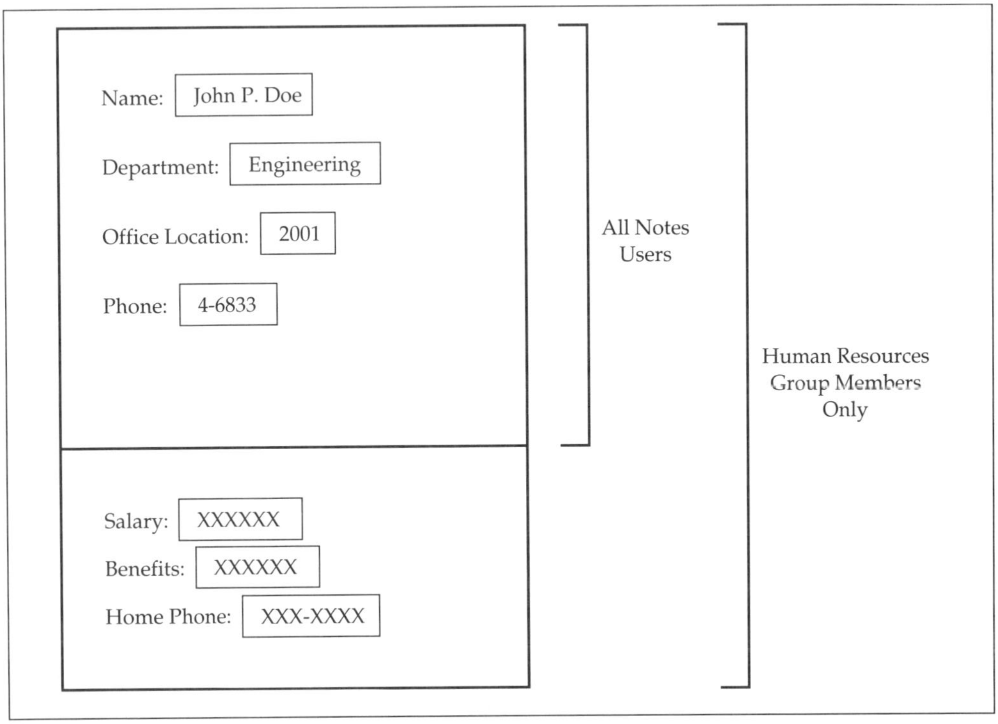

Figure 10.6: People who belong to the *Human Resources* group can see the confidential fields; other cannot.

encryption is not a foolproof security measure, but it does provide another layer of defense against information falling into the wrong hands. You can choose from three levels of database encryption security: simple, medium, and strong. The stronger the level of encryption, the harder it is to break but the slower it is to encrypt and decrypt during authorized use.

Replication

Usually, you don't spend all day every day in your office. You engage in such activities as business trips, conferences, and visits to clients. You may work at home part or all of the time. In the past, it has often been difficult for people who are not in the office to stay connected. The telephone was really the only way to get the information they needed to do their work. Whether you are working at home or on an airplane at 30,000 feet, Notes makes it possible for you to work with information that is shared by you and your co-workers. Notes allows you to make a copy of data to your laptop computer and then, even if not connected to a network, you can work on and update the data. Later, when you have reconnected to the network, Notes will synchronize the changes with the shared copy of the data, resolving any conflicts between the two copies. This replication capability places Notes in a unique subcategory of the groupware realm. None of the software mentioned elsewhere in this book handles replication as Notes does, so Notes has an important advantage over other groupware products.

Replication gives you the power to store a copy or copies of your database on several different servers or workstations and automatically synchronize the data at regular intervals. Typically, a shared Notes database is in as many as three places: the Notes server of origin, a workstation(s), and a remote Notes server(s).

Location 1: The Server of Origin When you want to share your database, you must put it on a Notes server. From there, the other people on your team can get to the information they need to have. If everybody who needs the data always works at a desktop machine that is connected to the LAN on which the Notes server is located, there may never be a reason to replicate the database.

Occasionally two people may work on the same document at the same time. Lotus Notes allows this to happen because it does not have the capability of *locking out* other authorized users from a document when it has been opened by another person. In cases like this, you must go back in and manually compare the two resulting documents for differences and reconcile them. This incapability for document lock-out makes Notes unsuitable for uses that require frequent real-time access to information in a database. For instance, a bank manager would not set up Notes for the tellers to use in processing transactions because it is unacceptable to have conflicting changes to a bank account record.

Location 2: A Desktop Computer or Laptop To work with a database when you are not connected to a Notes server, you will need to replicate a copy to your computer's hard drive.

Replicas of shared databases can be partial or full. Just as you might think, a partial, or selective, replica contains only the documents in a shared database that are of interest to you. You specify the documents you want before starting the replication process. A full replica is an exact copy, like a snapshot, of the source database.

Any time somebody needs the information and built-in functionality of a particular database but does not have the capability of connecting to a network, replication is the answer. For example, imagine that a construction supply salesperson visits a client on a construction site to estimate a job. She may need to be able to tell the contractor how many feet of copper cable are in the warehouse and available for next day delivery. If Notes has replicated the warehouse inventory database to a laptop before she goes to the site, the salesperson has access to this information. She can then go ahead and fill out an order within the database that marks the specified amount of cable as sold. When the salesperson reconnects to the network, the order is replicated to the shared copy of the database. Now other salespeople can see the new inventory information and make their own replicas on their laptops.

Location 3: Replicated on Another Server The appeal that Notes has to large, multinational corporations—for example, Federal Express—is that the same database can *live* on one server in Memphis, on another in Bonn, and on another in Tokyo. These copies can contain the same information and be kept in synch by replication (see Figure 10.7). Distributing the databases to servers closer to the people who need them reduces reliance on the company WAN, speeds access

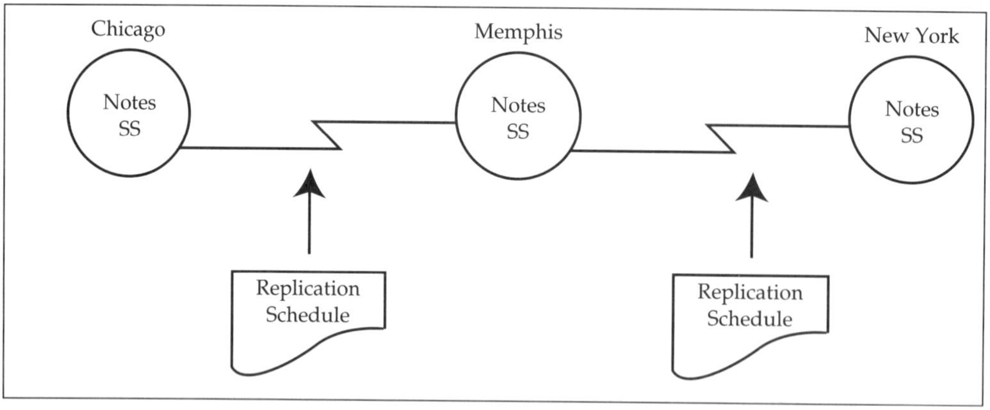

Figure 10.7: To keep replica databases in synch, the Notes administrator sets up a schedule for replication based on factors such as frequency of update to the database and network performance.

to the data, and reduces the load on the individual Notes servers. For example, if you work for FedEx in Memphis you might have an important discussion database that is replicated on a local Notes server in Memphis, on a Notes server in New York, and on another Notes server in Chicago. When one of your co-workers in Chicago adds a new topic for discussion, you want that topic to show up in the Memphis and New York copies of the database. Likewise, when you respond to that topic, you want your response to show up in the Chicago and New York Notes servers.

To make sure that all these changes show up in all copies of the database, the Notes administrator sets up a replication schedule among the three servers. The administrator might set up the schedule so that the servers are replicated every two hours on a staggered schedule. The Memphis server calls the Chicago server at 8:00 A.M., at which time all the changes made to the Memphis database since the last call are transferred to the Chicago database and vice versa. Then at 9:00 A.M. the Memphis database calls the New York server and they exchange updates to the database. Now both Memphis and New York contain the same information as Chicago did at 8:00 A.M. When Memphis calls Chicago again at 10:00 A.M., the New York updates are replicated to the Chicago server. This type of a schedule maintains a reasonable level of synchronicity among the three offices. To make these scheduled replication sessions as efficient as possible, only the individual fields in documents that have been changed will be replicated.

Sophisticated E-mail

As noted at the beginning of this chapter, Notes derives its power from more than just having a multitude of capabilities and features. The elegant integration of these essential features renders all of them more useful and powerful. This is especially true for Notes Mail. Notes Mail is not very impressive on its own, compared with many other e-mail systems. However, with the click of a button, this simple tool can mail any document in a Notes database to another Notes user. Even if that document includes fancy Notes features such as an expense report with formulas, buttons that perform certain actions, or links to other databases, the recipient need only open the e-mail to view the information and make use of the features included with the document. Or if you prefer that the recipient view the document within the database itself, you can place a link to the specific document in an e-mail message. Readers have only to double-click a button that takes them to the appropriate database and document. Links in Notes, called DocLinks, are similar to Web hyperlinks.

A Notes e-mail database, a personal mailbox, installs automatically for every new user. The personal mailbox database is just a Notes database with specialized views and forms designed for dealing with e-mail. It is stored on the Notes server, but only the user can access it. As mentioned, the personal mailbox database comes with several different built-in views. These views are the key to managing e-mail messages in Notes, allowing you to view by category, author, date, size, attachments, and more.

You can encrypt Notes e-mail just like any other document in Notes. Another security feature built into Notes Mail is the ability to *sign* outgoing e-mail messages (see Figure 10.8). All individual Notes users are assigned unique identification information in their *user.id* file when they are certified by the Notes administrator. When an e-mail message is signed, Notes attaches this information to the message. When the recipient opens the message, Notes validates the attached user information against the address book on the Notes server. This check ensures that the message has not been intercepted and altered somewhere along the way.

Have you ever worried that an e-mail message you sent didn't make it to its destination? Notes can ease your mind by allowing you to request notification of arrival when you send an e-mail message. You can even be notified when the message has been opened by the recipient.

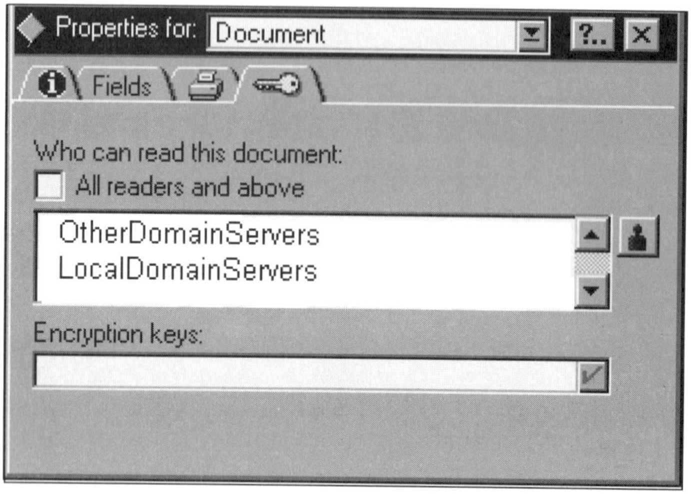

Figure 10.8: Notes gives you the option to sign and/or encrypt each e-mail you send to another Notes user.

You may send e-mail out of the Notes system to Internet e-mail addresses only if your Notes server attaches to a special type of computer, known as an SMTP gateway. When Notes e-mail leaves the Notes system through a gateway, many of the features of Notes Mail are lost. For example, if you send an encrypted message from Notes to an Internet address, the message will not be encrypted when it passes from the gateway to the Internet.

Notes Application Development: Modifying and Making Your Own New Databases

Things change. Groupware needs to be able to adapt to meet these changes. It should support ad hoc work groups as well as established business processes. You can develop brand-new databases from within your Lotus Notes client. Creating a very simple database from a template is easy.

When your boss puts you in charge of a new project, wouldn't you love to have a tool that you can tailor to the specific needs of the project? For example, what if your manager asks you to lead a task force to design a better way to handle customer requests for product literature? How can you use Lotus Notes to help you meet this challenge?

Notes includes tools for creating custom databases. The range of difficulty in designing these custom databases varies depending upon whether you use one of the templates included with Notes or start from scratch. If you use a template and make only minimal changes, it is fairly easy. If you start from scratch, although not altogether impossible, it can be difficult. Notes includes a set of commands and a formula language that you can use to customize your databases. This language has the look and feel of the commands and formula language for Lotus 1-2-3. Learning the commands, however, is not very intuitive or easy for the average computer user. If you decide to make any but the most simple changes to the database's design, you will probably need to get an experienced Notes application developer's help to do it.

Templates You can easily put into action some of the common tasks of Notes databases just by opening one of the templates or example databases that ship with the program. An example database is like a cookie cutter. Template databases provide canned databases with all the views, forms, and scripting for a particular task built in.

The first thing you might do to get the ball rolling on your product literature task is to create a Notes discussion database. This database provides a place for the members of the task force to brainstorm about ways to handle customer requests for literature. To make it happen, all you do is open up Lotus Notes, choose *New Database* from a menu, name the database something like *Product Literature Delivery Task Force*, give the members access to your database, and save it on your Notes server. Next you send e-mail to the members of the task force telling them that it is available. Then, presumably, the task force members can start sharing their thoughts and ideas about how to approach the literature distribution problem. It is a virtual meeting. As in a physical meeting, each member of the task force listens what others have to say and shares his or her own opinions. Unlike in a physical meeting, however, the participants do not have to be in the same room at the same time. People can participate at their convenience.

Eventually the discussion in the database might reveal that the biggest problem your company has in distributing literature to customers pertains to keeping track of which customer has requested what literature. Once you discover this, the customer tracking database (another Notes template database) might provide a good solution to the problem.

The customer tracking template included with Notes enables you almost immediately to put in place a customer tracking system. Each new customer added to the database must have the customer description and contact fields completed. The database tracks action items, phone call reports, incoming correspondence, outgoing correspondence, meeting reports, and other miscellaneous activity regarding the customer. By setting up a database based on the customer tracking template, you have most of the application development that you need.

Custom Database (Notes Application) Development When the template databases provided with Notes are not sufficient, you can always modify them or design and develop a custom Notes application. A Notes application is simply a Notes database(s) designed or customized to help people do their jobs. If an organization decides to use Notes to develop its own internal applications, it can do one of three things:

- Hire a full-time programmer/developer. This option is still better than the old way of hiring programmers to create applications using a programming language, because it is much easier to develop Notes applications.
- Contract the development of applications to a Notes development consultant.
- Purchase prefabricated third-party Notes applications.

In the example from above about product literature requests, you might need to make some subtle changes to the customer tracking template to tailor it to your exact needs. For example, you might want to add a field that lists all your product literature publications with check boxes beside them. When a customer requests a particular brochure, the person entering the request into the database need only click in the box next to that brochure. When your employee saves the document, you have a permanent record of the customer's request. You will also want to add a script to the template that fires off e-mail to the marketing department when a new request comes in, letting those people know that they need to send the requested brochure to that customer. To add these features, the template must be customized.

Many large organizations already employ programmers who develop stand-alone applications designed to assist workers with their jobs if regular off-the-shelf software does not have the required capabilities. This method of doing business creates highly customized applications, but it is expensive to keep all the programmers around. It can take weeks or months to develop a new application when the need arises. After an application has been written, implementing changes can be a monumental undertaking. Notes offers a better alternative.

When a company decides to use Notes for developing its custom applications, it can lop off large amounts of the development time and resources it expended by doing a project the old way. Application developers have a robust environment in Notes to create the tools that organizations need. Notes provides formulas, @functions, and a scripting language (LotusScript) that make it relatively easy to create an application with work flow capabilities or automated tasks. Once the people in the organization become familiar with the Notes client interface, they can easily start using new Notes applications.

Multiplatform Capability Notes runs on a variety of platforms. Personnel in the advertising department can run it on their Macs just as well as the number crunchers in accounting can run it on their PCs running Windows or OS/2. There is also a version of Notes for the Unix operating system. This is another advantage to producing companywide applications inside Notes. You do not have to develop a separate application that runs on each platform.

NOTES AND THE INTERNET

With Release 4, Notes includes features that show the Lotus intent to blend the capabilities of Notes with the Internet. They provide a Web browser for viewing other people's Web documents as well as a tool for creating and managing your own Web site. The Web browser makes switching between documents in a Notes database and Web documents very easy. Because of the way it is designed, however, it suffers a performance lag, compared with other Web browsers, the first time it visits a Web site.

Browsing the Web

Release 4 integrates a hybrid Web browser into the Notes client. The Web browser relies on the Notes server to retrieve HTML files from

Web servers (the files that are viewed with the Web browser). Regular Web browsers communicate directly with the Web servers. The extra steps involved in sending a request for a Web document to the Notes server, then on to the Web server, then back to the Notes server, and finally back to the Notes client slow the performance of the browser significantly the first time a Web site is visited. However, the Notes server stores all the Web documents it visits in a Notes database. The next time any Notes client requests the same page, the download speed is faster because the document is transferred only from the Notes server to the client, saving a trip across the Internet. Unfortunately, if the document has been modified since the last visit, the user does not receive the updated document. A user must specifically request that the document be refreshed from the source on the original Web server to ensure that the content being viewed is up to date.

One feature of the new Web browser in the Notes client is a direct result of its reliance on the Notes server to actually go out and fetch the Web documents from the Web servers. The administrator of the Notes server can set it up so that certain parts of the Internet are not accessible from the Notes client browser. For example, if the company management doesn't want employees wasting company time, it can block access to sites it deems frivolous or offensive. Of course, whether this feature is a benefit or a curse depends on your own perspective. It is also notable that since Notes may be on a non-TCP/IP network, the browser in the Notes client gives users Web access even though they are not directly connected to a TCP/IP network.

InterNotes and WebPublisher

The first Lotus attempt to integrate the advantages of Notes with the Web came in the form of InterNotes. InterNotes provides documents in Notes databases to Web browsers by automatically converting the Notes documents into HTML documents at regularly scheduled intervals (HTML is the language used to format documents for use on the Web). When a document is changed or added to the Notes database, the Web documents will reflect the changes and additions after the next scheduled publishing interval. An InterNotes-enabled Notes server must also be running and must be connected to the Internet (see Figure 10.9).

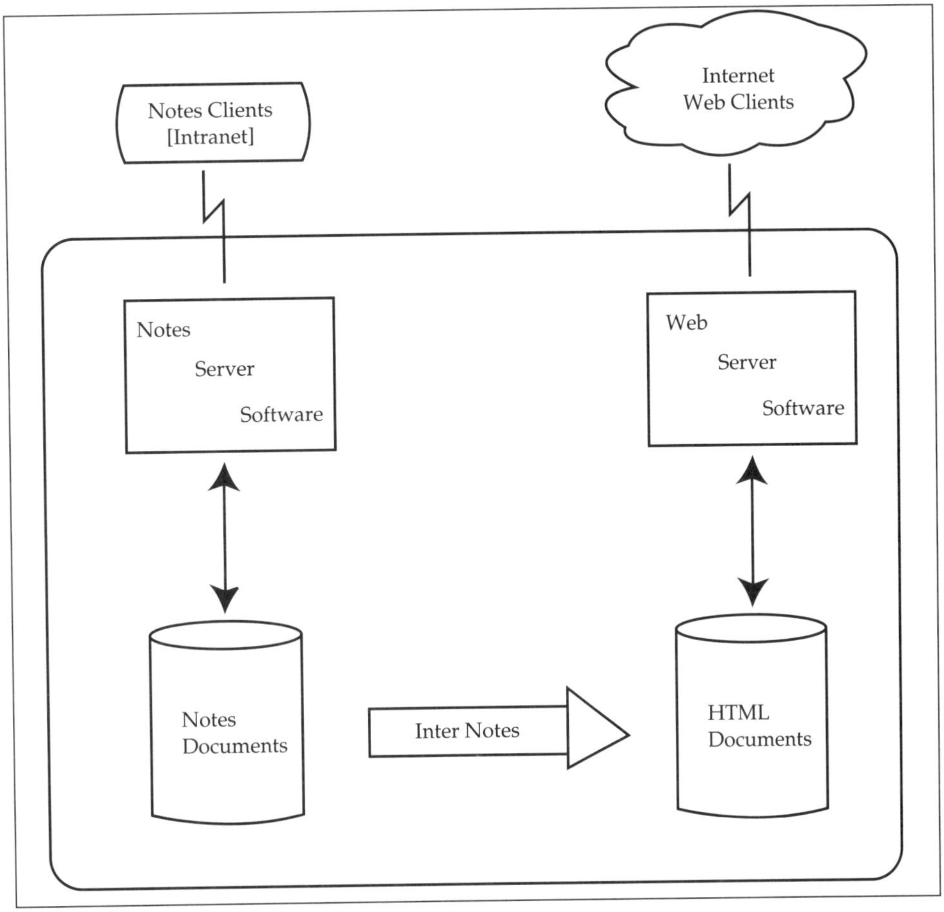

Figure 10.9: InterNotes helps a Notes server work with a Web server to publish Notes databases on the Web.

InterNotes works by recreating the views and document that are in a database into HTML. One HTML file is made for every document and view in the database. You can select only the views that you wish to publish. As with views in a regular Notes database, users must click on the document they wish to read. The images in Figures 10.10 and 10.11 show a view of a sample Notes database published using InterNotes in the Notes client and in a Web browser. Clearly, what the user sees in both cases is very similar.

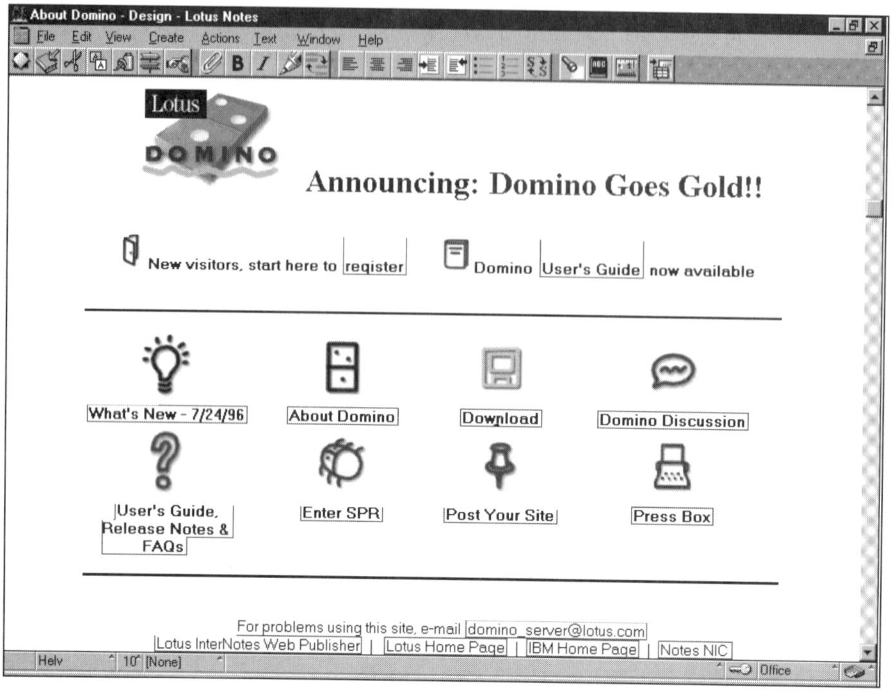

Figure 10.10: The Notes client displays a database like this.

Having the InterNotes document management capabilities power your Web site can be a great benefit. Using InterNotes to create a presence on the Web can provide advantages over other site management methods. The management of a large Web site can be tremendously complicated when it grows beyond a few dozen documents, and Notes' built-in document management processes can be helpful. You can design the Notes database containing the documents to be published on the web to be as complex as you wish. For example, the database can require that managers electronically sign off on new documents (or changes to documents) before they are published on the Web. This way, nothing inappropriate, under development, or confidential will be made available to the public without management approval. You can also create a view of the database that puts a small *New* icon out beside all documents that have been added within the last 48 hours and another icon that reads *Updated* to let readers know what's new and what's been updated in the last two days. Also, the full text of any database that has been indexed and is published using InterNotes may be searched through a Web browser.

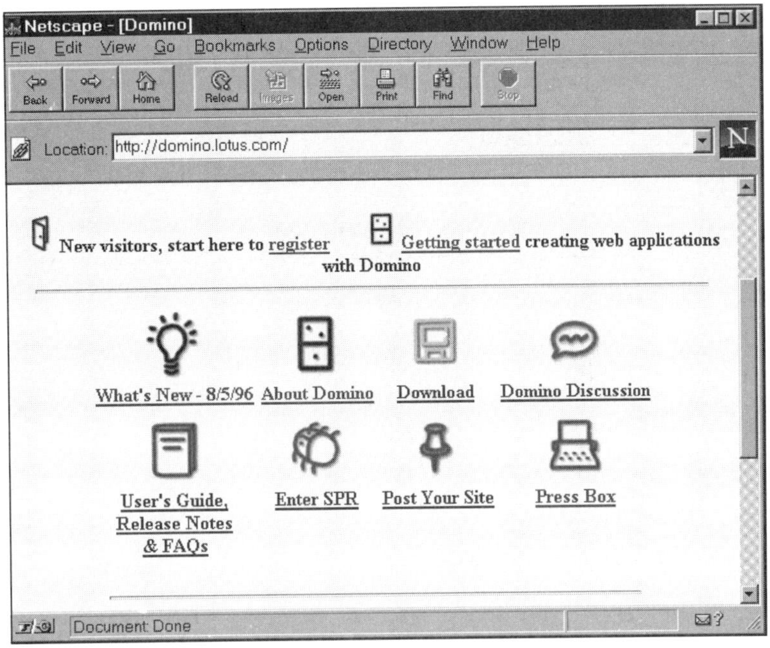

Figure 10.11: A Web browser displays the same database in a similar fashion.

InterNotes does almost all the HTML coding (the coding used to make files displayable by Web browsers). The creator of a document does not have to know how to use HTML. All that the creator of the document must do is use the standard Notes editor to type in and format a document. InterNotes takes care of the rest. If you desire, you may set up your database so that all text of a certain size in your Notes document will correspond to similar HTML heading levels. For instance, you can specify that all text that is 20 points or greater in your Notes document appears as a level one heading in the HTML document, while all text that is exactly 16 points appears as level two headings in the HTML document. InterNotes also translates tables that you have created in your Notes document into HTML tables.

Another nice feature of InterNotes is automatic graphic translation. Web browsers are able to display only certain graphics files that are in certain formats designated by the file extensions .GIF and .JPG. In a normal Notes document, though, you can have other types of image files in rich text fields. When you publish one of these documents with

InterNotes, image files in other formats such as Windows bit maps (BMPs) are automatically converted into the Web standard GIF format.

Finally, InterNotes allows you to publish interactive forms on the Web. When a user fills out the form fields in a browser and submits it, InterNotes saves the values in a regular Notes document. An example of where this is useful is an order form for customers. Customers can access your company site over the Internet with any Web browser. When ready to place an order, they simply use the Web browser to fill out the form with their name, company, address, and order. When they click on the *submit* button, the order is sent to the Web server. InterNotes converts the submitted information into a regular Lotus Notes document in a customer orders database. You can then use the work flow features in Lotus Notes to process and fill the order.

Domino

Lotus has continued to integrate the Web with Notes by building a Web Release 4.5 of the Notes server. This hybrid Notes server, called Domino, builds on the older InterNotes technology that required that a separate Web server run simultaneously with the Notes server. Domino extends the capabilities of InterNotes beyond merely publishing documents and fill-out forms. Web users may make use of many Notes applications over the Internet (or an intranet) by using a Web browser instead of a Notes client to access the server. Domino provides Web access to many Notes security features, including the capability of restricting access down to the field level when creating new documents. This means that almost any of the work flow applications your company develops in Notes, which previously required a Notes client, can now be used over the Web with a regular Web browser.

SUMMARY

Lotus Notes is different things to different people. Notes elegantly integrates a cluster of software tools, e-mail, a shared database structure, and sophisticated application development capabilities. All of this together makes Notes the world's leading groupware product. Lotus has attempted to combine Notes' strengths (security, work flow, document management) with the Internet's (open access, wide and increasing popularity, rapid development) to stay at the top of the competitive groupware market.

Chapter 11

SECURITY

This chapter explores business security needs and outlines the features needed to provide such security.

INTRODUCTION TO SECURITY

In the summer of 1996, American movie audiences were dazzled by one of the most elegant fictional computer break-ins ever filmed in *Mission: Impossible*. In the movie, Agent Ethan Hunt slithers into an ultrasecure CIA computer room through an air duct, lowering himself inch by inch to avoid setting off the motion detectors in the room. Temperature sensors, floor weight detectors, and countless other safeguards also protect the room. As he dangles from the ceiling, he enters into the system the stolen password that he has obtained, copies an exceptionally sensitive database to a tape, and almost escapes without detection. This incident is *hacking* taken to a new level.

Fortunately, you probably do not need to protect your organization's data quite as well as the CIA must. Hundreds of lives are probably not at stake if the data is compromised. However, there may be thousands of dollars worth of lost revenues if your leading competitor is able to steal your price list for the upcoming season and undercut your pricing. Or you may lose hundreds of hours recovering data after a break-in by a malicious hacker. Then again, you may lose nothing of value if a stranger infiltrates your system and reads all the files. Herein lies the first lesson of security: it is a balancing act between the value of time and resources spent protecting data and the value of the data itself.

Presumably though, much of your company's information is valuable. When you have something valuable, it makes sense to protect it. That's what security does. Before you pour your company's knowledge into that groupware system, have a plan. A good backup system can often avert total disaster, but a little preventive maintenance up front can pay off in saved time, data, and heartache.

This chapter discusses computer security in a business scenario. It introduces you to the issues involved in computer security so that you will gain an awareness about security that is sufficient for you to begin evaluating your organization's security needs. The actual nuts and bolts of installing security measures—from passwords to firewalls—is left to other more comprehensive sources. The Internet has hundreds of sites devoted to this topic on all levels of sophistication.

WHY DO YOU NEED SECURITY?

When you put a communications line into the back of a computer, you are installing a doorway into that computer. Whether that door is wide open or locked shut depends on how you choose to secure your computer. Your need to dead-bolt that door depends upon how concerned you are with the following issues:

- **Confidentiality**—Preventing confidential or private information from falling into unauthorized hands. For example, if you are conducting an ongoing virtual conference on the development of a new product, you will not want your biggest competitor to be able to read the conference.
- **Data integrity**—Making sure that the information available to authorized people is legitimate, untainted, and reliable. The popular example of a threat to data integrity is a computer virus that invades a system and randomly deletes or changes data.
- **Availability**—Making information accessible to the people who need it. If your server crashes, the information on that server is unavailable, and information that is unavailable is of very little value. Security can help you make sure that your people have access to the data when they need it.

The threats to confidentiality, integrity, and availability of data come from many places. Most companies are concerned with threats from outside sources. Fewer companies take the necessary steps to protect computer resources from the threat from within. Disgruntled employees can cause more trouble than hackers. Corporate denial of this threat is a real problem.

The Threat from Outside

Any connection between your computers and an outside network is a potential security hole. If your network is a totally private TCP/IP intranet, it is less vulnerable than if you choose to use the Internet itself for all your corporate communications. A private intranet can be attached to the Internet fairly securely with a firewall as a buffer between the networks, but even that is not fail-safe.

Corporate Espionage Many competitors would love to have an inside track to your company's plans, financial information, and client lists. If you are not cautious, your intranet can provide this information. Unscrupulous businesses have been known to intentionally gain access to and poke around in competitor's files. A firewall, described later in this chapter, can help combat this type of access.

It will probably be easier for a competitor to find a vulnerable employee within your company and bribe that person for the same information. Computer security should only be a part of any organization's more comprehensive security plan.

Hackers *Hacker* is an often misunderstood term. A hacker is usually someone who is interested in the way complex computer systems operate. Therefore, not all hackers are a threat to your company. The only ones you need to worry about are the ones interested in gaining access to your system. Once they get in, they may just look around—or they may wreak havoc.

Viruses Viruses are probably the most significant threat from the outside to your company's computers, especially to the PCs on employees' desktops. A computer virus is a program that finds its way onto a computer's storage device and produces unexpected and often undesirable effects. These effects can be minor annoyances such as unwanted messages that appear randomly on your screen, but they can also be devastating occurrences such as corruption or deletion of data stored on the computer. When your intranet is connected to the Internet, the likelihood of encountering virus programs increases. You should never trust any application or file provided from an untrusted source such as e-mail attachments from unknown people. Several vendors offer excellent antivirus software. It is well worth the small investment.

The Threat from Within

Even a computer that is not connected to a network can be subject to security breakdowns. The computer in the *Mission: Impossible* scene was not connected to a network because the data on it was deemed too sensitive to risk an intrusion from over a network. Nevertheless, Agent Ethan Hunt was able break into the CIA system. Part of the reason he got in was that he knew where to look for the information he wanted. He was a former employee. He knew the security mechanisms in place around the computer. All he had to do was get around these mechanisms one by one. Half the challenge to breaking in is knowing the system. Who knows the systems better than the people who work with them every day? In some situations, a trusted employee can become your computer system's enemy.

Disgruntled Employees Some companies live in a state of denial. They refuse to believe that their own employees will do anything to intentionally harm the company. On the contrary, employees can be the biggest threat to the security of your computer system. Employees typically possess all the keys they need to cause real damage: passwords, physical access to machines, and knowledge of the locations of strategic files. An employee may be motivated by greed, resentment, or just curiosity to violate security standards on your system by reading or sharing confidential files, physically damaging hardware, or hiding data.

For example, if your client list happened to include famous or noteworthy individuals, an employee with access to files pertaining to clients might read the information just out of curiosity. This very scenario was reported by an IRS investigation of employees who—just for their own entertainment—read tax returns filed by movie stars, politicians, and friends.

One way to combat this threat is to carefully assign the rights and privileges of individual employees. Do not give access to key files to people who do not need it. Of course, you have to balance this policy with the need for open lines of communication within the organization. Also, it is a good idea to promptly remove a terminated employee's access (login and password) from systems when there is reason to believe that he or she may feel resentment or hostility.

Human Errors Not all security threats result from an intentional attack. For example, think about an average data entry clerk. When you have to process hundreds of computerized transactions every day, it's easy to make a mistake and punch the wrong key occasionally. Many errors in the contents of a database are simply the result of unintentional human errors. The best way to prevent errors is to have error-checking logic built into the software. For example, if one space on an electronic application form is for the social security number of the applicant, you can program the software used to fill out the form so that it beeps and displays an error message to a person inputting the data improperly (e.g., entering eight digits for a nine-digit Social Security number).

The Threat from Nobody

Sometimes a significant threat to computer security does not come from a person at all. For instance, what if your company's building has a fire? Computers and heat of several thousand degrees do not mix well. The key to recovering from losing all your data in such a disaster is maintaining current backup copies in an off-site location. Other threats are broken water pipes, power outages, civil unrest, and natural disasters.

Security Solutions to Investigate

This chapter does not detail how to implement security solutions, but the following sections introduce some precautions you may wish to investigate more, depending on your security needs.

Authentication

The goal of authentication is to make certain that people trying to access a computer are actually who they claim to be. Usually, this is accomplished by requiring the person to know something—most commonly a password. Although it provides a good first layer of defense, this technique alone is not adequate unless you want only minimal protection for data. Passwords are too easy to compromise, either through systematic guessing or through carelessness on the part of users.

Most Web servers include the ability to require a user name and password to be entered when a document is requested from a protected directory. When you enter the password in a Web browser, the password is not displayed on the screen (usually the case with other systems as well) so that someone looking over your shoulder as you type the password cannot see what it is. Figure 11.1 shows the dialog

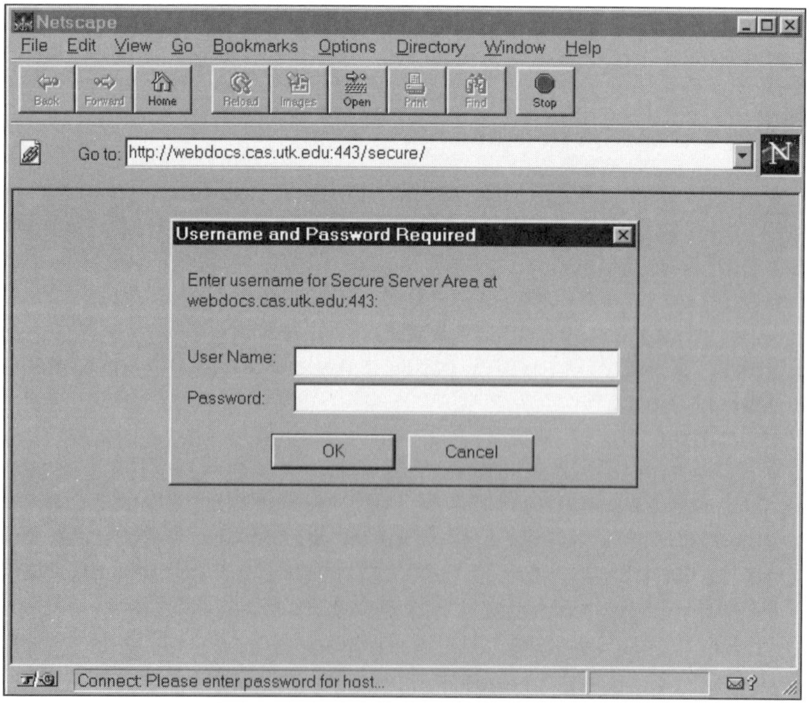

Figure 11.1: A Web server will demand a user name and password when a browser tries to access a secure directory.

box that demands a user name and password from a browser trying to access documents in a secure directory on a Web server.

Good passwords should be at least eight characters long. They should *not* be regular English words, your name, the names of your family members and pets, or social security numbers and birth dates. However, combinations of such items can be effective passwords. For example, you might combine the first two letters of the month of your birth, the last two digits of the year of your spouse's birth, and the last four digits of your child's social security number to get a pretty good password. Say you were born in December, your spouse was born in 1962, and your child's social security number was 123-45-6789. Your password according to the scheme above would be "de626789." This password would be hard to guess but fairly easy to remember.

Another way that authentication can work is by requiring the user not only to know something, but also to have something. This something can be a special electronic certificate that is unique to the user. The certificate is carried by the user on a floppy disk or stored on user's hard drive. An example of a user certificate is the Lotus Notes *user.id* file, which a person must have to log in to a Notes server. This method adds one more level of confidence to the authentication process.

Access Control

Once you have been authenticated by a Notes server, there are usually more security levels involved before you are allowed to read or modify files on the server. For example, in Notes users can be assigned different levels of access to a database. Users' access levels determine what they can do with the database. Those with Reader access can read but not modify documents. With Designer access, a person can modify all documents in the database as well as the design of the database itself.

Another type of access control is especially useful for limiting access to your Web server. You can specify when you are setting up your Web server that only machines within a certain Internet domain can access the server. For example, if your company's Internet domain is *xyz.com*, all the computers in your company will have *xyz.com* as the last part of their Internet address (e.g., *computer1.xyz.com*). (See the chapter on TCP/IP for more details about domain names.) If you set up your server so that only computers with Internet addresses ending *xyz.com* can access it, only the people in your organization can access the documents on that Web server.

Encryption

Many of the security measures available to you operate by preventing unauthorized people from accessing information. Encryption is different because it protects information from prying eyes, even if the file containing the information has been compromised, by making the content unreadable. The only way to read an encrypted file is to unscramble it using an electronic key. One popular encryption package is Pretty Good Privacy (PGP). PGP is distributed for free on the Internet. Notes also has an easy-to-use, built-in encryption feature.

Both PGP and Notes use encryption systems that are based on the *public key* system. A key is a unique electronic identifier that contains a string of characters. The software uses the string to scramble messages. In traditional encryption schemes, the same key is used to encrypt and decrypt the message. In a public key encryption system, you use a public key and a private key. You freely distribute your public key to people with whom you wish to correspond. Those individuals may then use your public key to encrypt messages to be sent to you. You can then decrypt the message when it arrives using your private key. You use your correspondent's public key to send an encrypted message.

ORDINANCE

There is an interesting note about the encryption scheme used by Notes and PGP. The encryption scheme, or algorithm, is very difficult to break. Encryption algorithms are considered to be ordnance under United States export laws. Because it is illegal to export most ordnance from the country, it is technically illegal to carry a laptop with PGP installed out of the country as well as to distribute it outside the United States over a computer network. Notes overcomes this limitation by producing two versions of Notes. The U.S. version uses the more powerful encryption method while the International version uses a less potent encryption method that is exportable. Many people feel that the laws that make it illegal to export the encryption methods are outdated and should be rescinded. In fact, there is some evidence that the laws have so stunted the development of encryption technology in the United States that other countries, particularly Japan, may have better encryption technology now.

Digital Signatures

Digital signatures, which provide a method for you to verify the authenticity of a message, use the same electronic keys as encryption. A signature created by PGP might look like this (this is a sample only):

```
----BEGIN PGP SIGNATURE----
Version: 2.6.2
iQCVAwUBL7jIOMUtR2oNv5BtAQGMBAQAn06z31ejZNZdcr722V/h77kI936H3Fqx
iob+FnZEyzQ4POATpuvNx45KUK4/mGd+uLPyCiJ9j90+VMBKS/+X5Ew7M3mtNKmA
HIxd5eKj4LXWRou1/cyk80J5al07xNipJ+95UB8KoeISUAqbGEDtCZ17q9bZOzUA
QEcw7vVxgcy=
=s8c6
----END PGP SIGNATURE----
```

A digital signature works by creating a checksum when a message is created. The checksum technique quickly determines if the content of an electronic message is the same after passing over a network as it was when it was sent. In a PGP digital signature, the checksum is encrypted with the private key of the sender. When the message is received, the checksum is decrypted by the recipient using the sender's public key. If the message has been altered, the checksum will show it much as a broken tamper-proof seal on a bottle of aspirin shows that it has been opened.

Backups

Routine backups of data are essential to good computer security. Backups should be made at regular intervals and archived on a rotating basis. For example, if you have a tape backup drive, you might make a complete backup of your server every night at close of business. You can keep each Friday's tape for four weeks and keep the tape from the last Friday of every month in a permanent archive. This requires you to buy plenty of tapes, but provides a good level of backup security. Keeping the archive allows you to go back to a known clean version of your data if you discover a major problem. For instance, a virus infection that goes unnoticed for several days or weeks will make worthless all the backups that you made while the virus was present but undetected.

Firewalls

If your intranet will connect to the Internet, you may wish to consider putting the network behind a *firewall*. Generally speaking, a firewall places a layer of protection between the Internet and your network by filtering the TCP/IP packets that move between the networks, as shown in Figure 11.2.

Because firewalls can be very complex to set up, network services companies now offer firewall services and consulting. The technology will improve and should become easier to use. If you choose to host your intranet with an Internet service provider (ISP), the ISP will provide firewall services for you for a fee.

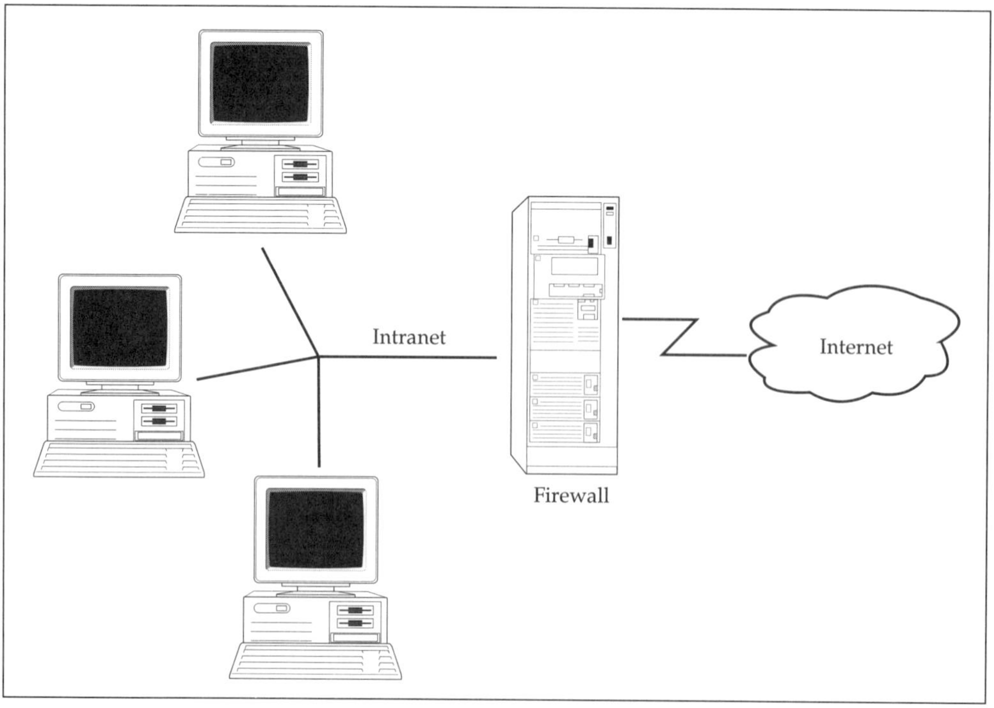

Figure 11.2: Firewall computers provide a buffer zone between your intranet and the Internet, keeping out unwanted intruders.

SUMMARY

The amount of time you spend on security for your intranet depends on your need for confidentiality, data integrity, and data availability. At least some level of security is needed for all intranets. Your Internet service provider, if your intranet is hosted by an ISP, can meet most of your security needs. Firewalls provide the maximum security for an intranet that is connected to the Internet, but they require a great deal of expertise to set up properly.

Chapter 12

DEVELOPMENT PLATFORMS

If simple delivery of information is enough to make groupware effective for you, e-mail is all you need. But when you need a program that can deliver information based on your instructions or need to create content that grabs someone's attention, you need more. You need the tools that can add interactivity and the true power of client/server computing to your groupware applications. This chapter looks at development platforms used by ordinary users, programmers, and third-party applications developers to enrich a TCP/IP groupware system.

Some of the options discussed below are beyond the capabilities of a casual user for developing applications. If you are not a programmer, it is still important for you to be familiar with these tools. The functionality added by new languages such as Java is already having a profound impact on the way businesses plan to use the Web. By being aware of these technologies, you can plan to implement them in your intranet. Customized and generic CGI scripts, Java applets, and ActiveX components are all available for purchase so that you can use them without having to learn the underlying languages.

REDUNDANT ALL OVER AGAIN

One of the things you are bound to notice as you learn about the different development environments is that many of these tools do exactly the same thing. For instance, you can make a form for visitors to your Web site to fill out using a CGI script, a Java applet, Lotus Notes applications, a browser plug-in, or a combination of them all. Each of these approaches will have advantages and disadvantages. CGI might be simple and quick, while a Java applet gives you advanced capabilities such checking the integrity of entries before the form is even submitted. A Java applet can run on any Java-enabled computer, but a plug-in written in C++ may work just as well.

Although definite trends are evident in the development community, no one can say for sure what the single *best* development environment is. Much of that depends upon how long the application you are developing needs to remain useful, and how fast you need to develop it.

HTML

Hypertext Markup Language (HTML) gives shape to the documents on the World Wide Web. Because it is a simple markup language, most people can learn how to create basic Web documents in just an hour or two. Read a $25 book, try a few things, and you're an expert in two days. Word processors and other programs now include features that save documents as HTML files. Using one of these programs makes the HTML tags invisible to the document creator and makes it easier for beginners to quickly create Web documents.

The Web consists of ASCII documents (marked up) and links. Documents are electronic files made available over the Internet by Web servers. Links are areas of a document on which a reader may click to get to related information elsewhere in the same document or elsewhere in another document on the Web. People who want to read the documents on the Web must use a program called a *browser* (e.g., Netscape Navigator or Microsoft Internet Explorer). The browser contacts the Web server and requests a document. The document travels across the network to the user's PC and is displayed by the browser.

HTML consists of tags inside angle brackets (for example, <H1> and </H1>). The tags inform the browser how to display the different elements of a page such as headings, paragraphs, links, and formatting. The sample below shows a simple HTML document followed by an example of how a typical Web browser displays that document (see Figure 12.1).

```
<HTML>
<HEAD><TITLE>Hugo's Cycling, Inc. Page</TITLE></HEAD>

<BODY BGCOLOR="#FFFFFF">
<IMG ALIGN="left" SRC="hugo-inc.gif">
<H1>Welcome to Hugo's Cycling, Inc.</H1>
Hugo's Cycling, Inc. is dedicated to providing high quality
cycling products at rock bottom prices. Click on any of the
areas below to
get product information and to find out how to order.
<P>
<UL>
<LI>
<A HREF="http://www.hugo.com/clothing.html">Clothing</A>
<LI><A HREF="http://www.hugo.com/components.html">Components</A>
<LI><A HREF="http://www.hugo.com/tires.html">Tires</A>
<LI><A
HREF="http://www.hugo.com/accessories.html">Accessories</A>
</BODY>
</HTML>
```

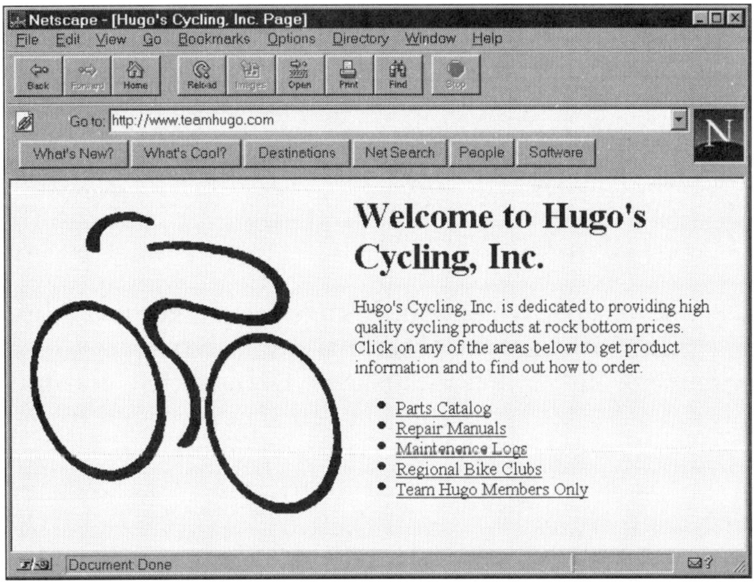

Figure 12.1: In this figure, a Web browser displays the HTML code from the example above.

A Web server accesses text documents. Text documents on a related topic marked up with HTML and *linked* together make up a *Web site*. The Web site's main page, known as its *home page*, is the first page that visitors see when they type in the *Uniform Resource Locator (URL)*, or Web address, for the site (e.g., http://www.whitehouse.gov).

The Web is a great way for businesses like a bicycle equipment manufacturing company to provide service to customers. For customers who have purchased a bike, you can publish the following:

- A catalog of the spare parts they need to maintain it
- Maintenance manuals and repair instructions
- Individual maintenance records to remind customers of when they need to get their bikes tuned up
- Lists of bike clubs, biking outings, and commercial bike tours
- A special section with restricted access for members of a specific bike club only

Customer service on the Web has unlimited potential. In addition, you can even sell at retail on the Web. HTML is the tool that you need to create a Web site for such a company.

HTML is suited to distributing information but by itself cannot do much beyond that. For instance, to produce a document that allows your Web site visitors to place an order for spare parts online, you will need to use additional programming. Your solutions might include one of a variety of tools developed to add interactivity to the Web: CGI scripts, Java, JavaScript, ActiveX, or a browser plug-in.

KNOW THE CODE

There was a time when cutting-edge word processors used cryptic tags similar to those of HTML. If you wanted to have nicely formatted documents you had to learn the tags. The same was true for Web documents in 1994. When the Web became popular in 1995, developers were quick to start producing HTML editors. The first ones provided buttons on which you click to insert HTML markups. Since then, graphical "what you see is what you get" (WYSIWYG) HTML authoring programs have become available. Most word processors now include the capability to save files in HTML format. Some use HTML conversion utilities. Others have built-in converters. All programs will have built-in HTML converters before long.

All this means that you don't *have* to know HTML anymore. Depending on what you need to do, you may be able to get away with simply using one of the HTML authoring programs to produce your HTML documents. But HTML is still a relative infant. It continues to evolve at a steady pace, a pace faster than software vendors can change their software. If you want your pages to use the latest in cutting-edge HTML effects, you must know how to open your HTML documents and edit them by hand. You must understand how HTML works to get the *most* out of it.

COMMON GATEWAY INTERFACE

HTML is the tool to use when you need to deliver information at a Web site. When you want to receive information from your visitors, you need to use something more. Besides hypertext links and e-mail, HTML by itself does not contain all the necessary programming for interactivity. The early pioneers of the Web recognized the need for this functionality and included a method to add interactive features to HTML documents on the Web by using Common Gateway Interface (CGI) scripts.

CGI scripts are programs that run on a Web server when called upon by a Web browser (see Figure 12.2). They tap the power of the

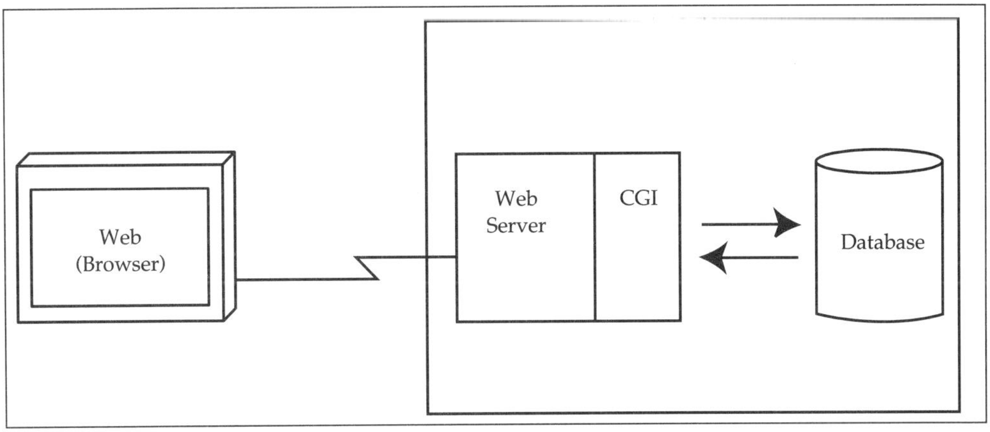

Figure 12.2: CGI scripts are programs that run with a Web server and provide interactive features for Web clients.

server computer and process information transferred to the server from the browser. Some CGI scripts format data submitted from a browser and then e-mail it to the owner of the server. The data is collected from visitors by the fill-in forms made possible by HTML forms markups.

CGI scripts can take data submitted from a browser, save it to a database, perform site searches, and generate custom HTML documents on the fly based on visitor input.

The most popular programming languages used for writing CGI scripts are *Perl* and *C*. Perl is a scripting language particularly adept at handling the strings of text transferred over the Web from Web browsers when a visitor submits an HTML form. Perl is widely used because it is relatively easy for programmers to use, and it is easily adaptable from one operating system to another. Programmers usually reserve C for more complex CGI applications, because it takes more time to develop a program in C than in Perl. Once compiled, however, C programs generally execute complicated processes considerably faster than Perl.

Both Perl and C are for programmers. Although nonprogrammers can learn HTML easily, programming languages are a different story. Fortunately, there are many CGI scripts written by other people available free or for sale that you can use with your intranet. Inevitably, however, you will probably hire someone to create some CGI scripts for your Web site. Many software vendors have integrated their software with the Web and supply their own CGI interfaces between their software and Web servers. Commercial Web servers often include some CGI scripts that provide basic functionality like comment forms, surveys, counters, image maps, and others.

JAVA

Java is a programming language developed by Sun Microsystems. Java programmers can create small application programs called *applets*. The applets are downloaded into a visitor's browser where they use the computing power of the visitor's computer to work rather than the computing power of the server. Full-fledged programs can also be created with Java, although they will presumably be larger and require longer downloading times than applets. Applets are embedded inside regular HTML documents on the Web. Java applets provide Web documents with never-before-realized levels of interactivity.

Instead of just text, graphics, and hyperlinks, a Web developer can now include spreadsheets, animations, dynamic financial charts, and a variety of other digital devices within an HTML document. Applix (http://www.applix.com) offers a sophisticated spreadsheet program and a word processor in Java.

Because any Java applet will run on any computer that has Java capabilities, Java provides an advantage to programmers who need to write programs for distribution over the Web. In the past, a separate program had to be developed for every operating system upon which a programmer wanted the program to run. With Java a developer can write just one program, and it will run on Macs, PCs, and Unix computers. The secret to this capability lies in the Java *virtual machine* (see Figure 12.3).

Java virtual machines are created specifically for an individual operating system (e.g., Mac or Windows 95). When Java code comes in over the network, the virtual machine interprets the Java code for the computer, enabling the applet to run as if it were designed just for that computer's operating system.

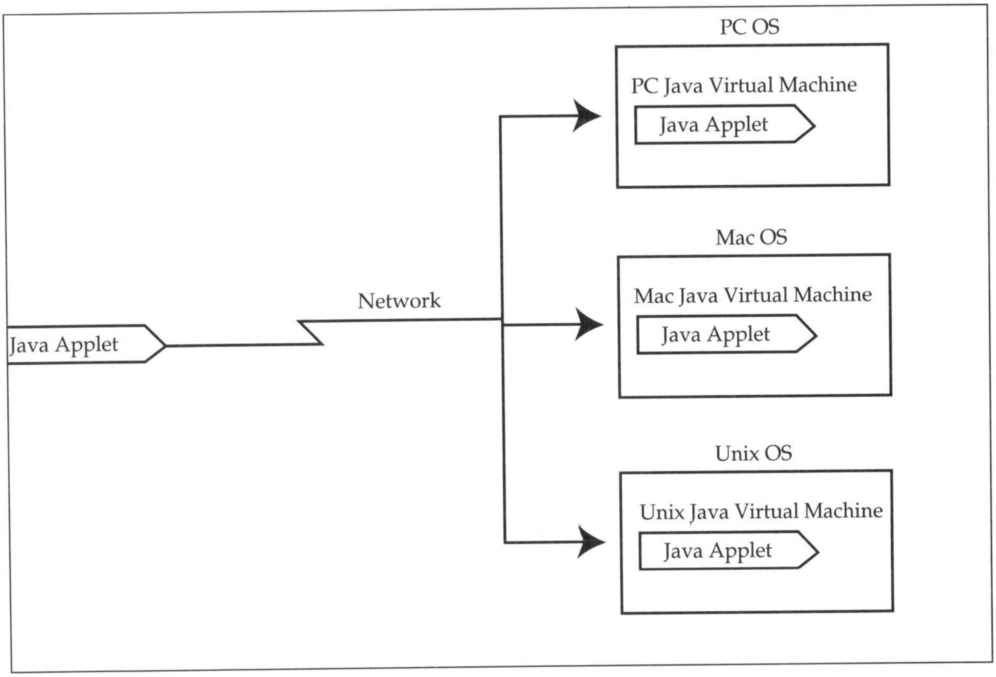

Figure 12.3: Java applets are interpreted and run on an operating system's Java virtual machine.

Java is a descendant of the C++ programming language and is not for novice computer users. Even with the many Java authoring tools available, you probably will not want to try to write a Java application without some programming experience or training.

JAVASCRIPT

Java and JavaScript are not the same thing. JavaScript is a scripting language. Java is a programming language used to develop stand-alone applications and applets. JavaScript can be used to tie multiple Java applets together within a Web document and allow them to interact with one another. Also, it can work alone to add basic types of interactivity to a Web document. For instance, a simple JavaScript can cause a button to change colors when a user passes the mouse cursor over it.

JavaScript can replace functions that are done with CGI scripts. The advantage to this is that the visitor's computing resources are used instead of the server's. Network usage is decreased because the client and server do not have to keep sending information back and forth once the JavaScript script has been downloaded to the client. Although JavaScript is easier for nonprogrammers to learn than Java, it still falls in the realm of the programmer.

ACTIVEX

ActiveX is described by Microsoft as a set of technologies designed to enhance Web documents. The technologies provide interactivity between Web documents and other applications either on the Web server or on the computer running the Web browser. For example, you could use ActiveX to allow a user to perform a query to a database connected to the Web server, to display a Microsoft Word document within a Web browser, or to provide a standard look and feel to the interactive tools embedded in your Web documents. ActiveX is an offspring of the same infrastructure technology as Object Linking and Embedding (OLE). OLE enables you to create interactive and linked documents within desktop applications such as Word, Excel, and other programs.

The fundamental building blocks of ActiveX include ActiveX Controls, ActiveX Documents, Active Scripting, Microsoft's Java Virtual Machine, and ActiveX Server Framework. These work with Java and other languages to enhance the interactive features available on the Web. Several tools are available for developing ActiveX functionality, including Visual Basic, C++, and Java.

ActiveX is not a programming language. It is a set of tools that programmers can work with (in conjunction with other tools) to enhance Web interaction. ActiveX is not cross-platform and runs only in Windows.

LOTUS NOTES

As discussed in Chapter 10, Lotus Notes provides a development environment for applications. In other words, it is a development platform by itself.

Nonetheless, Notes can effectively connect to the Web and take advantage of the Web as a development platform too. The Notes Domino software allows most applications created in Notes to be used

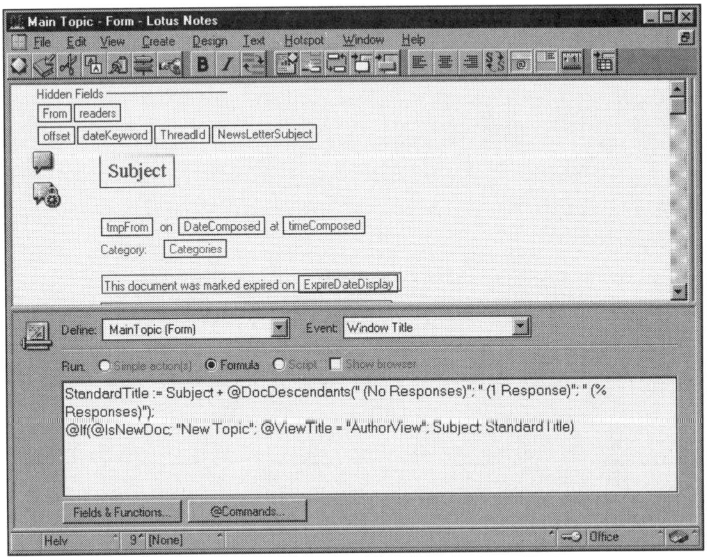

Figure 12.4: Lotus Notes contains a robust application development environment that is accessible over the Web.

over the Internet through access to the Notes Domino server with a Web client. Domino maintains a Notes application's functionality across the Web, including security down to the field level. You can rapidly develop work flow and other applications in Notes and then allow workers to access the applications with their Web browsers.

VRML

VRML is an acronym for Virtual Reality Modeling Language, which enables you to create 3-D graphical presentations for display through a Web browser. VRML is still undergoing rapid development but may soon provide a new way for you to move through cyberspace. Imagine being able to walk through a virtual office that appears in 3-D, pick up a pen from the table, write a memo, and send it. VRML holds great promise for making the visual aspects of navigating through the Web more interesting and efficient, but for now its groupware applications are limited. Because of the intensive graphics, VRML awaits greater bandwidth to realize its potential.

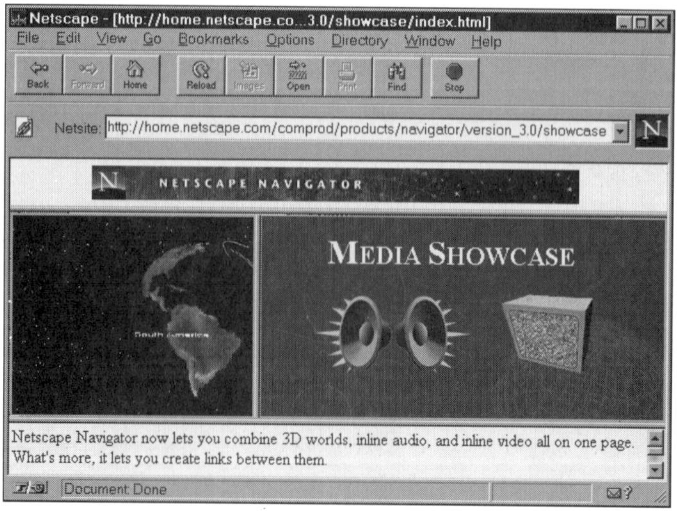

Figure 12.5: Plug-ins extend Web browser functionality.

PLUG-INS

Plug-ins are small programs that extend the functionality of a program. Browsers such as Netscape use plug-ins to extend their capabilities. Some plug-ins provide the ability to play audio files, and others let you embed video clips in your pages. Plug-ins can be created through Java or other programming languages.

Some examples of useful business plug-ins are given in the list below.

- **Address Book**—A plug-in can let you browse a company-wide address book located on a Web server from within your Web browser using customized controls and search capability.
- **Calendar**—You can use a plug-in created by your Web calendar system's vendor, which enables you to make updates to your calendar or shared calendars.
- **Spreadsheet**—Imagine placing a dynamically updated Excel spreadsheet in a Web document. You can build in formulas that allow your employees to do calculations for clients on the spot, even if the formulas *change hourly*.
- **Viewer**—In the old days of the Web, a few months ago, you needed to download a separate program to read, view, or play certain files outside your browser. With a plug-in, instead, you can read, view, or play such files from within your Web browser. For instance, the Macromedia plug-in, Shockwave, will play multimedia presentations created in Director, Macromedia's multimedia authoring program.

SUMMARY

The Web is now more than just a spiffy new online interactive multimedia document publishing system. Because there are many different approaches to creating programming for the Web, it has become a development platform. In fact, so many software developers are writing programs for the Web, it is quickly becoming a *robust* development platform.

Lotus Notes is also a development platform. Specifically, it is a groupware development platform that has grown to dominate the groupware market over the years. By embracing the Web, Lotus Notes continues to be fine and competitive groupware as well as a viable groupware development platform.

The Web and the other Internet protocols are the real story, however, and 1997 will see TCP/IP groupware competition heat up considerably. Already, much TCP/IP groupware is available. Although the Web is the primary infrastructure of interest for the Internet, other protocols, particularly MIME e-mail, contribute to group work programming too.

Although it seems at times that this book talks about the Internet and the Web as if intranets are not included, that is definitely not the case. Remember that programs that work on the Internet will work on an intranet too, *even if the intranet is not connected to the Internet.*

The primary infrastructure for intranet application development is the Web. This is particularly true because the other Internet protocols can be used through the Web's HTTP protocol. Thus, in a sense, the Web embraces the other protocols and dominates. The list of techniques to make your Web documents more powerful keeps growing. HTML documents working with CGI scripts on Web servers provide the most basic form of extended interactivity. New technologies such as Java and ActiveX are extending Web interactivity by enabling the creation of small but powerful applets that travel over the network. Eventually full-fledged Java programs (applications, not applets) will travel over the network to be used through people's browsers; some are already available. And there are the browser plug-ins that play non-TCP/IP programs. This rich digital environment has unleashed perhaps the most competitive period in software history at a time when the ubiquitous TCP/IP network (the Internet and intranets) promises to connect everyone in business, soon. A more ideal environment for the emergence of groupware as a viable business medium cannot be imagined.

Chapter 13

INTRODUCTION TO TCP/IP

A network *protocol* is software that enables network communications. Computers on the Internet use a whole family of protocols to accomplish basic but essential tasks in the communication process. This family of protocols is usually referred to as TCP/IP, which is short for Transmission Control Protocol/Internet Protocol, although most people use the term TCP/IP in a generic way to refer to the whole family of Internet communications protocols. This chapter briefly describes some of the most common protocols in TCP/IP. After reading this chapter, you will have a basic familiarity with the terminology and technology underlying the TCP/IP tools described later in the book.

WHAT IS A PROTOCOL?

Think about the last telephone call that you made. Whenever you have a phone conversation with someone, certain assumptions and underlying information are responsible for the success of the call. For instance, you must know a telephone number you can dial to make the other party's phone ring. When that phone rings, the person must recognize it as a signal that someone is trying to communicate and answer it. The initial part of the conversation is usually spent with both parties identifying themselves. Only when these conditions have been met does the transfer of information begin. During the conversation you must both follow generally accepted rules of conversation.

Only one person should speak at a time. Cues like voice inflection and word syntax help you recognize when it is time to speak and how to respond. Computers must follow similar conventions, or *protocols*, in order to make network communications possible.

The TCP/IP protocols are based on *open standards*. This means that the technical specifications used to write the protocol software are available to anyone. Open standards enable developers to create software for any type of computer that is able to interact successfully with TCP/IP software on other platforms. Developers have written TCP/IP software for every major computing platform in use today, including Unix, OpenVMS, CMS, Windows, Windows 95, Windows NT, Macintosh, and others.

OPEN STANDARD?

Just because TCP/IP is based on open standards doesn't mean that it works the same on every platform. On Macs TCP/IP services are handled through an extension to the system (MacTCP or OpenTransport). PCs running on Windows 3.11 must use special collections of TCP/IP software called *stacks*. There are several TCP/IP stacks offered by commercial vendors, or you can find them free on the Internet. Fortunately, Windows NT and 95 have TCP/IP services integrated into the operating system, so you do not have to use stacks. Unix also has TCP/IP tightly integrated with the operating system. Unix is ubiquitous on the Net because it was the first operating system to adapt TCP/IP as its primary networking protocol. Thus, it has a jump-start on the other operating systems in the creation and refinement of TCP/IP applications.

A typical Internet user may never need to understand how these protocols work together. For many computer users, someone will come and install the necessary software and hardware on their workstations, and they will begin using TCP/IP programs. However, if you are in charge of configuring your own computer and setting up your own network, or if you are just interested in how it all works, you will want to understand at least basic TCP/IP. That way you will be able to ask the right questions when you start setting things up.

FAMILY TIES: TCP/IP LAYERING

As you now know, TCP/IP is a family of protocols that work together to provide communication services. When data passes over a network, there are several different tasks for the protocols to accomplish.

- Managing the destination address of the data
- Controlling the way that electronic information is sent over the network wires
- Breaking the data up into pieces (packets) that are manageable and reassembling them once they arrive
- Compensating for the different ways computers on the network store and display information
- Dealing with unexpected problems or failures with the communication process.

TCP/IP handles all of these challenges by dividing responsibility for each task among different software components. These components work together smoothly because they exist in a layered hierarchy. The layers pass data from one to another, either from the user down to the network or from the network up to the user. Figure 13.1 shows a simple diagram of how this layered system works.

Upon completion of its responsibility, each layer attaches *header* information to the original data. Next, the layer below determines

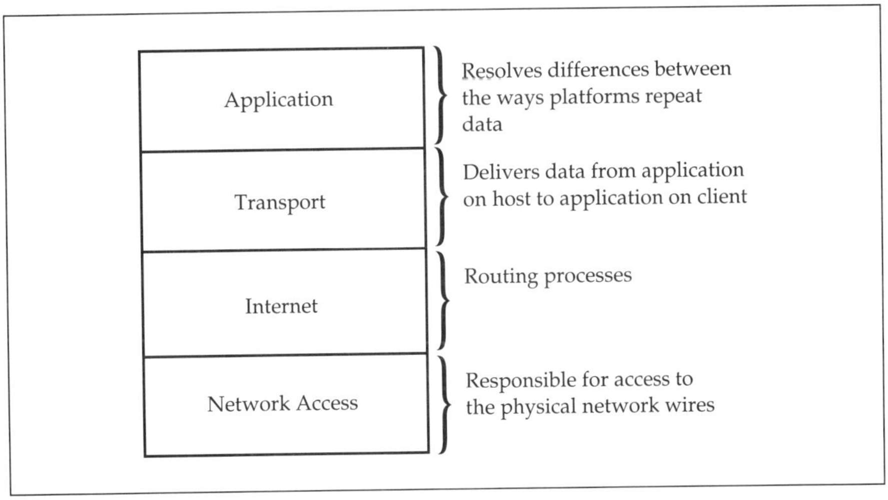

Figure 13.1: Each layer of the TCP/IP family contains protocols specifically designed to accomplish a specific task in the communications process.

how the data should be handled at that point. To try to envision how this works by imagining that the data being sent across the network is a package that you are sending from your office in Sioux City to a colleague in New York.

The package itself represents the data. The contents of the package are neatly contained within a cardboard shipping box. Once you have sealed the package, you give it to your executive assistant and tell your assistant where to send the package.

Your assistant represents the next layer in the process. The assistant types the name and address of the recipient onto a mailing label, places the label on the package, and then passes it on to the company mail room.

The mail room is yet another layer with a specific task. The mail room weighs the package and affixes proper postage to prepare the package for a successful trip through the U.S. Postal Service network.

Finally, a letter carrier picks up all the letters and packages in the mailroom and delivers them to the post office. From there the package travels to its destination based on the work done by each of the people representing the layers. Note that the letter carrier, your assistant, and the mail room clerk are not concerned with the content of the package. The only thing the assistant needs to know is the name and address of the recipient, and all the mail room needs to know is the weight of the package. The Postal Service cares only that a valid address is on the package and that the proper postage is affixed. Similarly, each protocol layer is not concerned about what kind of data is being transported. Only the information that a particular layer needs to get its job done is important to that layer.

Each TCP/IP layer actually consists of multiple protocols. Not all the protocols are used by every TCP/IP application. As the data moves through the layers, each protocol adds information relevant to its purpose in the communication process. Just as each person involved in mailing the package added important information, each TCP/IP layer adds important information as *headers* to the data *packet*. Figure 13.2 illustrates how each layer tacks its own information onto the original data. The process of tacking on this information is known as *encapsulation*.

When the data arrives at its destination, it travels back up through the layers of the receiving machine's TCP/IP software. Each layer

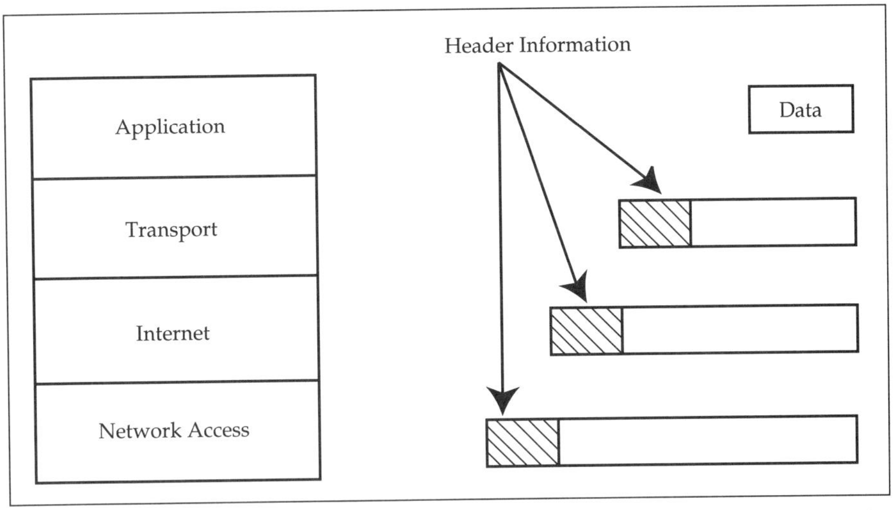

Figure 13.2: Each TCP/IP layer adds its own header information to the packet.

reads the header information provided by its counterpart on the sending computer. Following this strict way of communicating is the only way that computers are able to transfer billions of information packages to one another over TCP/IP networks like the Internet every day.

IP ADDRESSING

A computer has to put an address on mail that it sends out just as you do. The addresses used in a TCP/IP network are series of numbers. These numbers designate which particular network a computer is on and where it is on the network. IP, the protocol in charge of making sure that messages are sent to the right place, uses these addresses to do its job. For this reason these numeric addresses are called *IP addresses*. Internet IP addresses are represented by four sets of three numbers separated by a period (for example, 121.122.123.124). The sets are actually numeric representations of hexadecimal numbers. This means that each set must be between zero and 255. This system results in millions of possible combinations for IP addresses, meaning that there can be millions of hosts attached to the Internet.

Internet IP addresses are not assigned to hosts randomly. There is a complex system of different classes for IP addresses. These classes are labeled A through E. Of the five classes of IP address, the most commonly used are classes A, B, and C. If you are setting up an intranet that will *never* be attached to the Internet, you are free to use almost any valid IP address (TCP/IP reserves some IP addresses for special administrative uses such as broadcasts to the entire network). However, if you think you might connect to the Internet, you should plan ahead by using IP addresses assigned by InterNIC, (Internet Network Information Center), the agency charged with providing addresses on the Internet.

Something to keep in mind is that your computer's IP address may not be the same from session to session. This is true if you dial in to an ISP that *dynamically assigns* IP addresses to computers as they connect. Your ISP has a whole pool of IP addresses from which to draw. However, there is a finite number of addresses in the pool. The number of customers your ISP supports may actually exceed the number of IP addresses it has. But not every customer is connected all the time. Therefore, the ISP is able to ration out the IP addresses on an *as-needed* basis. When you finish your session and hang up, your computer releases the IP address back to pool for the next customer who dials in to use the service.

From time to time it will be important for you to be able to figure out what your IP address is during a session. For example, if you run a Web server on your PC during a temporary period that you are connected to the Internet, the only way you can tell people how to access your Web server is by telling them your computer's IP address. The IP address is always stored temporarily in your computer when you establish a connection to your ISP. Where you can find it on your machine depends on your operating system and connection software.

KEY TCP/IP PROTOCOLS

You need to be familiar with a few important TCP/IP protocols as you learn more about using TCP/IP tools in a groupware system. This section introduces some of the essential components of the TCP/IP suite and describes the tasks handled by each of these important components.

Internet Protocol

Internet Protocol, or IP, figures out the route that the data will take across the network. IP seeks to send each message via the most efficient and most reliable route possible.

WHEN DO YOU USE THE INTERNET?

The Internet is a packet network. You use the Internet only when you are sending or receiving packets. With your browser you can sit and stare at that nice new Buick for a half hour at the General Motors Web site and not use any Internet resources. The only time you use the Internet is when you click on a hyperlink to switch to a new Web document. At that time, the text and graphics for the new document are downloaded into your browser. As soon as that download is finished, you are no longer using the Internet until you switch to the next Web document.

In contrast, the telephone requires a dedicated circuit. If you are talking with someone, and there is a 30-second pause in the conversation when no one talks, you are still using that telephone circuit during that time. The telephone is not a packet network; it is a constant connection.

What communications resources do you use with the Internet? First, you use the telephone, a dedicated circuit, because you need it to connect to your ISP's computer. That dedicated circuit, however, extends only from your computer to your ISP's computer. For most people, that is a local phone call. You are tying up only local phone resources. Second, your ISP provides your connection to the Internet, and you use Internet resources too. But you only use the vast worldwide Internet resources when you are sending or receiving packets. You use the local telephone resources constantly as long as you are on the line.

For instance, it is easy to envision that in doing research on the Web where you stop to read documents often, you might use the Web only 25% of the time you are online. Perhaps less. The remaining 75% of the time you are reading, and there are no packets flowing. Think about your activities. What percentage of the time is the Internet juggling packets for you?

Transmission Control Protocol

Transmission Control Protocol (TCP) has many responsibilities in the communications process. TCP is in charge of making sure that the data sent over a network arrives in the same condition it was in when it left the sending computer. TCP also manages the resending of information when it is corrupted somewhere along the route.

Another important job of TCP is to break up large messages into more manageable chunks, known as *datagrams*, before sending them across the network. TCP also reassembles the datagrams when they arrive at the destination computer.

User Datagram Protocol

User Datagram Protocol (UDP) is similar to TCP in that it deals with ensuring the reliable transport of data between machines on a network. UDP differs from TCP because it does not open a connection between the sending and receiving machines during the transmission of the data over the network. Instead, UDP relies on the receiving machine to be available when the packet arrives.

Domain Name System

Every computer attached to the Internet has its own unique numeric address known as an *IP address*. An IP address looks something like this: 128.169.202.47. Naturally, it might be very difficult to remember the address of a particular machine on a network that has thousands of computers attached to it. Fortunately, the Domain Name System, or DNS, allows for the association of Internet addresses (based on words) to the numeric IP addresses. These word-based addresses are known as *domain names*. For example, if you worked for Sullivan Milk Inc.; in the sales department, the domain name address of your desktop computer might be pc1.sales.sullivanmilk.com. This domain name would in turn be associated in a central database with the IP address of your machine, 128.169.202.47. When you enter a domain name into a TCP/IP application, the DNS translates it to an IP address for you by looking it up in a database (see Figure 13.3).

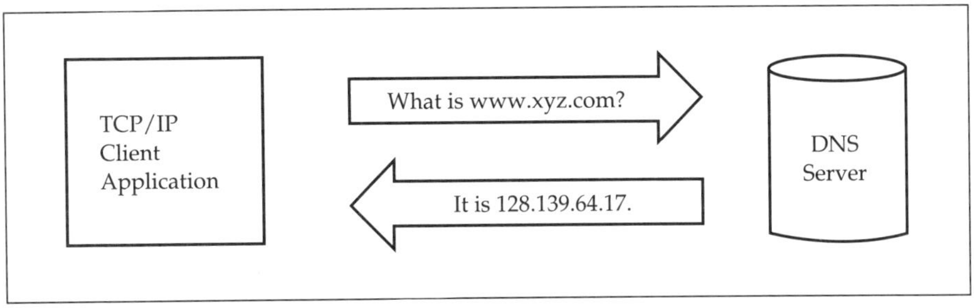

Figure 13.3: DNS provides a way for TCP/IP applications to figure out the IP address of a computer based on its domain name.

Simple Mail Transfer Protocol

Simple Mail Transfer Protocol, or SMTP, transfers mail among different mail hosts on the network. When you send e-mail to someone over the Internet, you are making use of SMTP.

Post Office Protocol

Some PC e-mail clients use Post Office Protocol (POP) to manage the transfer of e-mail between mail host computers and local client computers. The other mail protocol discussed above, SMTP, requires that computers be turned on and attached to the network around the clock. POP enables you to check for mail on an SMTP mail host (i.e., your ISP's computer) only when you want to. So, your PC does not always have to be running.

In addition to SMTP and POP are POP2, POP3, IMAP4, SMTP, and others. Why is there a need for several separate e-mail protocols? All these different protocols result from the different needs people have for reading, storing, and otherwise handling their e-mail.

If you have a computer attached to the Internet and your friend has a computer attached to the Internet, why can't you just send e-mail from your computer to your friend's computer? The reason lies in the way Internet e-mail works. SMTP is the primary TCP/IP mail protocol. All hosts that send and receive Internet e-mail use SMTP. Your ISP (an SMTP host) holds your outgoing mail in a queue and sends it to your friend's ISP (an SMTP host) at regular intervals. Your friend's ISP then holds the incoming e-mail until your friend logs into the SMTP host and reads the e-mail.

Looking at the way two different users, Sam and Sally, use e-mail can show you how different people have needs for different mail-handling protocols. Sally works primarily while logged into her company's Unix system. The system is always on and always connected to the Internet. The mail facility built into Unix that uses SMTP is all that Sally needs. The host stays on at all times and is always connected to the Internet. When new mail comes to the host addressed to Sally, it is held for her until she logs in and reads it. The mail stays on the Unix server until she deletes it.

Sam works primarily on his desktop PC. His PC is turned on from only 9:00 A.M. to 5:00 P.M. while he is at work; if someone tried to send e-mail directly to his PC after 5:00, it would bounce. For this reason, Sam has his e-mail sent to his account on the Unix system. Sam could use the same client as Sally, but he would have to log in to the system every so often all during the day just to read e-mail. Instead, Sam uses a *POP client* that runs on his PC (see Figure 13.4). The POP client is configured to log in automatically to the Unix system (which is also running POP server software) every 30 minutes and check for new mail addressed to him. If there is new mail, it is downloaded to his PC's hard drive and deleted from the Unix server. If not, the client simply closes the connection and tries again on the next half hour. POP is the what allows this interaction to take place.

Telnet

The Telnet protocol is an application used to log in to remote computers. For example, if you have an account on a Unix computer in California, you can log into your account using Telnet from a computer in New York while there on a business trip. Because you are connecting over the Internet, there are no long distance charges.

One of the primary reasons for logging in to another computer is to get to resources on the other computer that are not available on yours. For instance, you can Telnet to the library electronic card catalog at many major universities to see if a particular book is available. In this case, your operate a database on the remote computer, the database containing the electronic card catalog. Another reason for logging in to another computer is to use software installed on that computer. Suppose you are a professor at a small university and you need to use

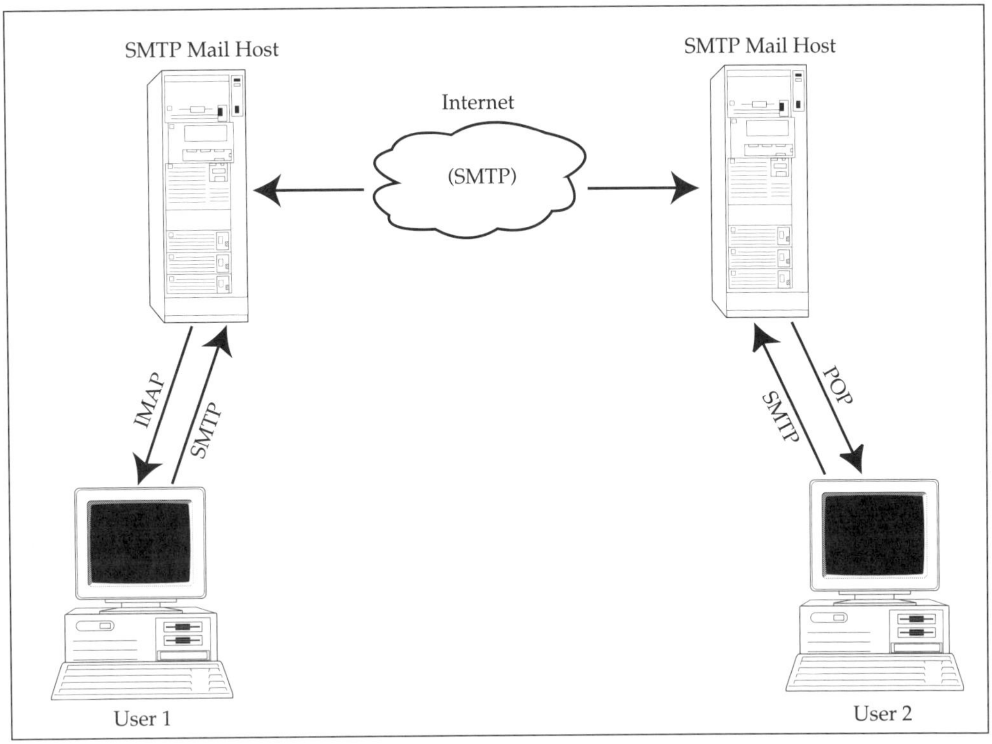

Figure 13.4: The different e-mail protocols in TCP/IP work together to provide flexible e-mail handling options.

a powerful and expensive statistics program to finish your research. Your university doesn't have it. You can get a guest account on a computer at a larger institution that does have the software, Telnet to that university's computer, and run the program.

File Transfer Protocol

File Transfer Protocol (FTP) lets you move files across the network from one computer to another. You must always log in to the remote computer. This requires a login name and a password. With normal FTP, you must have an account on the remote computer (the FTP server) to log in and transfer files to or from the server. You get an account by making arrangements and perhaps paying a fee. Many sites on the Internet, however, provide FTP servers open to the public, *anonymous FTP*, which allow you to log in without an account. For such servers the login name is *anonymous* and the password is *guest* or perhaps your e-mail address. (The remote computer tells you the password.) Once you have logged in, you can download documents, software, and other files to your computer.

Anonymous FTP sites are also appropriate for private use. For instance, your company can set up an anonymous FTP server to provide its employees with the capability to leave files for outsiders to download. You can leave a large file (one so large you don't want to sent it by e-mail) for someone with whom you are working to download from your company's anonymous FTP server at that person's convenience and without having to get a login name and password ahead of time.

ANONYMOUS FTP SERVER

Setting up an anonymous FTP server can be a challenging proposition. If fact, unless you are an experienced network administrator, you probably should not do it. There are great security risks involved in letting strangers log in to your system without providing some type of authentication. An inadequately set up FTP server can be an open invitation to your system for a hacker. Instead, why not let your ISP manage all the risk for you? Most ISPs will provide you with your own anonymous FTP site. This way you can provide anonymous FTP service for your employees to use without the headaches of server maintenance and security. If you have more large files to distribute than will fit into the hard disk space your ISP provides you at a reasonable rate, negotiate an agreement with your ISP to co-host a hard drive for you. You can supply your ISP with a 500MB SCSI-2 hard drive for less than $200, have adequate space, and because you are supplying the hard drive space, perhaps get a reasonable monthly rate for the anonymous FTP server services.

Hypertext Transfer Protocol

Hypertext Transfer Protocol (HTTP) is the protocol used by the Web. HTTP allows for the transfer of files containing all types of media, including audio, video, text, and more. It also controls the interaction between Web browsers and Web servers.

Gopher

Before the Web introduced the point-and-click interface to the Internet, the best way for people to find information was Gopher. Gopher is a menu-based system that organizes information in a hierarchical fashion. The menus contain hyperlinks to documents and to other menus to make navigation easy. The documents are plain ASCII text. The thousands of Gopher servers continue to hold vast amounts of information as they are widely used in the academic community. Most Web browsers have the capability to retrieve information off Gopher servers using the Gopher protocol. Instead of entering a web address (such as http://www.cosmonaut.com) into your Web browser, you enter a Gopher address (gopher://gopher.cosmonaut.com) to view a Gopher document in your Web browser.

Other Protocols

There are other protocols that handle network error messages, Usenet newsgroups, and more. The important thing to remember is that all these protocols work together to provide network functionality over a TCP/IP network.

SUMMARY

A network protocol is software that handles communications procedures among computers according to agreed-upon conventions. TCP/IP is the commonly used term for the suite of protocols used by the Internet and other TCP/IP networks. TCP/IP is based on open standards, making it a very widely used and flexible suite of protocols. In order to connect to a TCP/IP network, a computer must be running a version of TCP/IP.

Chapter 14

IMPLEMENTATION

If you are convinced that your company needs to use TCP/IP groupware, how do you make it happen? Before you go in and tell your boss that you have decided to install a company intranet, you need to think about everything involved in setting one up. You have to think about what kind of network you will use. Will it be Ethernet? Will it be a simple bus network? Should you get everybody a modem and an account with a local ISP? Next, you have to think about the hardware your company already has in place. Do you have Macs and PCs? Do you have all PCs but from different vendors? Also, how much time and money can your company devote to setting up and maintaining its network? All these factors must be considered.

The example programs described later in this book require a TCP/IP network, and your network must run TCP/IP to be an *intranet*. This chapter briefly introduces some of the considerations involved in setting up a TCP/IP network. Of course there is not room in this book to detail the ins and outs of developing the infrastructure for an entire computer network. You should use this chapter as a starting point in the research of your intranetworking options. Consider it a cheat sheet and study guide for the pop quiz your boss will give you when you march into the office and proclaim, "We need an intranet!"

NETWORKING CONSIDERATIONS

Some people say that *intranet* is just another word for a *LAN*. Many of the companies who used to make software for local area networks have suddenly turned into self-described *intranet solution providers* by integrating TCP/IP into their products. Although a basic intranet essentially performs many of the same functions of a traditional local area network, there are some key differences. For instance, you cannot readily attach a traditional LAN to the Internet without a gateway to serve as a translator between the two. Telling the difference between an intranet and a LAN is like trying to distinguish cable television from radio. The difference is scale and features. An intranet uses the exact same protocol technology as the Internet. New software tools for the Internet are being developed by thousands of companies. With an intranet you can take advantage of all these new programs and easily tie into the Internet. In other words, instead of depending on just one vendor to produce new and more useful software for your groupware system, you have a whole industry dedicated to the process.

Of course, setting up a TCP/IP network is every bit as challenging as any other kind of network installation to a communications neophyte. The key to success in setting up your intranet is understanding your company's needs and getting help when you need it.

Instant Intranet: Just Add TCP/IP

If your company has a LAN, you may already have part of your intranet in place. You might even already have the necessary hardware in your desktop machines if the network interface cards can support TCP/IP. Many network cards can work with TCP/IP with the proper software driver installed. You certainly already have the cables in place that connect the computers. *TCP/IP is nonexclusive.* TCP/IP can run alongside many LAN protocols on the same network (known as *piggybacking*). You need to install and configure the TCP/IP software on the PCs and servers in your organization. Once all the machines are successfully set up, you can begin using the TCP/IP applications discussed in this book.

An alternative to piggybacking TCP/IP with your existing LAN is to configure whatever other networking operating system you are running so that it sends its packets in TCP/IP form. For example, if you have a Novell NetWare LAN, you can set it up so that when

NetWare sends its packets over the network, they are encapsulated in TCP/IP packets. Once the packets reach their destination, the TCP/IP headers are stripped off, leaving the regular NetWare packets to be dealt with as usual.

Planning an Intranet from Scratch

If you do not have a LAN yet, you have a little more planning to do. You need to select an operating system for your server machines, keeping in mind that you may hook your intranet into the Internet eventually. You will want to choose an operating system for the servers that can scale up to handle a larger number of users. Windows NT Server and Unix are both good choices.

You will also have to take into account hardware considerations. Some of these are discussed in the next section.

Setting up your intranet can be a very complicated process if you are not familiar with networking. In most cases you should bring in a consultant to help you plan and install your network. This is especially true when you are setting up a LAN to run TCP/IP in conjunction with another networking protocol or if you plan to connect your intranet to the Internet.

HARDWARE CONSIDERATIONS

If you will be starting from scratch, you may have an advantage from an administrative point of view. You will have a say in what hardware makes up your intranet. For simplicity's sake, you may want to standardize on a hardware platform for workstations in your organization, although it is not a requirement. This way you need to learn how to set up and maintain only one type of computer. For instance, you might decide to purchase only Pentium 166MHz machines with 16MB of RAM, or perhaps you would prefer to use all Macs. When a problem pops up on one machine, you can solve it and be alerted to the potential problem in the other similar machines. You have to deal with only one hardware vendor as well.

Configurations

The specific configuration of your PCs will, of course, depend on your needs. If you plan to use teleconferencing software, you will need sound cards and speakers. If you want videoconferences to take place on your intranet, expect to acquire individual video cameras (cams) for the top of each monitor. You will also need network interface cards (NICs) in all your computers.

Servers

You will want one computer, or possibly more, dedicated to being a server(s). For instance, an internal Web server for light use by three or four employees can be an old 486 machine with 8MB of memory. If hundreds of people will be attaching to your internal Web server, you need more computing horsepower. Do you plan to connect your Web server to the Internet at anytime? If so, you can forget using that old 486. Nothing less than a Pentium with plenty of memory and hard drive space will do.

SOFTWARE CONSIDERATIONS

If you are not an old pro at setting up servers, it might be a good idea to start with one piece of functionality at a time when implementing your groupware system. Since e-mail is perhaps the most important component of your system, why not set that up first? Make sure that everything works as planned. Let your users learn how to use it. After e-mail is in place, add an internal Web server with essential documents and services for employees. When you plan to phase in these services over time, you have the benefit of observing how the new software affects network performance. Another advantage is that the users of the system will stay interested in the groupware project because it is constantly improving without becoming overwhelming.

INTRANET CHECKLIST

The lists in Tables 14.1 and 14.2 present a generic framework of hardware and software components for a small intranet that will also be attached to the Internet through a dial-up connection to an ISP. This sample intranet provides an internal Web server but relies on the ISP mail host to provide POP mail services. The lists represent average configurations.

Table 14.1:. Intranet Hardware Components

Web Server	Pentium, 16MB, 1GB hard drive, Network Interface Card (NIC)
Internet Gateway (router)	386, 8MB, NIC, phone line interface (e.g. modem, ISDN); check with your ISP for specific requirements.
Network Cables	Twisted pair or coaxial cables, depending on distance between computers, number of computers, NIC type, etc.

Table 14.2: Intranet Software Components

Web Server	Windows 3.11, TCP/IP stack, HTTP Web server, CGI scripts (optional)
Internet Gateway	Windows 3.11, TCP/IP stack, dial-up software for connecting to ISP (PPP), routing software, firewall software

Windows NT Alternative

Another alternative for your intranet server's operating system is Microsoft Windows NT Server. Network managers view NT as the robust, multithreaded environment found in Unix combined with the graphical user interface (GUI) of Windows 95. Windows NT is a strong choice for business servers because it addresses the following needs:

- Stability—Windows NT handles different tasks in isolated memory segments. This means that if one program goes awry, it generally won't crash the whole server as happens on other operating systems. This kind of reliability can mean a lot to someone who has had to get up in the middle of the night to reboot an essential server. NT also has built-in network monitoring capability. You can keep an eye on your network's performancc.
- Ease of Management—NT provides *Wizards* that take you step by step through administration tasks such as creating user accounts, managing folders, adding and removing programs, and administrating network clients. It is also possible to remotely administer an NT Server using a Web browser.

- Web and Intranet Service—Microsoft has tried to build NT Server as the complete intranet platform. The latest version ships with a Web server (the Internet Information System), FrontPage (a Web site creation and maintenance tool), Internet Explorer (Web browser), and the NT Domain Name Resolution server (DNS service). An NT Index server that provides full text searches on HTML and MS Office documents is available for free download from the Microsoft Web site.
- Gateway Services—NT has TCP/IP, IPX (Novell's protocol), NetBeui (another protocol), AppleTalk, PPP, and other protocols included in the operating system. This means that your NT server can be a gateway between your old networks and your new ones. It can also be your network's connection point to the Internet (i.e., you can get by without a router, although having a router offer added benefits).
- Security—NT provides higher levels of security than most organizations will need. Administrators can restrict access to files, folders, network devices like printers, and more.

Although you certainly do not have to use Windows NT for your intranet server, it offers the advantages enumerated. Substitute NT for Windows 3.11 and the router listed for the average system above, and you will have a capable system.

You should note that Windows NT Workstation may not make a capable TCP/IP server. At press time Microsoft had disabled NT Workstation's digital TCP/IP server capabilities and then legally disabled such capabilities in its licensing agreement. Your best bet is the considerably more expensive Windows NT Server.

Client Computer Recommendations

Table 14.3 shows the recommended client computer configuration.

Table 14.3: Client Computer Recommendations

PC	Pentium, 16MB, multimedia capability (sound card, speakers, microphone, cam), Network Interface Card (NIC)
PC Programs	Windows 95, Web browser and plug-ins, POP e-mail client, FTP client, Telnet client, drivers for NIC

CONNECTING TO THE INTERNET

Once you have decided to connect your intranet to the Internet, there will be even more work to do. Will you use a dedicated connection to the Internet for your company and maintain all the server hardware and software yourself? Would you be better off using a simple dial-up account through an ISP, saving you the headaches of server and network maintenance but perhaps at a loss of some flexibility? The answers depend upon your budget, expertise, and intranet goals.

Are You Dedicated? In a dial-up arrangement you must use your modem to dial in and connect every time you want to use the Internet. You can use any phone line to do so. Getting a special phone line is neither a necessity nor even desirable.

If you are on a LAN, you are connected to your network around the clock. If your LAN is to be connected to the Internet and provide around-the-clock service to the LAN users, you need a dedicated line; that is, a line that is dedicated to that use and is always in use (like a never-ending phone call). Naturally, there's a substantial difference in price between dial-up lines and dedicated lines.

Line performance is always a consideration in setting up networks. For instance, if you use an ISDN line that offers four times the performance of an analog line, it seems as if you have a real performance advantage. But bandwidth is not the entire story. The number of people using the line simultaneously is an additional factor. It's a statistical evaluation. The more people likely to be using the line at the same time, the worse the performance will be for a particular line.

For instance, if you have a dedicated ISDN line (see below) connecting your intranet to the Internet, and one person downloads a file from the Internet, that person will experience four times the performance of an analog line. If, instead, four people use it simultaneously via your network to download files, each person will experience performance comparable to that on a normal analog line. What is the likelihood of four people downloading files at the same time? Suppose you do a study that shows for every 55 employees, there's a likelihood that four will be downloading files at the same time. You have determined that a dedicated ISDN line will provide 55 people with the equivalent of a normal analog line. Naturally, there will be peak-use periods when the intranet connection to the Internet slows down and off-hours periods when it provides blazing performance. Although evaluating line performance is not as simple as illustrated here, you need to know that there's a direct correlation between performance and the number of users.

If you elect to get a dedicated Internet connection for your LAN, you can plan to invest in some more hardware and software. You will have to have a gateway machine, or *router*, that connects your in-house network to the incoming line. You will probably want some firewall software providing a buffer between your network and the outside world. Also, if you register your own domain name (e.g., *yourcompany.com*), you will have an expense for InterNIC registration. This covers your first two years. Thereafter, it costs $50 annually to renew your right to exclusive use of your domain name (see *Your Own Domain Name*, below). Last, you will have to arrange for the connection to the Internet through an ISP. Your connection options vary widely as do prices, but you can count on a substantial monthly charge for anything faster than an ISDN connection (discussed below).

Don't Throw Away That 286 PC Yet A router is a decidedly unglamorous device. It routes packets. Network lines are inevitably slower than computers. Why not rehabilitate your 286 (clean the dust off it), invest $30 in routing software, and get yourself a perfectly capable router? You may need more than that if you have a large and busy network, but why spend $2,000 for a router until you need it?

An Alternative Plan

Of course, if all that planning, expense, and maintenance seems an undue burden, you do have other alternatives. What if you work at a small firm in which every employee has to wear many hats? Perhaps *you* wear all the hats! You do not want to learn how to manage a network. You want to be able to send e-mail to clients and subcontractors but don't really need e-mail in-house to communicate with your coworkers. You would like to have access to the Web and perhaps a Web presence of your own. Finally, there is not a huge amount in the budget for new computers, but you can afford an extra phone line and three or four fast modems for the PCs you already have.

You have two basic connectivity options.

- A SLIP (Serial Line Internet Protocol) or PPP (Point to Point Protocol) dial-up connection to an Internet Service Provider
- An ISDN (Integrated Services Digital Network) connection to an Internet Service Provider

SLIP and PPP are protocols used to run TCP/IP applications over a modem connected to a regular telephone line. ISDN is a faster connection method that uses special equipment to get better performance out of a regular telephone wire. To get the most for your money, check with your local ISPs for rates and services (they probably advertise in your paper's Sunday business section).

By taking the ISP route, you are leaving the day-to-day management of the servers up to the service provider. This can be a major convenience but can limit the kinds of tools you use to get work done. For instance, an ISP may not be willing to let you implement custom CGI scripts on the Web server it maintains.

For browsing the Web, you will need to get at least SLIP or PPP Internet access, so you will want at least a 33.6 modem. Also, be sure to look into the Internet services that your long distance company may offer. The service should include at least one e-mail account for each individual in your organization.

Another alternative for your company might be ISDN access. ISDN is faster but more expensive and more complicated to set up initially. Your telephone company will have to become involved with the negotiations between you and your ISP. Keep in mind that a faster connection means that employees save time, particularly for Internet-intensive activities. ISDN is available today in almost every urban area. A special modem required for ISDN access can cost from $200 to $1200.

SLIP, PPP, and ISDN connections are adequate for browsing the Web, using e mail on an ISP mail host, and using other TCP/IP clients such as Telnet and FTP. If you want to add videoconferencing over the Internet to your list of TCP/IP tools, you should consider ISDN the minimum acceptable connection type.

A Twisted Pair Your phone line is a *twisted pair*, two very small copper wires twisted together. If it is used in an analog mode, the maximum speed is 33.6 kilobits per second, which is roughly about 3.6 kilobytes per second. Normal phone service is analog. ISDN uses one twisted pair and offers a maximum speed of 128 kilobits per second, or about 12.8 kilobytes per second over two B channels.

You can use each ISDN B channel separately or use both simultaneously. For instance, you can connect to the Internet at 64 kilobits per second on one B channel while simultaneously talking to someone over the phone on the other B channel. To access the Internet at 128 kilobits per second, the two B channels must to be bound together. Each B channel is a separate phone line with its own phone number.

For offices in which installing extra twisted pairs is not financially feasible, ISDN offers the opportunity to double the number of phone lines while increasing speed (bandwidth) at the same time. Binding two B channels enables you to use a high-speed (high-bandwidth) line on an existing twisted pair.

To use an ISDN line, you need the following:

- A network termination device called an NT1.
- A power supply. There is no power over ISDN lines as there is for analog lines.
- A terminal adapter to connect devices such as phones and computers to the line.

Fortunately, these items come as a package in the form of an ISDN modem. It's not really a modem; *modem* is a marketing name for the public. Because ISDN modems are collections of different devices wired and programmed together for different purposes, you will want to be careful when you purchase one to make sure you are getting what you need for your system. Here are some features to look for:

- External ISDN modem. If you get an internal modem (for inside your PC), when you turn off your computer, the ISDN line is off too. An external ISDN modem has its own power supply, stays on around the clock, and supplies power to the ISDN line around the clock.

- Analog phone port. ISDN phones are very expensive. You will want your ISDN modem to have an analog phone jack to enable you to plug in your analog phone line. The analog phone jack should be rated for the number of phones you expect to use on that line (a six-phone capacity is not unusual).
- Built-in NT1. You don't want to have to buy this device as an extra.
- Terminal adapter. An ISDN modem is a terminal adapter.
- Built-in 33.6 kilobit analog modem. If you want to have faxing capability in your computer, you will need this. If you just want to connect a fax machine to an analog phone line, you will not need this.
- Binding capability. You will want to be able to bind the two B channels together for maximum bandwidth when you need it. This is a complex feature provided by ISDN modem software.

You can find an ISDN modem with the above features now for under $700. ISDN modems with minimal features currently sell for under $300. Make sure you're getting what you need for your office. In regard to TCP/IP software, most dial-up connection software treats an ISDN line as a fast analog line, so there is nothing special you have to do to use your ISDN modem with your existing communications software.

ISDN lines are as trouble-free as other phone lines once they are set up properly. Getting set up can be difficult. The phone company sets up a twisted pair as an ISDN line for you. It's then reasonably easy to connect your analog phones to your ISDN modem and have them work immediately. Beyond that, however, there are no guarantees. Getting your ISDN system to connect properly with your ISP for Internet use can be a challenge to your sanity if you do it yourself, or to your pocketbook if you have a consultant do it. Bon voyage!

Your Own Domain Name

You might be interested in having the ISP help you register for your own domain name. This enables you to choose a unique identifier on the Internet with your company's name in it. For example, if your company is Sullivan Milk Inc., you might register for the sullivanmilk.com domain name. The advantage to this is that your e-mail address will be employeename@sullivanmilk.com instead of employeename@mailhost.isp.com. Also, your Web page address can be `http://www.sullivanmilk.com` instead of `http://www.isp.com/users/sullivanmilk/`. One problem you might encounter is that the name sullivanmilk.com has already been taken by someone else. Domain names have to be unique, so you might have to get creative if your first choice has already been taken (for example, sullivan-milk.com or sullivanmilkinc.com).

Your Own Web Site

Your ISP will undoubtedly offer Web site hosting services. Essentially, you are getting storage space on an ISP's hard disk, Web server service, and a connection to the Internet. It is a good idea to shop around to see who gives you the most disk space and the best technical support for the money. Some ISPs will help you get started in creating your own HTML documents. (See Chapter 12 for information about HTML.) Many ISPs will also design and create the site to your specifications for a fee.

Allowing your ISP to manage the day-to-day maintenance of the Web server leaves you free to manage your business without having to learn a lot of new skills. You get the benefits with a minimum of hassle, but give up some of the flexibility that managing your own servers and network can provide.

Consider a Co-Host The largest expense, other than personnel, in maintaining a network system connected to the Internet is the phone line. ISDN is not adequate for heavy traffic. A T1 line (equivalent of 26 twisted pairs with a bandwidth of 44.6 kilobits per second) or a fractional T1 line is a desirable alternative. Unfortunately, T1 lines are quite expensive. You will pay based on the distance between you and your ISP as well as other factors. Thus, you pay the phone company a generous monthly fee. But that's not all. A T1 line uses a prodigious amount of Internet resources provided by your ISP, and you will pay your ISP a generous fee each month too. You might be better off by sharing a T1 line and getting the benefits without the costs.

You can *co-host* your network server computer on your ISP's premises. Your computer is connected to your ISP's network by an Ethernet card. Your ISP's network is connected to the Internet via a T1 line. Thus, you have a full-bodied connection to the Internet. You can administer your server computer remotely. Every so often you may have to call your ISP and ask someone to physically reboot your computer, but otherwise remote operation should work smoothly.

What does this system give you? It gives you great flexibility. You can run whatever software you please, including standard Internet servers (e.g., Web server), special servers, groupware programs, Web-database applications, distributed software (e.g., Java programs and applets), CGI programming, and the like. Co-hosting can be a inexpensive way to have maximum flexibility in building a robust network system.

There are two disadvantages to this system. First, you must maintain your Internet software (e.g., Web server, e-mail host server), a job otherwise done by your ISP. Second, your company's employees will have only dial-up service if your are going to use this system as your office network. You may want to co-host a server computer even if you don't use it for your office network. It gives you maximum flexibility in running a Web site and operating groupware such as Web chat, Web conferencing, and authoring software.

SUMMARY

When implementing your intranet, you must consider hardware requirements, software requirements, and service requirements (such as Internet service and network consulting). After you have set up your intranet, introduce new services gradually so that users have an opportunity to learn the new functions and are not overwhelmed.

Chapter 15

COMMUNICATIONS

The programs in this chapter will help you form a core of essential services for your organization's intranet. The first is Eudora, an e-mail client. The second is SLMail, a SMPT and POP3 e-mail server. The purpose of this book is not to give complete instructions for each program covered, but to cover the implementation of sample functions to give you an idea of how the programs work. These programs are Windows programs and not difficult to use.

For Eudora, you will add a name and a group to the address book and attach a file to an e-mail message. These are two simple but powerful groupware functions. For SLMail, you will set up an auto-responder and a mailing list. The auto-responder automatically sends out a specific text document (in e-mail form) in response to e-mail sent to a specific e-mail address. You can use this robot feature creatively for a variety of purposes. With the mailing list feature you can create a convenient-time conference.

For readers who do not have and will not use these programs, it's worth your time to follow through the instruction anyway. It will give you a better idea than you had before regarding the management of intranet software. This is particularly true if you have not run any server software before. Server software is new to most computer users, just as intranets and the Internet are new. In the future, however, people who thought they would never run a server (didn't even know what a server was) will find that it has become a client/server world. Many average computer users will be operating servers soon, if not on their intranet server computer, then from their own desktop PC. This chapter and the next few chapters will give you an idea of what you're getting into.

If this book had been written as the popularity of the Web started to swell at the end of 1994, it would have undoubtedly contained sample programming for command-line interface Unix programs so obtuse as to be brain numbing. Yet this book goes to press less than two years later, and there are dozens of easy-to-use Windows and Mac programs available, both servers and clients. This is a time for you to try your hand at operating a server, and the servers to which this book introduces you. SLMail in this chapter and others in the following chapters are servers relevant to group work.

EUDORA E-MAIL CLIENT

Eudora is an e-mail program distributed by Qualcomm of San Diego, California (http:/www.qualcomm.com). *Eudora Pro* is Qualcomm's commercial offering, and *Eudora Lite,* distributed free over the Internet, is a scaled-down version. Buying Eudora Pro for about $60 is well worth the expense. With Eudora Pro you get mail filtering, easy file attachment, spell checking, excellent documentation, and more. You will get a great deal of use out of the address book and the file attachment capability.

When you need to communicate with two or more people on a regular basis, it can be inconvenient to type in each e-mail address every time you want to send an e-mail. Eudora's address book has *nicknames* and *groups* features that can make reaching groups of people easier for you. The typical Internet e-mail address looks something like this: msmith@mail.eng.bigchem.com. Obviously, it can quickly become unreasonable to try to remember more than a few of these addresses. Eudora's nickname feature allows you to assign people easy-to-remember *aliases* (substitute names or nicknames). When you want to send a person mail, all you need to remember is the nickname that you assigned. For example, say the address above (msmith@mail.sales.bigchem.com) is the e-mail address of Mary Smith at BIG Chemicals (a major supplier of chemicals used in swimming pools). You frequently send Mary mail because she is your primary contact at BIG. Rather than typing in the long address every time you e-mail Mary to place an order, you just create a nickname for her in Eudora. That way all you have to type in the *To:* field is *Mary*.

When you realize that BIG may not be providing you with the most competitive prices, you decide to correspond with several chemical vendors at once to get the best price. Whenever you are ready to place an order, you send e-mail to Mary at BIG as well as to Sean Forest at EnviroChem (forest@envirochem.com) and to Gilda Majors of Quality Chemicals (gilda@aol.com). Of course, you make a nickname for all of these people so that you do not have type any of the addresses when you want to mail them individually. When you want to send them all the same message, however, you still have to type in each nickname at the top of the message, unless you make a group.

To save the aggravation of typing in all those nicknames, you can make a group called *ChemSales* in the Eudora address book. The ChemSales group has the nicknames of Mary, Sean, and Gilda in it. Once you create the group, all you have to do is type ChemSales in the *To:* field and all three salespeople will receive the message.

Finally, Eudora's quick recipient list feature makes it possible to put any group or nickname that is in the Eudora address book under a menu in Eudora. With the quick recipient list you do not even have to type in the nickname or group. Just choose the nickname or group from the quick recipient list in the *Send* menu, type the message, and click on the send button.

The following sections show you step by step how to setup the Eudora address book and also how to send attachments with your e-mail messages.

Address Book

Adding Nicknames to Your Address Book In this example, you will add a Nickname for Mary Smith to your Eudora address book.

1. Start Eudora by choosing Eudora from your start menu (see Figure 15.1).
2. From the Windows menu, choose *Nicknames* (see Figure 15.2).
3. Click the *New* button.

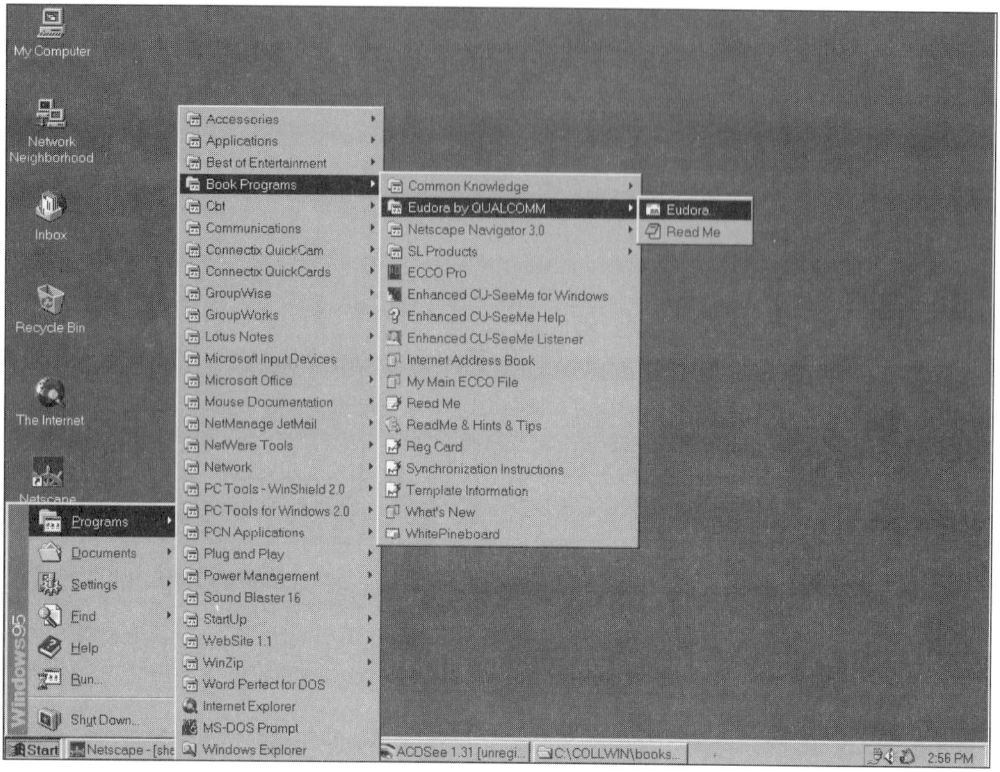

Figure 15.1: Choose Eudora from the start menu.

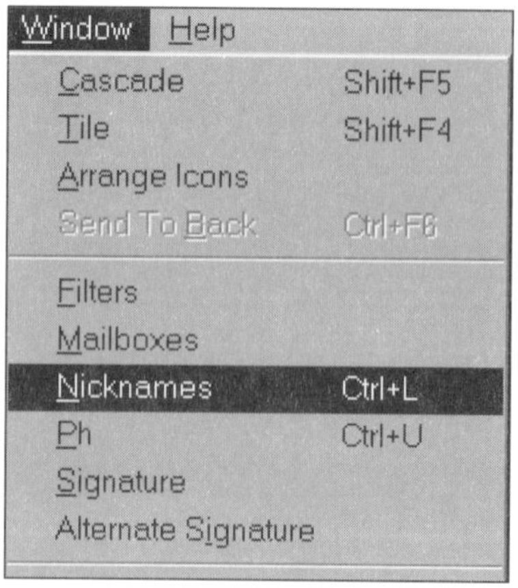

Figure 15.2: Select *Nicknames* from the Windows menu.

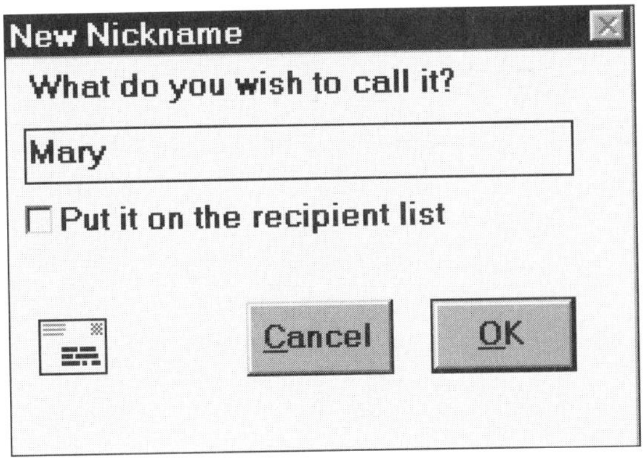

Figure 15.3: Type in a unique nickname for this person.

4. Type the nickname you want to use for this person in the dialog box that appears (see Figure 15.3). The nicknames you use must be unique (i.e., you may not have multiple nicknames of *Mary*).
5. Click the *OK* button.
6. The cursor will appear in the *Address* section of the dialog box (see Figure 15.4). Type in the person's e-mail address (msmith@mail.sales.bigchem.com).
7. Click in the section titled *Notes* (or press the Tab key).
8. You may type in any notations you wish to associate with this person (see Figure 15.5). These notes are for your personal use only. Eudora does not send the notes with any e-mail generated with this nickname. Type in *BIG Sales Rep* now.
9. Close the *Nicknames* window.
10. Click the *Save* button when Eudora asks if you want to save your changes (see Figure 15.6).

You have successfully added a new nickname. Now you can send an e-mail to Mary Smith at BIG Chemicals just by typing *Mary* in the *To:* field.

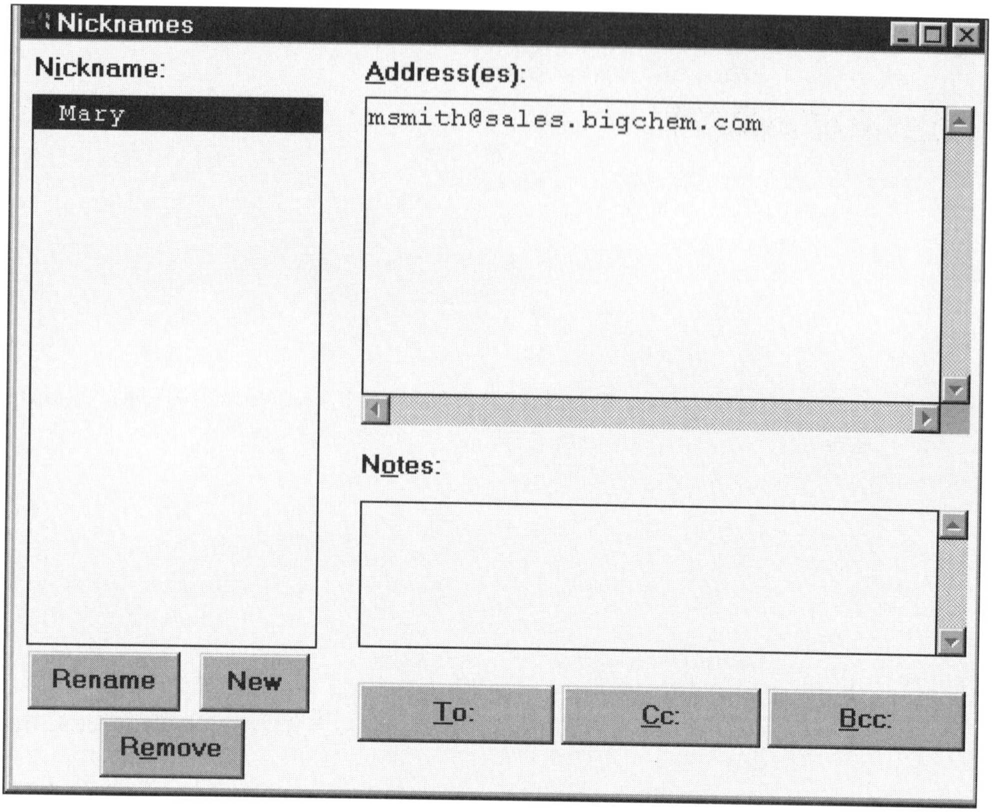

Figure 15.4: Type Mary's e-mail address into the *Address* section of the dialog box.

Adding Groups to Your Address Book Now you are ready to create the *ChemSales* group that contains the e-mail addresses of all the pool chemicals salespeople. Groups are simply nicknames that contain more than one e-mail address. You will put this group on your quick recipient list so that you can send e-mail to the group by choosing them from the Message menu.

1. Choose *Nicknames* from the Windows menu in Eudora (see Figure 15.7).
2. Click the *New* button.
3. Type in the name of the new group: *ChemSales* (see Figure 15.8).

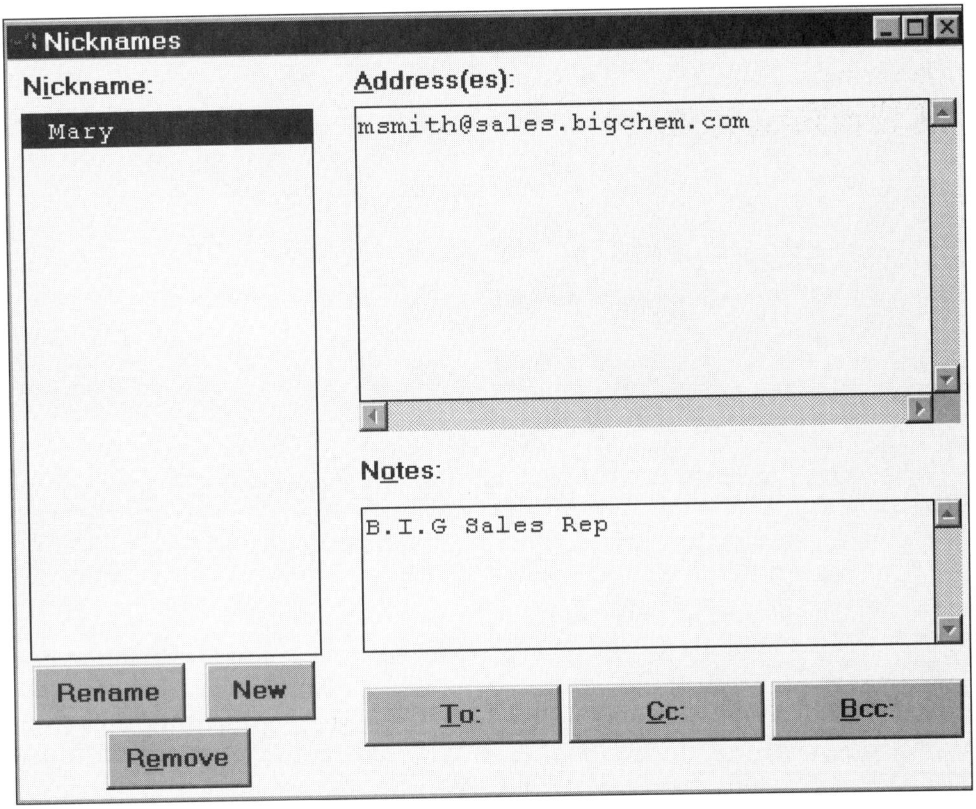

Figure 15.5: The content of the *Notes* section does not show up on mail sent using the nickname.

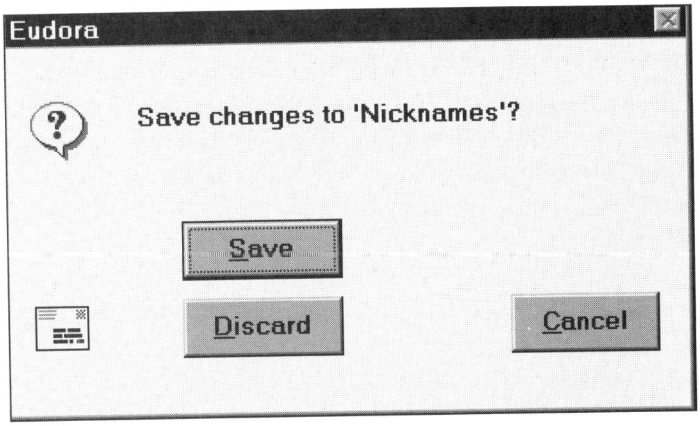

Figure 15.6: Click the *Save* button to save your changes.

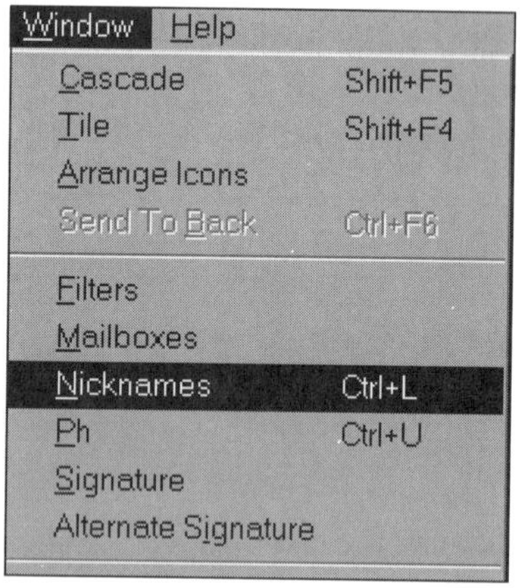

Figure 15.7: Select *Nicknames* from the Windows menu.

4. Click in the box next to the words *Put it on the recipient list* (see Figure 15.9).
5. Click the *OK* button.
6. The cursor will appear in the *Address* section of the dialog box. This is where you type in the e-mail addresses or nicknames of the all the people who will receive mail addressed to this group. Type, *Mary, forest@envirochem.com,* and *Gilda@aol.com.* Be sure to place a comma between the new e-mail addresses or nicknames (see Figure 15.10).
7. Click in the *Notes* section.

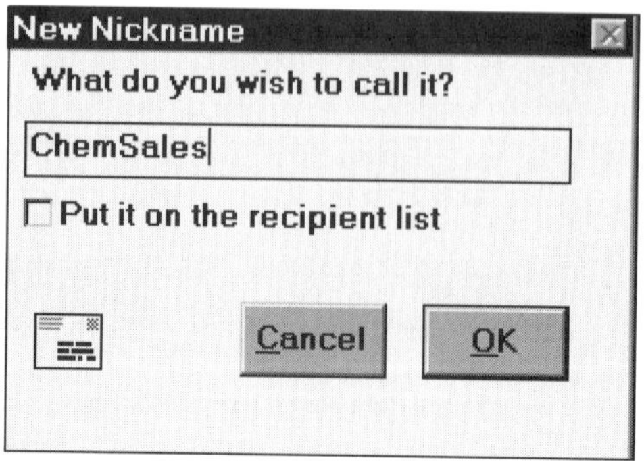

Figure 15.8: Type in your unique name for this group, *ChemSales*.

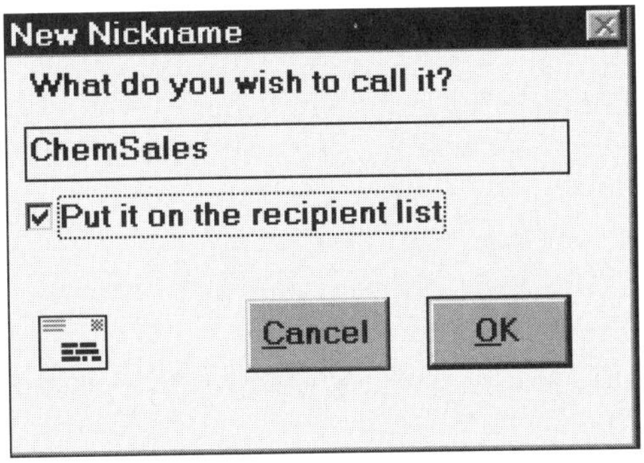

Figure 15.9: Click in the checkbox beside *Put it on the recipient list.*

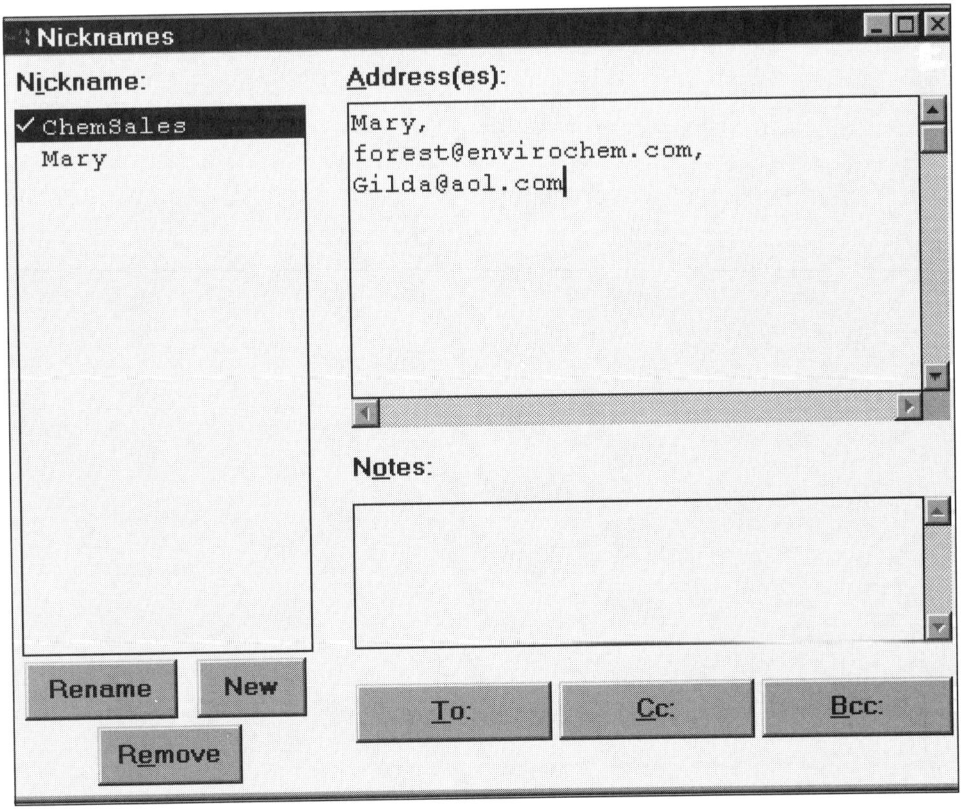

Figure 15.10: Include the e-mail addresses or nicknames for each person who will receive mail sent to the group, separating them with commas.

8. You may type in any notations you wish to associate with this group. These notes are for your personal use only. Eudora will not send the notes with any e-mail generated with this nickname (see Figure 15.11). Type in *Chemical Salespeople* now.
9. Close the *Nicknames* window.
10. Click the *Save* button when Eudora asks if you want to save your changes.
11. To send mail to the *ChemSales* group, simply choose *ChemSales* from the *New Message to* submenu in the Messages menu (see Figure 15.12). Eudora automatically inserts *ChemSales* into the *To* field for you (see Figure 15.13). You can also put regular nicknames in your quick recipient list.

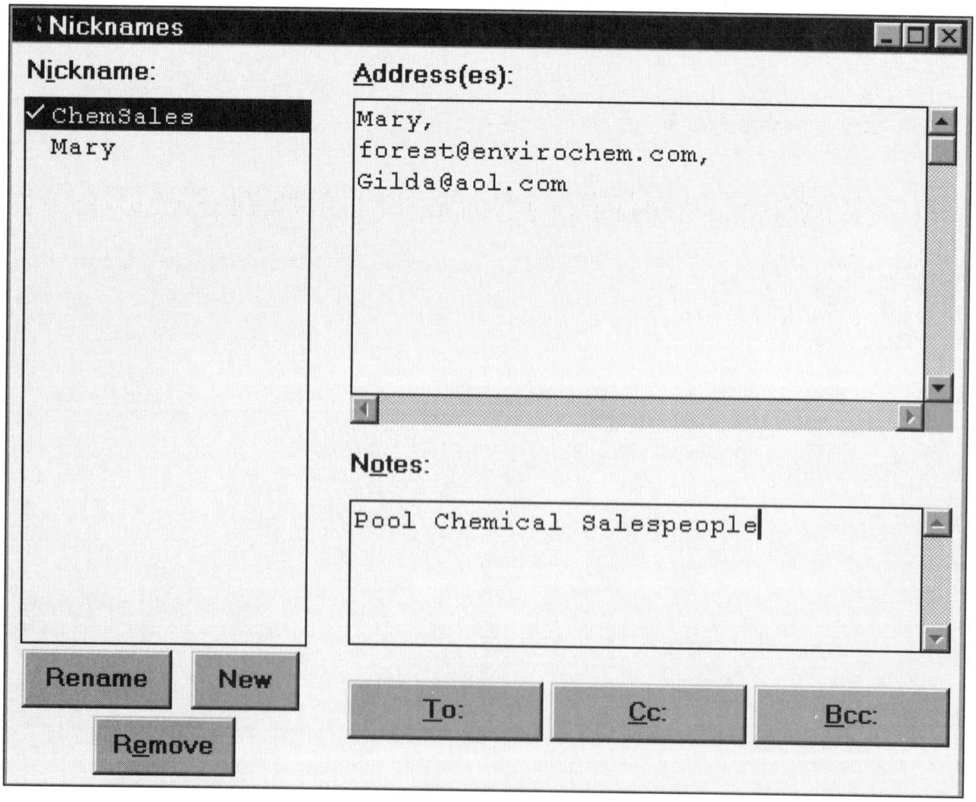

Figure 15.11: The content of the *Notes* section does not show up on mail sent to the group.

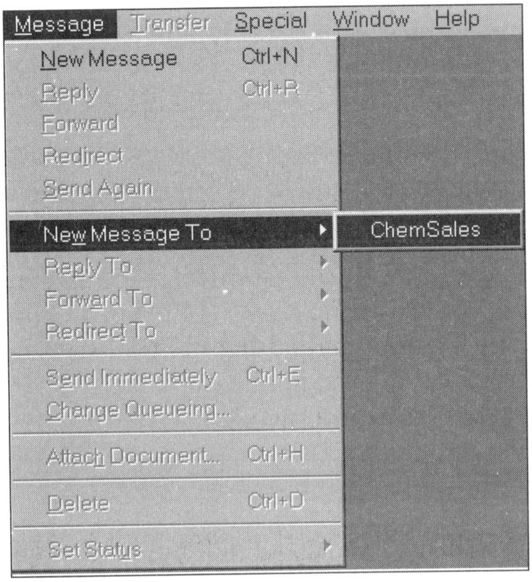

Figure 15.12: To send mail to ChemSales, just choose it from the *New Message to* submenu under the Messages menu.

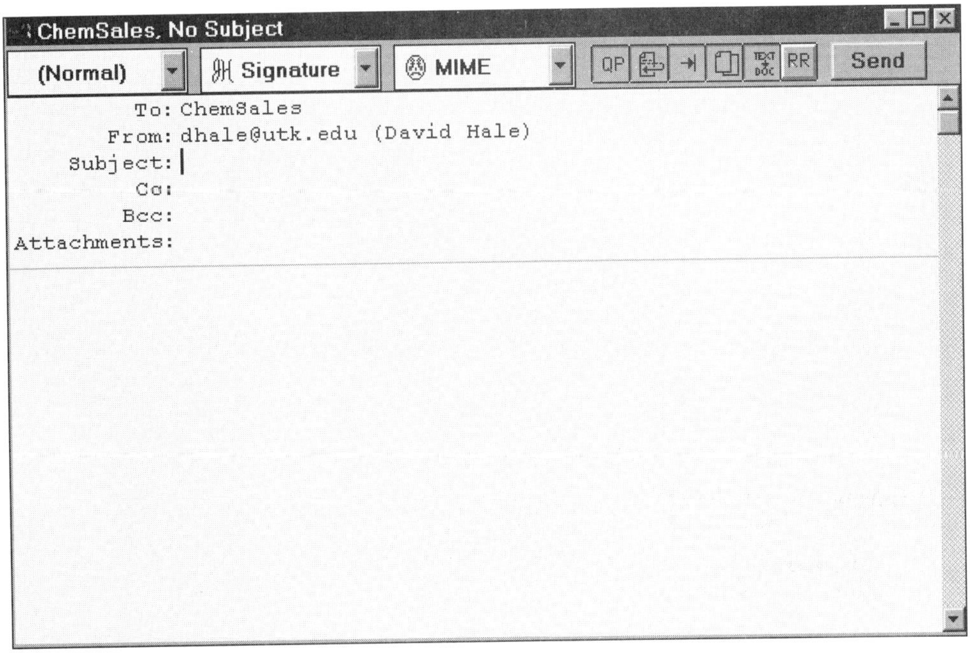

Figure 15.13: *ChemSales* is inserted in the *To* field for you.

Using Attachments in Eudora

Sometimes you will need to send attachments with your e-mail messages. You can attach word processing documents, spreadsheets, graphics files, and other types of files very easily with Eudora. The steps below describe how to attach a Microsoft Word file called *resume.doc* to an e-mail message in Eudora. The resume.doc file is on your computer's hard drive in the C:\documents\personal directory.

1. Choose *New* from the Message menu (see Figure 15.14).
2. Click in the *To:* field.
3. Type in the e-mail address of the recipient (see Figure 15.15).
4. Click in the *Subject* field.
5. Type in the subject of your message, *Application*.
6. Choose *Attach Document* from the *Message* menu (see Figure 15.16).

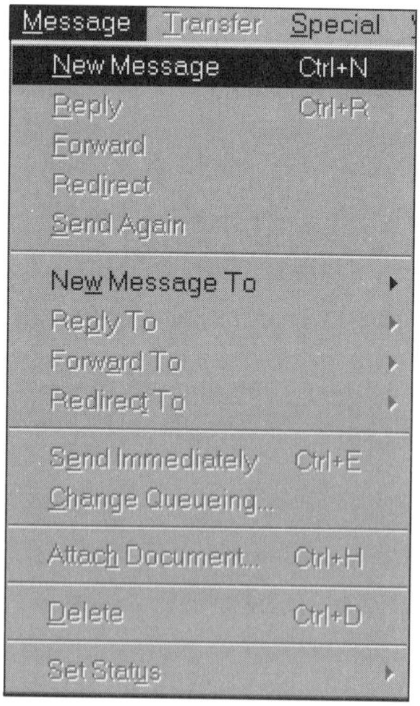

Figure 15.14: Create a new message.

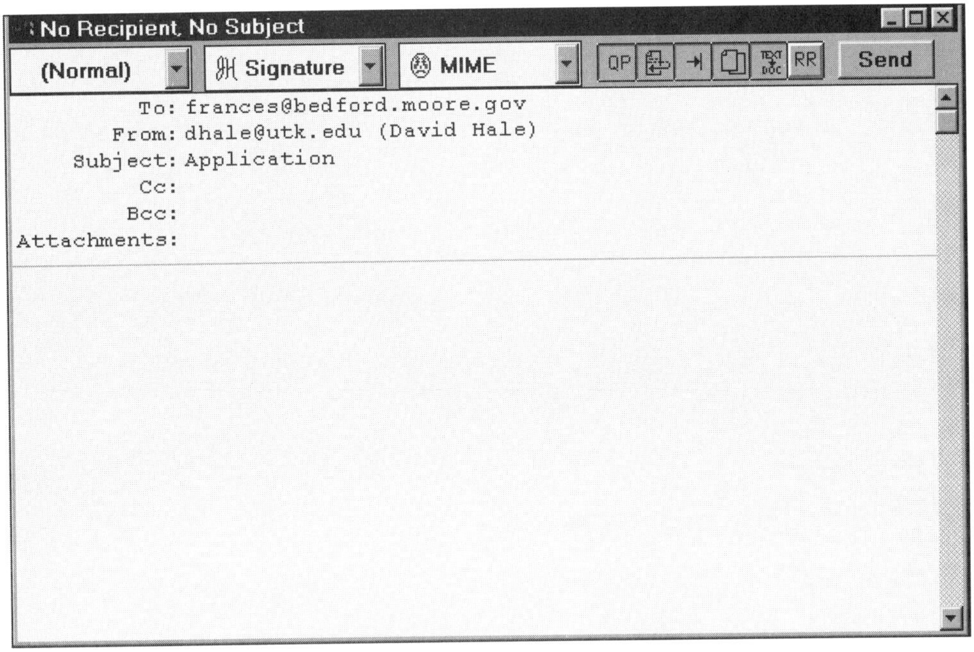

Figure 15.15: Type in the e-mail address of the recipient.

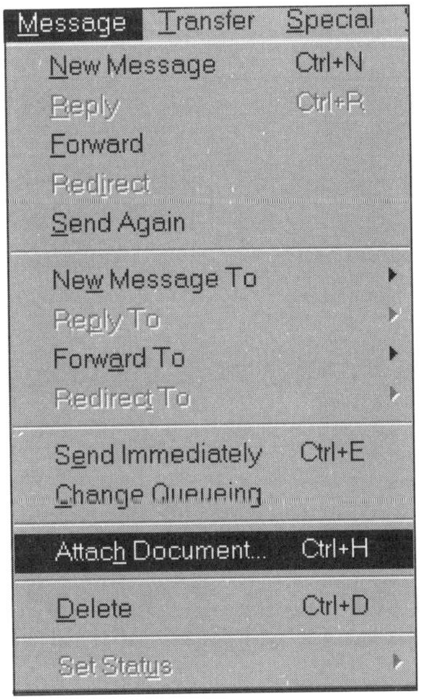

Figure 15.16: Choose *Attach Document.*

7. Find the file using the standard dialog box that appears and select it (see Figure 15.17).
8. Click the *OK* button.
9. The path to the file and the filename will appear in the *Attachments* field of the e-mail message (see Figure 15.18).
10. Click in the *Message* field of the message window and type the body of your e-mail message as you normally would.

You have attached the file *resume.doc* to the e-mail message, and you are now ready to send the message. Remember, the person to whom you are sending the document must also be using a MIME-compliant e-mail system. Otherwise, your attachment won't go through to the recipient.

SLMAIL E-MAIL SERVER

SLMail is a full-featured e-mail server distributed by Seattle Labs in Seattle, Washington. With versions for Windows 95, Windows NT, and

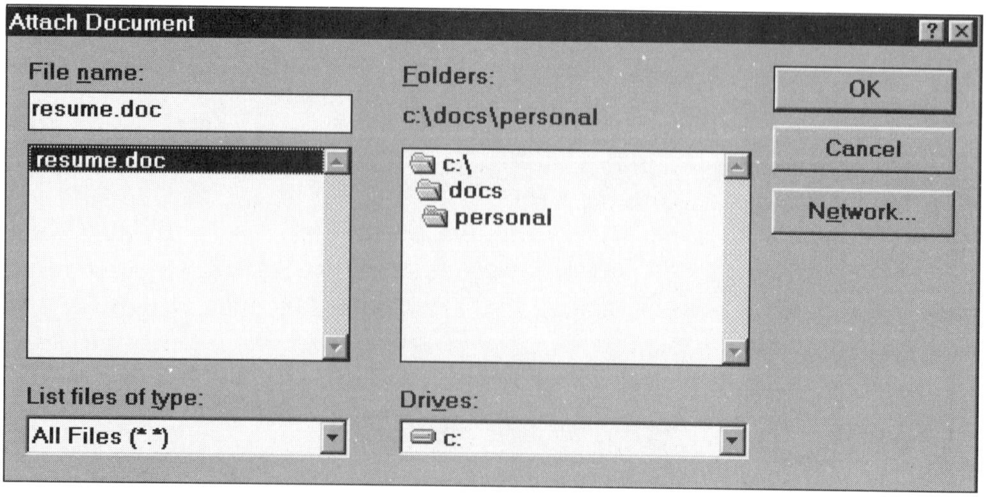

Figure 15.17: Select the file you wish to attach from the dialog box.

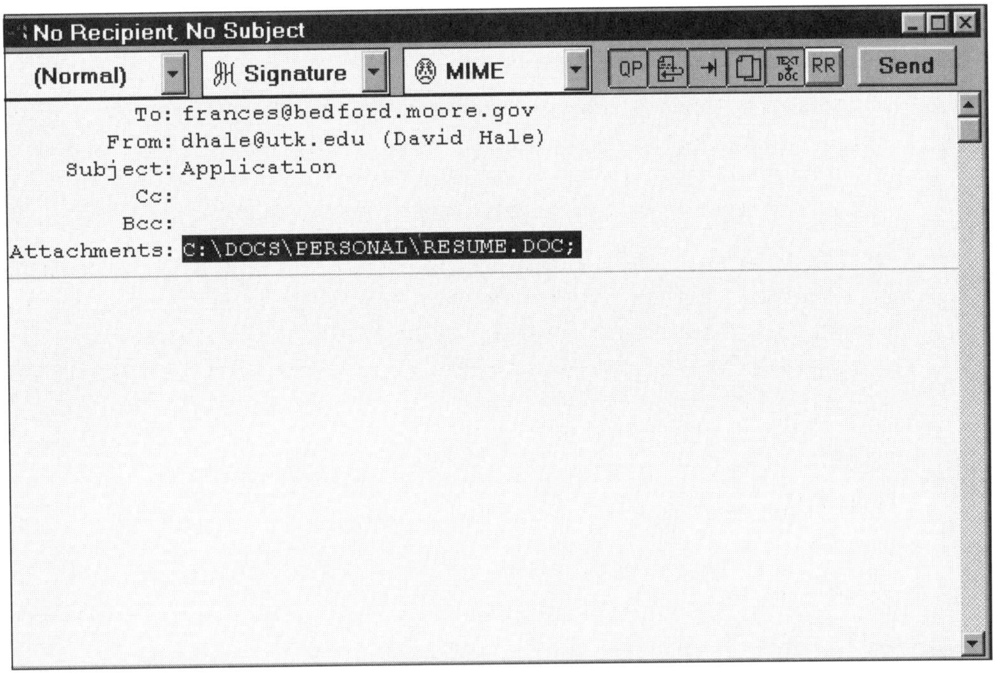

Figure 15.18: The complete path and filename appear.

Windows 3.11, SLMail provides the features that any small to medium-size organization needs in a mail server, including auto-responders, mailing lists, and account management. SLMail supports the SMTP and POP3 mail protocols. Using POP3 you can set up Eudora on each user's desktop computer to check into the SLMail server for new e-mail on a regular basis.

Many businesses like to offer customers the chance to send e-mail requests for additional information about the company's products. To provide immediate feedback to their customers these businesses often use an *auto-responder.* An *auto-responder* is a special account on an e-mail server that automatically responds with a predetermined message whenever it receives e-mail. For instance, you can have an account called *info* that automatically mails out a brochure to a customer-based e-mail request sent from the customer to the *info* account (info@your.company.com).

The example below describes how to set up an auto-responder in SLMail. This auto-responder will automatically send a price list for the

Shoestring Window Company when someone sends e-mail to prices@shoestring.com. The name of the file is prices.txt, and it is in the C:\docs\prices\directory.

Setting up an Auto-Responder

Follow the steps below to set up an auto-responder:

1. Choose *Users...* from the *Configuration* menu. The System Users dialog box will appear (see Figure 15.19).
2. Select the contents of the *User ID* box and type in *prices,* the name for the account.
3. Click the radio button beside *Auto-Responder* in the *System Users* dialog box.
4. Click the *Add* button to add the new account.

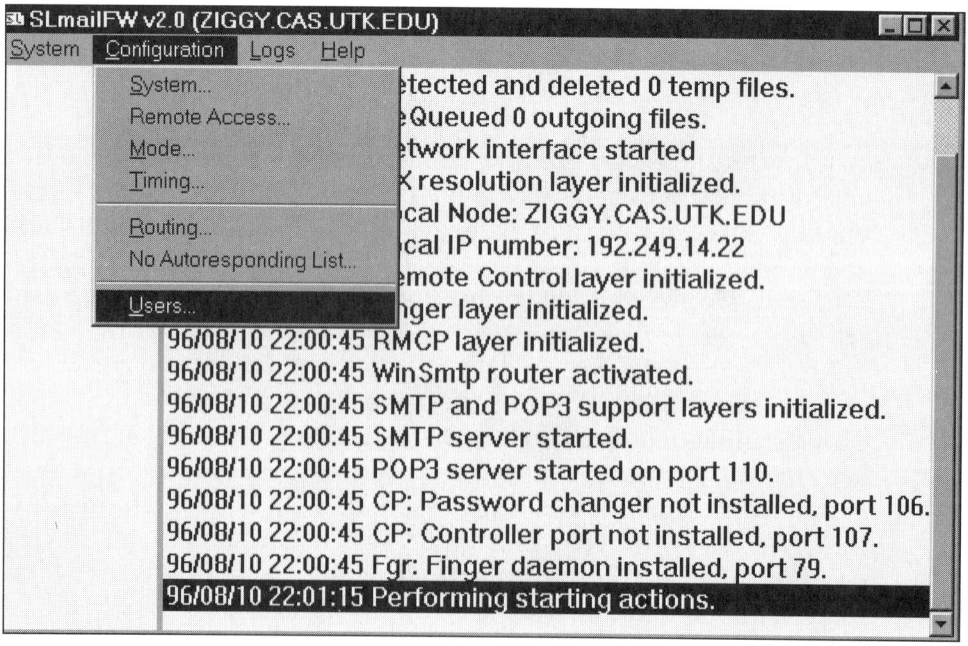

Figure 15.19: Choose *Users...* from the *Configuration* menu.

5. Two fields will appear: *Responder Name* and *Responder*. The *Responder* field is filled in automatically for you, based on the User ID you specified for the auto-responder account (see Figure 15.20).
6. Type a short text description of your auto-responder in the *Responder Name* field (e.g., *Shoestring Windows Price List*) (see Figure 15.21).
7. You must now specify which file is sent when a request comes in to prices@shoestring.com. Click on the *Show Configuration* button to continue. (Note that you must click the *Add* button

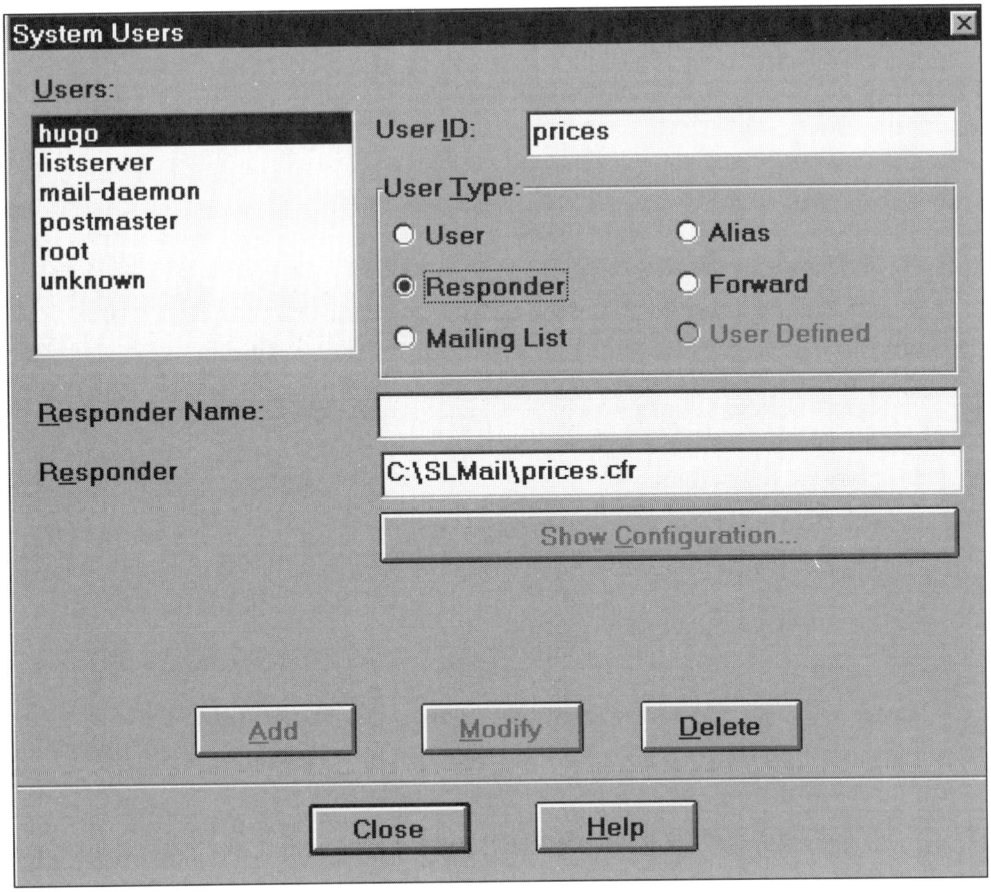

Figure 15.20: The *Responder Name* and *Responder* fields will appear.

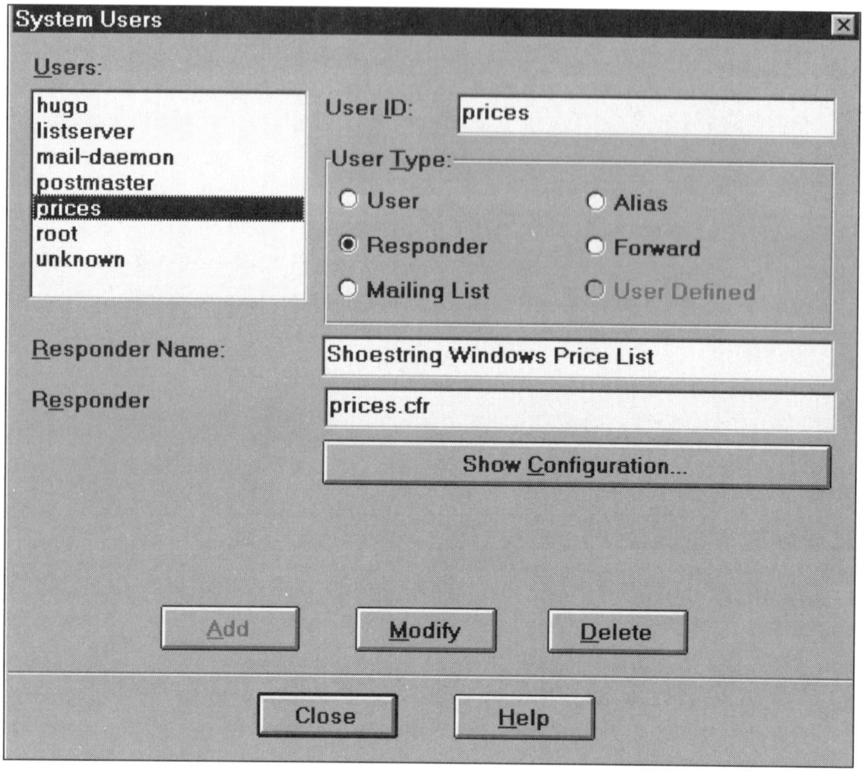

Figure 15.21: The new auto-responder account has been added but not configured.

before the *Show Configuration* button will become active.) This brings up the *Configure Auto-responder* dialog box shown in Figure 15.22.

8. Deselect the checkbox beside *Send Files Only On User's Request*. That option is used for a different type of auto-responder.
9. Click the *Edit Responder Items* button.
10. Another *Configure Auto-Responder* dialog box appears (see Figure 15.23). Type *Shoestring Windows Price List* in the box beside *File Identifier*. This is a text description of the file.
11. Click the *Browse* button (see Figure 15.23).

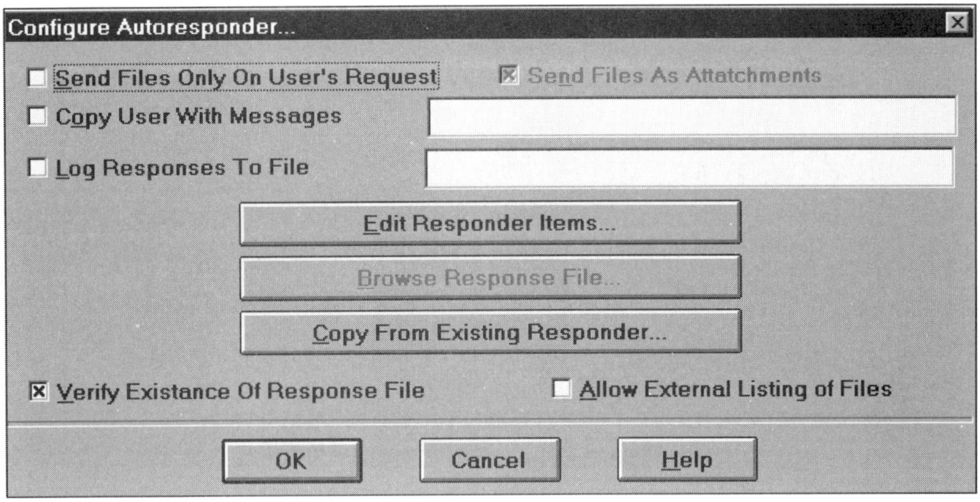

Figure 15.22: In the *Configure Auto-Responder* dialog box specify the file sent by your auto-responder.

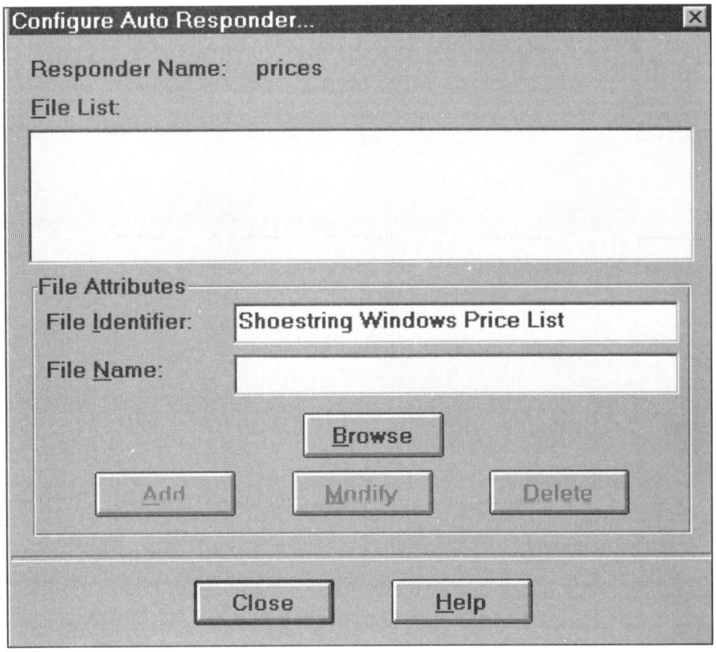

Figure 15.23: Enter your file identifier and then click the *Browse* button to select the text file that the auto-responder will automatically send.

12. Select the file C:\docs\prices\prices.txt (see Figure 15.24) and click *OK*.
13. Click the *Add* button.
14. Click the *Close* button.
15. Click the *OK* button.
16. Click the *Close* button.

That's it. Now when your customers send e-mail to prices@shoestring.com, they will get the contents of C:\docs\prices\prices.txt back in an e-mail message.

Setting up a Mailing List

The simplest form of convenient-time conferencing is an e-mail mailing list. SLMail lets you easily create and manage mailing lists. The steps in this section explain how you can create a mailing list for discussions about company policies and procedures for use by your company. The name of the list will be *policy-l*. Employees will be able to

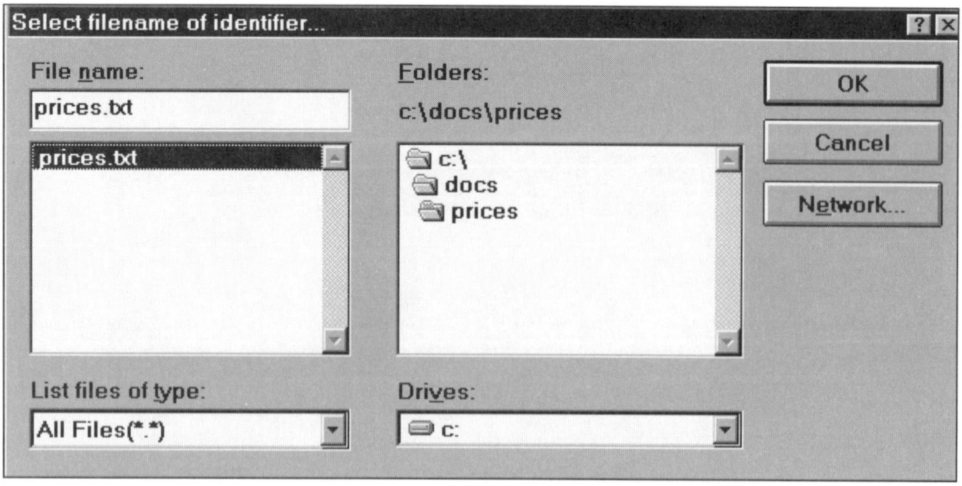

Figure 15.24: Select the text file.

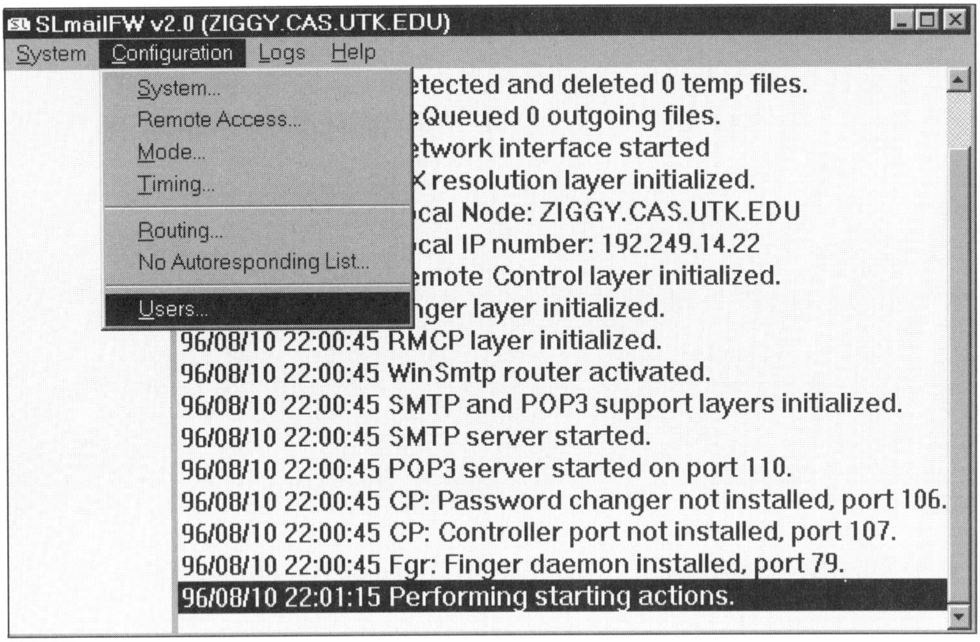

Figure 15.25: Select *Users.*

add themselves to the list using regular listserv commands (included in the SLMail documentation). The listowner or manager of the list will be the head of Human Resources at Shoestring Windows, Kelsey Vaughn (user ID *kelsey*).

1. From the Configuration menu select *Users* (see Figure 15.25).
2. Select the contents of the *User ID* field and type in the name of the list, *policy-l*.
3. Click the radio button beside *Mailing List*.
4. Click in the text field beside *Listowner*. Type in the user ID of the list owner, *kelsey* (see Figure 15.26).
5. Click the *Add* button.

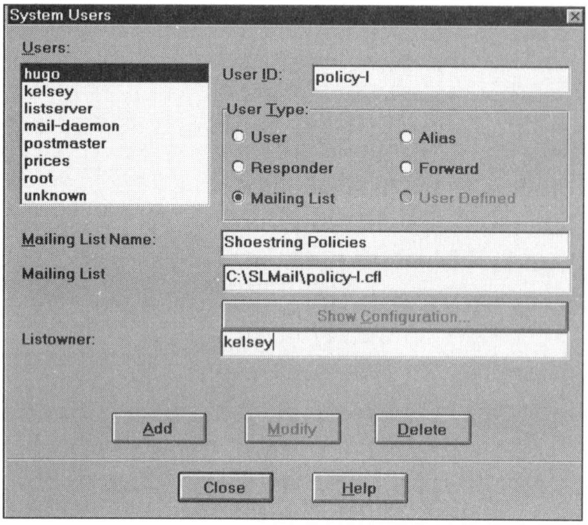

Figure 15.26: The user *kelsey* is designated as the owner of this list. Listowners must have accounts in SLMail.

6. You must now configure the mailing list features. Click on the *Show Configuration* button.
7. The *Mailing List* configuration screen appears. You have many options for your list. The *policy-l* list is closed, meaning that people who are not members of the list cannot send messages to it. The default configuration shown in Figure 15.27 is adequate for this mailing list.
8. Click the *OK* button.
9. Click the *Close* button.

There are many options available to you with an SLMail mailing list. The Listowner can moderate discussions, allowing only those contributions that are relevant. You can allow users to receive the posts to the list in *digest* form. Digests are once-a-day mailings of all contributions to the list over a 24-hour period in one big e-mail message. Some people prefer to manage high-volume lists by receiving them in digest form. Experiment with the features to customize your mailing list to get the performance you need.

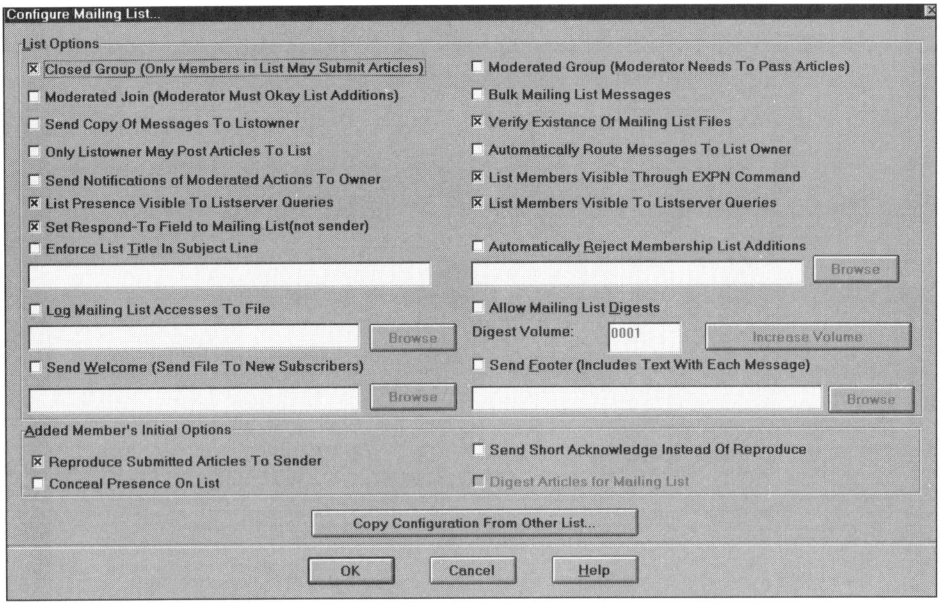

Figure 15.27: This list is closed to people who are not members of the list but it is not moderated.

SUMMARY

E-mail is an essential component of an intranet. You and your co-workers will use it to exchange files and communicate efficiently. If you don't want to manage your own e-mail server, you should rely on your ISP's e-mail services.

Chapter 16

WORK MANAGEMENT

Work management software must tend to many details yet remain easy to use. It must be able to handle simple tasks as well as complex ones. It must store and retrieve work meta information, and it must perform one or some of the functions that fall under work management. It is challenging to build software that is flexible enough for groups to tailor to their work processes.

GROUPWORKS

Not many programs can handle all five types of work management software outlined by the book. FTP GroupWorks comes close. It offers a to-do list, scheduling, work flow, task management, and project management. All are well integrated with each other. Within a project are shared calendaring, personal and shared to-do lists, contact management, schedule assignment, and management. Tasks assigned to you in one of the projects to which you belong also show up in your personal work space list. GroupWorks provides an intuitive way to keep track of multiple projects at once in a shared environment.

GroupWorks provides your team with a central location for discussion of any new project it undertakes. The manager of the project can assign tasks as needed. Everyone on the team has a place to come and see how the project is progressing. GroupWorks uses the metaphor of tabbed index cards for the different categories of work in a project. The example below shows how Hugo, a foreman at Stepp Construction, a renovation and construction firm, will use GroupWorks to manage a large team project like the renovation of an old house.

1. The foreman, Hugo, chooses New from the File menu as shown in Figure 16.1.
2. Next he types the name of the project in the Name for New Project box as shown in Figure 16.2.
3. Hugo chooses the start and end dates from the section at the bottom of the dialog box (see Figure 16.3).
4. He clicks the *OK* button, then clicks *OK* again.
5. A new project screen appears as shown in Figure 16.4. On the top tabbed card, the *Overview* card, are the name of the project, start and end dates, the overall description of the project, important milestone markers for the project, the names of the team members assigned to the project, and a space for attaching files related to the project.

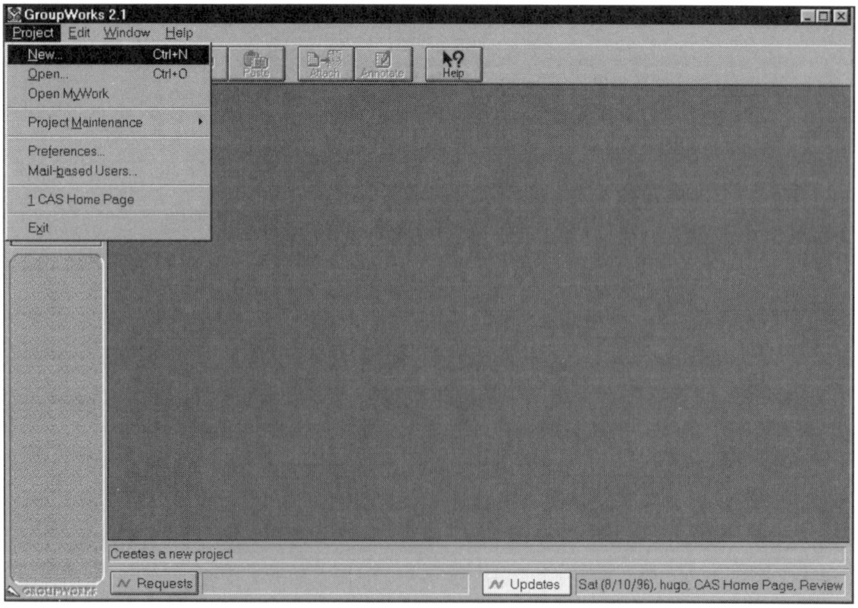

Figure 16.1: Creating a new project.

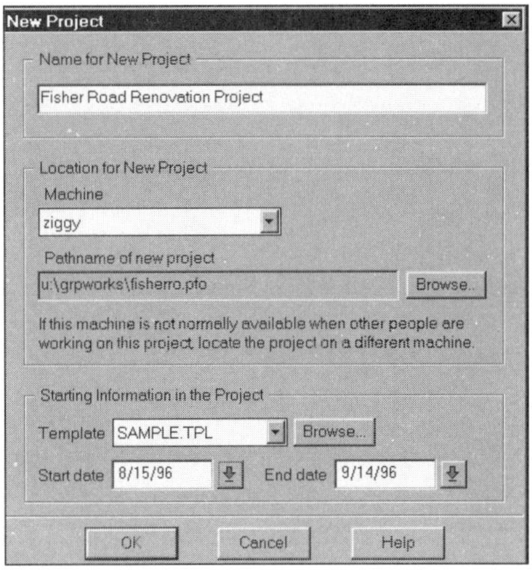

Figure 16.2: This project is called *Fisher Road Renovation Project.*

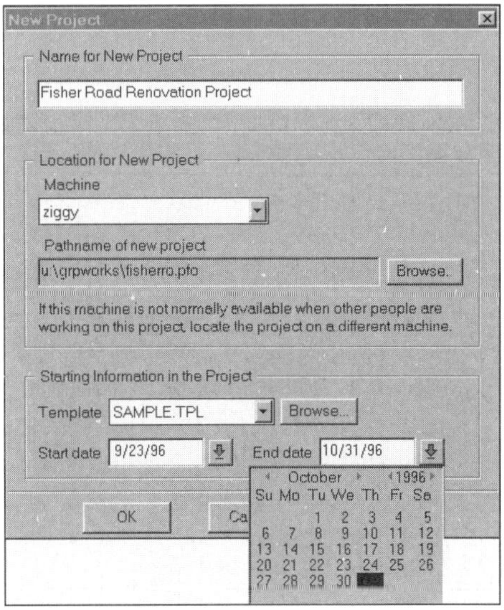

Figure 16.3: The Fisher Road project begins on September 23, 1996, and ends on October 31, 1996.

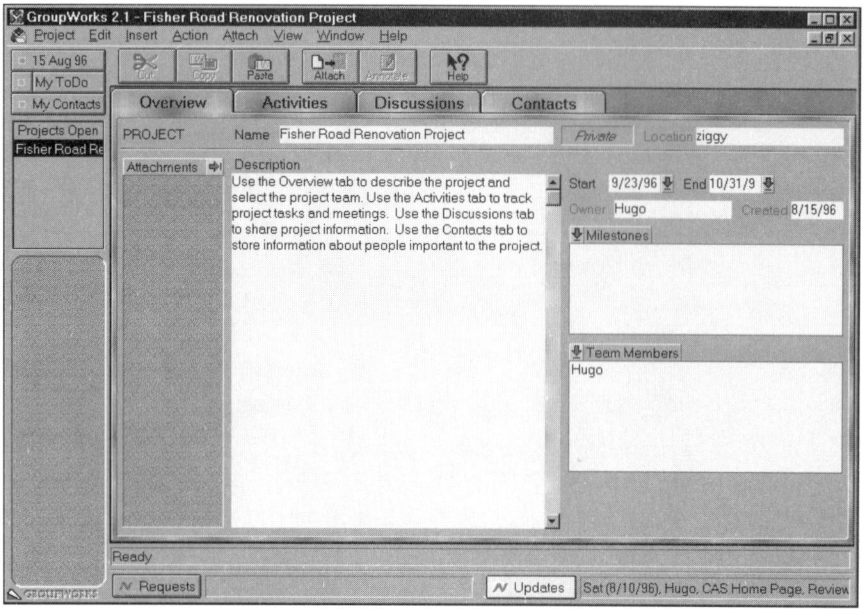

Figure 16.4: The tabs along the top of the screen provide access to the different cards that make up the project.

6. Hugo types in a description of the project in the *Description* box. He then begins to add the names of the members of the team. To add names, he just clicks on the arrow beside *Team Members,* as shown in Figure 16.5. Anyone in the Team Members list can see the project.
7. Hugo wants to include a note with directions to the house. To do this he chooses *Attach Note...* from the Attach menu and then types in the title of the Note and the text (see Figure 16.6). When he is done, he clicks the *Update* button as shown in Figure 16.7.
8. Next, Hugo adds the milestones for this project. *Milestones* are important dates during the course of the project that can be used to gauge the project's progress. To add milestones, Hugo clicks on the arrow beside Milestones. Once in the Milestones window, he types a description of the goal in the *Description* box, selects the date when it should be reached, and clicks the *Add* button (see Figure 16.8). When he has added all five milestones for this project he clicks the *OK* button.

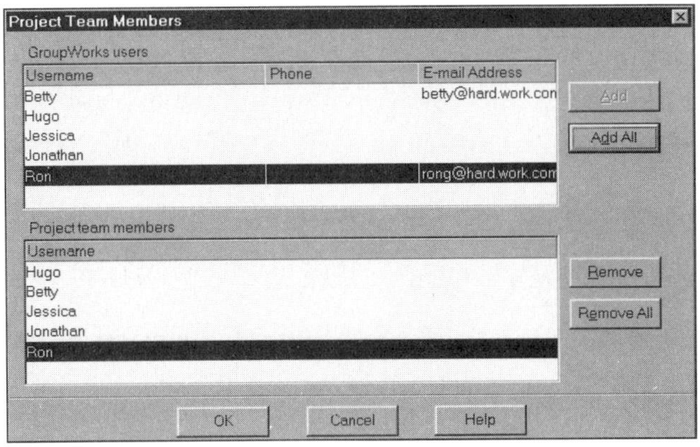

Figure 16.5: Putting people on the Fisher Road project by clicking the *Add All* button and then the *OK* button.

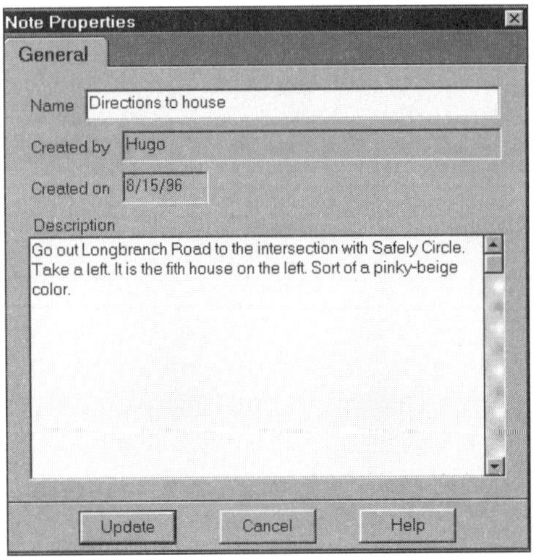

Figure 16.6: Providing directions to the house by attaching a note to the overview card.

9. The Overview card now holds the key information about this project (see Figure 16.9). Anyone new to the project can come to this page to get an overview of the goals of the project.
10. Now Hugo is ready to move on to the *Activities* card, which provides a time line for individual activities, or tasks, that make up the project. Team members can assign one another

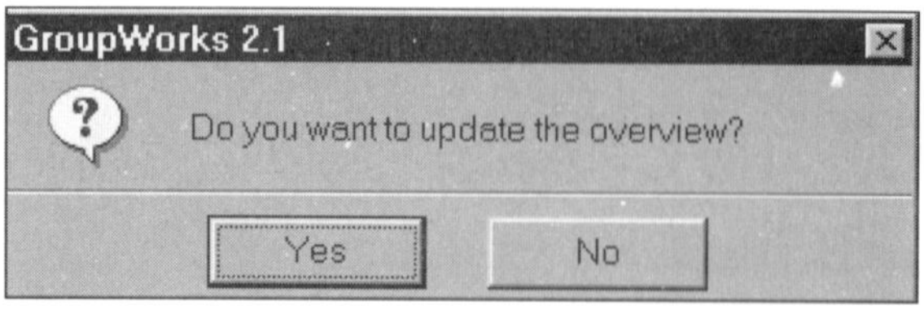

Figure 16.7: Clicking the *New* button to update the card with an attachment.

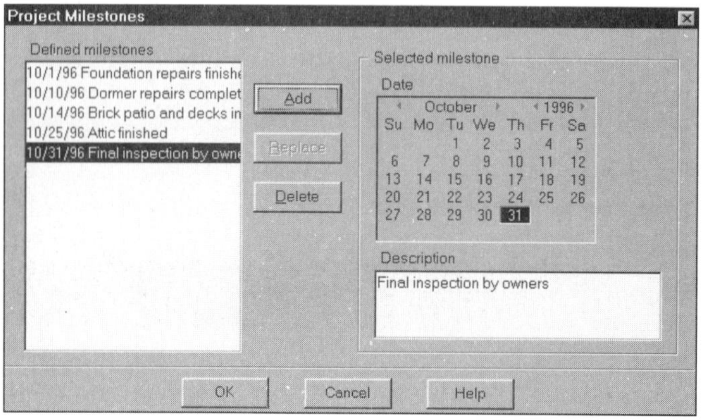

Figure 16.8: There are five milestones for the Fisher Road Project.

tasks. Hugo wants to assign the foundation project to his foundation specialist, Ron. He clicks the *Task* button in the toolbar. He types the name of the task in the *Name* box, enters a textual description in the *Assignment* box, assigns the project to Ron by clicking the arrow beside Assignees, and selects the start and end dates for the task. When the task is ready, Hugo clicks the *Publish* button in the toolbar so that the rest of the team can see the changes to the card. Also, people who are assigned tasks receive an individual notice of their new tasks when the card is published. You can see the Activities card in Figure 16.10.

11. Hugo leaves it up to Ron to assign to his assistant Jonathan the subtasks that will be necessary to complete this task. To assign a subtask, Ron selects the foundation task and clicks the *SubTask* button. The procedure thereafter is the same as a regular task. Ron's subtasks and some of the other tasks are shown in the updated Activities card in Figure 16.11.

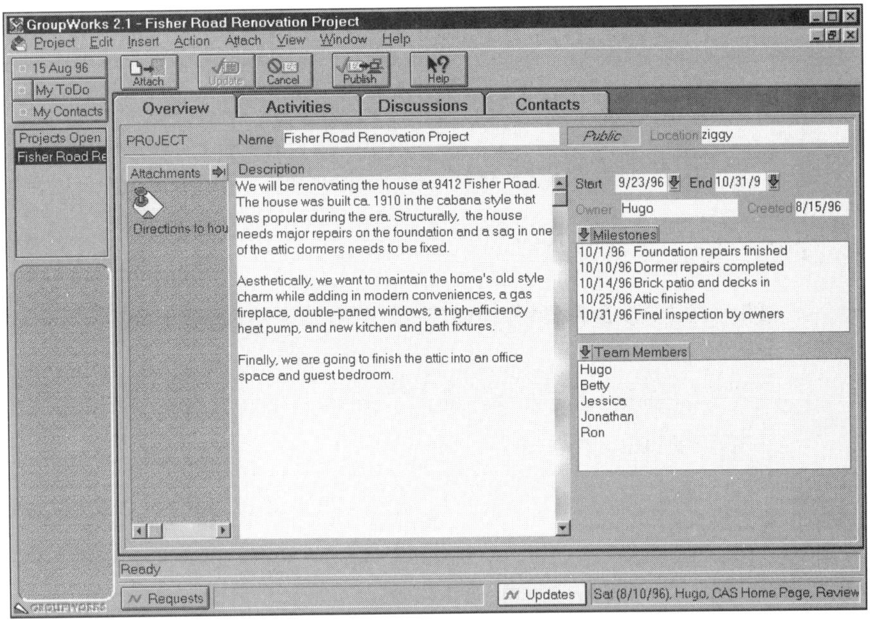

Figure 16.9: The Overview card holds all the essential data about a project.

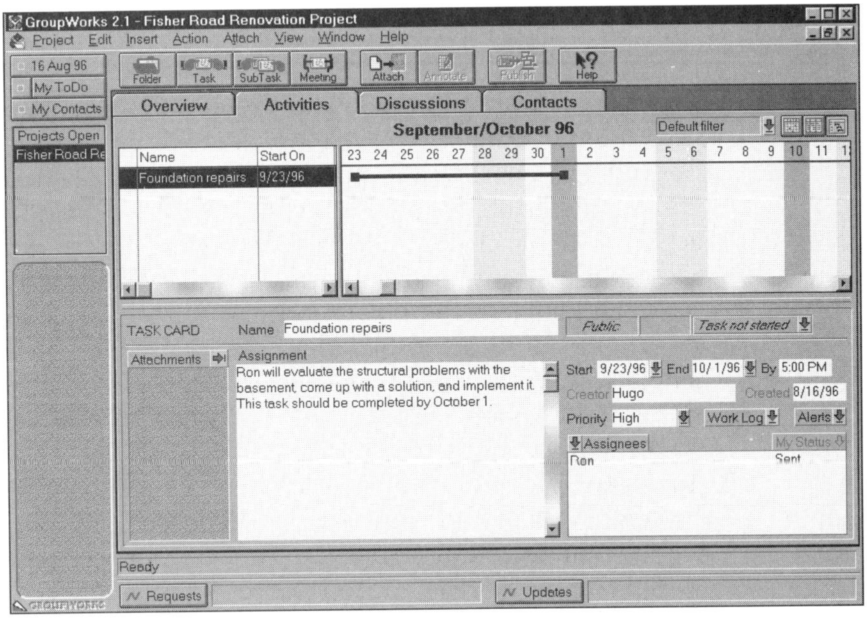

Figure 16.10: The first project is added to the Activities card.

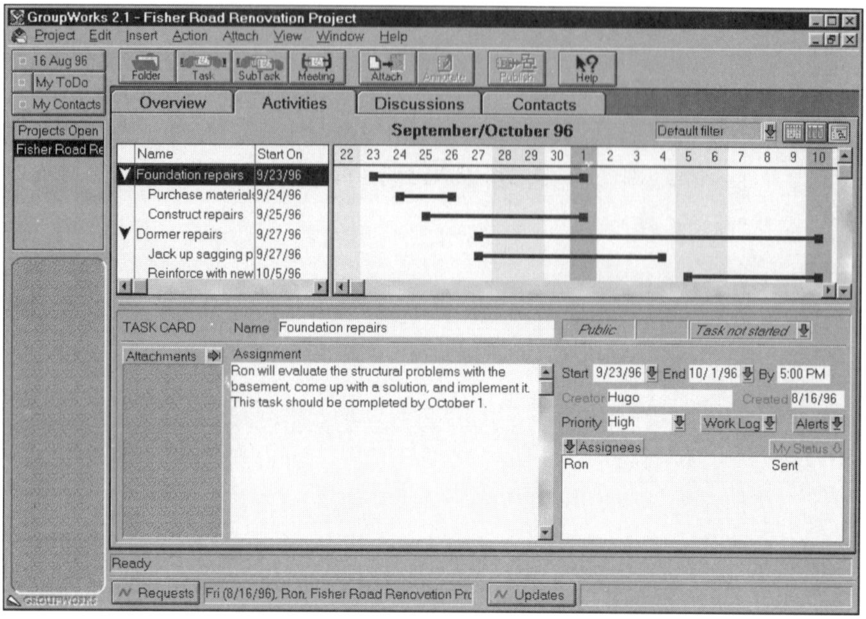

Figure 16.11: The time line view of the Activities card gives a graphical representation of the project's scope.

12. Figure 16.12 shows the outline view, also available through the Activities window. The outline shows details about start date, end date, priority, completion status, assignees, and more in a tabular layout.
13. The next card is for discussions about the project. Jessica starts a topic about the trouble she is having with one of the jigsaws. Hugo replies that he may have a solution for her. Betty and Ron, in the meantime, are discussing the relative merits of treated lumber with Jonathan in another thread. Jonathan has embedded an Excel spreadsheet into his response to Ron's response. To compose a new topic, Jonathan just clicks on the *Topic* button. To respond, push *Reply,* and for responses to responses, push the *Reply-Reply* button. Figure 16.13 shows the discussion card for the Fisher Road Project.
14. Figure 16.14 shows the Contacts card. Any team member can share a contact on this card. If you need to track phone calls for billing purposes, it's built into this card as well.

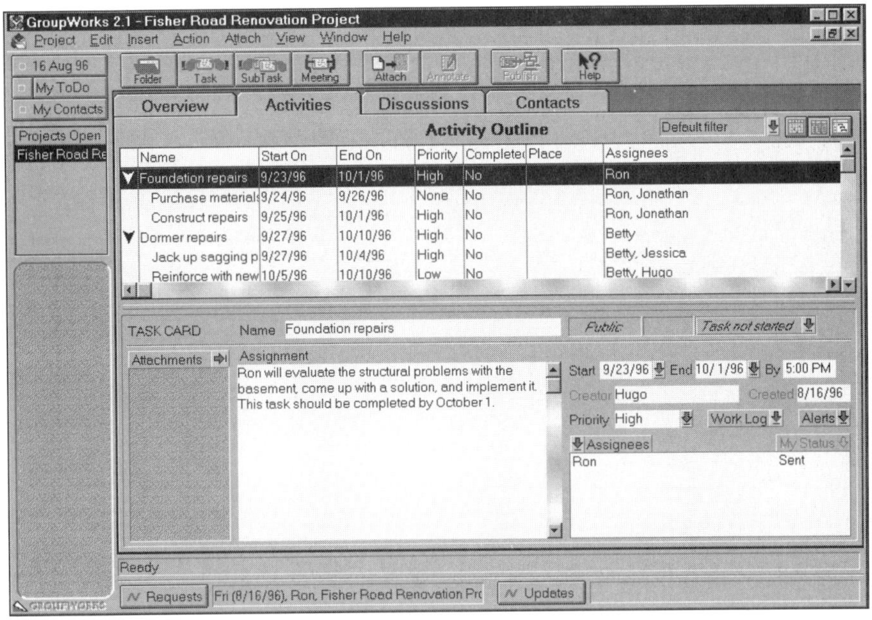

Figure 16.12: The outline view of the Activities window is shown.

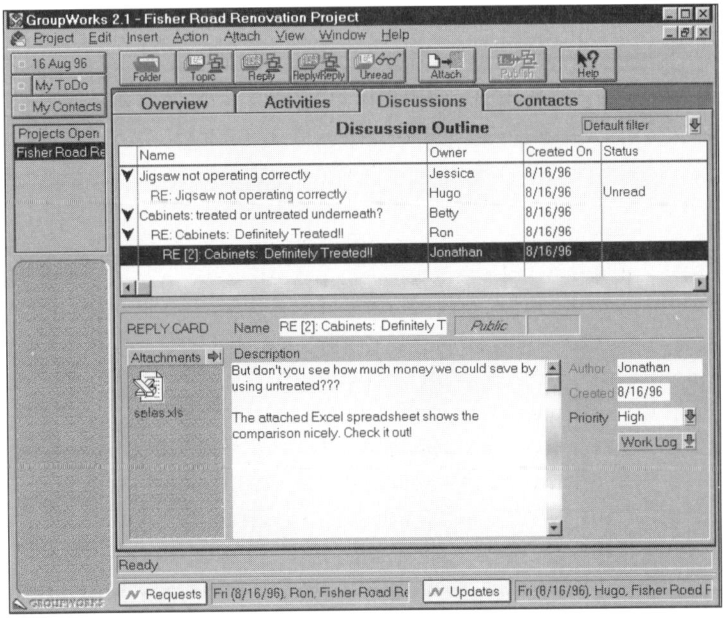

Figure 16.13: Unread discussion topics are highlighted in blue until they are read.

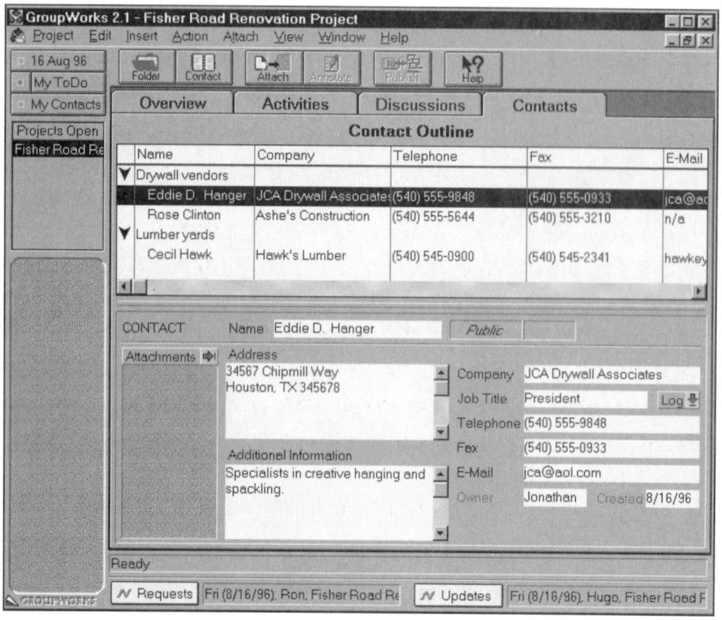

Figure 16.14: The Contacts card manages addresses, phone numbers, e-mail addresses, and phone call logging.

GroupWorks is limited by its ability to run only on Windows, Windows 95, and Windows NT. If you have a single Mac or Unix computer in your organization, it will not work for you. Another way that GroupWorks could be improved is by integrating the client into the Web.

ECCO PRO

When you are working on a new project, do you often write ideas, notes, and outlines on a notepad as you work? Many people work like this. ECCO Pro exploits the metaphor of a notepad in helping you to organize information, manage your time, and work with others. ECCO Pro is a software product of Netmanage, a major producer of TCP/IP software. Netmanage is currently adding TCP/IP functionality to ECCO Pro that should be implemented through a program named ECCO Share by the time you read this. The new ECCO Share will provide cross-server sharing of the functionality contained in

ECCO Pro as well as replication services. ECCO Pro's superior calendaring and work management features are deserving of consideration.

ECCO Pro is more than a personal information manager. It provides calendaring, scheduling, project management, address books, billing records, Internet address management, and correspondence tracking. A convenient feature of the program is its ability to share information among these functions and even with other applications like word processors. If you are typing a letter in your word processor and need the address, you can just click on ECCO's ever-present *shooter* icon in your menu bar and shoot the information right into the letter. Need to schedule an appointment with someone in your address book? Just drag that person's address book entry into the time slot on your calendar, and you are done (see Figure 16.15). All the information that you have about the person in address book is now available in the calendar as well. Any changes you make in either location show up in both places, making information sharing a powerful feature.

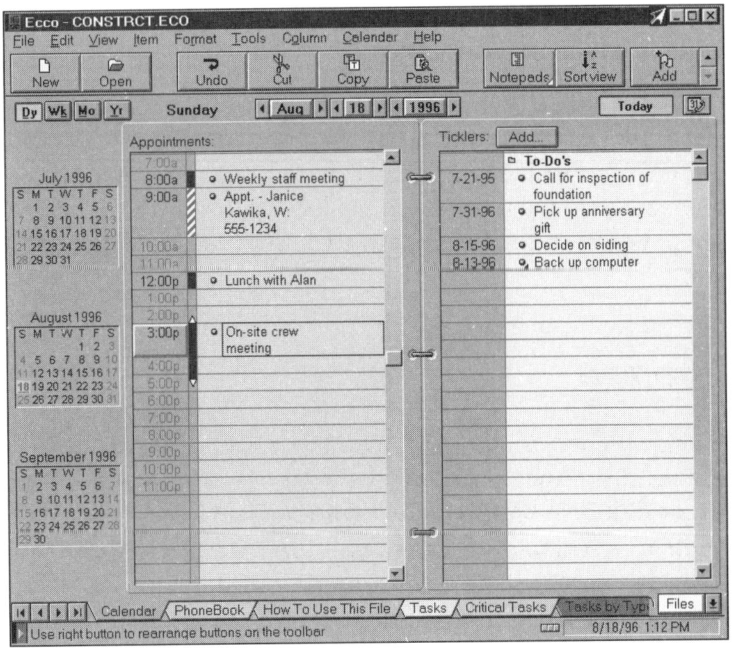

Figure 16.15: ECCO Pro can link your calendar to all the other information in your information manager.

Your project notepad can contain multiple customized columns to help you manage the project. For instance, the notepad in Figure 16.16 includes a Gantt column to track progress on a construction project.

Today you can share information with others using ECCO on a LAN through file sharing. This capability makes the calendaring and project management features particularly powerful groupware. ECCO Share will bring this seasoned software to intranets where you can take advantage of its proven capabilities. In the future it will also become more closely integrated with the extensive array of TCP/IP programs offered by Netmanage.

SUMMARY

Work management is a fast-growing area in groupware. The many available programs offer different combinations of the criteria covered in Chapter 5. In late 1996 and in 1997, many new group work programs that offer work management will become available.

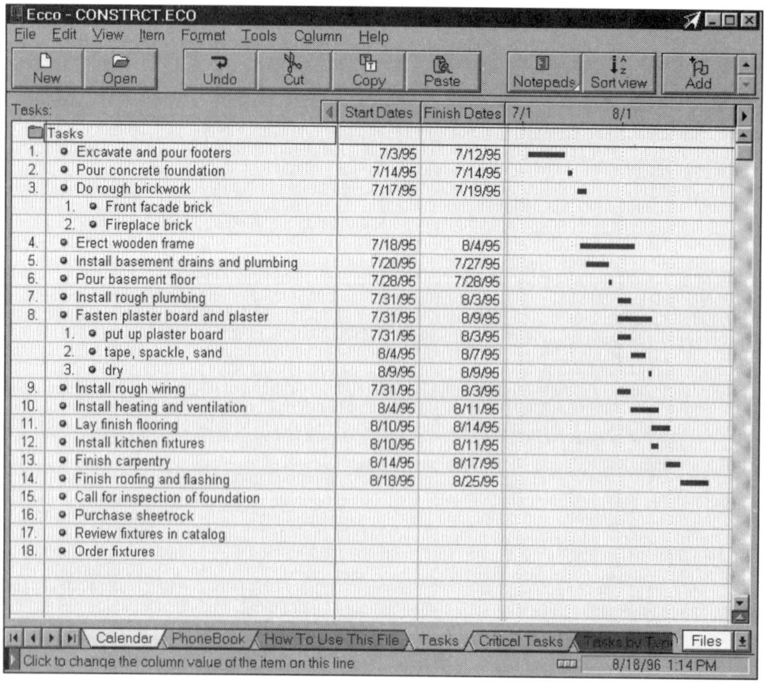

Figure 16.16: ECCO Pro uses a notepad to help you manage projects.

Chapter 17

CONFERENCING

Conferencing comes in two varieties: real-time conferences and convenient-time conferences. Convenient-time conferences go by such names as mailing lists, Usenet, forums, clubs, discussion groups, newsgroups, Listservs, and roundtables. Real-time conferencing includes the Internet Relay Channel (IRC), Web chat, phone conferencing, and teleconferencing. And then there's the white board.

At one time you had to depend on your ISP to use these types of programs. Now they are available in easy-to-use GUI programs. You can administer one of these programs yourself whether for the Internet or for an intranet.

THREE CONVENIENT-TIME CONFERENCES

The following sections explain the specifics of Majordomo, Cold Fusion (Allaire), and Netmanage, three convenient-time conferences.

Majordomo

Majordomo is a common name used to refer to traditional Internet mailing lists. These are generically referred to as *Listservs* (named after Listserv, one of the original mailing list programs). Majordomo is popular among ISPs and is widely available. It is easy to have your own mailing list provided by an ISP for about $10 per month. An example of a ListServer is shown in Figure 17.1.

Setup Setup is easy with Majordomo because the ISP does most of the work. You are the mailing list administrator. Your biggest job is to choose a name. The first inclination is to choose a name that suits the purpose at hand. If it is a temporary project, however, you might regret the choice of names later, and it might cause you to change the name. Pick a generic name that assumes you'll keep the mailing list a long time and use it for many different activities.

You control your Majordomo mailing list with e-mail messages. Majordomo itself resides on the ISP's computer (or the server computer on an intranet). There is no client. Your e-mail program is, in effect, the client.

The ISP will ask you whether you want to moderate the mailing list. If you do, all e-mail traffic will come to you first, and you

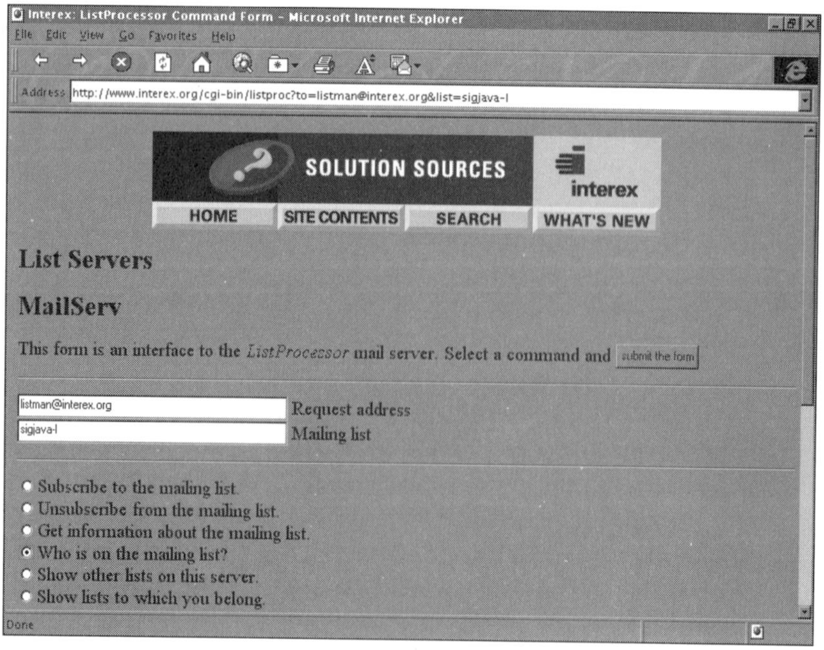

Figure 17.1: Sample ListServer.

determine whether it will be sent to the mailing list. If the mailing list has much traffic at all, this can be a big job, so it's better to leave the list unmoderated. In addition, moderation may dampen the enthusiasm of participants. Moderation is a built-in delay as well as censorship. Neither goes over well, but in some situations, moderation is appropriate.

Once you're ready to go, you have to understand two things:

- Send all administrative commands to: `majordomo@isp.com`. This is administration.
- Send e-mail to: `listname@isp.com`. This is content.

Majordomo is easy to use, but sometimes it's confusing if you don't keep the above addresses straight. The first is for administering the mailing list. The second is for participating in the mailing list.

Public Mailing List A public mailing list is one open to the public. There are two ways to handle a public mailing list. First, allow anyone to subscribe to the list without approval. People can send a *Subscribe* e-mail message to Majordomo, and Majordomo adds them automatically. Second, allow anyone to send a *Subscribe* message to Majordomo, but require all subscription messages to come to you for approval.

Private Mailing List For a private mailing list, you usually send the *Subscribe* e-mail message on behalf of participants by sending an e-mail message to Majordomo with a list of participants to be subscribed. When you want to shut down the conference, you delete everyone by sending an *Unsubscribe* e-mail message with the names of all subscribers in it to Majordomo.

Single Mailing List A single mailing list may be all you need. It can be an ongoing conference for a department at your company, and it can also be a one-month conference for a project that is to be done at the end of a month. Perhaps the mailing list lies idle for a month, and then you use it for a new project that lasts a couple of months.

Multiple Mailing Lists Suppose you play a role in three different group projects with three different work groups simultaneously. You will need three mailing lists. It costs a little more, but it provides a capable conferencing environment. Your role in getting the mailing lists set up is minimal. The ISP does all the work.

Reusable Mailing List Is a mailing list reusable? Sure. Unsubscribe the old participants, and subscribe the new participants. Think of your mailing list as an ongoing digital resource that you can use for your group work as you need it.

How Majordomo Works When a participant sends an e-mail message to the mailing list, Majordomo automatically sends the message out to everyone on the mailing list. Suppose you are the head of a Seminar Committee that will offer some seminars under the sponsorship of the North Bay Multimedia Association. There are two subcommittees, Education and Marketing. These are unrelated activities, so you use two mailing lists. One you name *edu-nbma* and the other *mkt-nbma*. Your ISP is North Bay Net (nbn.com). To program Majordomo, you send e-mail messages to *majordomo@nbn.com.* Your subscribers participate in the mailing list by sending e-mail messages to *edu-nbma@nbn.com or mkt-nbma@nbn.com.* For instance, when a participant sends a message to `edu-nbma@nbn.com`, Majordomo receives the message and sends it to everyone on the mailing list.

How Participants Use Majordomo For conference participants, Majordomo is simple to use. A participant merely sends an e-mail message addressed to *edu-nbma@nbn.com* (see Figure 17.2).

The message will be sent by Majordomo to everyone on the mailing list. Every participant receives all messages sent to the mailing list. It is up to each participant to file the message away for future reference. There is no automatic message filing feature. Participants can use any e-mail client to participate. When you receive a message, it shows in your e-mail client as coming from the person who sent it.

Specifics As the mailing list administrator, you subscribe and unsubscribe participants for a work group. You do this with e-mail.

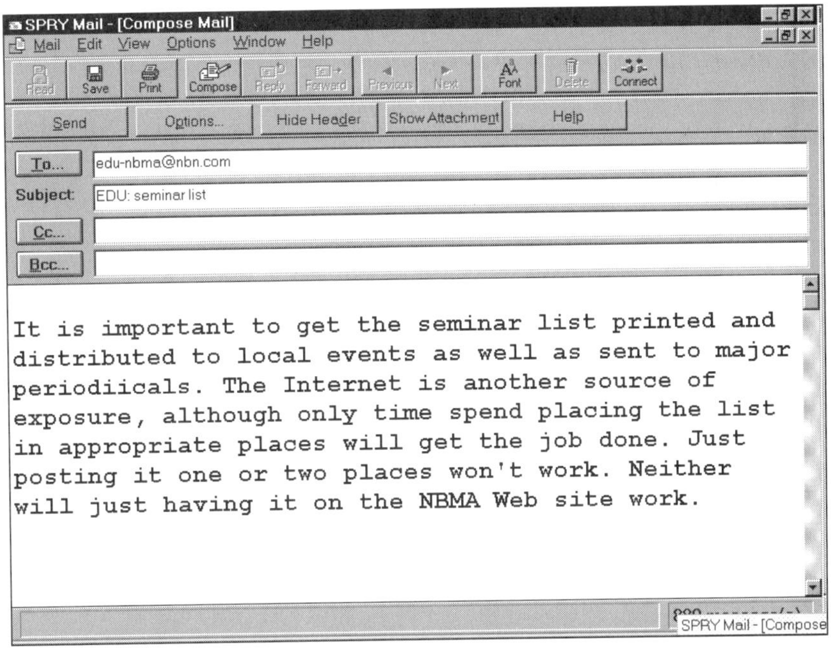

Figure 17.2: Sending a message to the Education Subcommittee online conference.

Subscribe The command for subscribing someone is the following:

```
subscribe [password] [mailing list name] [participant e-mail
          address]
```

You can subscribe as many participants as you want in one e-mail message (see Figure 17.3). Use one line for each.

Keep in mind that the ISP has set up everything for you. All you have to do is subscribe the participants, and you're in business. Only you know the password to make the *Subscribe* command work.

Unsubscribe To take a person off the mailing list, use the unsubscribe command (see Figure 17.4).

```
unsubscribe [password] [mailing list name] [participant e-mail
            address]
```

Again, you can also unsubscribe numerous participants at one time.

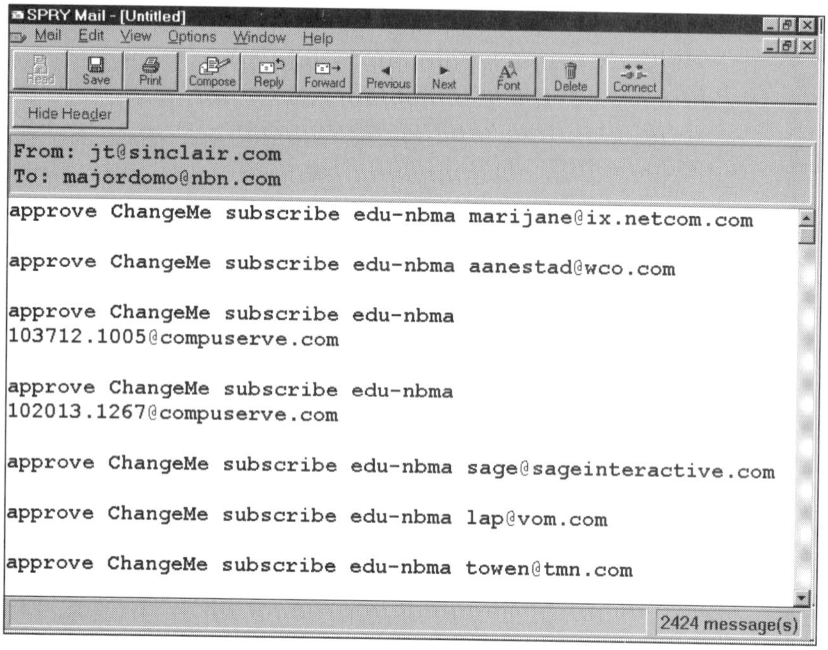

Figure 17.3: Setting up a mailing list for a work group.

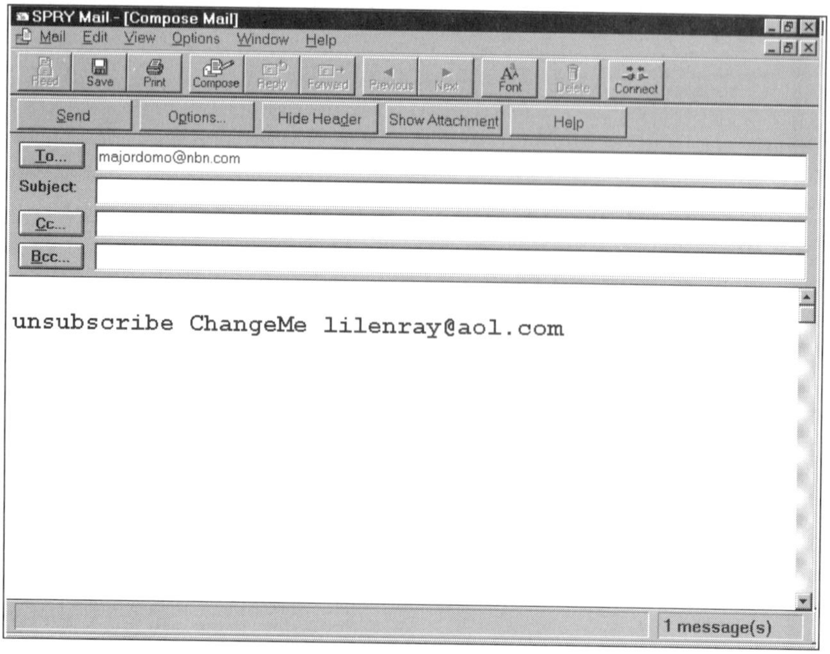

Figure 17.4: Unsubscribing a participant.

Participants What if participants try to do something—like subscribe or unsubscribe? If they do, it doesn't work, because they are not on a public mailing list. The e-mail message comes to you. You can approve or disapprove it by sending the appropriate e-mail message to Majordomo (see Figures 17.5 and 17.6).

List At any time, any member of the mailing list can get a copy of the mailing list by requesting it from Majordomo in an e-mail message.

```
who [mailing list name]
```

Majordomo will send the entire mailing list (see Figure 17.7).

Information For new subscribers, Majordomo is careful to send information on using a mailing list as well as a copy of mailing list commands. Thus, you do not even have to indoctrinate new subscribers in the technical details. It is wise, however, to ask all members to preface all *Subject* lines in their messages with a special code. For the Education Committee mailing list messages, for instance, use *EDU:*

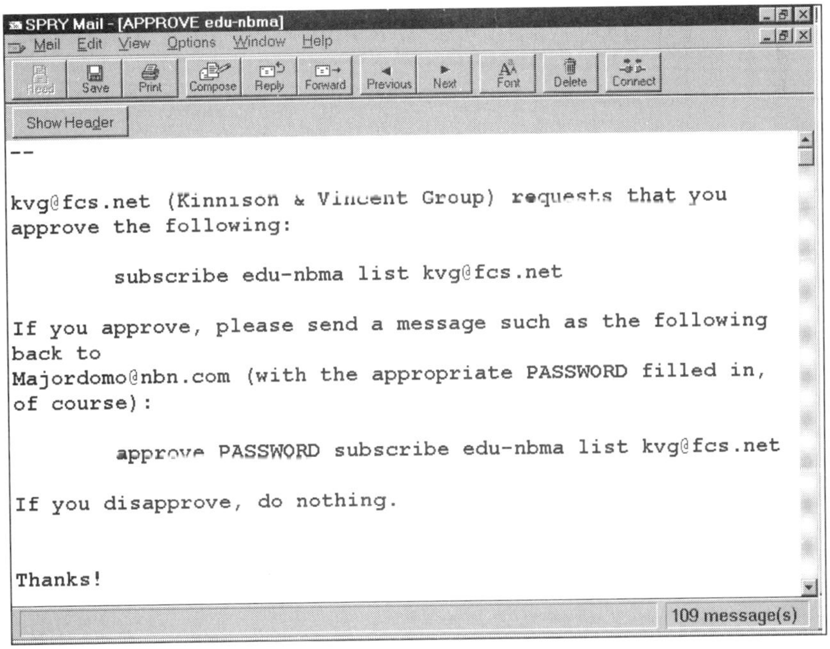

Figure 17.5: An e-mail request to subscribe comes to you.

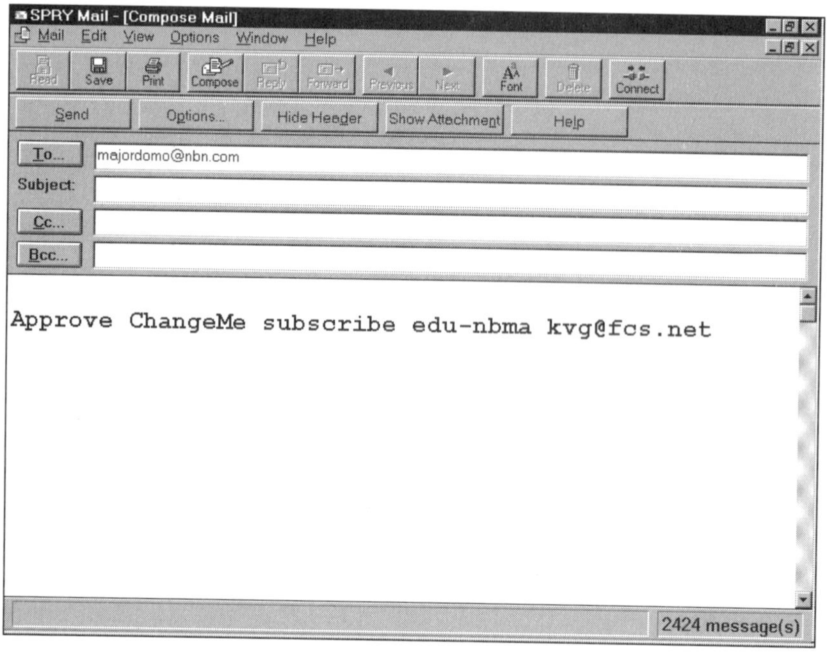

Figure 17.6: You approve the subscription.

Summary—Majordomo As you can see, you administer a Majordomo mailing list via e-mail. The administrator is the only one with a password and thus the only one who can enable subscriptions, unsubscriptions, and approvals. The figures above give you an idea of how you administer Majordomo but do not tell the whole story. Majordomo also sends useful confirmation messages to you every time you send a command and otherwise helps you. There are about a dozen commands you can use to get various tasks done.

The most difficult part is remembering to send administrative e-mail messages to `majordomo@nbn.com` and e-mail messages for the work group to `edu-nbma@nbn.com`. Although a mailing list is not the ideal system for conferencing—it contains no threads and requires everyone to handle e-mail traffic—it works. It's inexpensive, easy to use, readily available from your ISP, and easy to administer. Try it.

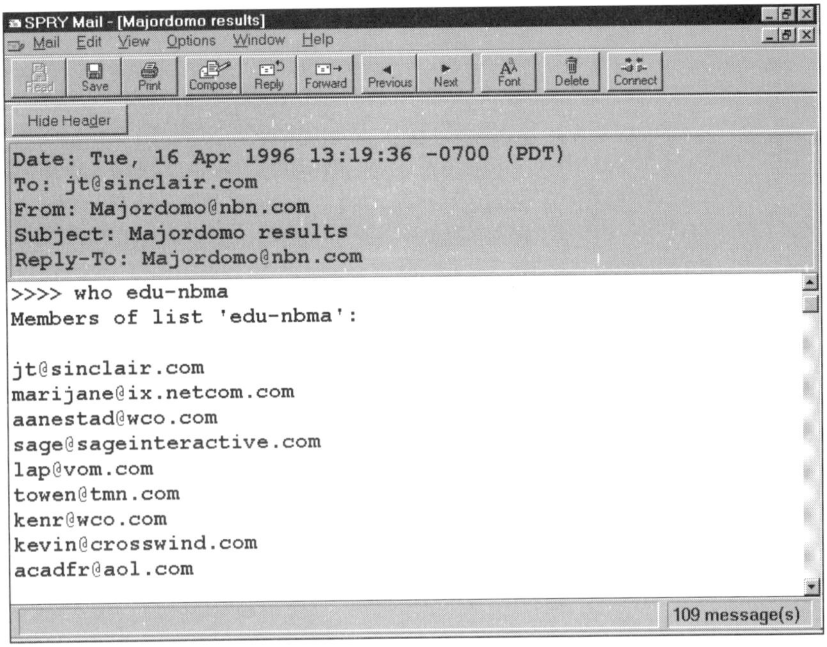

Figure 17.7: Majordomo will send you the mailing list, if you are on the list.

Cold Fusion (Allaire) Forums

Cold Fusion is a Web-database development tool (see Chapter 19). To use Cold Fusion (Allaire) Forums, you must have Cold Fusion and a Web server installed on your PC. WebSite is a good choice because Cold Fusion is bundled with WebSite Pro, which is an attractively priced package. Installing Cold Fusion is easy. Installing Allaire Forums is considerably more complicated, although not difficult, and will probably require a few hours of your time. You must learn a portion of the program to complete the installation. Once installed, however, it's easy to use for participants, and the administration, although more complicated than that for Majordomo, is not difficult.

Allaire Forums is a threaded conferencing system. Postings (messages) are similar to e-mail messages. The difference is that the messages don't come to you. You must go to the *Conference* where the messages are posted in *Forums* to read them. If you want to post a message (which is equivalent to sending an e-mail message), you must do it at a Forum.

Suppose you are the manager of a real estate investment group and have been evaluating income properties in Denver. Now you go to Seattle to look at income properties there. You have had ongoing e-mail exchanges with members of the group and decide it would be better to administer a few Forums—better and less trouble for you and better for the group members, too. Once you have Allaire Forums installed, you look at the administration of the Forums. The first thing you do is log in as the administrator. You see four choices (see Figure 17.8).

Under *User and Group Security* you can create, modify, and assign privileges to users and groups. This is where you assign login names and passwords and also assign certain users to specific groups. Under *Conference Management* you create, modify, and assign properties to forums and conferences. You populate conferences with forums and start forums by sending a beginning message. Click on the *Conference Manager* button and then the *Create New* button (see Figure 17.9).

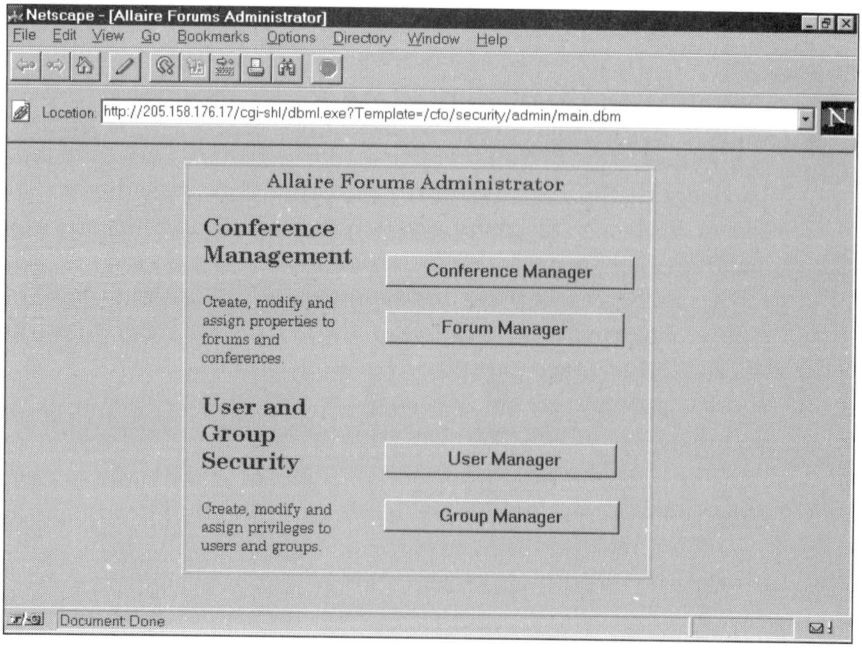

Figure 17.8: Administrator's page.

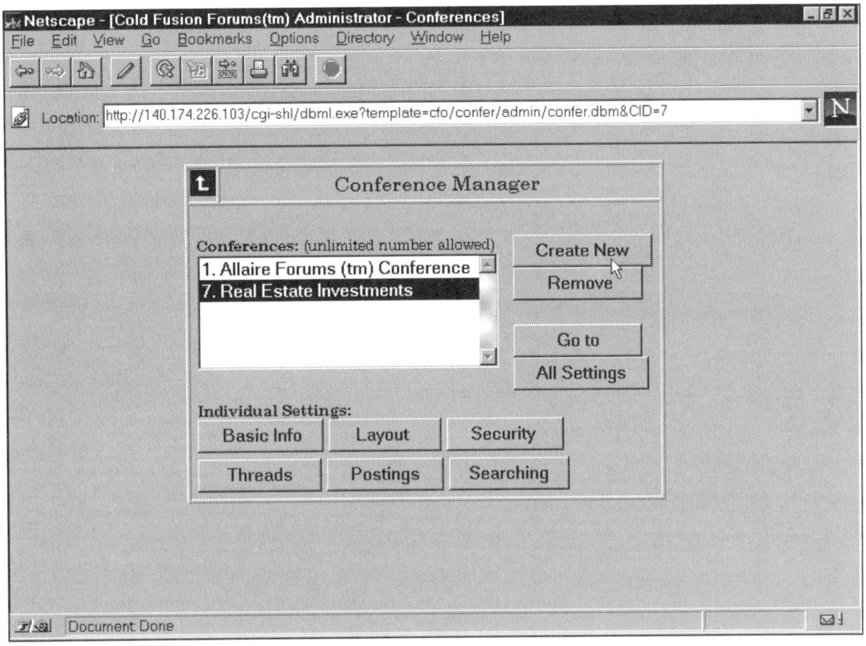

Figure 17.9: Start a new conference.

You get a screen where you can start a new conference. At the top, type in the name of the conference, *Real Estate Investments*. Then use *Add New Forum* to add *Denver*, *Property Types*, and *Seattle* forums. Then *Select* each of the forums you have created (see Figure 17.10). Now you have a new conference with three forums set up. Click on *Finish* to complete the process.

Clicking on the Finish button returns you to the first Conference menu where you can tune your new conference. Using the six buttons at the bottom, you can set the layout and structure for your conference. Click on the arrow in the upper left-hand corner to return to the main menu (see Figure 17.11).

Now select *Forum Manager* to tune the new forums. The four buttons at the bottom provide for setting up the forums. Choose *Seattle* and *Basic Info* (see Figure 17.12).

Fill in the description and click on Finish (see Figure 17.13).

You can set up a moderator, set messages for reading only, or set messages for reading and writing (see Figure 17.12 above). When you finish with all three forums, return to the main menu. Your new

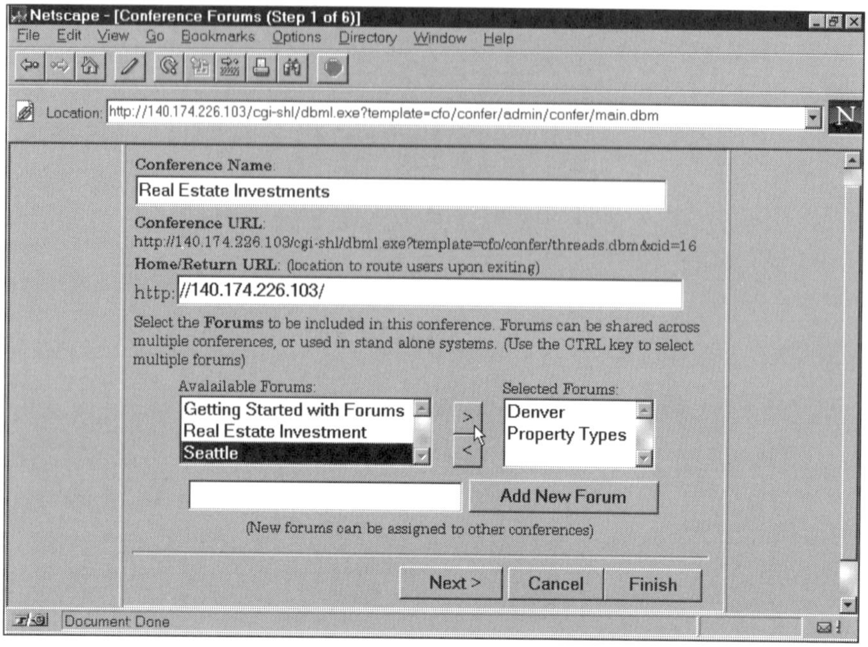

Figure 17.10: Start three forums in the *Real Estate Investments* conference.

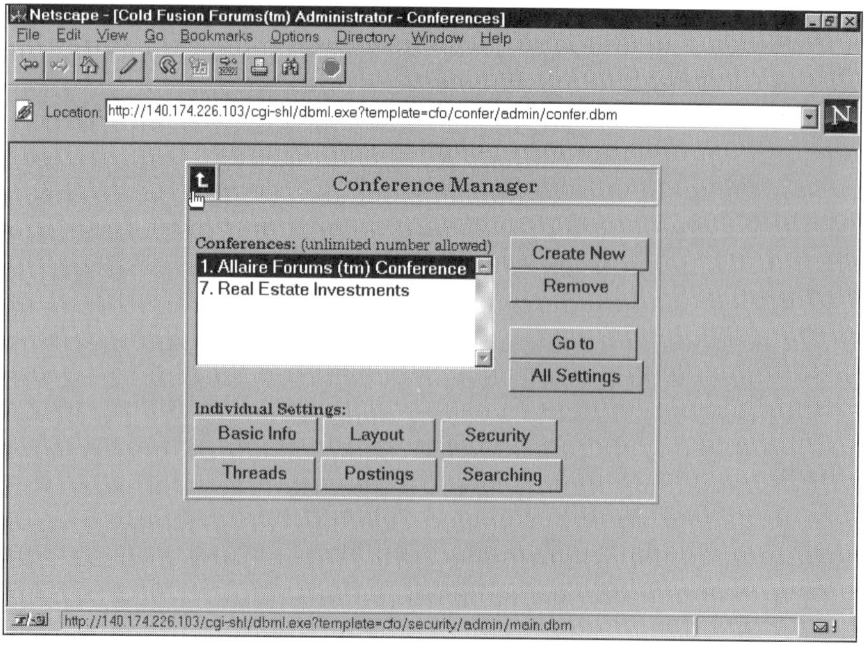

Figure 17.11: Tune your conference with the bottom buttons and return to the main menu.

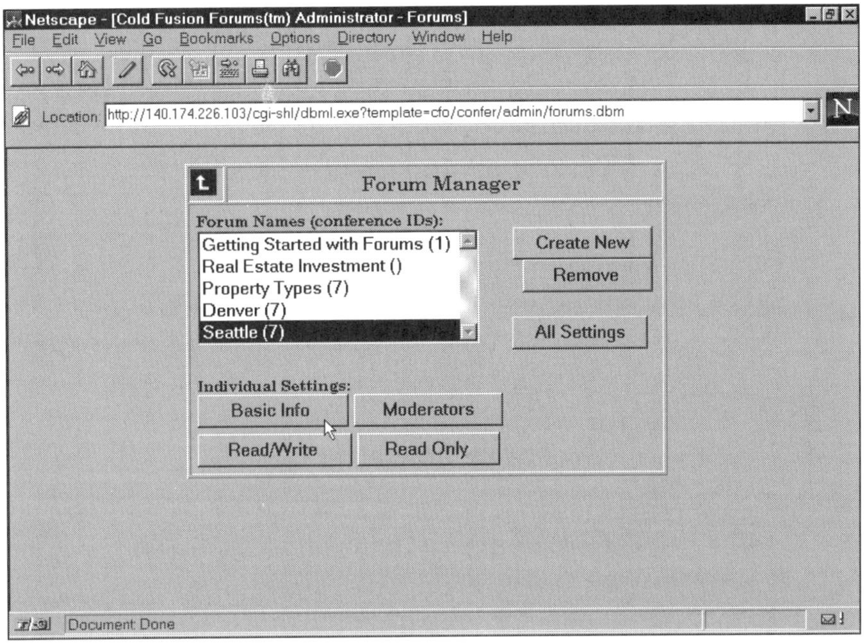

Figure 17.12: Tune the forums.

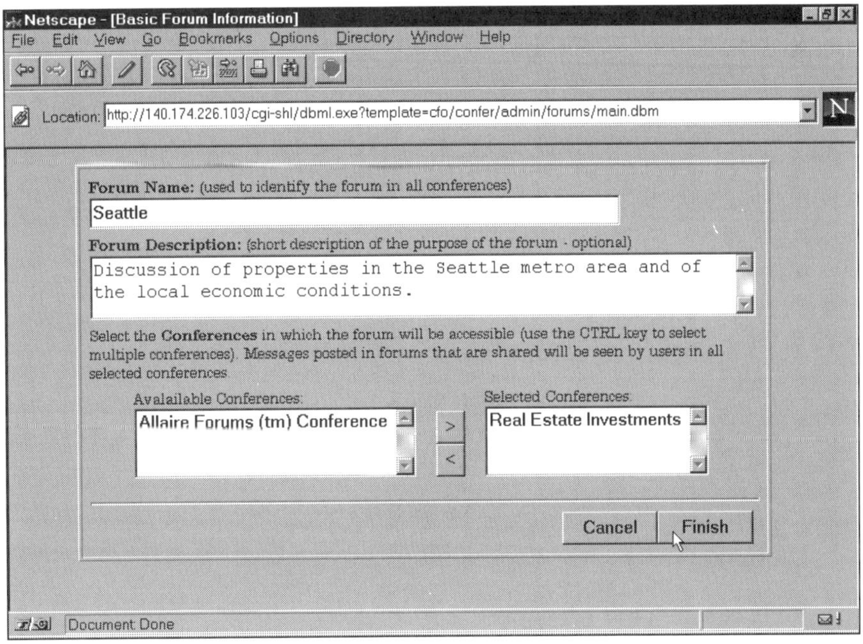

Figure 17.13: Add information on the forum and return to the prior menu.

forums are ready for action. Close the administrative function of Allaire Forums.

Next access the forums as a participant. You will have to enter the proper network address. Try:

```
../../cgi-shl/dbml.exe?template=cfo/confer/threads.dbm&cid=7
```

or

```
000.000.000.000 (your IP number)
```

The number 7 in the first address indicates the number assigned to the conference. If these procedures don't seem to work, it may be for one of the following reasons:

- You're not connected to a network.
- You don't have a Web server running.
- You are in *Open File* mode with your browser.

Once you connect properly, you will see something like the chart of forums and threads shown in Figure 17.14.

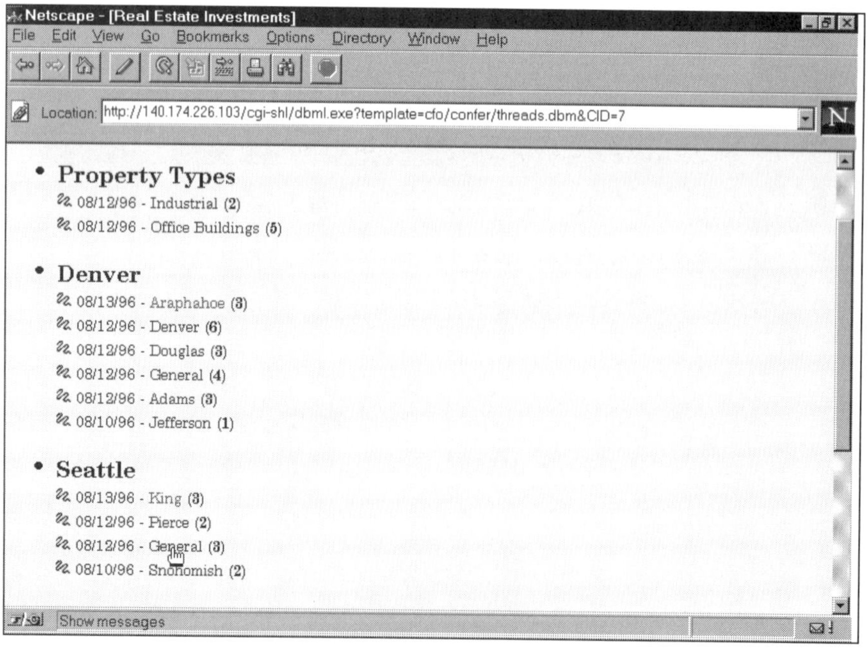

Figure 17.14: The forums and threads.

Choose the thread *General* under the Seattle forum. This thread shows three messages with the first words of each message displayed (see Figure 17.15).

Click on one of the messages in the list of postings, and it will take you to the full message (see Figure 17.16).

You can read the message and post a reply. You will get the message form (see Figure 17.17).

Write a reply message and post it (see Figure 17.18).

Now you have added another message to the thread (see Figure 17.19).

Finally, you can start a new thread, say one for Salt Lake City (see Figure 17.20).

As you can see, it's easy to use Allaire Forums either as the conference manager or as a forum participant.

Summary—Allaire Forums Allaire Forums is the first of a series of functions that Allaire plans to introduce in its Cold Fusion series.

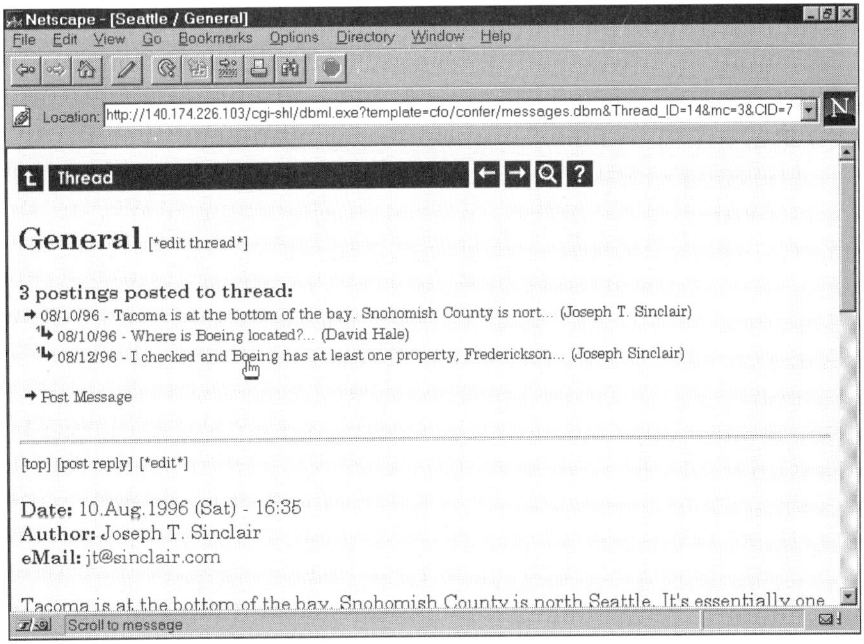

Figure 17.15: Messages as posted.

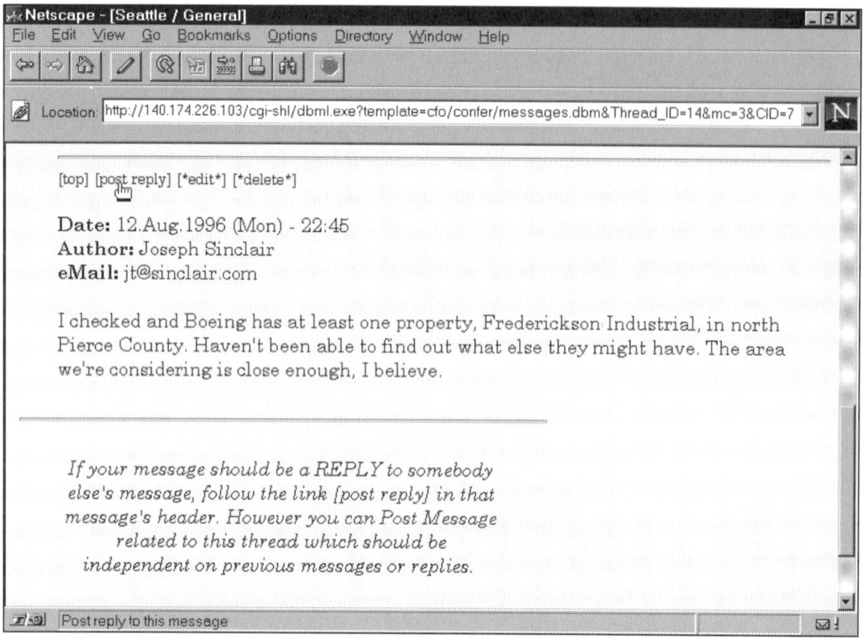

Figure 17.16: Full message.

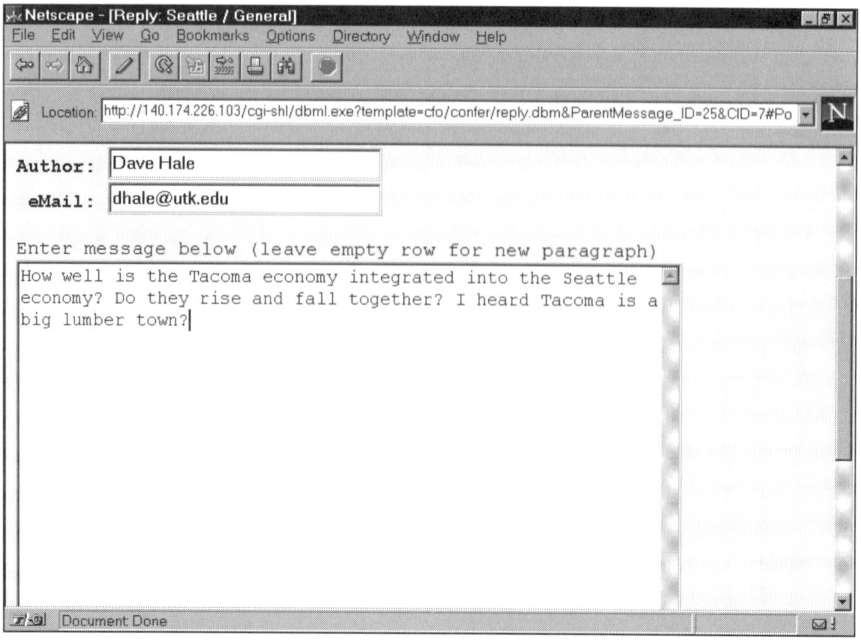

Figure 17.17: Write a reply.

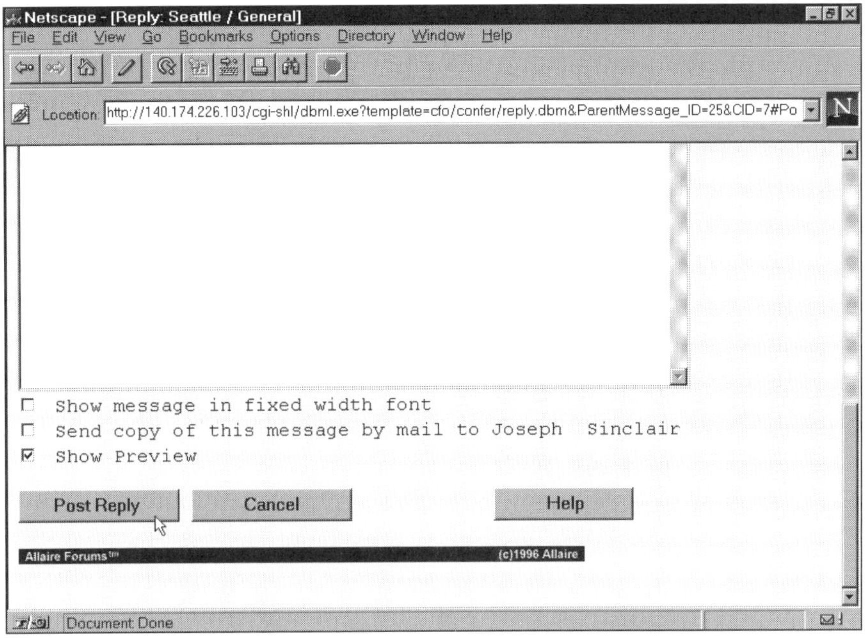

Figure 17.18: Post the reply.

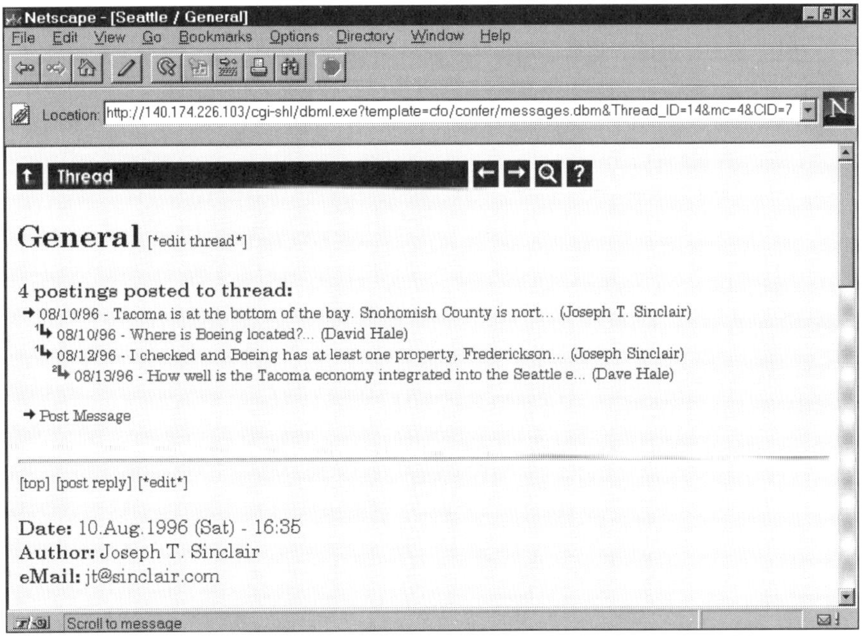

Figure 17.19: A new message on the thread.

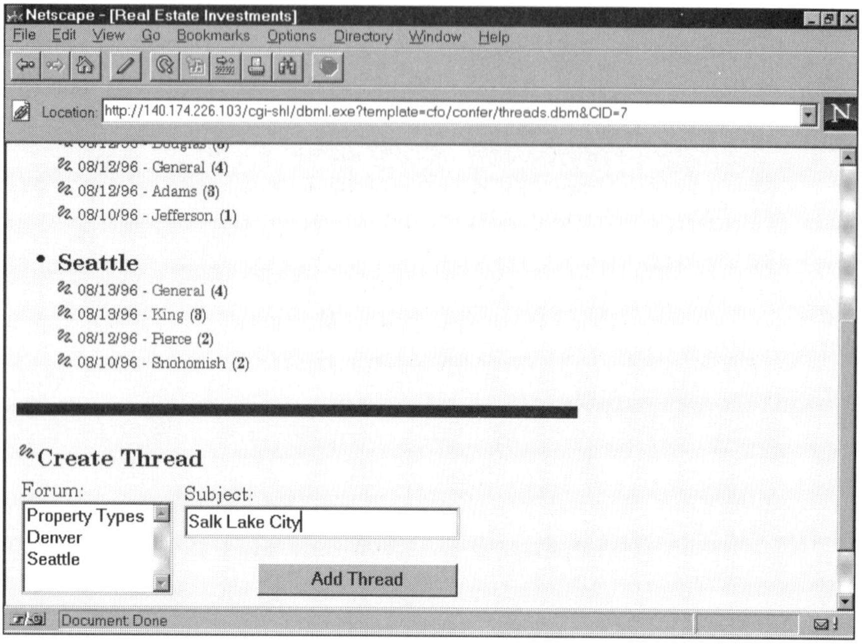

Figure 17.20: Start a new thread.

(Cold Fusion is a Web-database development tool.) After it is set up, Allaire Forums is easy to administer and easily used by forum participants. Because it is a Web program—programmed with CGI scripts—you need a Web server to make it operate. You also need Cold Fusion and Perl Win 32 to make it operate (Perl Win 32 is bundled with WebSite). The combination of Cold Fusion and WebSite is easy to install and use. Allaire Forums is a useful groupware addition.

Netmanage Forums

The Allaire Forums program is an easy-to-operate and effective program, but it operates through the Web using CGI scripts. That's almost like a workaround. After all, there is an Internet protocol for conferences, and it's the one Usenet uses for newsgroups (discussion groups): Network News Transport Protocol (NNTP). You can't use Usenet for your private conferences, but there's no reason you can't use NNTP and an NNTP server. In fact, Netmanage offers the Intranet Forum Server, which is an NNTP server. You can access it with any news reader such as the one included in the Netscape browser (see Figure 17.21).

There's no reason to include instruction in this book regarding the use of Usenet, because it is a feature of every basic Internet book. The use of Netmanage's Intranet Forums Server on your intranet, or even on the Internet, works much the same as Usenet. The only difference is that you will have to set up the server.

The Forum Server, a multithreaded news server, complies with the Internet standard for Usenet news servers (NNTP), giving it some distinct advantages:

- Any Usenet-compliant client (reader) can be used to access the forums. Newsreaders are built in to the Netscape Navigator and Microsoft Internet Explorer. There is no need to install yet another client on your desktop computer.

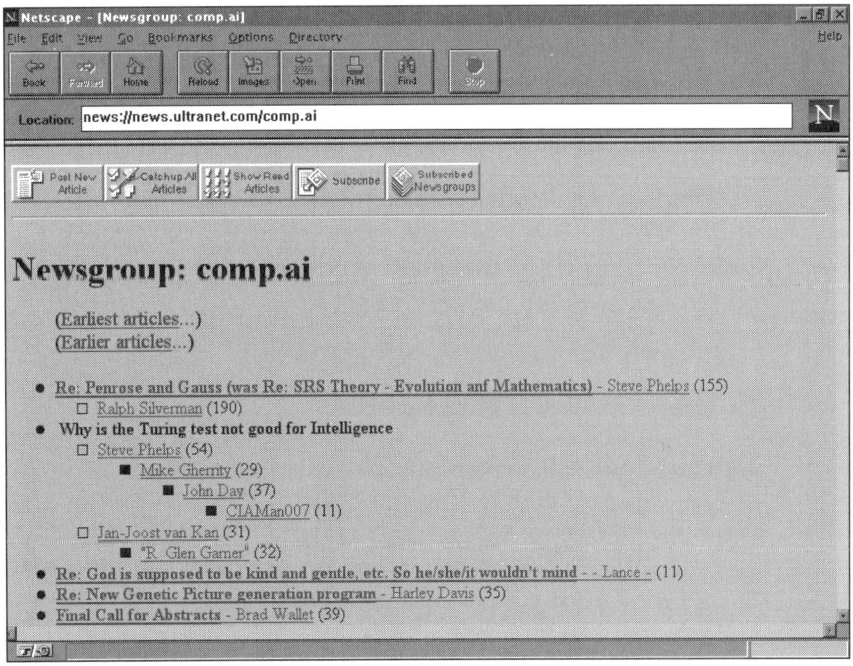

Figure 17.21: Newsreader in Netscape browser.

- You can attach your news server to a feed from an ISP. This means your employees can have access to the thousands of Usenet news groups on the Internet (or just some of them, if you prefer). This opens up another rich information resource.
- NNTP is highly reliable. It has been around for years and has been refined to perfection.
- The Forum Server runs as a service on the Windows NT platform, which means that it starts automatically when the system is booted. Also, it uses minimal system resources on your server computer.

Once you have installed the server, you need to set up access levels and then create the groups you wish to host on your news server. To create a new group, open a DOS window and change to the *C:\nmservers* directory.

Next, type *NEWSCTL NEWGROUP group.name rest creator* where *group.name* is the name you want the group to have. The *rest* parameter and the *creator* parameters are optional. The rest parameter can have one of three values:

- y—New postings to the group are allowed.
- n—New postings to the group are *not* allowed.
- m—The group is moderated. New postings are first sent to a moderator, who decides if they should be added to the group.

When you have added the group, you need to issue the command *NEWSCTL RELOAD* to make your changes take effect. More details about configuring the server are provided with the documentation, but the server is not difficult to set up.

A REAL-TIME CONFERENCE

Netscape CoolTalk by InSoft is a real-time audio and data conferencing program designed to work over a TCP/IP network. CoolTalk's audio conferencing feature enables users to speak and listen simultaneously (*full-duplex*). Cool Talk also includes chat and white board programs. A *chat* tool lets you hold a real-time text conversation with someone else over an intranet or the Internet. The *white board* provides a shared space on each user's desktop for real-time drawing, graphics sharing, and even text sharing.

Netscape distributes CoolTalk as a helper application to the Navigator Web browser and plans to distribute a plug-in for using the CoolTalk technology directly within the browser. To gain an appreciation for the potential usefulness of CoolTalk, imagine that two real-estate developers are considering the purchase of income property in the Seattle metro area. Bill lives in Detroit and Hugo lives in Atlanta. The pair decide to have a CoolTalk conference to discuss the prospects in the area. Bill's computer does not have a sound card so they elect to use the chat tool and white board instead of the audio feature.

A CoolTalk Conference

At the agreed-upon time, Bill launches CoolTalk and attempts to begin a conference. To do this, he chooses *Start* from the Conference menu, as shown in Figure 17.22.

The *Open Conference* dialog box appears. Either Bill must know the domain name of Hugo's computer, or Hugo must be available on an IS411 public server (discussed later). Bill knows Hugo's domain name is real.estate.com, and his user ID on his Windows NT workstation is HUGO. Bill types in `HUGO@real.estate.com.` He then clicks the *OK* button (see Figure 17.23).

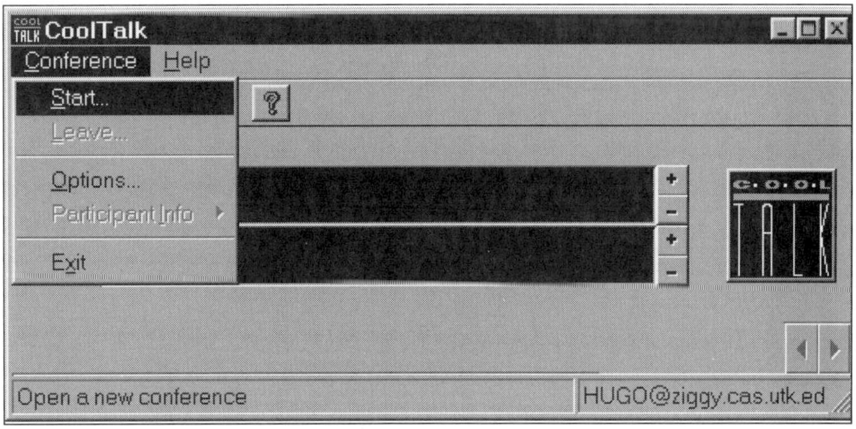

Figure 17.22: Choose *Start* from the Conference menu in CoolTalk.

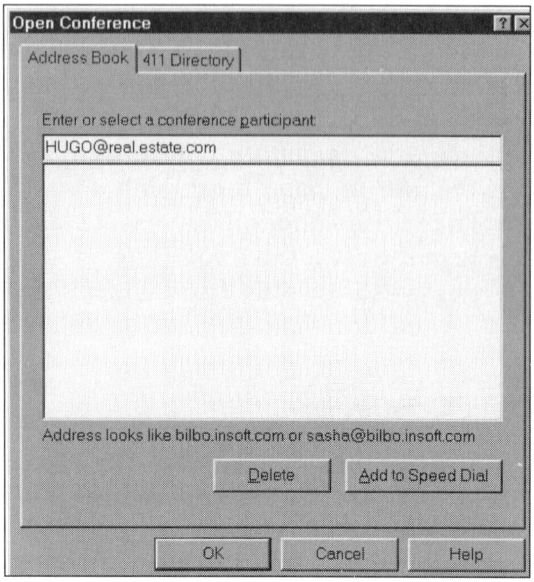

Figure 17.23: Type in the domain name of your correspondent's computer preceded by the user ID and the @ sign. Then click *OK*.

COOLTALK MINI-FAQ
WHAT IS AN IS411 PUBLIC SERVER?

An IS411 Server is a service that enables you to find other CoolTalk users. You can also provide your name and address to other users on that server. In order to use an IS411 server, you will need to supply its host address to CoolTalk. Netscape provides an IS411 server, which you can use to find someone with whom to talk.

So I just type in the e-mail address of the person I want to talk to?

No! CoolTalk provides a peer-to-peer connection. This means that your Internet-attached desktop computer is connecting to the computer of the person with whom you are conferencing. If you are conferencing with someone on a Unix, Windows 95, or Windows NT machine, that person will have a user ID assigned. Although this has the look of an Internet e-mail address (i.e., user@domain.com), there is no way of knowing whether the computer on which the person is conferencing has a mail server. If the computer is Windows or Unix, you will just enter the computer's domain name or IP address. This is not an e-mail address.

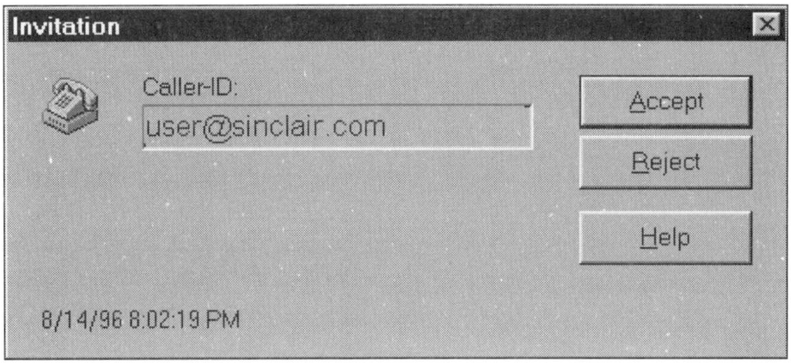

Figure 17.24: Alert for an incoming call.

As soon as Bill clicks OK, the box in Figure 17.24 appears on Hugo's screen, provided he is running CoolTalk or CoolTalk *WatchDog*, which alerts CoolTalk of incoming calls.

If Hugo does not answer the call within about 20 seconds, the connection is dropped, and a missed call message like the one in Figure 17.25 is displayed.

Hugo is at his computer, so he simply clicks on the *Accept* button to begin the conference. The screen in Figure 17.26 is the standard CoolTalk interface. Notice that there is now a picture of Hugo on the right side of the window (the picture is an optional feature).

Bill clicks on the typewriter icon in the main CoolTalk window to initiate a chat session. He types his first message into the bottom half of the screen (*Personal Notepad*). After he is finished typing, he clicks the send button in the toolbar. The message moves from his *Personal Notepad* to the session *Log File* window (see Figure 17.27). Hugo can

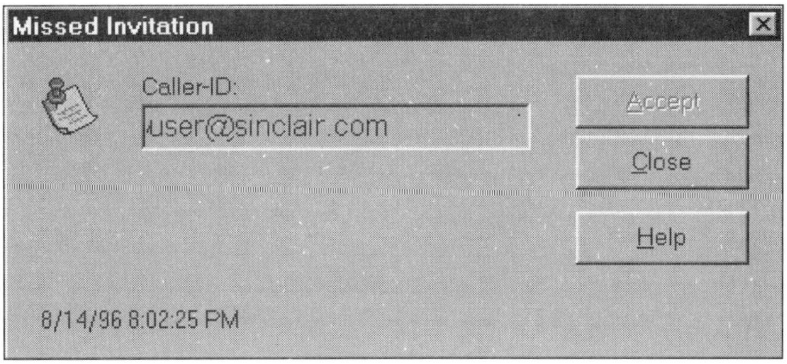

Figure 17.25: When your computer is running CoolTalk or Watch Dog and you miss an incoming call, CoolTalk displays this message.

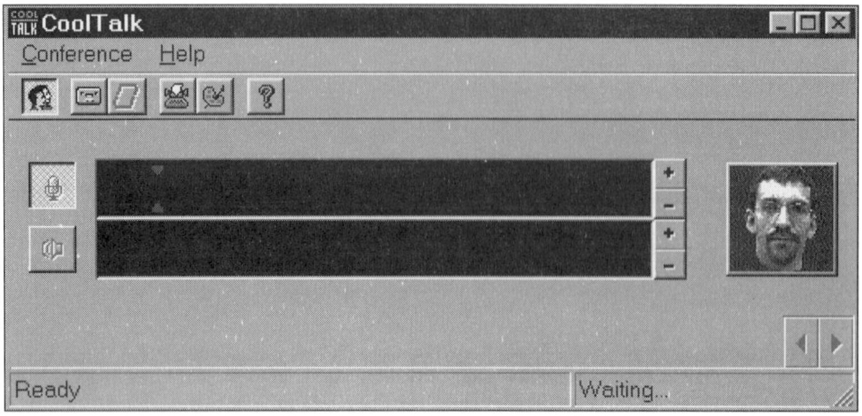

Figure 17.26: When you see the other party's face, you know the conference has begun.

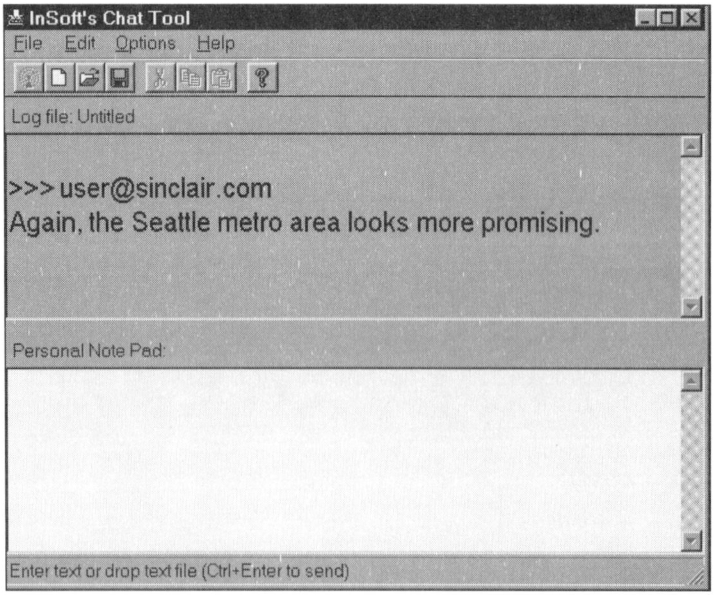

Figure 17.27: The view from the screen after the correspondent's message has been typed and the *Send* button has been clicked.

now see the message too. CoolTalk automatically adds the user@domain.name information as a preface to each transmission.

Hugo types his response inquiry (*What's the cap rate there?*) into his *Personal Notepad* (see Figure 17.28).

When Hugo clicks the send button, his message moves to the *Log File* (top) part of the window, and both parties can see the message as it appears in Figure 17.29.

Bill responds to Hugo's inquiry about the cap rates in the Seattle area by offering to put them on the CoolTalk white board, as shown in Figure 17.30.

Hugo tells Bill to go ahead and post the numbers to the white board (see Figure 17.31). (All of Bill's comments will appear in the *Log File* in the remainder of the figures, with Hugo's responses in the *User Notepad*.)

Bill clicks on the main CoolTalk window, then clicks on the *White board* icon (the icon with a palette on it). He chooses the text tool from the toolbar, clicks in the white board window, and begins typing in the cap rates. Each line is transmitted to Hugo's screen as soon as Bill presses the *Enter* key. Figure 17.32 shows what both people see when he is finished.

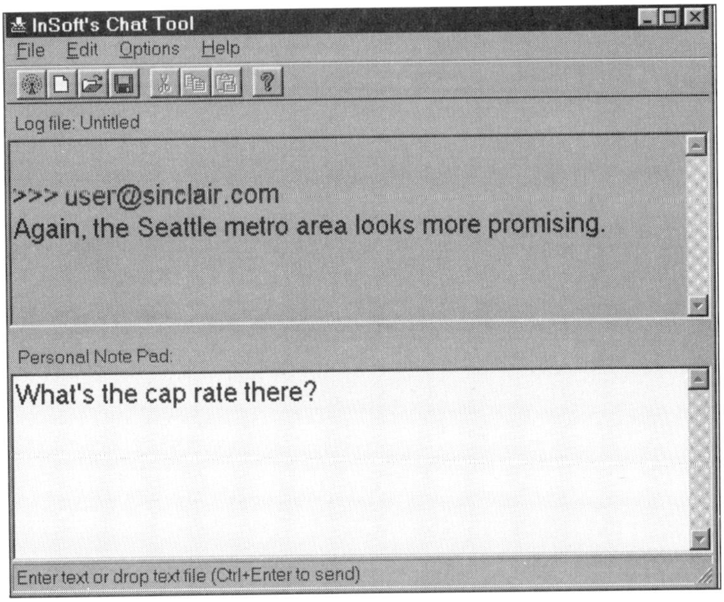

Figure 17.28: Message being typed but before being sent.

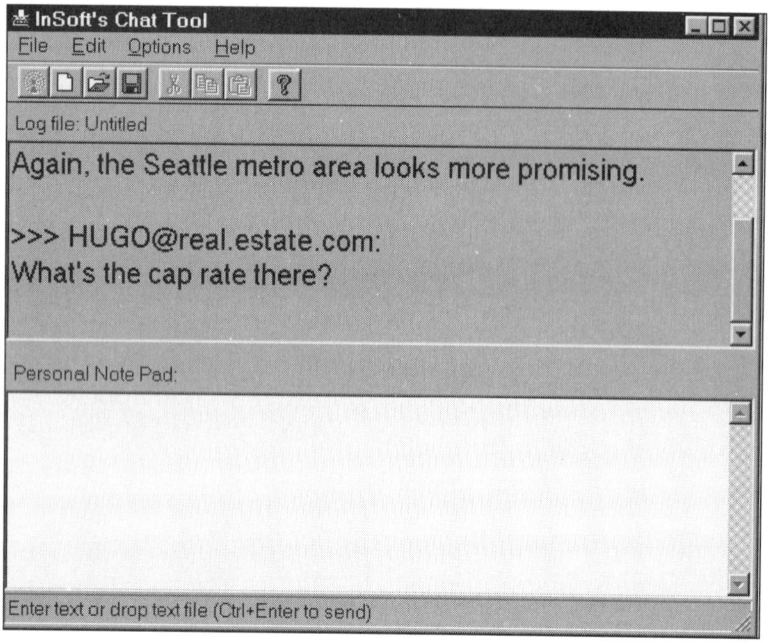

Figure 17.29: The response appears in the top of the chat Window after it has been sent.

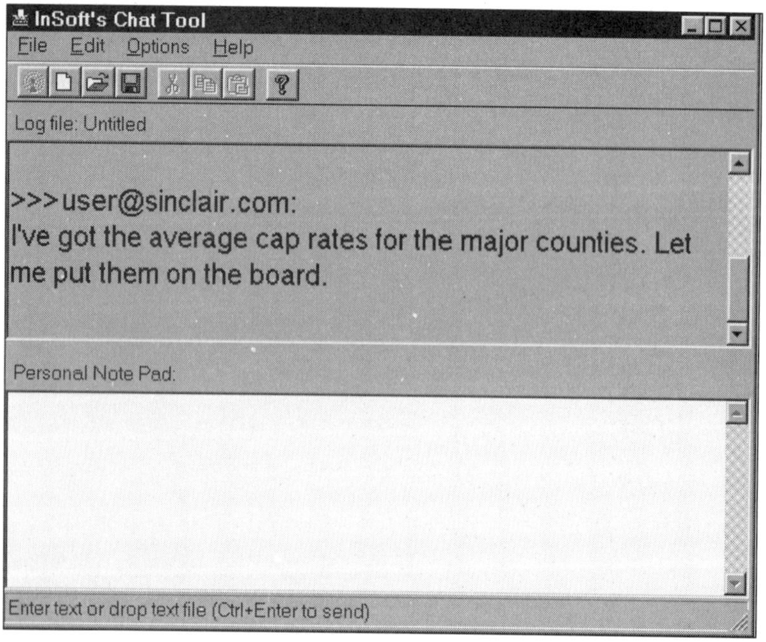

Figure 17.30: Offer to put information on the white board.

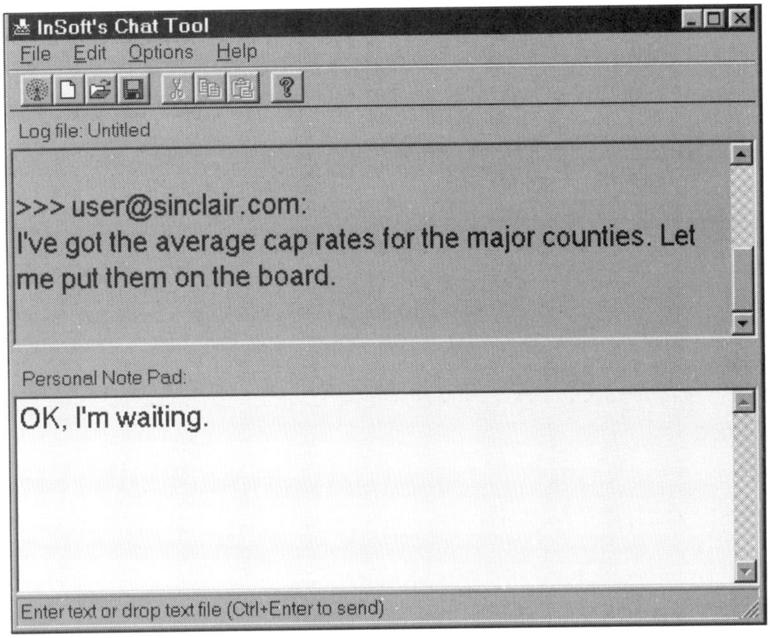

Figure 17.31: Ready to use the white board.

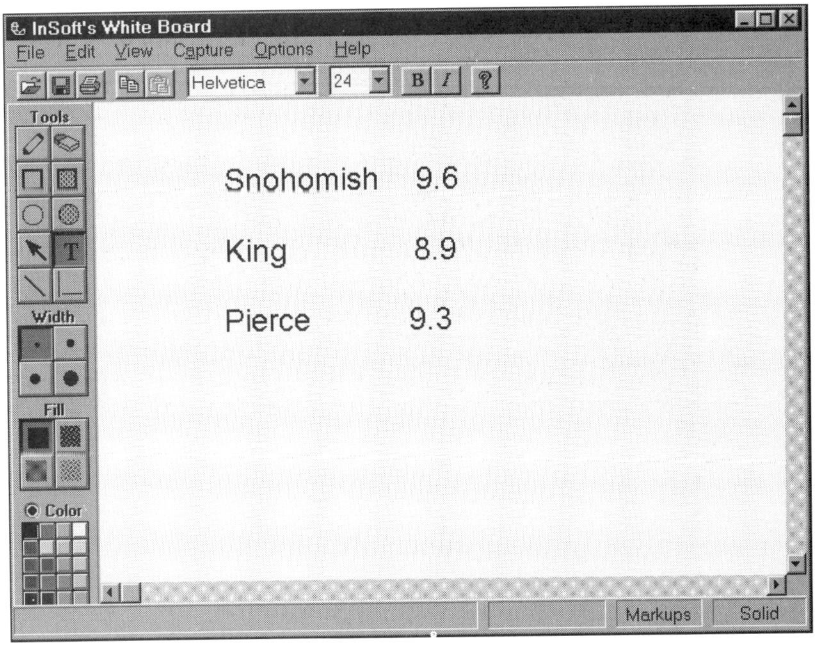

Figure 17.32: The white board is used to display the cap rate numbers.

When finished, Bill clicks back on the chat window and types his commentary on the numbers (shown in the *Log File* section in Figure 17.33). Hugo's response is shown in the *User Notepad* of the same figure.

Bill responds to the concern expressed by Hugo, and Hugo asks where Pierce county is located (see Figure 17.34).

Bill describes where Pierce County is (see Figure 17.35), and then draws a sketch of the region on the white board to add context to his answer (see Figure 17.36).

Hugo is not clear on some details about the map so he switches back to chat to ask for clarification (see Figure 17.37).

Bill provides the clarification in Figure 17.38, and Hugo asks where Boeing is.

The exchange continues to its conclusion as shown in Figures 17.39 through 17.40.

When they are finished with the conference, they simply choose *Leave* from the Conference menu.

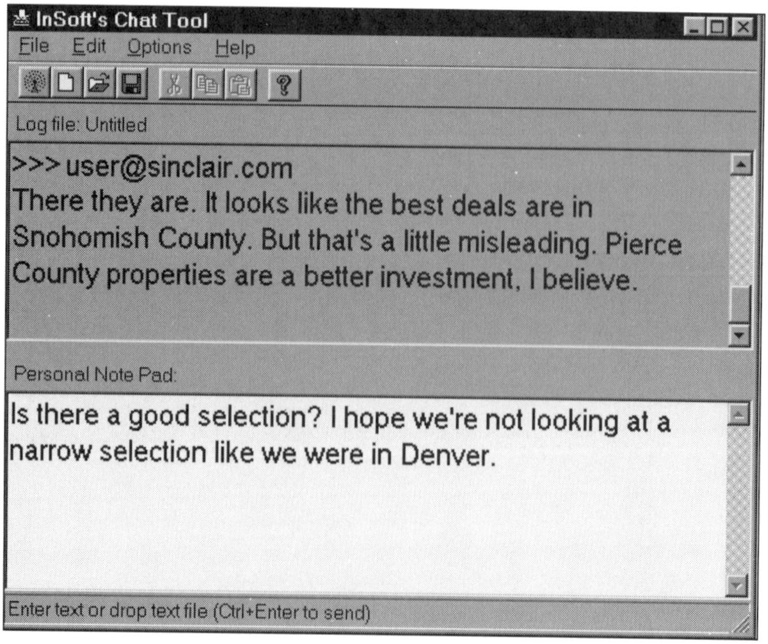

Figure 17.33: Comments on the cap rates. Response is shown in the *User Notepad.*

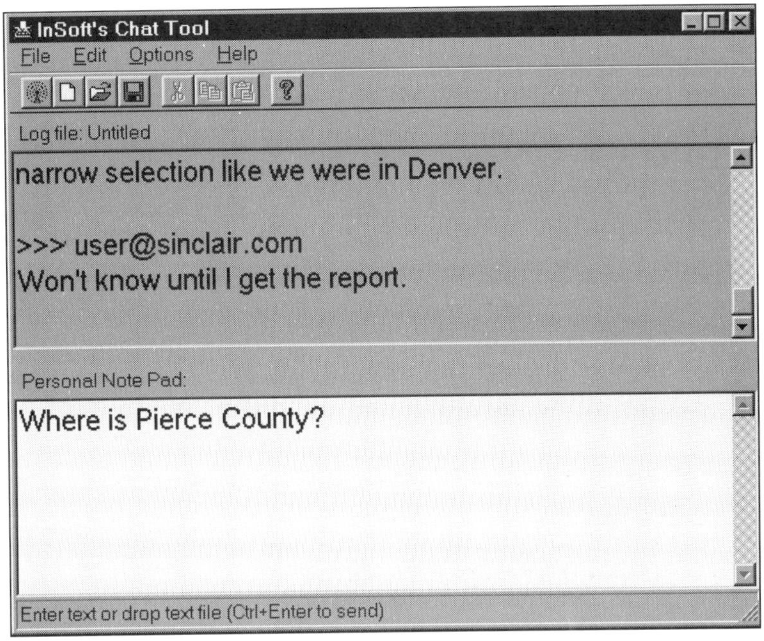

Figure 17.34: A question about Pierce County.

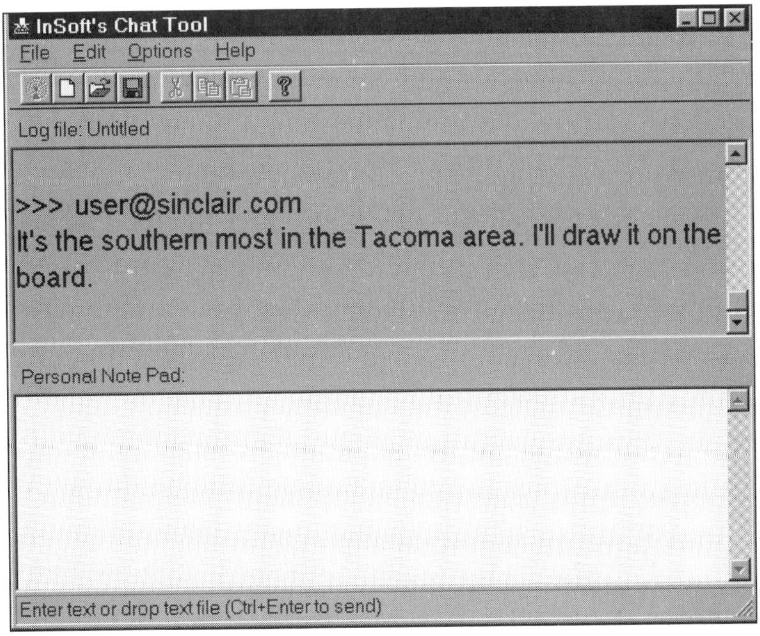

Figure 17.35: Answer and offer to draw a map.

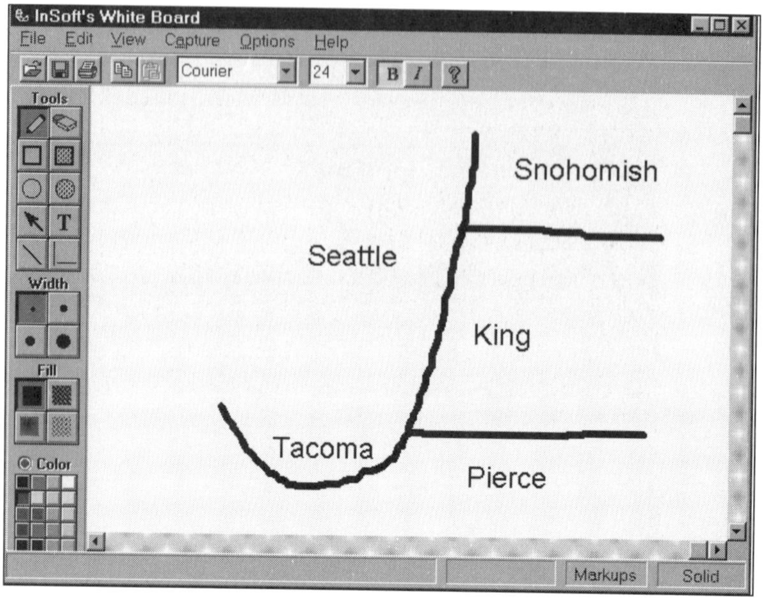

Figure 17.36: Sketch of the Seattle region on the white board.

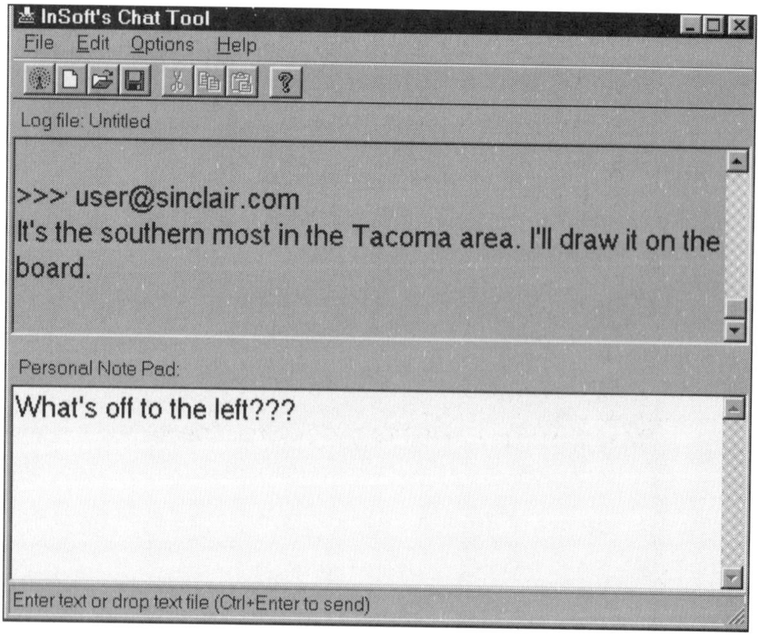

Figure 17.37: Request for more details about the map.

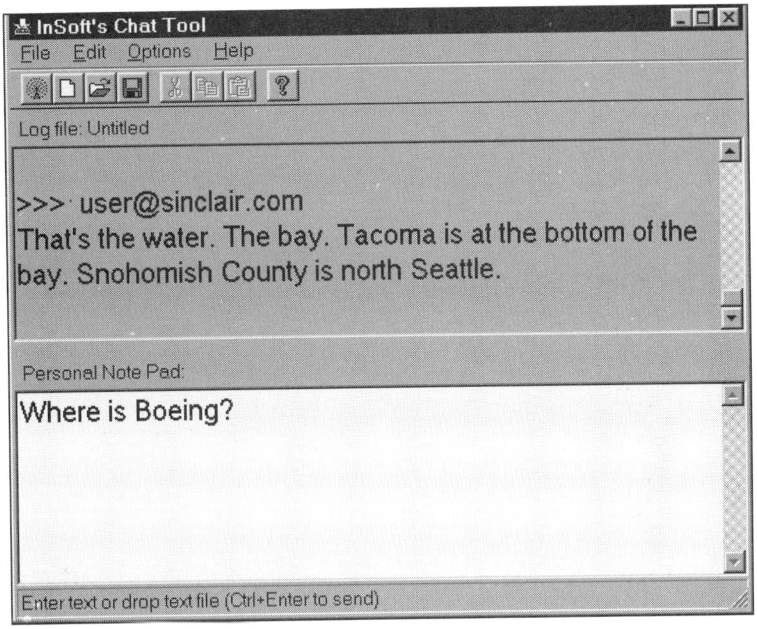

Figure 17.38: More conversation.

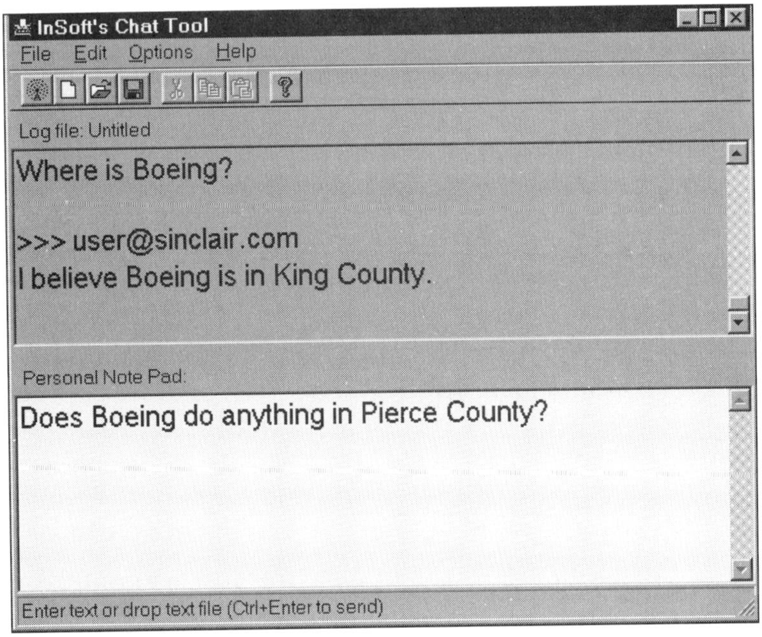

Figure 17.39: The exchange continues.

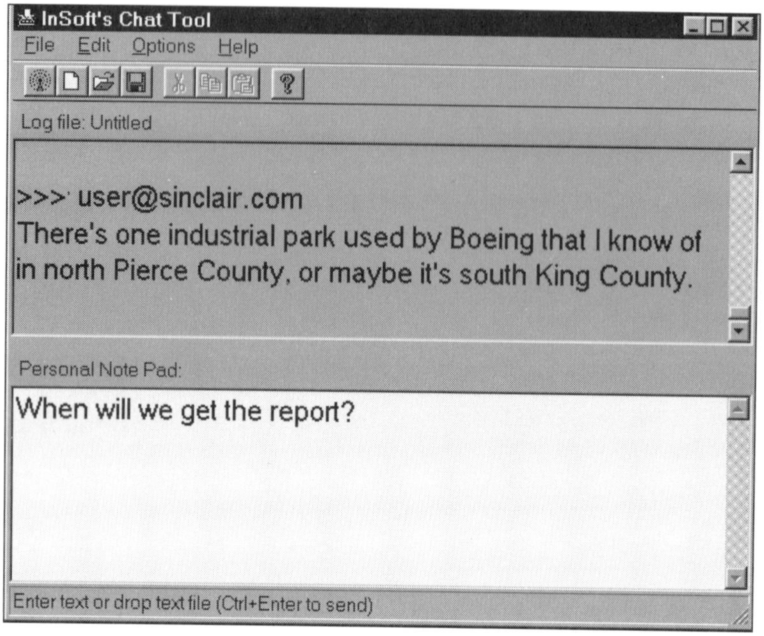

Figure 17.40: The last exchange.

GRAPHICS

In addition to drawing and text, you can use the white board to share graphics. Copy a graphic from anywhere, and paste it onto the white board. Your correspondent will see it soon after you paste it.

The combination of CoolTalk's white board and audio conferencing capabilities takes remote conferencing to a new level. Microsoft has also introduced a program like CoolTalk for its browser. The ability to draw a picture on someone else's screen to describe what you are saying enhances the conferencing experience. It brings participants one step closer to working as if they were in the same room when they might be half-way around the world from each other. For instance, a Help Desk technician in San Francisco can use the white board to look at a the configuration screen (i.e., screen shot graphic) of a user in Minneapolis to troubleshoot problems.

SUMMARY

There is no shortage of easy-to-use conferencing programs for you to use for your intranet or even over the Internet for dispersed co-workers. Whether real-time or convenient-time, conferencing is easy to install, operate, and use. And it's a great groupware technique.

Chapter 18

PUBLISHING

Business publishing is undergoing a metamorphosis. Dynamic documents such as employee manuals and directories are no longer trapped in static media such as books. Now you can put your manuals on your intranet (internal Web site) and update them at will. Your intranet becomes a 24-hour-a-day information center for employees, allowing them to access the information day or night to get the most up-to-date information. This information is important to your organization's continuing success. You need a Web server that is reliable, easy to set up, and easy to maintain. Some of the new generation of Web servers include tools that check your site for bad links, provide graphical maps of your site's layout, and have built-in CGI scripts. The first section of this chapter describes how to set up *WebSite,* an easy-to-use Web server that runs on either Windows 95 or Windows NT. By following this example you'll see many of the issues you'll encounter in setting up your Web site. There are lots of other servers, but the situations described here are likely to be the same as those with other products.

The Web changes business publishing, but for the foreseeable future there will remain a need for hard-copy documentation as well. Documents for printed distribution can still benefit from your intranet. A collaborative editing tool (authoring program also known as a collaboration program) lets you leverage the power of your desktop computer and network. An authoring program associates changes to a document with the people who make them during the editing process. You need to be able to consolidate changes between two copies of the same document as well as add formatting to the documents so that they will look their best and be easy to read.

You have a variety of options. Your word processing package may have sophisticated document collaboration features. For instance, recent versions of Microsoft Word enable you to compare multiple revisions of the same document and accept or decline suggestions from other editors. But word processors do not take care of these processes automatically nor do they use your intranet. ON Technology's *Common Knowledge* gives you strong word processing capabilities combined with an intuitive authoring environment that works over your intranet. The second section of this chapter details how people can work together to produce a document in Common Knowledge, which runs on Windows.

WEB PUBLISHING WITH WEBSITE

Publishing on the Web doesn't have to be difficult. The current generation of Web servers helps you produce full-featured Web sites without your having to know any programming languages, markup languages, or scripting languages. You do not need to waste your time trying to figure out the best way to write CGI scripts. You can create Web documents with conversion programs, and you can set up WebSite almost effortlessly.

WebSite is one of the easiest Web servers to set up and run. It provides a graphical map of your site to ease maintenance and a built-in capability for handling CGI scripts, interactive forms, searching, and page counting.

Using WebSite

You can use WebSite straight out of the box to make a site with some big-time intranet functionality. All you need to get started is an IP address. Once the IP address is plugged in and the server is started, you have a Web site. The section below gives you details on how to plug in your IP address, set up a portion of your site so that only certain people can get access, create a searchable index of your site, and make sure that every link in every document on your site is good.

Hooking Up Your Site

Your server computer must have an IP address before you launch WebSite. If you are on a TCP/IP intranet, that is taken care of. If you are connecting to the Internet, you will need to establish the connection and be assigned your IP address before beginning by following these steps:

1. Start up the Server Properties executable that is installed with WebSite (see Figure 18.1).
2. If you don't have an IP address and you will be running the Web server for only yourself, make up an IP address and type it in (see Figure 18.2). If you have a dynamically assigned IP address (i.e., you have a different IP address each time you connect to your ISP), determine what it is after you get online, and type it in for a temporary online session. If you have a permanent IP address, type it in the Server Name box.
3. Click the *Update* button, then the *Close* button.

Congratulations! You have a Web site.

Locking Out Unwanted Visitors

This section describes how to control access to one portion of your site by enforcing password authentication. You might do this to allow premium clients added services like extended documentation. You can also set up part of the site for access by employees in your finance department only, for instance. This type of password authentication is useful for blocking out unwanted casual visitors, but should not be relied upon as the sole source of protection for highly sensitive data. Applications that involve confidential information should be put on a secure Web server, which encrypts the information sent between the client and the server. O'Reilly and Netscape both offer secure Web servers. See the section in Chapter 11 on VeriSign for more information about secure Web servers.

You can apply access control in WebSite to any URL path, but not to individual documents. If applied, it affects the URL path (i.e., the current folder) and all subpaths (subfolders) below it. WebSite allows you to create individual user IDs as well as groups of users who can be

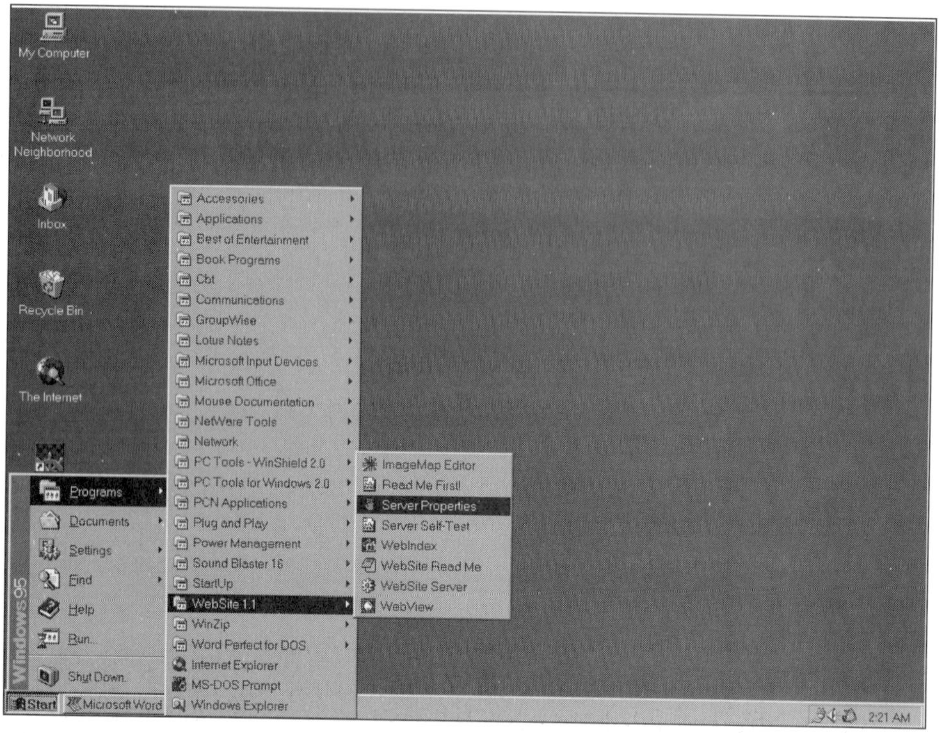

Figure 18.1: The Server Properties program is found in the WebSite folder of your *Start* menu.

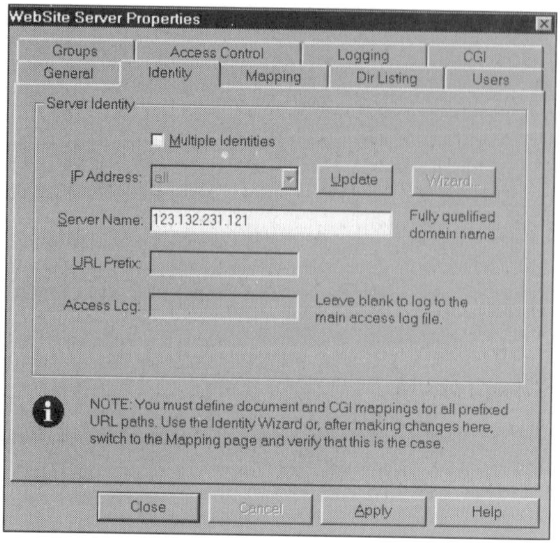

Figure 18.2: Enter your IP address.

granted access to certain parts of your site. Access can be granted or denied by IP address or domain name as well.

The steps below explain how the XYZ Trading Company can create an area for the private departmental policies and planning information on its Web server that is accessible by only the members of the Export department. Using the features described above, Spencer, the XYZ Corporate Webmaster, can create an *Export* group. The members of the group (and no one else) will have access to the files in the *policies* folder.

1. Spencer begins by starting the Server Properties executable from the Start menu (see Figure 18.3).
2. Spencer selects the *Groups* tab in the Server Properties window, as shown in Figure 18.4. (*Realms* are a way of organizing your site's groups. This example uses the default realm in WebSite, Web Server.)

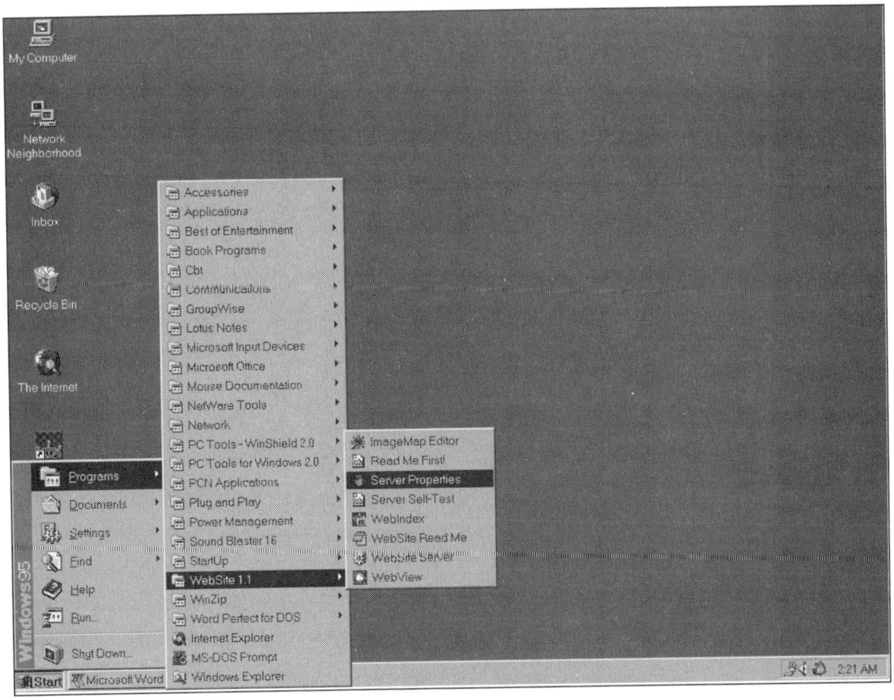

Figure 18.3: Launching the Server Properties program.

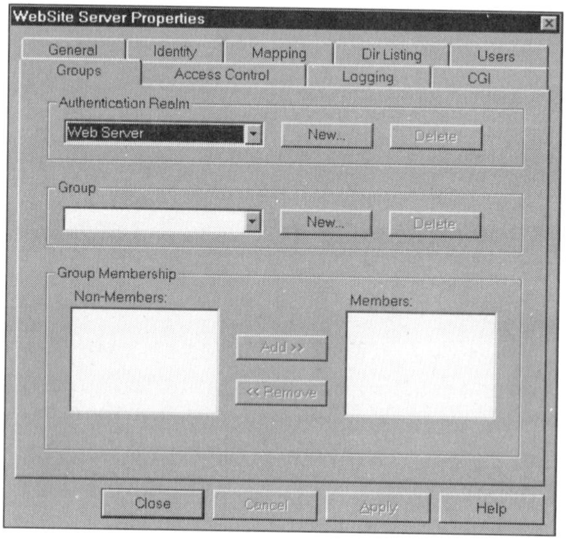

Figure 18.4: To create the *Export* group, choose the *Groups* tab.

3. He clicks the *New* button in the Group area of the window to create a new group. He then types in the name of the group (see Figure 18.5) and clicks the *OK* button.
4. Before he can add users to the new group, Spencer must create new user IDs for the people in the Export department: Melissa, Donald, Jane, Susan, and Michael. He clicks on the *Users* tab and then the *New* button in the User section of the window (see Figure 18.6).
5. Spencer types in the first user ID for Melissa and a password. He then clicks the *OK* button (see Figure 18.7).

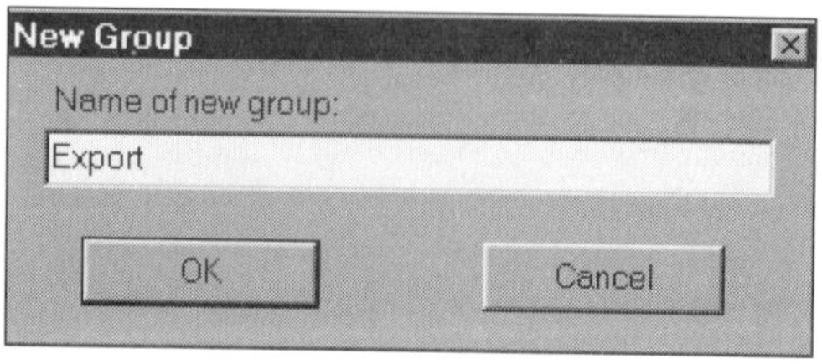

Figure 18.5: Entering the name of the new group.

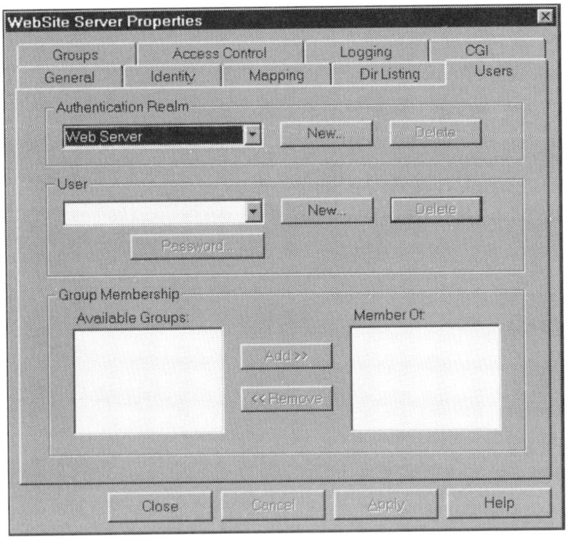

Figure 18.6: Click the new button to add a new user.

6. Spencer repeats the process for each of the team members.
7. Spencer then switches back to the Groups window by clicking the *Group* tab. He chooses the *Export* group from the Group menu. He clicks on the first user ID under *Non-Members* (Donald) and clicks the *Add* button (see Figures 18.8 and 18.9). This places Donald in the *Export* group.

Figure 18.7: The new user's password must be entered twice to confirm it is correct without being shown on the screen.

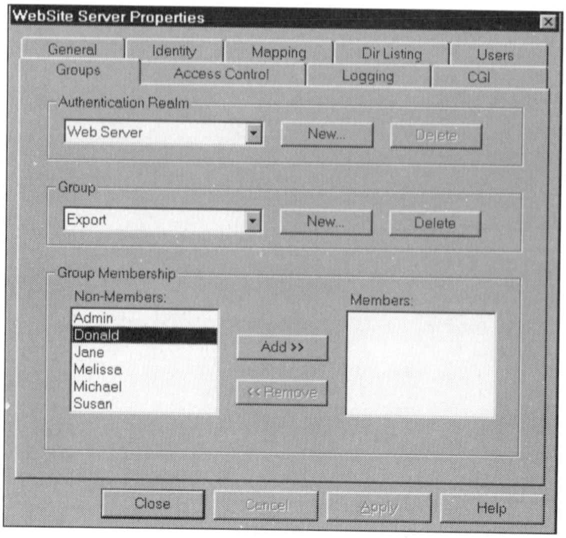

Figure 18.8: Donald is moved from the *Non-Members* box.

8. Spencer repeats step 7 for the remainder of the users until all the names are entered, as shown in Figure 18.10.
9. Now that the *Export* group is set up, Spencer can grant the group access to the *policies* directory. He clicks the *Access Control* tab. He needs to create a new URL Path, */policies*, so he clicks the *New* button, types in */policies* (see Figure 18.11) and clicks *OK*.
10. In the Authorized Users & Groups area, Spencer clicks *Add*. This opens a pop-up dialog box.
11. He selects the user or group (groups appear in brackets [ ]) that is to be allowed access to the selected URL path, in this case *[Export]*, and clicks *OK* (see Figure 18.12).
12. Only the users and groups that appear in the *Authorized Users* box are allowed access to the specified URL Path, unless no users or groups are listed at all. In that case, *everyone* is allowed access (subject to other possible access control methods such as IP address or host name filtering).

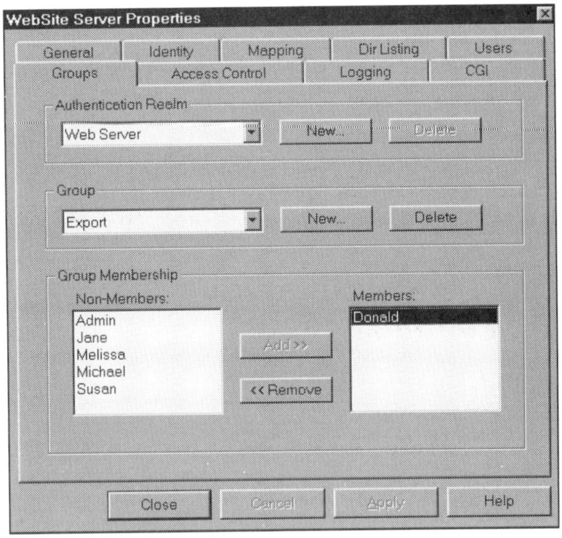

Figure 18.9: Donald is moved to the *Members* box.

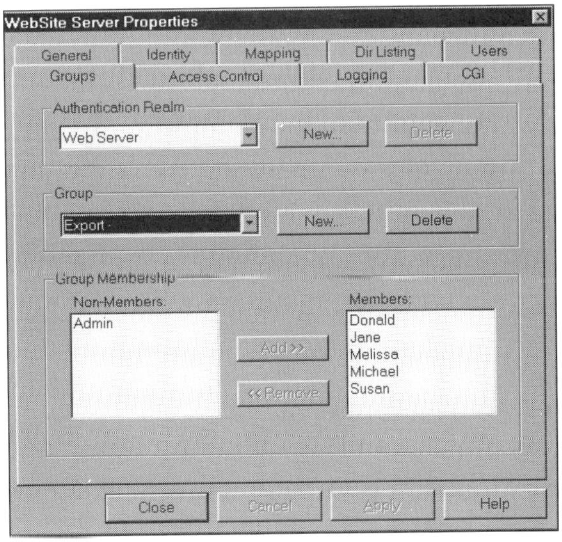

Figure 18.10: The *Export* group now contains all the user IDs.

13. When Donald wants to access the export department's policies area, the server now demands that he enter his user ID

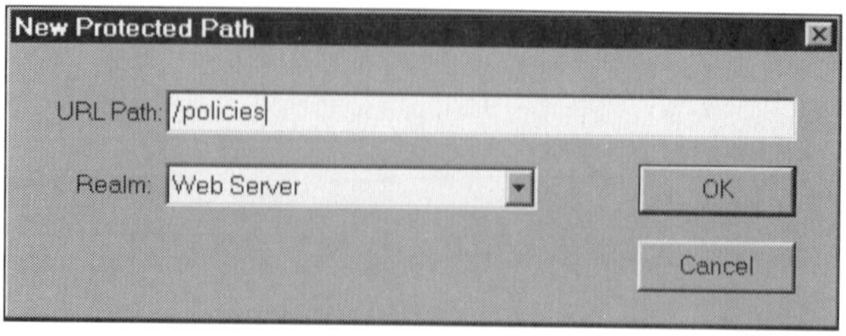

Figure 18.11: Adding the new URL Path, */policies*.

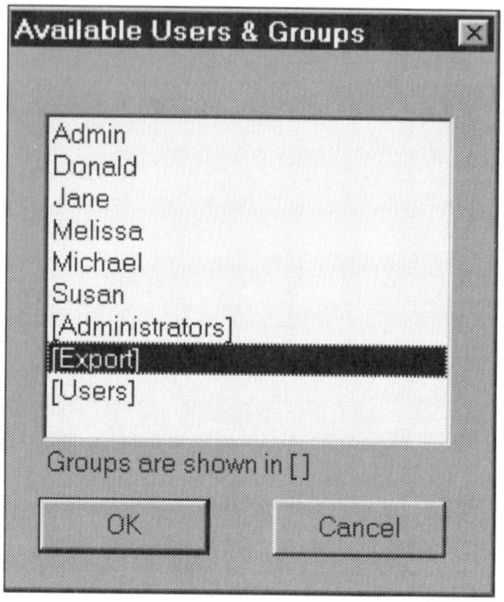

Figure 18.12: The *Export* group is authorized to access files in the */policies* folder.

and password as shown in Figure 18.13. Figures 18.14 and 18.15 show what users see when they enter incorrect and correct passwords.

Helping Out Visitors with Text Search

A Web site can quickly accumulate mountains of information on many topics. Well-planned and well-executed page design are essential to making a site with hundreds or thousands of links useful to visitors. Even with good design, though, finding a document in a large site can be tedious. Often the most effective way to find something is to let the search engine find it for you.

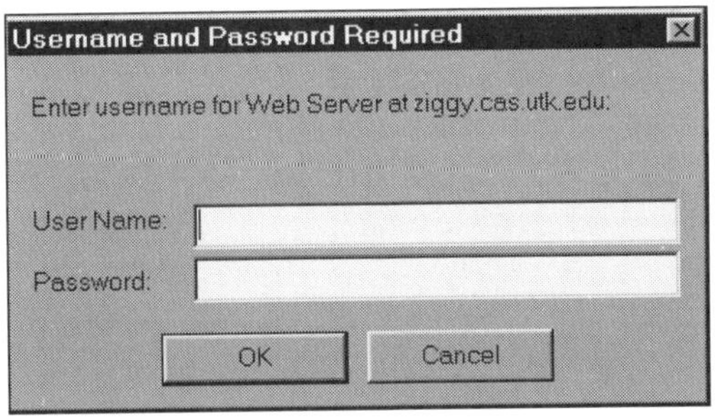

Figure 18.13: The server demands authentication.

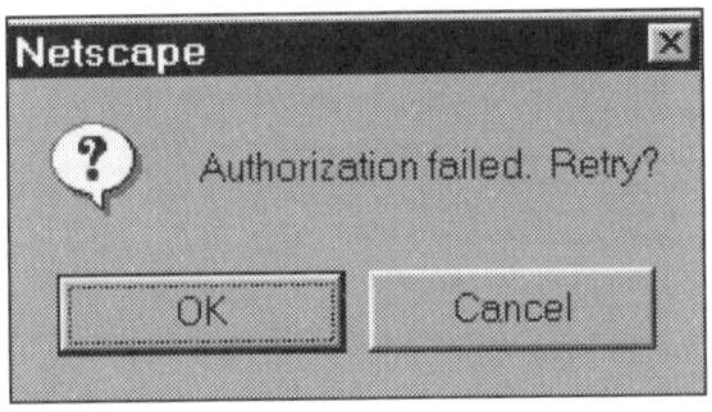

Figure 18.14: This is what a user who enters an invalid user ID or password sees.

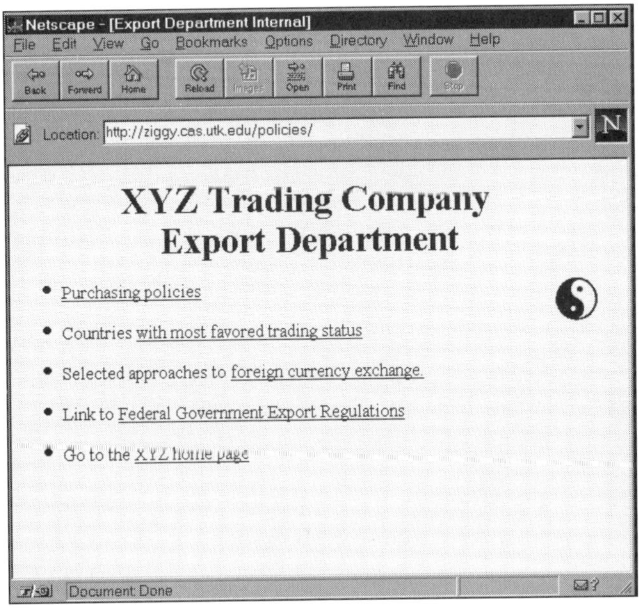

Figure 18.15: This is what Donald and other members of the *Export* group see after entering their user ID and password correctly.

WebSite includes a search engine and a tool used to index the contents of your site. The search engine is able to search much faster through an index than through each document. The steps below describe how to build an index that will cover the whole Web site. Spencer does have the option of indexing only parts of the site, if need be.

1. Spencer chooses the WebIndex tool from in the WebSite folder on the Start menu (see Figure 18.16).
2. The *WebIndex* screen appears. There are three tabbed sections in this screen. URLs on the left are excluded from the index; URLs on the right will be included (see Figure 18.17).
3. To include the whole site in this index, Spencer clicks the *All* >> button. Every URL path on the server is included. He then clicks in the *Index Name* box and types *XYZ Full Index* (see Figure 18.18).

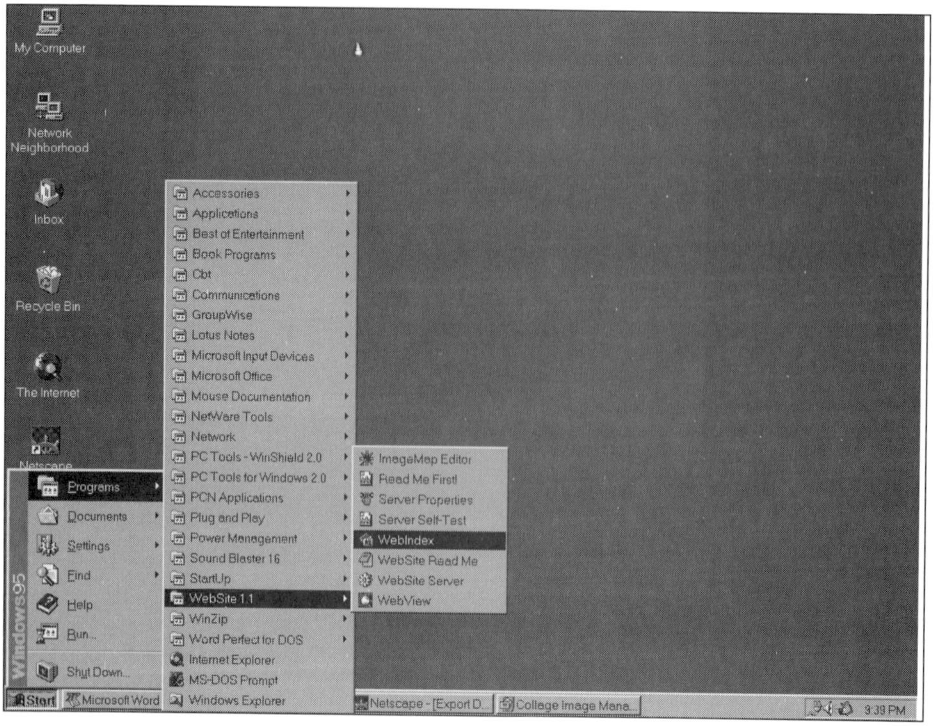

Figure 18.16: Choose WebIndex from the Start menu.

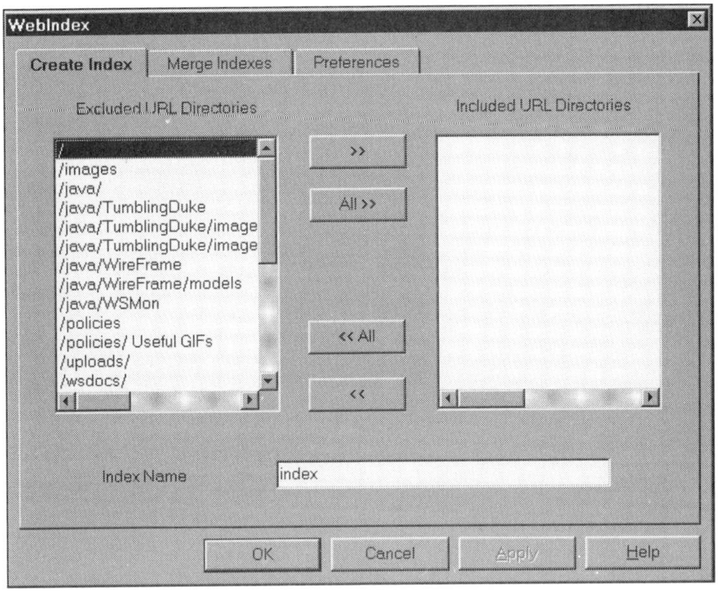

Figure 18.17: No URLs have been included in this index yet.

4. Spencer clicks on the Preferences tab.
5. Under Preferences (shown in Figure 18.19) Spencer can specify the following details about his index:

- **Index Files of Type**: Use this option to specify file-extension of the files you want to be fully indexed.
- **Index only File Name**: The file types in this list have only their file names indexed, not their contents.
- **Ignore Words**: Use this to specify a list of words to be ignored during creation of the index. You may use either WebIndex's default internal list or a list of your own. The words in the list must be separated by spaces, and the list can include multiple lines.

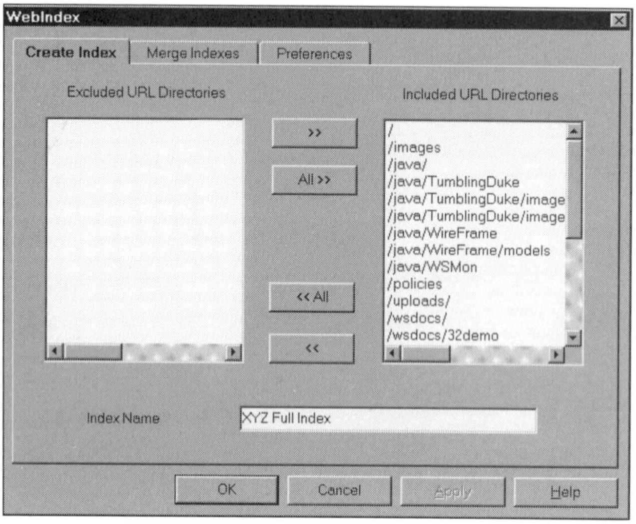

Figure 18.18: This index (*XYZ Full Index)* will contain the contents of every URL path on the server.

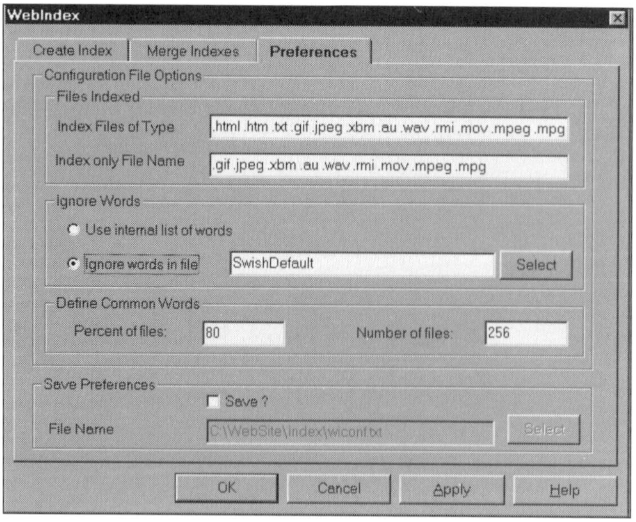

Figure 18.19: The Preferences screen is used to make your index searches more efficient.

- **Define Common Words**: You can define how WebIndex will determine common words, which are not indexed, by specifying the percentage of files in which a word appears and the number of files in which a word appears. For example, the default specifies 80% and 256. This means that WebIndex will omit words that appear in more than 80% of the files or more than 256 files.

- **Save Preferences**: You can save your preferences for reuse when you create another index.

6. After specifying his preferences, Spencer clicks the *Apply* button and the *OK* button.
7. Now that he has an index, Spencer must create an HTML interface to his index. To do this, he will need to use the *Find Form* wizard in WebSite's *WebView* program (see Figure 18.20). Spencer starts the program by choosing it from the Start menu.
8. Spencer specifies which file will contain the search form, *search.html*. He has already created a blank file called

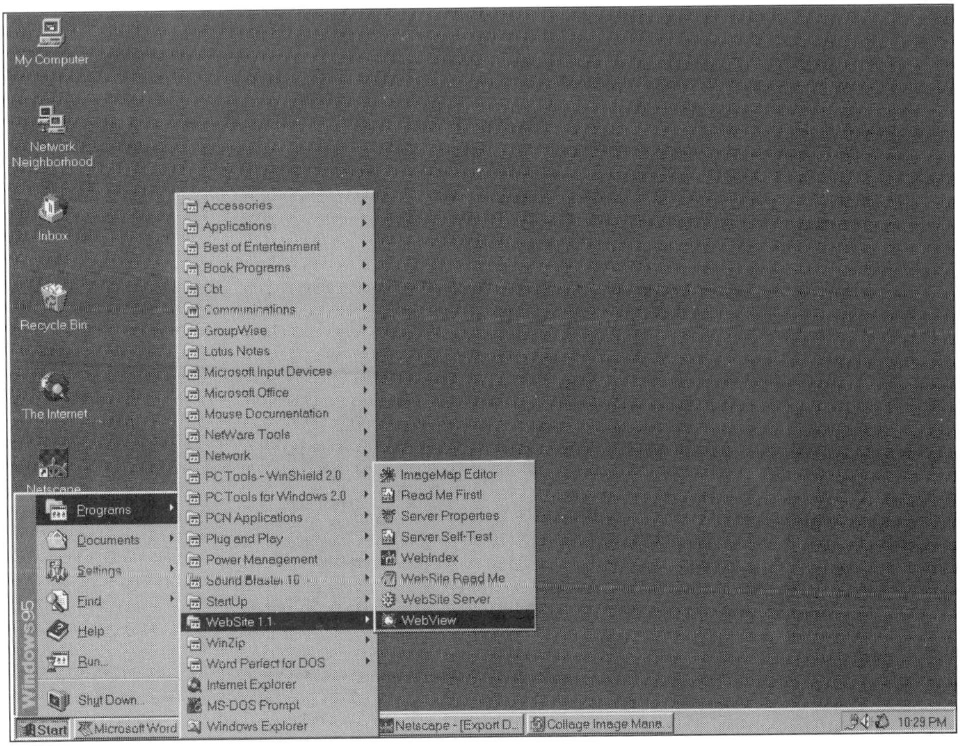

Figure 18.20: Launching *WebView*.

search.html in the *htdocs* directory and put a link to it on the XYZ home page. Spencer clicks on search.html in the window and then chooses *Wizards* from the Tools menu, as shown in Figure 18.21.

9. Next he selects *FindForm* from the dialog box that appears (see Figure 18.22) and clicks *OK*.
10. He clicks *OK* again to permit the wizard to overwrite the blank *search.html* file (see Figure 18.23).

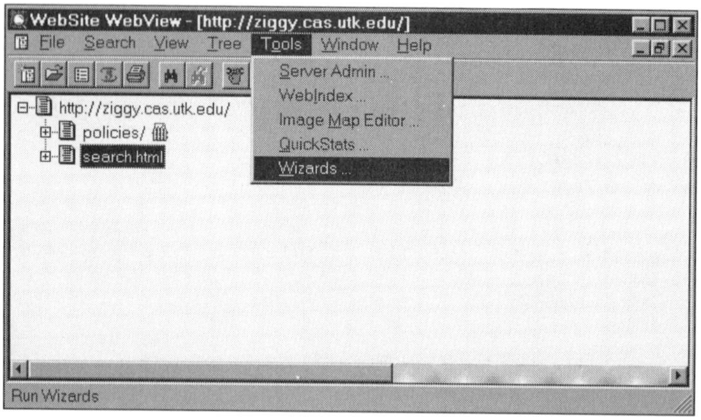

Figure 18.21: Select *search.html* and choose *Wizards* from the Tools menu.

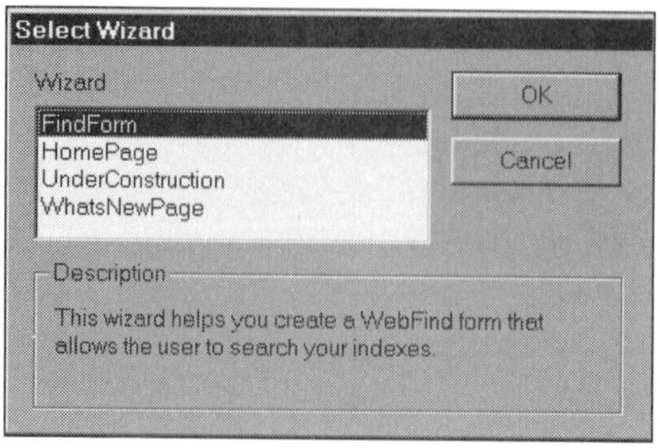

Figure 18.22: Choose the *FindForm* creation wizard.

11. In the *Title* section of the window, Spencer types *XYZ Search Page*. In the *Header Paragraph* section he types an explanation of the page's purpose (see Figure 18.24). He then clicks *Finish.*
12. Now, when a visitor clicks on the link to the *search.html* file the document in Figure 18.25 is displayed.
13. If the user enters a search on the word *policy*, the document in Figure 18.26 is returned.

Searching provides a valuable service to your site's visitors. It can make your documents easier to navigate and more useful.

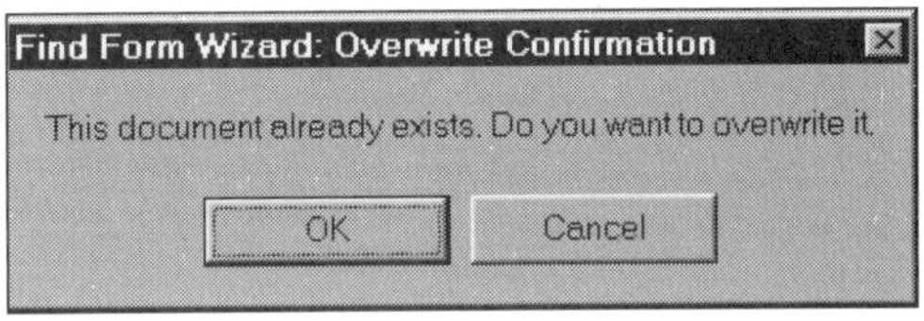

Figure 18.23: Click *OK* to allow the wizard to proceed.

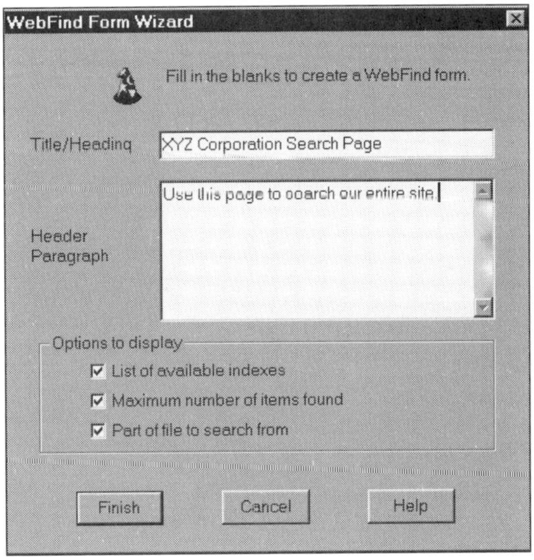

Figure 18.24: The final screen of the wizard enables customizing a search page.

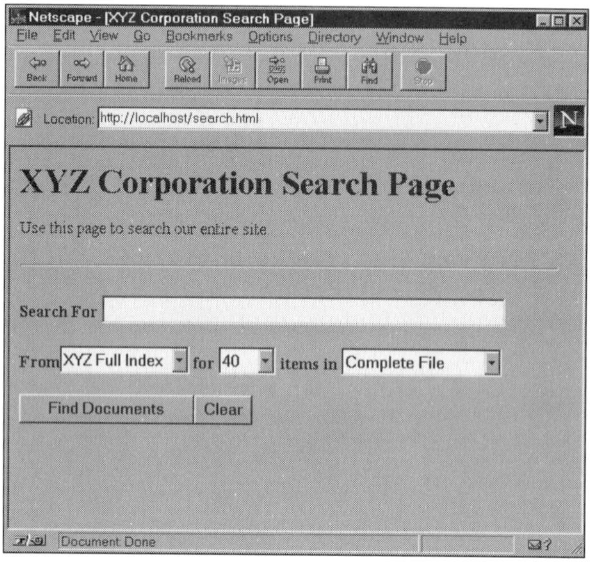

Figure 18.25: The search page gives the user options about how detailed the search will be.

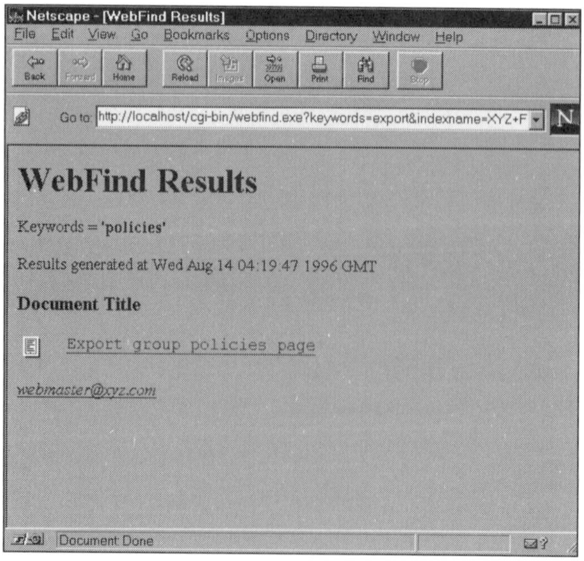

Figure 18.26: The search results page found one match and provides a link to it.

DOCUMENT COLLABORATION WITH COMMON KNOWLEDGE

Common Knowledge is a client/server system that can run on TCP/IP. The Common Knowledge server is the repository for all the documents on which your team is working. The documents on the server are the *master documents*. Each team member has a copy of the Common Knowledge client on his or her desktop computer (PC or Mac) and is granted an account on the Common Knowledge server. When a team member opens a document off the server, a *local document* copy is created on his or her hard drive. All changes by the author are saved to the local document until the author is ready to make the changes available to the others. When ready, the author *updates* the document. All other authors are made aware of the changes in a variety of ways (an audible tone or a symbol in the menu next to the document) the next time they open Common Knowledge. Master documents appear under the *Public* folder in the Common Knowledge window. New documents that you prefer not to make available to others in the work group appear in your personal folder that uses your name as its title.

The steps below outline how four members of the Shoestring Window Company's Marketing department (Alex, Caroline, Megan, and William) can collaborate on a press release announcing new pricing for the company products. The marketing department already has a Common Knowledge workgroup called *Marketing* set up on its central Common Knowledge server.

1. Before she can access the Common Knowledge server, Caroline must be authenticated by entering her user ID and password (see Figure 18.27).
2. Caroline, the advertising manager, creates a new document called *Price List Press Release*. To do this she chooses *New* from the File menu, as shown in Figure 18.28.
3. A New document window appears as shown in Figure 18.29.
4. Caroline then types in the text of the press release (see Figure 18.30). She uses the ruler and menu options to format the document to her liking.

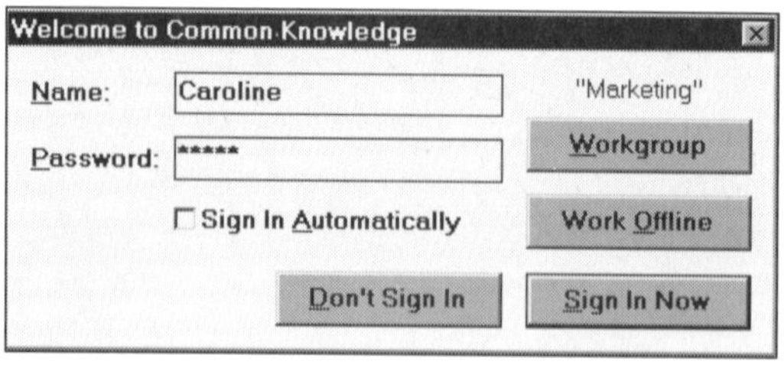

Figure 18.27: The Common Knowledge server requires a user to enter a user ID and password before gaining access to the documents in a workgroup.

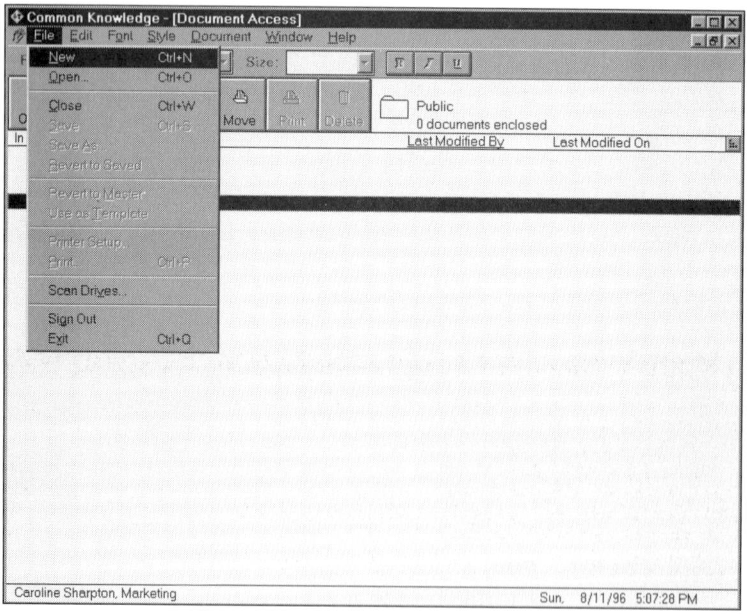

Figure 18.28: Choosing *New* from the File menu.

5. She then presses the *Update* button to distribute the document to others on the team. The *New Document* dialog box appears (see Figure 18.31). Caroline is already in the *Document Participants* section as the creator of the document.
6. Caroline types in a name for her document, *New Price Press Release*.

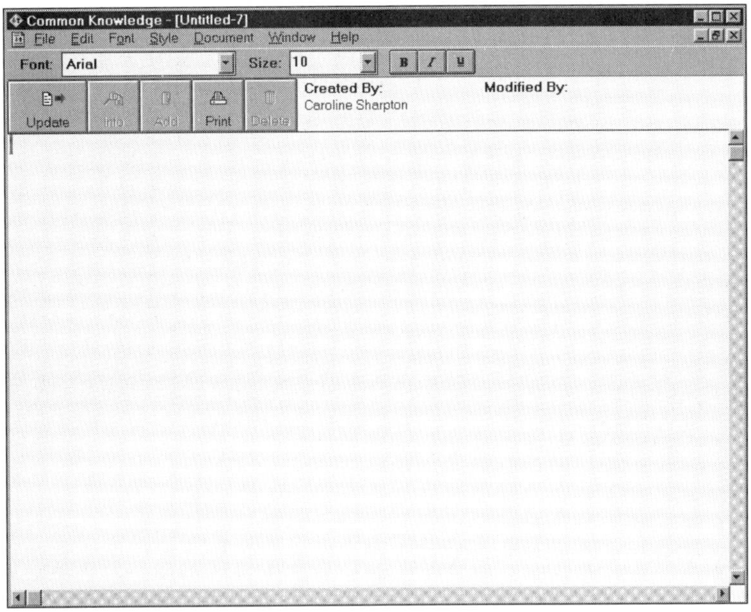

Figure 18.29: A new blank document appears.

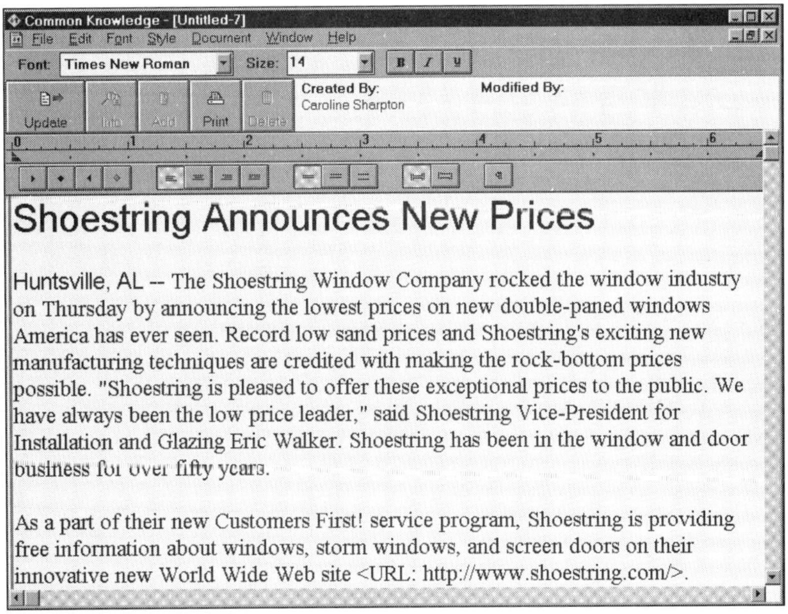

Figure 18.30: Creating the press release.

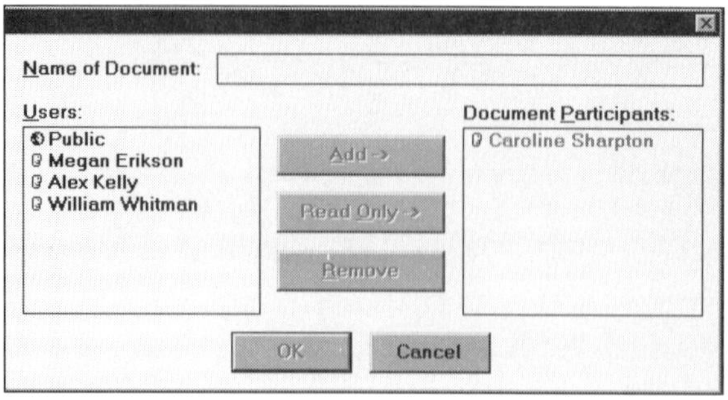

Figure 18.31: The *New Document* dialog box helps in distribution of new documents.

7. She then selects *Public* from the *Users* list (because she wants everyone who appears in the list to have access to the document) and clicks the *Add* button (see Figure 18.32).
8. She clicks the *OK* button. The document is saved. When she closes the press release, it appears in her personal folder in the *Document Management* window because she is the document's owner (see Figure 18.33).
9. Next, William opens his Common Knowledge client and sees that there is a new document in his public folder (see Figure 18.34). The solid black document icon to the left of the document title indicates to him that it is new.
10. William double-clicks on the new document to open it. He immediately realizes that he needs to make some changes to

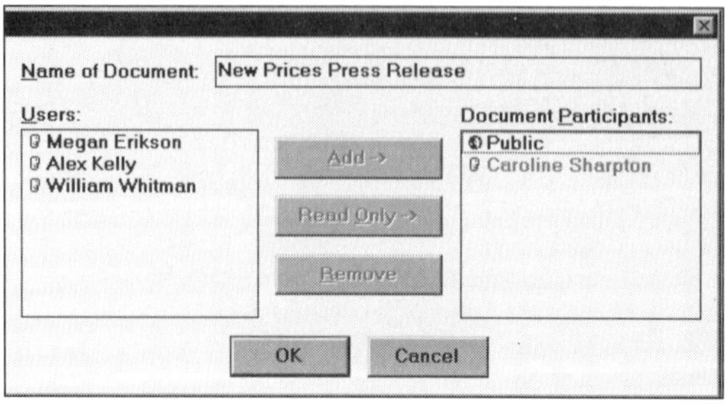

Figure 18.32: Everyone in the Users list is added when *Public* is added to the *Document Participants* list.

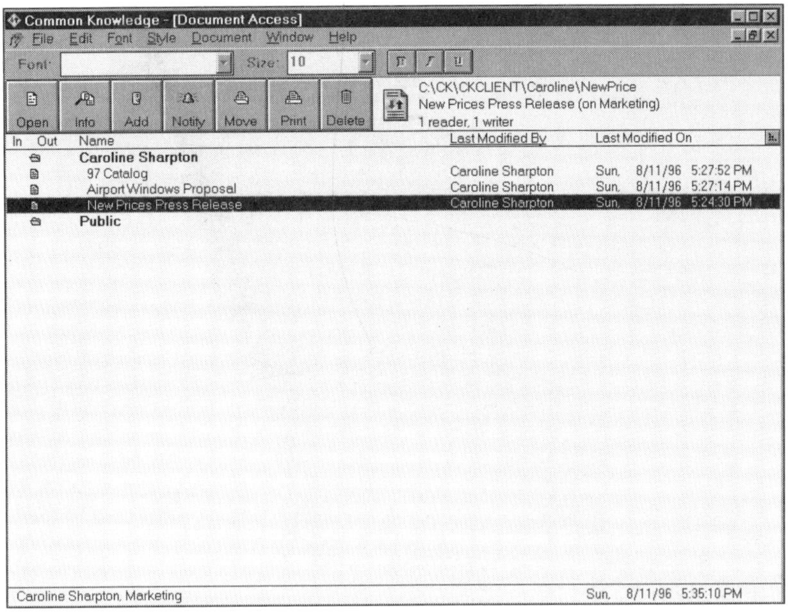

Figure 18.33: *New Price Press Release* appears in the personal folder.

the wording of the first paragraph. Changed paragraphs show up with a gray vertical change bar in the left margin (see Figure 18.35). Also the *Modified By* field in the upper right-hand corner of the document window shows that William was the person who most recently modified the selected paragraph. When he is finished, William closes Common Knowledge.

11. When Megan gets to work, she opens up Common Knowledge on her Macintosh to see what is new. She also finds the new press release document and opens it. Being a very artistic person, Megan decides that a catchy graphic should go at the top of the release. She simply copies the image to the clipboard in her graphics program to the document and clicks on the *Update* button (see Figure 18.36).
12. Alex, who viewed the document earlier, logs in to find that there are new changes to the document. The black arrow to the left of the document indicates that there are incoming changes (see Figure 18.37).
13. Alex is dismayed to see that no one has yet thought to put the new prices in the press release. He decides to place a table in

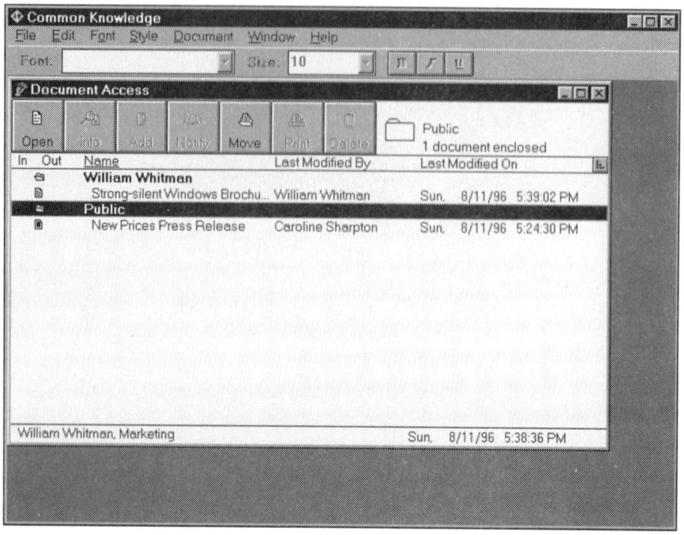

Figure 18.34: The solid black document icon indicates a new document.

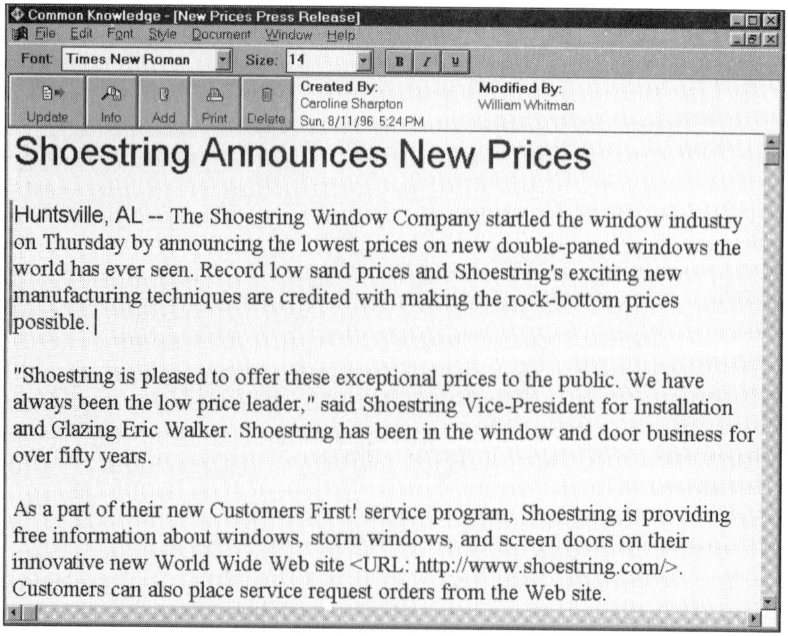

Figure 18.35: Changes are indicated by the gray change bar.

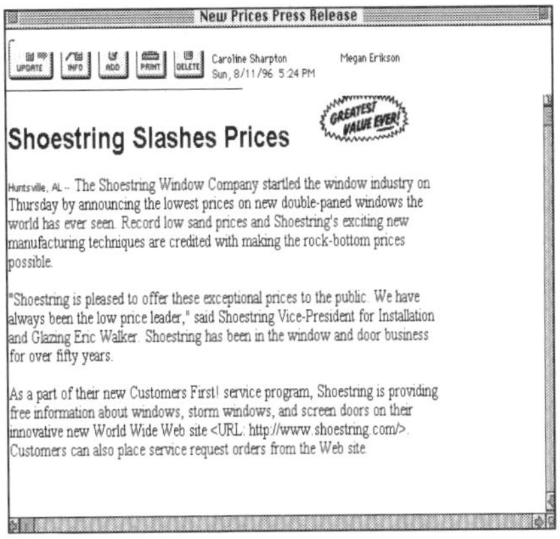

Figure 18.36: Adding a graphic to the document.

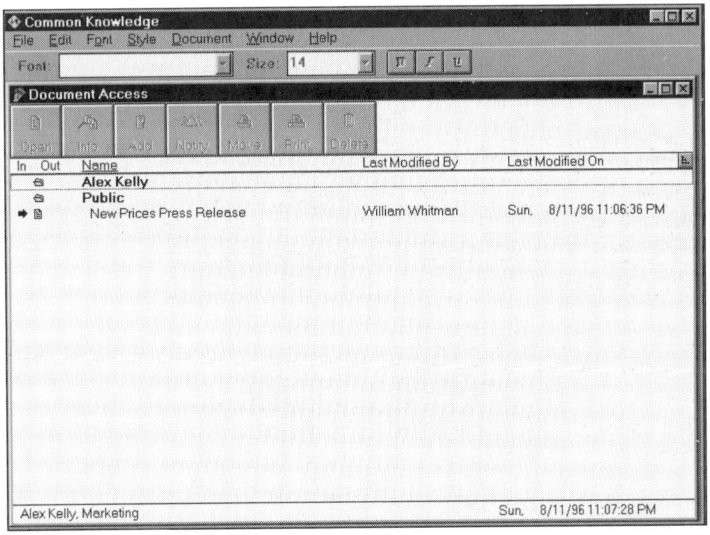

Figure 18.37: The black arrow indicates changes to an existing document.

the document that compares the old prices on selected items with the new prices. To place a table in the document, Alex simply selects *Input Table* from the Edit menu (see Figure 18.38).

14. Alex indicates that his table should have two columns and six rows (see Table 18.39). He then clicks the *OK* button.

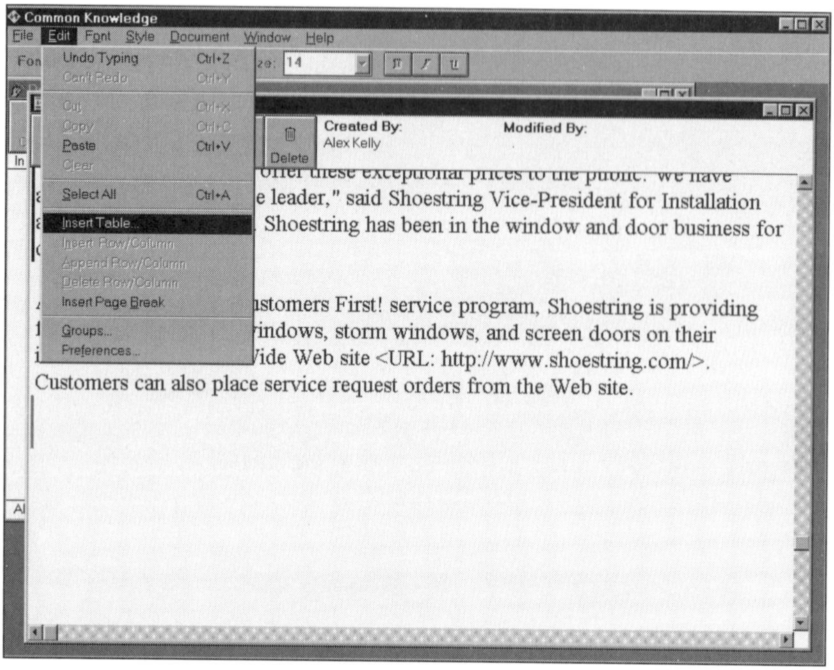

Figure 18.38: Inserting a price comparison table.

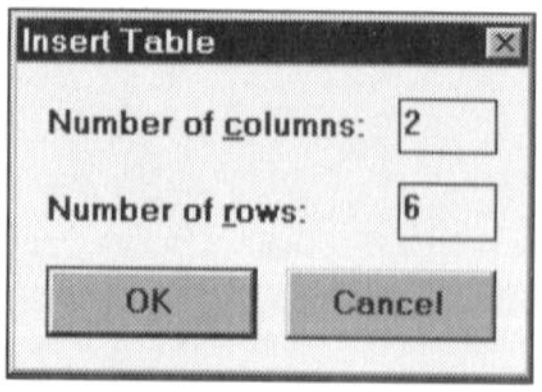

Figure 18.39: This dialog box requests details about the new table.

15. When the new table appears, Alex realizes that he should have created three columns: one for the name of the item, one for the old price, and one for the new price (see Figure 18.40).
16. Alex selects one of the columns by clicking and dragging over it and chooses *Insert Row/Column...* from the Edit menu (see Figure 18.41).

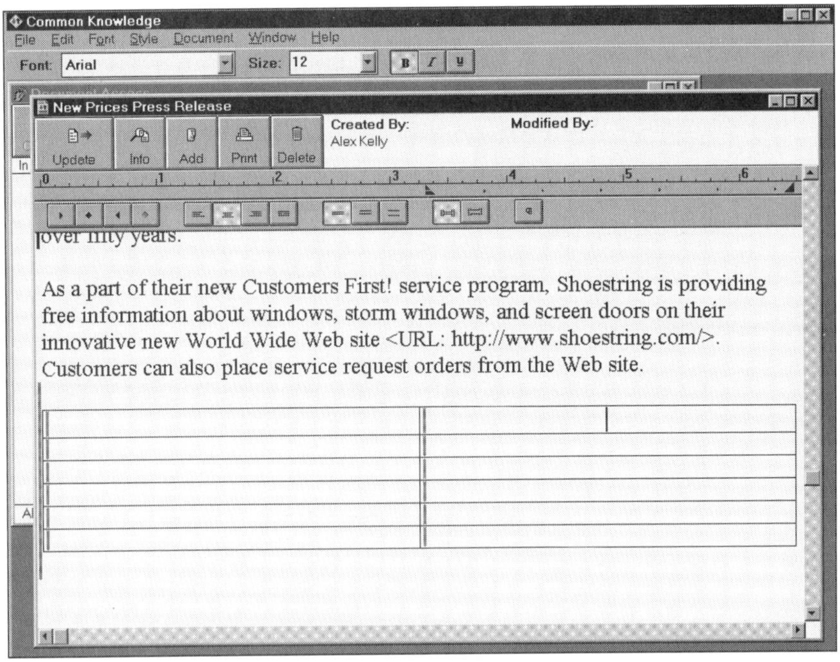

Figure 18.40: This table needs to have a column added to it.

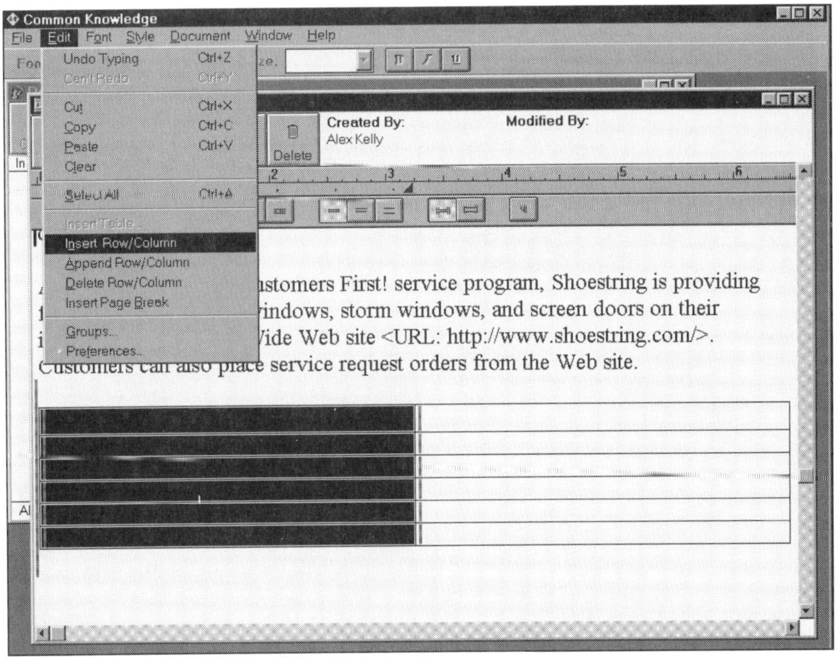

Figure 18.41: Elect to insert a new column.

17. Alex selects column from the dialog box (see Figure 18.42) and clicks the *OK* button.
18. Alex adjusts the column width by clicking on the column boundary and dragging. Finally, he puts the information into the table.
19. When Caroline logs back in to the Common Knowledge server the next day, she sees that her press release has been updated, as shown in Figure 18.44.

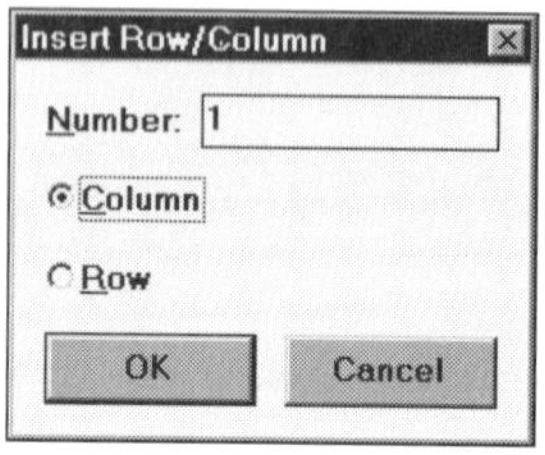

Figure 18.42: The Insert Row/Column dialog box appears.

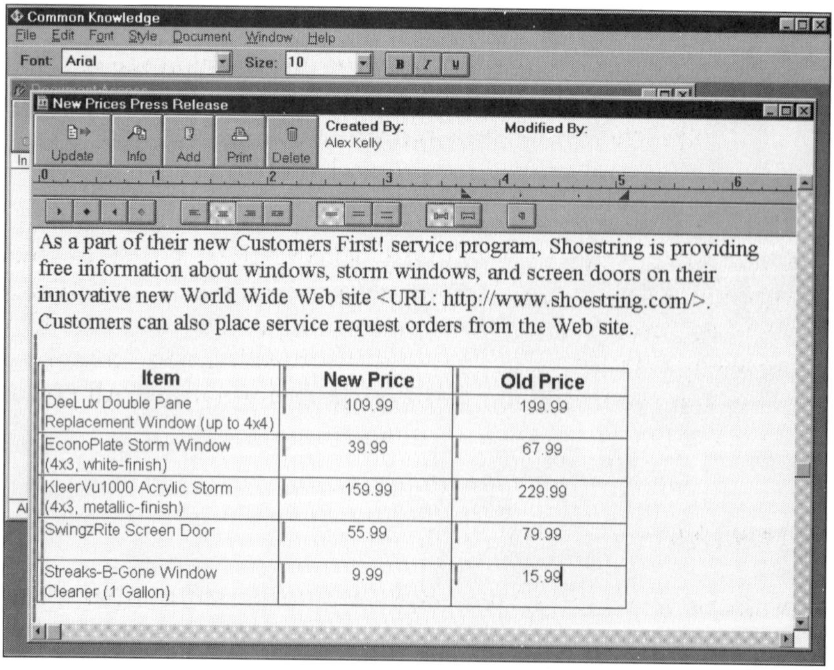

Figure 18.43: The price information is inserted into the table.

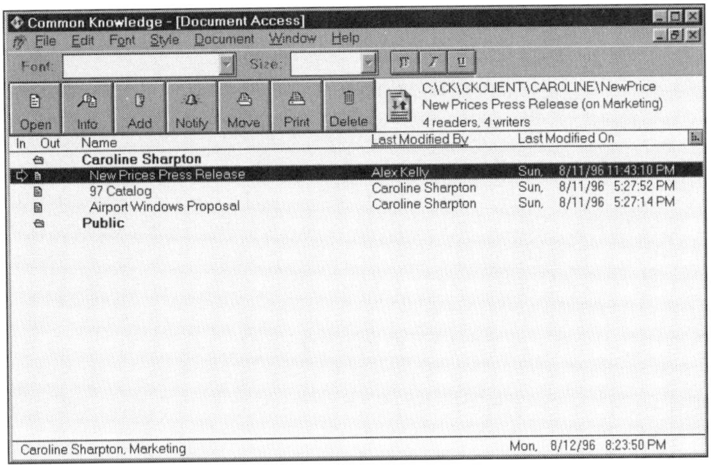

Figure 18.44: A black arrow indicates a change to the document.

20. To see who on her team has contributed to the document, Caroline clicks the *Info* button in the toolbar. The screen shown in Figure 18.45 lists all people who have been involved in editing the document.
21. Caroline closes the Document Information screen. She is satisfied with the results of the document and is ready to print it. She clicks the *Print* button in the toolbar and clicks *OK* to print out a copy (see Figure 18.46).

You can see how easy it is for your team to collaborate on document publishing in Common Knowledge. Changes made to Common Knowledge documents are instantly made available to everyone involved in the project over the intranet. Common Knowledge takes care of revision consolidation, distribution of changes, revision history, and document formatting. All you have to add is the talent.

EMISSARY

Emissary is a useful Web browser incorporating other clients and development tools, all rolled into one program. In edit mode, you can compose and edit HTML documents as if Emissary were a word

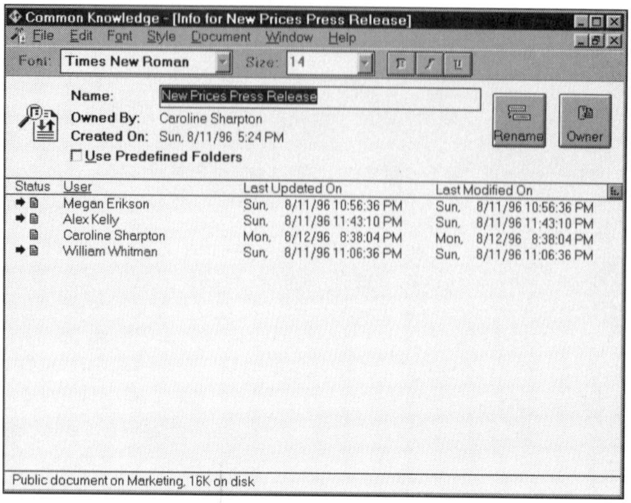

Figure 18.45: The Information screen shows who has edited the document.

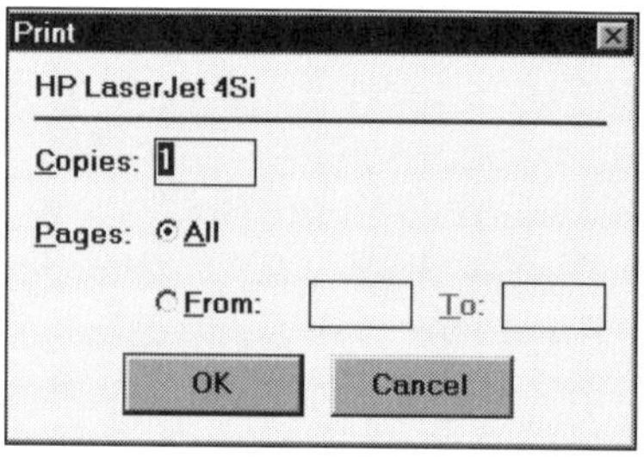

Figure 18.46: Click *Print* to get a hard copy of the team's product.

processor. No HTML is needed. In e-mail mode you can even send HTML documents and e-mail with embedded objects—the recipient needs Emissary to receive such e-mail. Many other browsers have emulated Emissary (e.g., Netscape Gold), but Emissary continues to be an innovation and useful multifeatured browser. Web browsers like Emissary and Netscape Gold with HTML authoring functions and other useful tools are handy for intranets where many employees are as likely to be Web publishers as they are to be Web site visitors.

SUMMARY

Installing your own Web server? It's really not too difficult, and doing it with WebSite is about as easy as it gets. Any PC user—perhaps even a novice—can do it. A few uses for a Web server, temporary or permanent, have been suggested in this book. Surely, you can think of many more uses. Install a Web server today, and try some of your ideas.

Groupware servers and systems can be easy to install and use too. As demonstrated with Common Knowledge, you don't have to be a programmer or network whiz kid to set up some groupware systems, although it doesn't hurt to have a network administrator available to answer basic questions.

TCP/IP programming has traditionally been the bailiwick of the Unix programmer/network operator. Times have changed. Today there are many TCP/IP programs available in versions for Windows and Mac. Many are easy to install and use. And there's no reason you can't start using them just as effectively as you use other programs.

Chapter 19

DATABASES FOR INTRANETS

In this chapter, three intranet database techniques are covered. First, the conversion of a database table to an HTML document through the use of Access and Access Internet Assistant is demonstrated. This is static publishing. Second, with Access, Cold Fusion, and WebSite, a query against the same database table is made. This is dynamic publishing. Third, a text search engine is shown finding documents on a PC.

ACCESS INTERNET ASSISTANT

The Access Internet Assistant is a free downloadable program at the Microsoft Web site (`http://www.microsoft.com`). Once installed, it becomes part of Access 7.0 (Windows 95 version).

The database to be published (*loanoff*) is an employee roster for a branch loan office. The table to be published (*employee*) contains the names, titles, home addresses, and other information for employees.

You load the database in Access first (see Figure 19.1). Then choose *Tools, Add-ins, Internet Assistant* (the set-up program places Internet Assistant on the menu) to get the publishing started.

This will bring you to an object dialog box. For *Object Type* choose *Table*. For *Object Name* choose *employee* (see Figure 19.2) and click on *Next*.

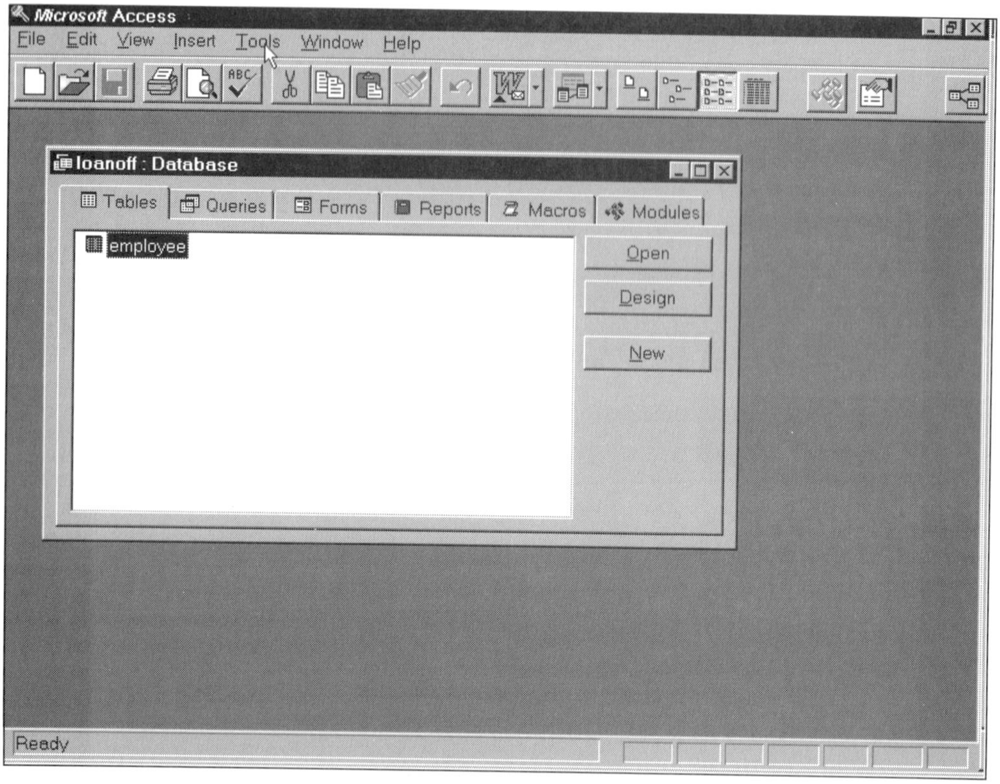

Figure 19.1: Employee database in Access.

You get to the *Template* dialog box (see Figure 19.3). Accept the default and click on *Next*.

The next dialog box is gives you your choice of folders for the file that will be created for the HTML document. Accept the default *IA95* folder and click on *Finish* (see Figure 19.4).

Internet Assistant puts the file in the *IA95* folder for you with the name *employee.htm*. Now you can use the *Open File* mode in your browser to access the file that will have the *employee* table in HTML format (see Figure 19.5).

This is a simple way to publish tables, queries, views, and reports on the Web. There are many conversion utilities for databases, and in the future, most database engines are likely to have converters built in.

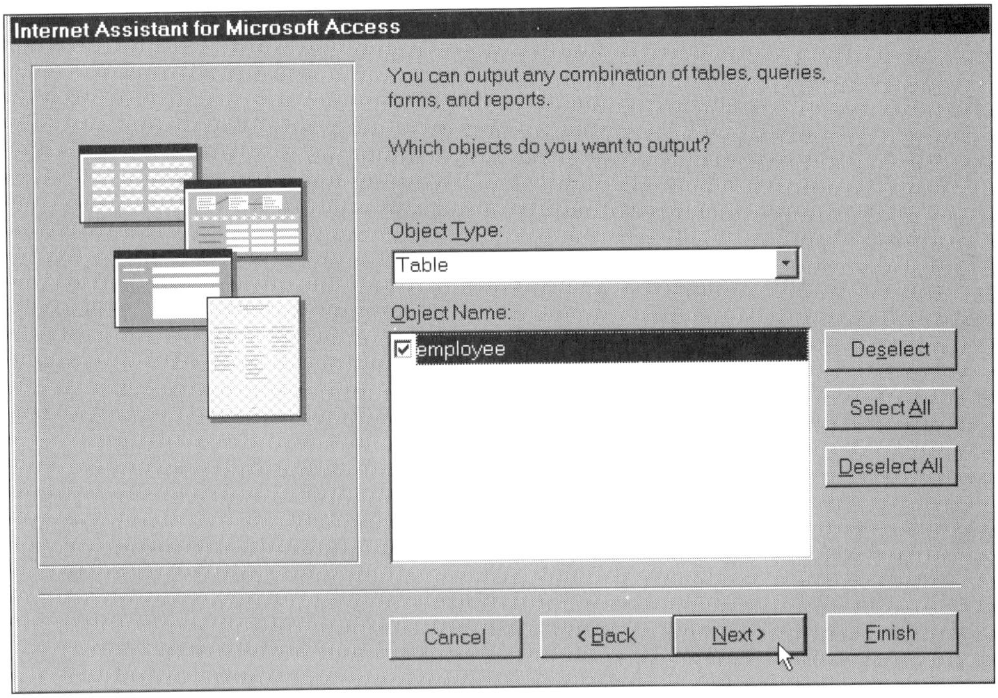

Figure 19.2: Object dialog box.

COLD FUSION

This introduction to Cold Fusion assumes that you have installed both Cold Fusion and WebSite. Both are available at their respective Web sites, and Cold Fusion is bundled with WebSite Pro. Cold Fusion also works with other Web servers. This project is to create an employee directory with each employee's address and phone numbers. By entering an employee's last name, you can query the database to get the employee's address and phone numbers. You will need three files to do this project:

- Web document with an HTML form section
- Template for the report (a second Web document)
- SQL query

For the first two, you will have to craft Web documents using HTML. You can create the query in Access. Although this is a simple

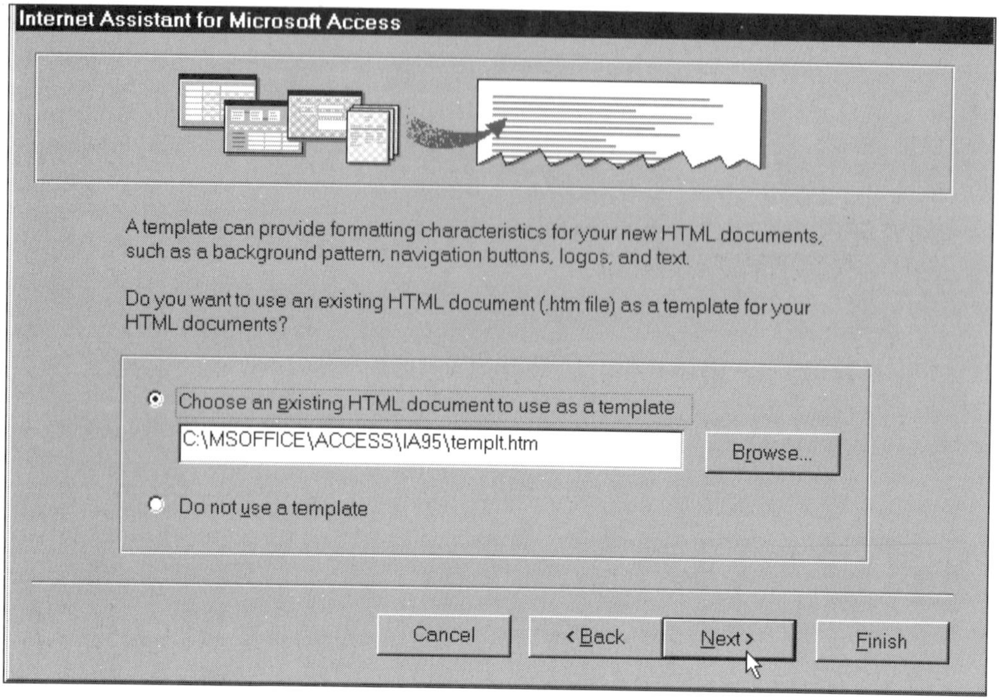

Figure 19.3: Template dialog box.

project, it will show you that creating a Web-database development does not necessarily have to be done by a programmer.

For the first document, just create a basic Web document. The HTML form is the important element in this document. The HTML source is given.

```
<HTML><HEAD><TITLE>Branch Office Employee
Directory</TITLE></HEAD><BODY>
<CENTER><H1>Branch Loan Office</H1>

<H1>Employee Directory</H1></CENTER>
<PRE>
```

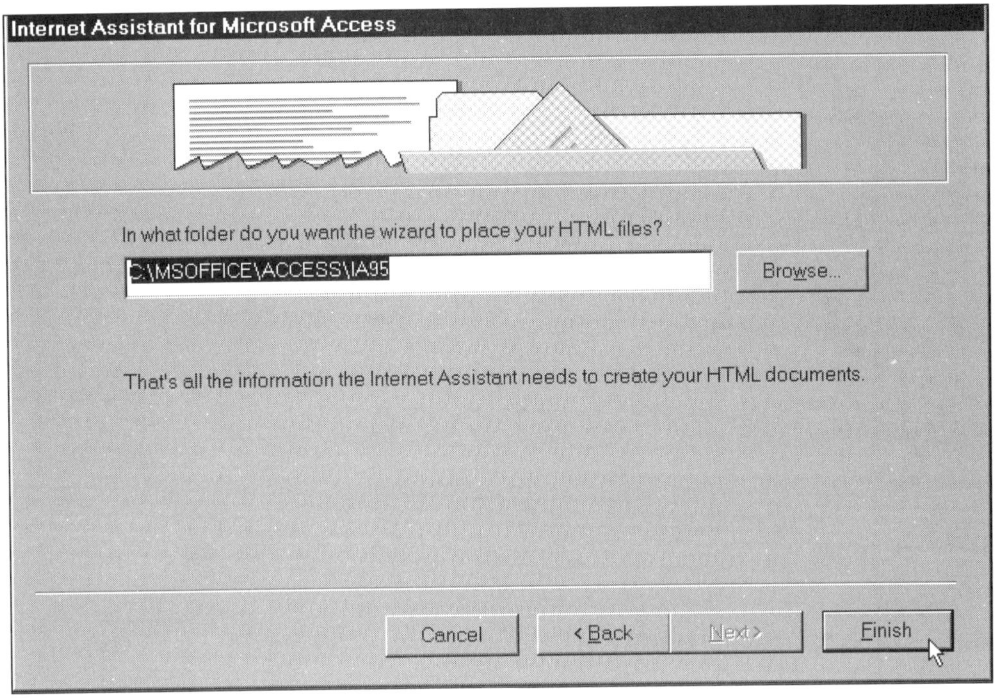

Figure 19.4: Choose folder to store HTML file.

```
</PRE>
<B>
Enter a person's last name and click on the <I>Submit</I> but-
ton to get that person's address and phone number.
<P>
<FORM METHOD="POST" ACTION="../../cgi-
shl/dbml.exe?template=addphone.dbm">
Last name: <INPUT NAME = "employeename">
<P>
<INPUT TYPE="SUBMIT" VALUE="  Search   "> <INPUT TYPE="RESET"
VALUE=" Reset  ">
</B>
</BODY></HTML>
```

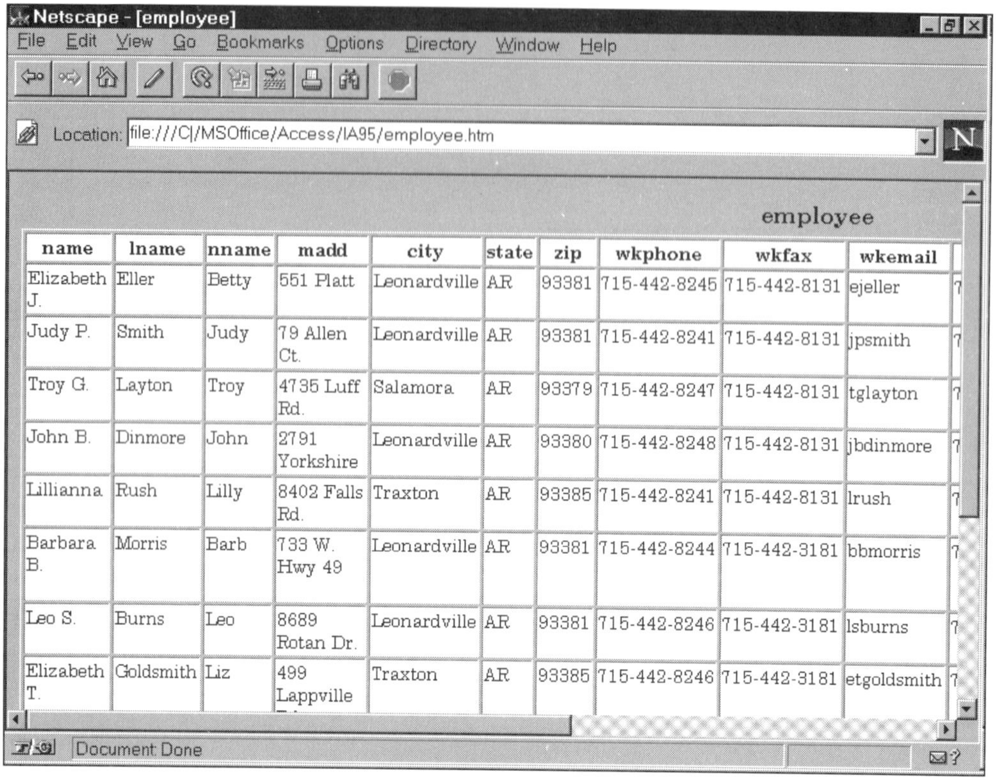

name	lname	nname	madd	city	state	zip	wkphone	wkfax	wkemail
Elizabeth J.	Eller	Betty	551 Platt	Leonardville	AR	93381	715-442-8245	715-442-8131	ejeller
Judy P.	Smith	Judy	79 Allen Ct.	Leonardville	AR	93381	715-442-8241	715-442-8131	jpsmith
Troy G.	Layton	Troy	4735 Luff Rd.	Salamora	AR	93379	715-442-8247	715-442-8131	tglayton
John B.	Dinmore	John	2791 Yorkshire	Leonardville	AR	93380	715-442-8248	715-442-8131	jbdinmore
Lillianna	Rush	Lilly	8402 Falls Rd.	Traxton	AR	93385	715-442-8241	715-442-8131	lrush
Barbara B.	Morris	Barb	733 W. Hwy 49	Leonardville	AR	93381	715-442-8244	715-442-3181	bbmorris
Leo S.	Burns	Leo	8689 Rotan Dr.	Leonardville	AR	93381	715-442-8246	715-442-3181	lsburns
Elizabeth T.	Goldsmith	Liz	499 Lappville	Traxton	AR	93385	715-442-8246	715-442-3181	etgoldsmith

Figure 19.5: The *employee* table as a Web document.

Cold Fusion uses CGI scripts (Perl). Notice that the line below indicates that the Cold Fusion CGI script *dbml.exe* will handle the query and put the resulting data into the template *addphone.dbm*.

```
<FORM METHOD="POST" ACTION="../../cgi-shl/dbml.exe?template=
          addphone.dbm">
```

The purpose of the above document is to get the input to make the query. Once the input is entered and the *Submit* button is clicked, the CGI scripts make the query to the Access database file, retrieve the data, place the data into the desired Web document, and publish the new Web document. This is a custom-made Web document created on the fly from a Web site visitor's input.

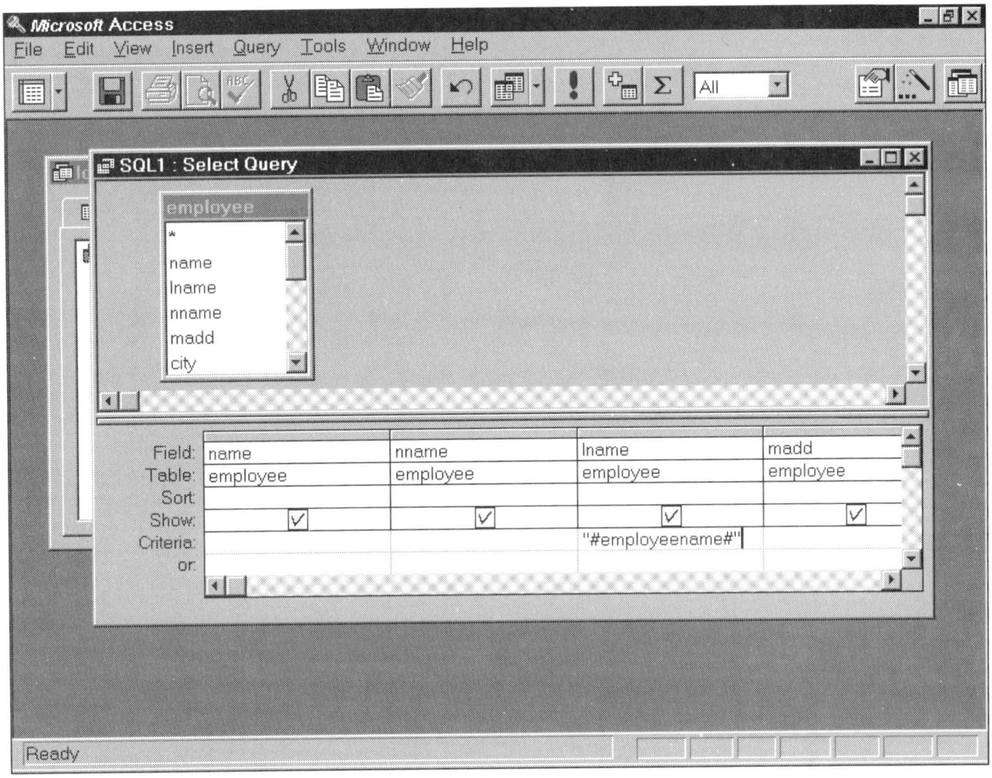

Figure 19.6: Access Query.

The second document is the actual employee directory. It contains the layout for the directory and the query. First, create the template, and then add the query. To create the template just make a simple Web document.

```
<HTML><HEAD><TITLE>Branch Office Employee Directory</TITLE>
</HEAD><BODY>

<CENTER><H2>Branch Loan Office Employee Directory</H2></CENTER>
<PRE>

</PRE>
<B>
<P>
```

```
<!--insert query plus output-->

</B>
</BODY></HTML>
```

To make this work, you must now create the query. To do so, open Access and open the *loanoff.mdb* database. Create a query that provides the following columns (fields) from the database:

name	first name plus middle initial
nname	nick name
lname	last name
madd	mailing address
city	city
state	state
zip	ZIP Code
wkphone	work phone
hmphone	home phone

The column that is the subject of the query is lname, and the variable to use for the query is *employeename,* which is required by Cold Fusion to be set off by the # character: #*employeename*# (see Figure 19.6).

Once you have the query set up, in the upper left-hand corner, click on the arrow to switch the query view to SQL View (see Figure 19.7).

Copy and paste the SQL query into the addphone.dbm document. Cold Fusion has a Database Markup Language (DBML) that is similar to HTML and easy for nonprogrammers to use. The DBML markup you need for the query is as follows:

```
<DBQUERY NAME="" DATASOURCE="" SQL="">
```

Name this query *person*. The data source is *loanoff* as set up in *Data Sources* (see below). And the SQL is the Access SQL query statement. The complete Cold Fusion query markup follows:

```
<DBQUERY NAME="person" DATASOURCE="loanoff"
SQL="SELECT DISTINCTROW employee.name, employee.nname,
employee.lname, employee.madd, employee.city, employee.state,
employee.zip, employee.wkphone, employee.hmphone
FROM employee
WHERE (((employee.lname)='#employeename#'));">
```

Notice that the quotation marks around #employeename# have been changed to single quotes. This is something you have to do manually. This query retrieves the data from the database. It takes another

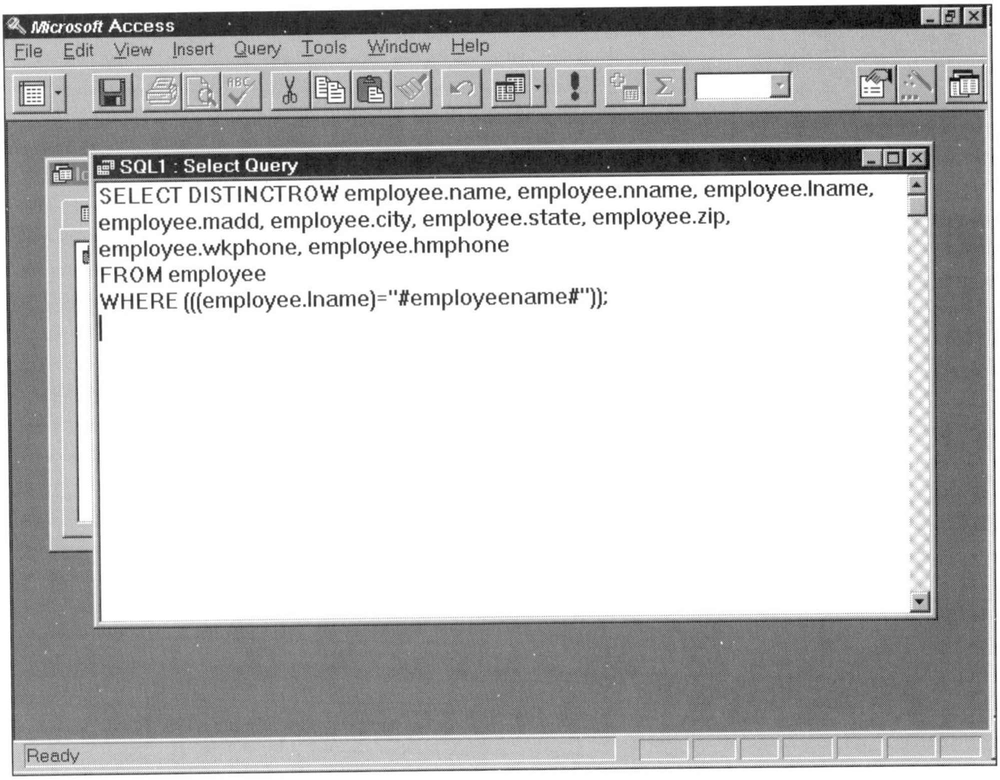

Figure 19.7: The SQL statement for the query.

DBML markup—an output markup—together with a template section to publish the data on the Web page. The markup follows:

```
<DBOUTPUT QUERY=""></DBOUTPUT>
```

The template section uses the Cold Fusion set-offs (#) with the database columns (fields) used as variables. It looks as follows:

```
<H3>#name# #lname# - #nname#</H3>
#madd#<BR>
#city#, #state# #zip#<BR>
#wkphone#<BR>
#hmphone#
```

When you put the template section together with the DBML markups, you get the following:

```
<DBOUTPUT QUERY="person">
<H3>#name# #lname# - #nname#</H3>
```

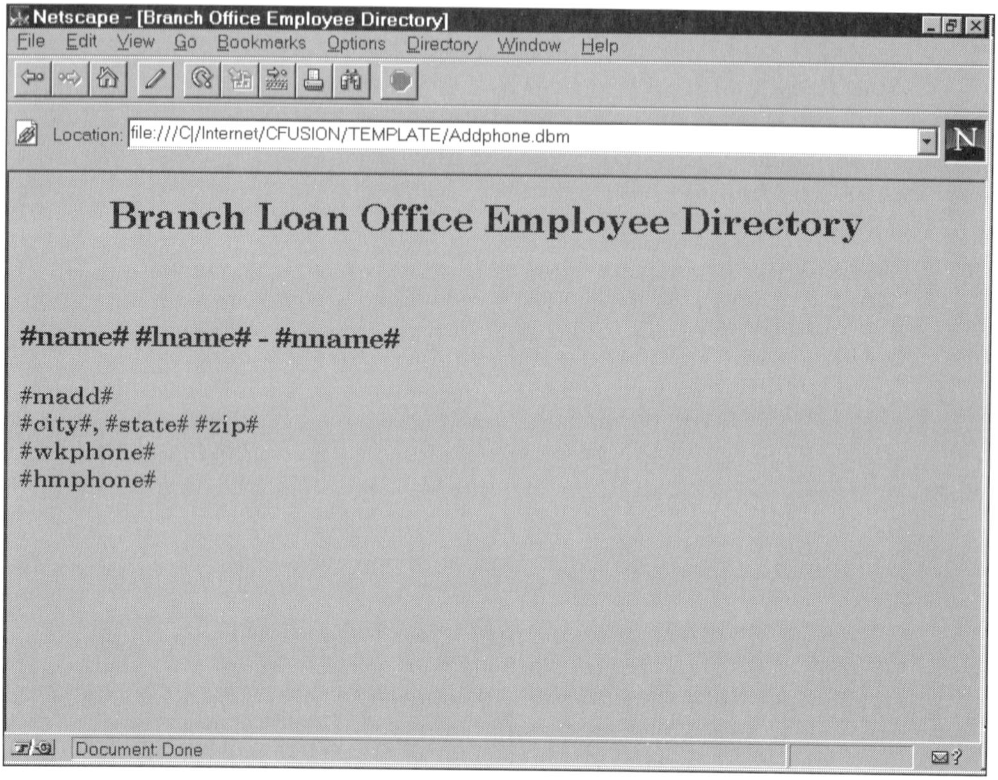

Figure 19.8: Add phone template in Web browser.

```
#madd#<BR>
#city#, #state# #zip#<BR>
#wkphone#<BR>
#hmphone#
</DBOUTPUT>
```

Thus, the *DBOUTPUT* markup publishes the data that the query called *person* retrieves. The query plus the output looks as follows:

```
<DBQUERY NAME="person" DATASOURCE="loanoff"
SQL="SELECT DISTINCTROW employee.name, employee.nname,
employee.lname, employee.madd, employee.city, employee.state,
employee.zip, employee.wkphone, employee.hmphone
FROM employee
WHERE (((employee.lname)='#employeename#'));">
```

```
<DBOUTPUT QUERY="person">
<H3>#name# #lname# - #nname#</H3>
#madd#<BR>
#city#, #state# #zip#<BR>
#wkphone#<BR>
#hmphone#
</DBOUTPUT>
```

The above query plus the output make up the middle section of the addphone.dbm template, which now looks as follows in its entirety:

```
<HTML><HEAD><TITLE>Branch Office Employee
Directory</TITLE></HEAD><BODY>

<CENTER><H2>Branch Loan Office Employee Directory</H2></CENTER>
<PRE>

</PRE>
<B>
<P>
<DBQUERY NAME="person" DATASOURCE="loanoff"
SQL="SELECT DISTINCTROW employee.name, employee.nname,
employee.lname, employee.madd, employee.city, employee.state,
employee.zip, employee.wkphone, employee.hmphone
FROM employee
WHERE (((employee.lname)='#employeename#'));">

<DBOUTPUT QUERY="person">
<H3>#name# #lname# - #nname#</H3>
#madd#<BR>
#city#, #state# #zip#<BR>
#wkphone#<BR>
#hmphone#
</DBOUTPUT>

</B>
</BODY></HTML>
```

When viewed in a Web browser, it looks as shown in Figure 19.8.

Note that Cold Fusion requires the extension of the template to be *.dbm* (i.e., *addphone.dbm*). So far, you have been in the *Open File* mode of your browser. Now you have to make sure of the following:

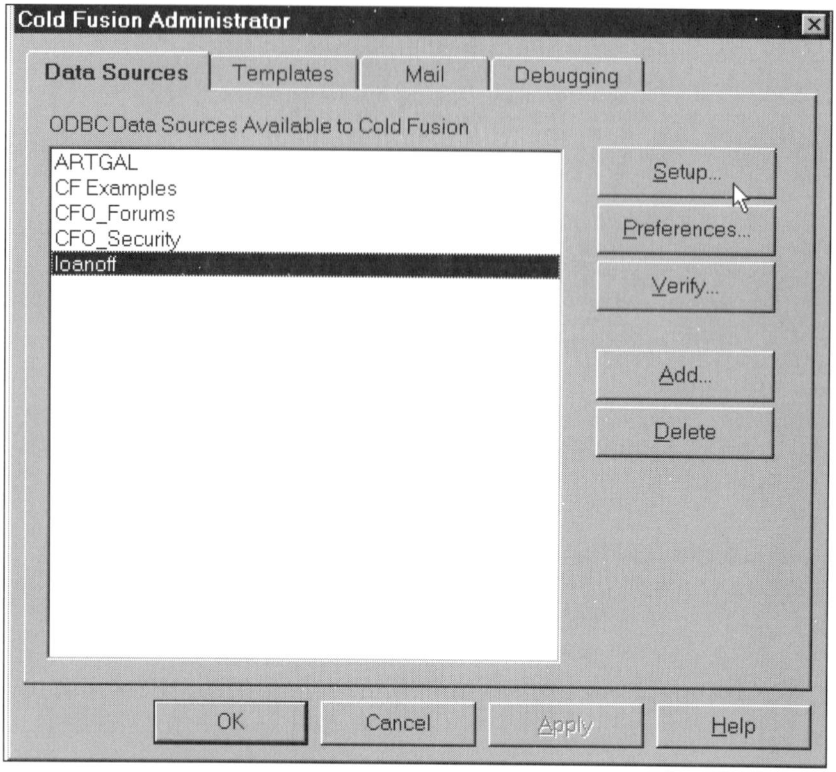

Figure 19.9: Install database in Cold Fusion.

- WebSite (or another Web server) is running.
- Cold Fusion is running.
- Your browser is in *localhost* mode (not *Open File* mode).

Next you install your database in Cold Fusion. Start the Cold Fusion Administrator. Go to *Data Sources* and choose *Setup* (see Figure 19.9). Go through the procedure for installing your database (*loanoff.mdb*) using the Cold Fusion Access ODBC database. Name the data source *loanoff*.

Now go to the first Web document (*loandir.htm*), type the name *Morris* in the input space, click on the *Submit* button, and you get the information for Morris (see Figure 19.10).

This is a lot of work. As with HTML, however, it gets easier and faster with practice. The point is that you don't have to be a programmer to do

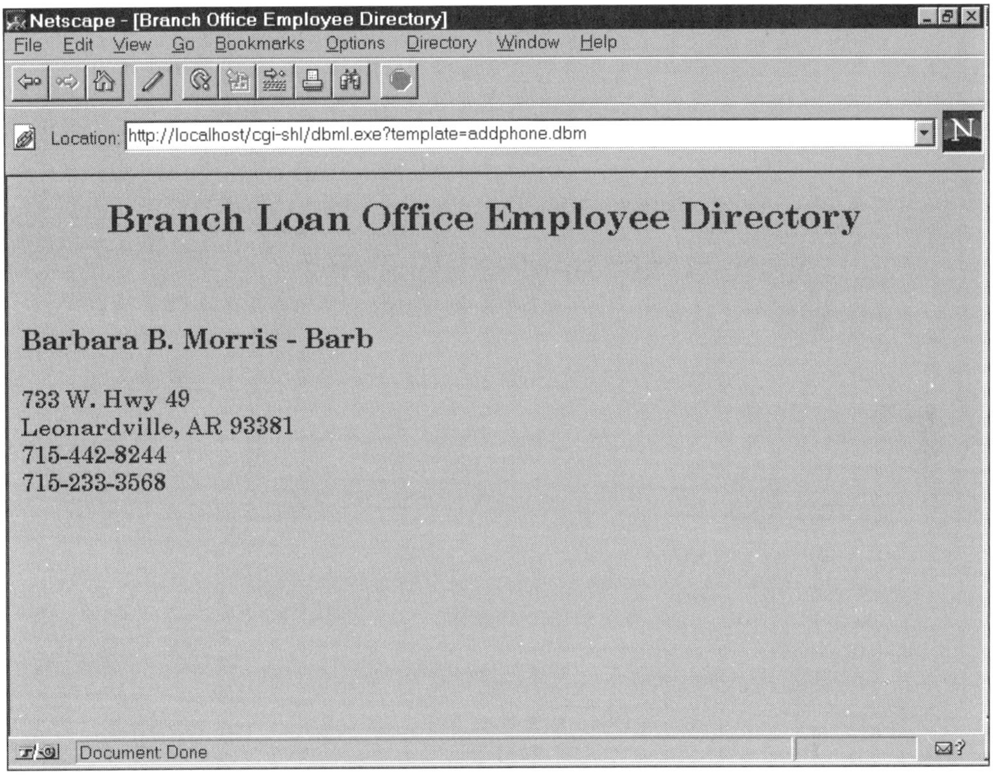

Figure 19.10: The results of the query on Morris.

this (you do need to know HTML), and it uses DBML, which is similar to HTML. Cold Fusion will offer an extended markup language in the future that enables you to incorporate groupware functions into Web pages as well as database functions.

COLD FUSION AND WEBSITE

This project was done with the use of Cold Fusion and WebSite. The *addphone.dbm* file goes in the Template folder (directory), which is a subfolder of the Cfusion folder. The *loandir.htm* and the *loanoff.mdb* files go in a folder you create (*loan*) as a subfolder of the *htdocs* folder, which is a subfolder of the *WebSite* folder.

QUERIES

Access does not create pure SQL queries. They are proprietary Access SQL statements. The only reason they work in the project above is that the Cold Fusion Access ODBC driver understands Access SQL.

Many Web-database development tools require you to furnish the SQL queries. They must be exactly correct SQL statements, and you cannot use Access to generate them. If you can't use Access, what can you use? Microsoft includes with Windows 95 a tool named MS Query, which will generate real SQL queries. It is very similar to Access, and you can use it to generate SQL queries for developing Web-database applications.

ALTAVISTA

Digital offers a desktop version of its famous AltaVista search function, which is a predominate landmark on the Web. You can use this version to search your own hard disk as well as to provide a means for visitors to search portions of your hard disk (Web site) when you are running a Web server or are otherwise online.

Because the text search capability of the WebSite software package is covered in another chapter, such capability will not be covered here too. Nonetheless, text search engines are appropriate to cover in a database chapter. If you look at a Web site as a document system, a document repository, and a database, a text search engine is a valuable means of finding the data you need—a valuable database tool.

AltaVista offers many filters for finding text; that is, it can find keywords in word processor files, e-mail, and ASCII documents as well as Web documents. It enables you, and potentially your visitors, to find information in text of all kinds on your hard disk. Digital Equipment wants you to think of AltaVista on your computer as being an extension of the prime-time AltaVista on the Web. Great idea.

Text search engines are fast because they do all their work ahead of time. The first step is to index the words in the documents for which you will use the text search. The text search engine goes through and indexes each word. This takes a considerable amount of time. After the words are indexed, however, the text searches go very fast. Without indexing, text searches would be slow. When you add a new document to the repository or an old document changes, new indexing must be done. This is impractical, but what is practical is periodic reindexing. The AltaVista text search engine enables you to schedule indexing.

Another thing to keep in mind is that there is no reason that your co-workers on your intranet or on the Internet must be restricted in their access to only Web documents. After all, the Gopher system is a huge repository of information that, when accessed, presents only ASCII text. All (or a portion) of your word processor files, e-mail files, ASCII files, and other text files can be made available for text searching by visitors (co-workers). When found, non-Web documents will be seen as ASCII text documents by Web browsers (unless they are binary files). Some files will look just fine and will be readable. Others will be unreadable because of the markups (e.g., word processor files). Once a visitor has found a document in which some desired information may be located, however, that document may be accessible and readable by some means other than through a Web browser. Thus, the text search has more utility than just searching Web documents.

SUMMARY

Easy access to data is important to many businesses. The intranet makes access potentially easier to potentially more employees potentially less expensive than ever before. Certainly, enabling access to data for members of a workgroup is an important concept in groupware, and Web and TCP/IP technology provide the means.

Chapter 20

CROSS-PLATFORM DOCUMENT STANDARDIZATION

Readability is the ultimate measure by which any document is judged. Typesetting is a finely tuned art that has been refined over hundreds of years. Although some digital systems do not provide very competent typesetting, you must still make the best of what's available. The lowest common denominator is ASCII text. It is ASCII text that goes into the Gopher system and also provides the basis for HTML programming. Thus, as a starting point, you must be able to produce ASCII text that looks good; that is, ASCII text that is easily readable.

DOCUMENT TYPES

The following sections describe document types (different formats). Starting with ASCII text, you can build an intelligent format that will translate easily into other formats. If you don't take the time and trouble to set up a system, your personnel will spend a lot of wasted time reformatting each time they have to use information in a new media.

ASCII Text

With ASCII text, you don't have much with which to work. It is very *minimal formatting,* similar to a typewriter. There are no half-lines or one-and-one-half lines. There is only one line size. There is only monospaced type and no bold or italic type. With monospaced type the characters are all exactly the same width. Notice that in the word "middle" the *m* is wider than the other letters. When the same word is written in ASCII text, each letter takes up exactly the same amount of horizontal space, including blank spaces. Because there is no underlined type in ASCII, you cannot even use underlining for *italics* as you can on a typewriter. Yet, you must still follow the normal typesetting guidelines for keeping the text as *readable* as possible. Do not use capitals or all capitals for emphasis in the text or in the headings. All caps are appropriate only for chapter titles and document titles. Keep in mind that this barely formatted type is the starting point for a number of electronic publishing and communication formats. Thus, you need to keep it *simple* and follow *good typesetting practices* (see ASCII version of this paragraph in Figure 20.1).

With ASCII text, you don't have much with which to work. It is very *minimal formatting* similar to a typewriter. There are no half-lines or one-and-one-half lines. There is only one line size. There is only monospaced type and no bold or italic type. With monospaced type the characters are all exactly the same width. Notice that in the word "middle" the *m* is wider than the other letters. When the same word is written in ASCII text, each letter takes up exactly the same amount of horizontal space, including blank spaces. Because there is no *underlined* type in ASCII, you cannot even use underlining for *italics* as you can on a typewriter. Yet, you must still follow the normal typesetting guidelines for keeping the text as *readable* as possible. Do not use capitals or all capitals for emphasis in the text or in the headings. All caps are appropriate only for chapter titles and document titles. Keep in mind that this barely formatted type is the starting point for a number of electronic publishing and communication formats. Thus, you need to keep it *simple*, and follow *good typesetting practices*.

Figure 20.1: ASCII version of the paragraph above.

The easiest way to create a standard ASCII document with your word processor is to set your margins at 1.25" left and right. Use Courier 12 point type and a line of space between paragraphs and between headings and paragraphs. Don't use any of the formatting provided by your word processor, and don't use characters from the extended character set (i.e., use only the characters that appear on your keyboard). The specifications in this paragraph will provide the best-looking documents in most situations. Disregard these specifications, and you may find translation difficult.

Be aware that in a standard document, the line breaks will be stripped and the text wrapped in most Internet applications. Therefore, it makes sense to arrange your text in simple full-width blocks as much as possible. This format is not very exciting, but nonetheless functional.

Gopher

In the Gopher system the text will look essentially identical to the way it looks as an ASCII document, because Gopher is not capable of displaying anything more than ASCII text. The only thing different may be where the words wrap.

HTML

HTML is a crude but attractive species of desktop publishing. The text will wrap differently in a Web document than in a Gopher document, because HTML produces proportionally spaced typesetting rather than ASCII monospaced typesetting. Web documents have an attractive typeset look. You can add formatting and headings to an ASCII document by using HTML markups. If you don't have a simple ASCII document with which to start, however, you will waste time.

E-mail

Transferring text by e-mail using the SMTP protocol produces a look similar or identical to the original ASCII document. Internet e-mail programs use ASCII text. Again the difference is in where the words wrap.

You should be aware of an important groupware technique; that is, copy text out of a word processor document or another program and paste it into an e-mail message. Just highlight the text with your mouse, choose *Copy* from the Edit menu, switch to your e-mail program, and choose *Paste* from the Edit menu. Because e-mail is ASCII text, a document prepared with clean ASCII text will survive this translation looking good.

Word Processor

When you print the standard document from your word processor, you will want to typeset it first. The text should be done in a readable serif typeface. The headings will be larger type, perhaps bold. With a full line of space between the paragraphs and also between the headings and the paragraphs, however, the document will not have a polished look (see Figure 20.2). You will need to make the lines after headings and the lines after paragraphs half-lines (see Figure 20.3).

Rich Text Format

Rich Text Format (RTF), first provided by Microsoft in the late 1980s, is ASCII text. It contains a large number of markups (using ASCII characters) that provide full-fledged typesetting and formatting for a document. An RTF document is approximately 30 to 40% larger than the same document in ASCII format. In other words, the markups create about 30 to 40% overhead. The added size is worth it, though, because RTF is cross-platform. For instance, RTF provides an easy way to transfer fully-formatted text between different brands of word processors and even between Mac word processors and PC word processors.

SIMPLE SYSTEM FOR A STANDARD DOCUMENT

This simple system is an example of a system you can devise to meet your organization's needs. If this system fits your needs, use it. Chances are it won't, and you will have to think through a system that fits you particular mix of printed and electronic documents.

Word Processor Formatting

Most documents start with a word processor. Because heretofore, everyone's concern was with making documents look good on paper, word processors—during the early days of desktop publishing—turned into desktop publishers. They took on functionality beyond just text authoring. Today, word processors do a great job of making documents look good. Unfortunately, some of the formatting may not work well for document conversion to electronic documents. This is an area of complexity well beyond the scope of this book. Nonetheless, the simple analysis offered below is intended to get your thought processes moving in a direction that will lead to solutions for your own particular document system.

Perhaps the most annoying problem caused by word processors is that they use line *spacing after* and line *spacing before* rather than using extra lines. This makes conversion to proper ASCII text difficult. Normally, you will probably have a half-line between paragraphs and also between a heading and the following paragraph. A full line goes between a paragraph and the following heading. The usual way to accomplish such a scheme is to leave out the full lines and add spacing (e.g., *spacing after*) to the lines. This simply enlarges (increases the height of) the last line of the paragraph or the line of a heading to a line and a half and does not add in a line. Unfortunately, when such a document is translated to ASCII, the ASCII version has no line spacing where it should be. A better practice is to leave in the full lines and change the lines between paragraphs and also between a heading and the following paragraph to half-lines (see Figures 20.2 through 20.5).

The secret of productive trout fishing, therefore, appears to be in the bugs along the streams.

Trout fishermen don't like bugs, however, so they tie flies to imitate them. It makes trout fishing a much cleaner sport and gives fly fishermen something to do during the winter months.

Fishing Is Scientific

As more and more Fish & Game biologists study trout, the scientific literature grows.

Figure 20.2: Paragraphs with full line spacing. This looks like amateur typesetting.

Figure 20.2 doesn't look quite right. The document in print should look like Figure 20.3.

The secret of productive trout fishing, therefore, appears to be in the bugs along the streams.

Trout fishermen don't like bugs, however, so they tie flies to imitate them. It makes trout fishing a much cleaner sport

```
and gives fly fishermen something to do during the winter
months.

Fishing Is Scientific

As more and more Fish & Game biologists study trout, the sci-
entific literature grows.
```

Figure 20.3: Paragraph with half-line spacing except between heading and preceding paragraph. This is better typesetting than in Figure 20.2.

If Figure 20.3 leaves the lines in, reduces the lines between paragraphs to half-lines, and reduces the line between a heading and the following paragraph to a half-line, the conversion to ASCII text will look as it should. See Figure 20.4 below.

```
The secret of productive trout fishing, therefore, appears
to be in the bugs along the streams.

Trout fishermen don't like bugs, however, so they tie flies to
imitate them. It makes trout fishing a much cleaner sport and
gives fly fishermen something to do during the winter months.

Fishing Is Scientific

As more and more Fish & Game biologists study trout, the sci-
entific literature grows.
```

Figure 20.4: ASCII version of paragraphs in which half-line spacing is used by a word processor for proper typesetting.

If instead, Figure 20.3 is formatted with the line spacing taken out and *spacing after* for paragraphs and *spacing before* for headings added, it will look exactly the same in print. When it is converted to ASCII text, however, it will look like Figure 20.5.

Keep in mind that the word processor document in Figure 20.3 can be converted to an RTF document and can be used by most word processors (both Mac and PC versions) as well as many of the text-based multimedia authoring programs. If the lines *have not* been taken out, the RTF document will be directly convertible to properly formatted ASCII text as illustrated in Figure 20.4. If the lines *have* been taken out and *space after* (and *space before*) used instead, the RTF document will translate into ASCII text as shown in Figure 20.5.

```
The secret of productive trout fishing, therefore, appears
to be in the bugs along the streams.
Trout fishermen don't like bugs, however, so they tie flies to
imitate them. It makes trout fishing a much cleaner sport and
gives fly fishermen something to do during the winter months.

Fishing Is Scientific
As more and more Fish & Game biologists study trout, the sci-
entific literature grows.
```

Figure 20.5: ASCII version of paragraphs in which the spacing between paragraphs and also the spacing between a heading and the following paragraph have been enabled in a word processor with an increase in the height of the lines (e.g., *space after* or *space before*) rather than with the addition of half-lines.

Simple System Conclusion

The standard document advocated in this chapter may not fit your requirements. Although it can be a useful document for many people, it is offered primarily as an illustration of what a standard document must do. You have your own unique typesetting schemes. The goal is to create a scheme that looks good in ASCII text, looks good in word processor printed text, looks good in RTF text, and is easily convertible among them all. Remember, if it looks good in ASCII text, it will look good in electronic formats like HTML. Your initial effort spent in developing standard documents will be rewarded by increased efficiency in preparing your Internet and intranet publishing and communication.

AUTOMATIC CONVERSION

Automatic conversion of a word processor document to an HTML document is a possibility. Plenty of software tools are available now to do it. In the future, such capability will be built into all programs. Unfortunately, unless the word processor documents are properly set up, the conversion will produce a document that requires tuning with an HTML editor. For instance, if you use the style *Heading 1* in your word processor, it is almost certain to translate to *<H1>* in HTML. In HTML *<H1>* is likely to create the largest heading, about 16 points. If you are using *Heading 1* in your word processor to typeset a paragraph heading at 12 points, when it is converted to HTML, it will look far too large and strong. Thus, you will have some editing to do.

Word Processor Templates

One method of avoiding the problem in the prior paragraph is to set up word processor templates that produce text that converts accurately. You can start by setting things up in an intelligent way and then experimenting. It will take some trial and error. Coordination between word processor templates and HTML programming is the goal. With proper coordination, your Web documents should look as good as your word processor documents.

Special Programs

There are special programs that go beyond straightforward conversion. They are designed to convert the documents in a documents system. They take a series of documents that are identically formatted and convert the entire series into a system of hyperlinked Web documents. They include detailed functionality for matching the formatting of the documents to be converted to HTML formatting that produces attractive Web documents. InfoAccess HTML Transit is a good example of such programs (see Figure 20.6).

Built-In Conversion Capability

Many programs already have built-in conversion capability. Soon, built-in converters will be a common feature of every program that produces text or numbers. Automatic conversion is not a complete answer as indicated above. Automatic conversion without some effort to match word processor formatting to HTML formatting will inevitably require tuning. In any event, coordinating word processor documents with HTML programming does not necessarily mean that conversion to ASCII text will proceed well. It all starts with ASCII text; that's the key. If the basis of a document is good ASCII text, conversions will be easier and more efficient.

STANDARD GENERALIZED MARKUP LANGUAGE

Unfortunately, the techniques offered so far in this chapter are just patchwork. Most people thinking about using an intranet and using groupware have reached a significant fork in the road. To choose one fork means continuing to use digital technology to crank out more and more paper. To choose the other fork means to use digital documents

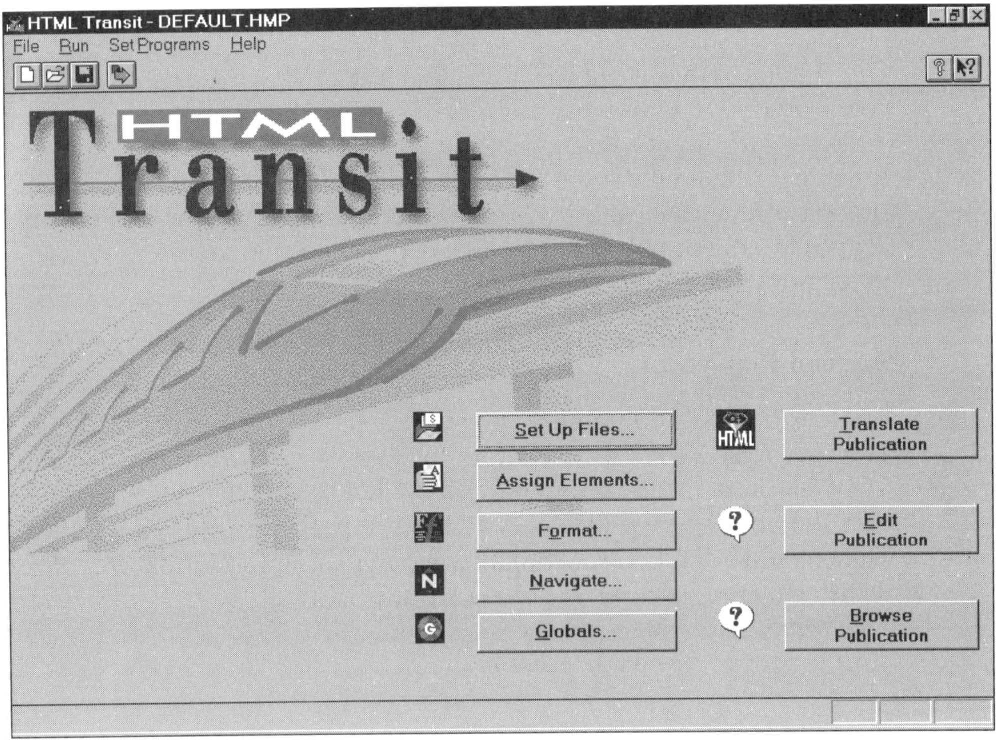

Figure 20.6: InfoAccess HTML Transit.

more and to begin to use digital multimedia technology. Standard Generalized Markup Language (SGML) is the ultimate—and perhaps inevitable—technology for the adept handling of documents in a world where you're not quite sure in what format the document will be viewed or published.

Repurposing

How can you be sure in what format your document will appear? Take a simple proposal to provide services in regard to a project. It contains information on how you will handle the project as well as a price for your firm's services. The company to which you are submitting it may want it attractively printed on paper but may want to post it on its internal Web server as well. And the company needs to send it in the form of e-mail (ASCII text) to distant places. After all, a lot of people must review it. The company in turn may want to take part of the information in your proposal and paste it into a proposal it is sending to another company.

Today such repurposing complicates things. How will you deliver a proposal that glides smoothly across all those formats? Moreover, *tomorrow*, your proposal will include some graphics, some embedded programming, perhaps some audio bites, or even some video clips. How will such a multimedia document glide smoothly across all those formats?

Suppose you have done a report on a topic for your boss and submitted it via e-mail. Your boss wants to publish it as a brochure for customers as well as publish it on the company's public Web site. In addition, your boss plans to propose that it be included in the company's annual report, which is to be published as a multimedia CD. You will be required to spice it up with some multimedia elements first. How will you make this document glide smoothly across all those formats?

You can begin to see how programs like Word Perfect, Microsoft Word, and Page Maker with their proprietary markup languages and dedication to print are crude vehicles for future multimedia digital documents. Even conversion programs (e.g., word processing to HTML) don't perform well unless the word processing templates are well tuned to conversion. Is there a better way? These are some of the questions SGML attempts to answer.

Structure Not Content

SGML is a technology that defines the structure of a document. It has nothing to do with content. The basic element of SGML is the Document Type Definition (DTD). You can use SGML to define any kind of a document. Once defined, the document has structure that works across all platforms. The DTD determines the markups and the rules of usage.

Think of a DTD as a template in a word processor but more sophisticated. Even while the document is being created, the template ensures that the document contains all required elements and follows the DTD rules. Subsequently, the template serves as a guide when one is searching the document for information. Markups identify each element of the document and can also serve as dynamic cross-references to other information (i.e., hyperlinks). In addition, the markups can describe the attributes of the information such as the source or the level of security required. For instance, if you are preparing a comprehensive report on insurance coverage, you can use markups to attribute various portions of the information included in the report to specific insurance companies. If your boss wants to know what information in the report came from Prudential, for example, an electronic scan of the document will show the text attributable to Prudential. In a thick maintenance manual for a complex machine, each safety section can be marked with a special safety attribute markup. Subsequently, a reader can electronically assemble all those safety sections into one safety document. Of course, the markups don't show when the document is published in readable format.

It might appear that this system relegates an information creator (author) to working within some sort of arbitrary confines. The DTD, however, is not as confining as it might appear. First, SGML enables an industry, a profession, or an institution to create a few or many standard document structures simply by engineering multiple DTDs. Second, it frees authors to concentrate on content rather than on document formatting for multiple platforms. Once a document structure is defined, an author simply learns the markups and the rules of usage. Then the author can spend time working on content, knowing that the document will work well across all platforms. In fact, the document on which an author works is an ASCII document.

For instance, HTML is an SGML DTD. As most readers know, HTML documents are ASCII documents to which markups (defined in the HTML DTD) have been applied. You don't have to put your HTML document on a Web server or on the Web to make it work. With a program that can read the markups (i.e., a Web browser), you can read any HTML document on your own computer. The browser, using the ASCII documents and markups, typesets the document in such as way that it adheres to the structure set forth in the DTD. It works well when the document is in your Windows PC; it works well in a Mac; it works well on a Web server in your ISP's Unix computer; and it's the same ASCII document.

REDEFINING HTML

HTML is a remarkable document-publishing system. The markups are relatively few and easy to use. The documents have multimedia with navigation capability. Yet, HTML leaves a lot to be desired because it is a rather crude desktop publishing system that needs improvement. Thus, Internet users have watched the HTML DTD be revised into version 2.0, with 3.0 now cooking, and some people are even thinking about what 4.0 should include. Although a DTD sets a standard for a particular activity (e.g., publishing on the Web), it is clearly not necessarily a standard cast in concrete.

In effect, you use SGML to define a smart digital document when you create a DTD. A smart document has the following attributes:

- Portable across multiple computers and operating systems
- Usable in various delivery systems
- Open-ended (i.e., accessible via various modes)
- Recognizes multimedia and supports a wide variety of deliverables
- Conforms to applicable standards
- Takes into account intellectual property issues

The smart document achieves seamless gateways as summarized by the statement, "Write once. Deliver anywhere in any manner." *Open-ended* as used to describe an SGML document means that anything might be done with it. Some of the possibilities follow:

- Transmit
- View
- Interrogate
- Search
- Typeset
- Print
- Play back
- Project
- Navigate (e.g., hyperlinks)
- Broadcast
- Translate

This view of a smart document or SGML document makes you realize that word processors (e.g., Microsoft Word) and page layout programs (e.g., Page Maker) are SGML-like technology but wholly dedicated to printing. Clearly, these proprietary mark-up systems will not be able to handle the document problems future unless they change substantially to accommodate multimedia and one of them becomes a standard. With the Web having set a standard of its own that is already pervasive, it seems unlikely a software company will be able to do so. Because HTML is an SGML DTD, it appears that eventually, SGML will provide the infrastructure necessary to support smart documents.

WORD PROCESSORS, ETC.

Could Microsoft Word be based on SGML? Could Word Perfect be based on SGML? If they were based on SGML, could they still compete? The answer to these questions is yes.

What are the benefits of documents created with SGML? The benefits have a lot to do with the following :

- SGML uses ASCII text, which is very portable. It is easily handled by any software without special processing.
- Writing and applying the markups are all an author has to do. Precise rules of usage (e.g., HTML) tell the author what to do. An author does not need to be concerned about page appearance. The appearance is taken care of in every medium. The processing is not part of the document, which also making the author's job easier. The processing resides in the programs that use the document.
- Industry standards can be built into the DTD. For instance, court systems run on documents that are created according to certain guidelines. A DTD or several DTDs can build a sound and flexible infrastructure for the multimedia information that will be used in courts in the future.
- The markups are multipurpose; that is, they can be used for navigation as well as for composition.
- The documents are reusable. They can be used in any medium and even for media that doesn't exist yet.

Were SGML to set the standard, authors would spend less time with reinvention. They can depend on DTDs and spend their time creating content.

A New Standard?

How close is SGML to setting a standard for the new world of digital multimedia documents? The Web is a persuasive indicator that an SGML DTD can provide useful infrastructure for publishing and communication. The federal government has been using SGML extensively for years and presumably will accelerate such usage as it moves further into the information age. Many governmental agencies have discovered SGML. For instance, the Securities and Exchange

Commission now requires corporations to submit financial reports in SGML format. Many more governmental agencies will discover SGML soon after they learn how much easier and less expensive it is to publish electronically than on paper. Many industries and corporations use SGML particularly for large publishing systems. And many businesses that contract with governmental agencies are now using or must soon learn to use SGML. It has gained a firm foothold and seems well on its way to making further gains.

DTDs

DTDs for complex documents or for document systems can take years to develop and perfect. For many businesses, this is a somewhat daunting and expensive prospect. Fortunately, industry groups, businesses, and software vendors that have developed useful DTDs often make them available for purchase. SGML authoring programs may come with helpful DTDs, just as word processors come with helpful style templates. You don't have to do it all yourself. Below is a DTD letter as it looks in print (see Figure 20.7). In Figure 20.8, you can see how it appears in the InContext SGML authoring tool.

```
August 11, 1996

Cragmore Publishing
3471 Highland Pkwy
York, PA 78530

John Preston:

Thanks for your quick reply to last week's letter. This order
is not so urgent. For the next session we will need 3 cases
of maintenance manuals to be delivered by August 23, same
address in Lancaster. Please consider this a confirmed order,
and please bill our Pittsburgh office. We appreciate your
good service.
Next time I'm in York, probably the week after next, I will
look forward to discussing our fall requirements with you.

Sincerely,

Sam Wenton
```

Figure 20.7: Letter as printed.

Is SGML for You?

Your word processor uses a proprietary markup language. In effect, it is an authoring program for that markup language. Your word processor does not ask you to supply the markups that it uses to format and typeset the documents. Instead, you use a Graphical User Interface (GUI) that makes everything easier and makes the markups transparent. It seems unlikely that you will give up that ease of use. On the other hand, before long you will be faced with all the new problems of handling multimedia documents that will be repurposed to who-knows-where? After struggling with that, you may decide that SGML is worth a try. What you need is a word processor that uses SGML as its markup language or a word processor that can at

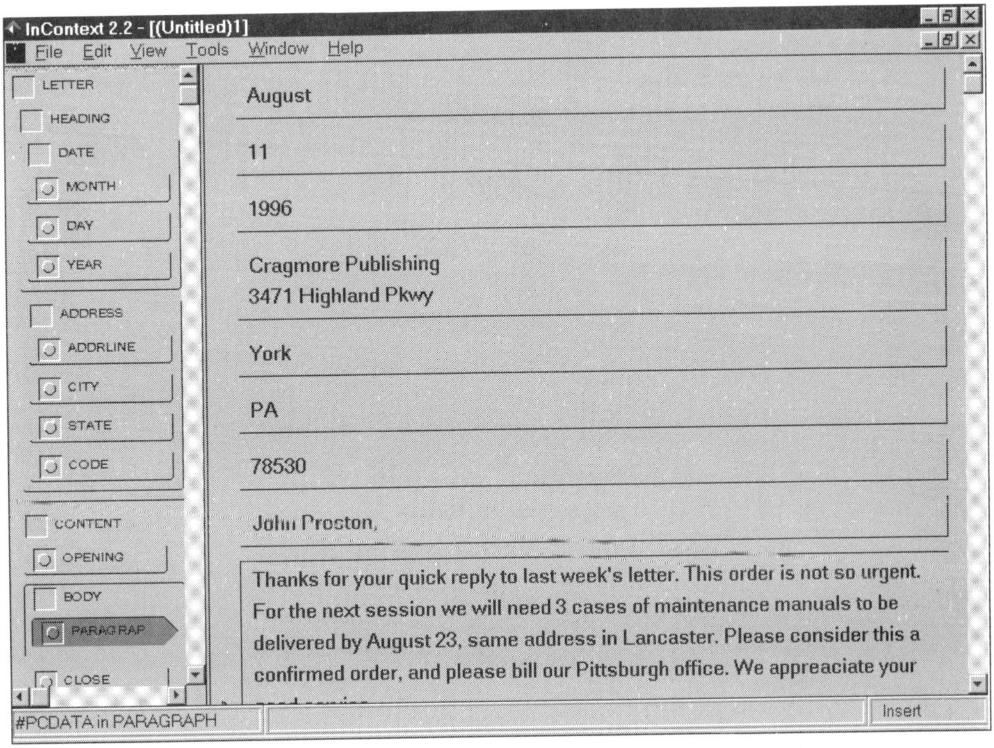

Figure 20.8: Letter in the InContext SGML authoring program.

least create, handle, import, and export DTDs and SGML documents (see Figure 20.9).

HTML shows that it is not easy to create an authoring program for a DTD. The first authoring programs for HTML were relatively crude. They are improving. Many people using HTML routinely would rather use an HTML editor than an HTML authoring program. One would certainly not say that about the Microsoft Word markup language. The Word authoring program (i.e., the Microsoft Word word processor) is easy to use, as are its competitors such as WordPerfect. Few people would choose to use a Word *editor* that merely helps them apply Microsoft Word markups. Until computer users start to see SGML authoring programs being sold as competitors to their favorite

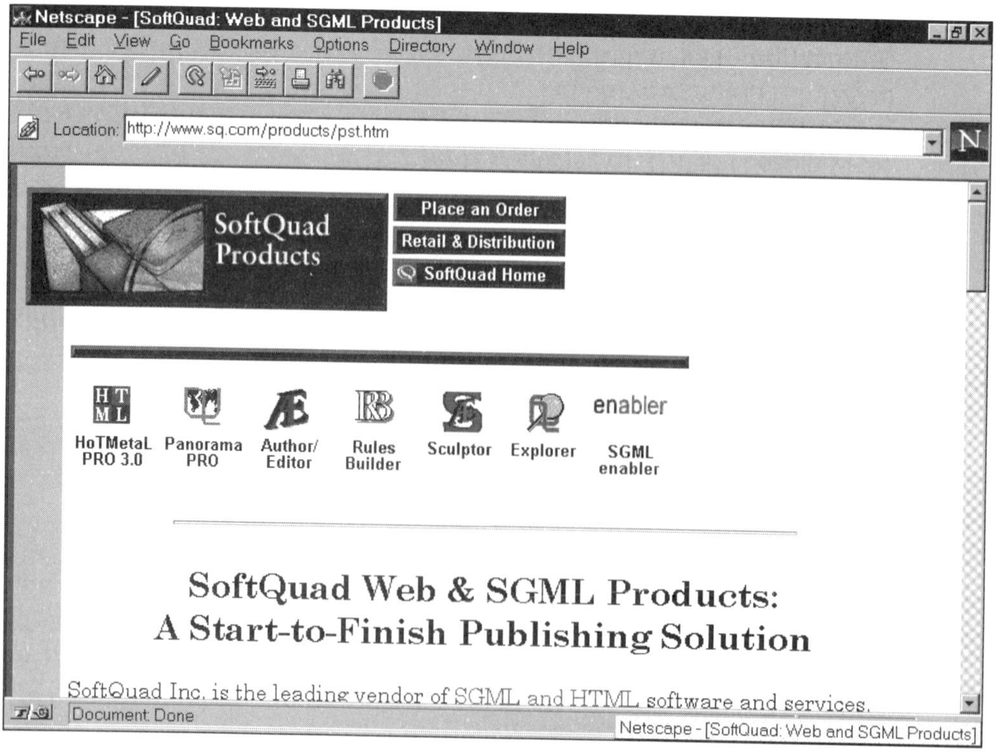

Figure 20.9: Soft Quad offers numerous SGML tools.

word processors (with similar ease of use and functionality), SGML will probably not be terribly alluring.

Some SGML authoring programs are now available. SoftQuad (`http://www.sq.com`) and InContext (`http://www.incontext.com`) both make an SGML authoring program, as do other software vendors. Soft Quad even makes an SGML browser for the Web (Panorama). Some word processors and desktop publishing programs now include SGML filters or converters. SGML is gaining ground but is not in the mainstream yet.

Currently, a serious pitfall to adopting SGML is the high cost of developing DTDs. If you need custom DTDs for your work, developing them can be as big a project as inventing HTML. Developing DTDs is the same as developing any other software, although it is perhaps more expensive because there are so few SGML programmers. The only financially feasible approach for small businesses is to use DTDs developed by others for standard uses such as letters, memos, proposals, reports, and the like. The ideal SGML authoring program will come with dozens of standard DTDs, just as a word processor comes with numerous style templates today. Should SGML become the new document standard, there will certainly be a lively commercial market for DTDs.

Many large organizations are now using or converting to SGML systems. They have the funds to finance the requisite efficiency gains they hope to realize from using SGML technology. It is more difficult for small organizations to convert if they feel it is necessary to develop their own DTDs. On the other hand, with a careful survey of the software market, you may be able to effectively use SGML in your business with standard shrink-wrapped DTDs developed by others. This book does not necessarily advocate that you use SGML today, but it's time to start thinking about it.

SUMMARY

Creating a cross-platform document system is a complex endeavor. The larger your organization and the more varied its paperwork, the greater the magnitude of the problem. It's not something you can ignore, however. The best way to avoid serious problems is to get organized up front. Establish a standard. Publish the standard. Teach employees, colleagues, vendors, and customers the standard and how to use it. Encourage everyone to follow the standard.

Remember that one of the most important aspects of a standard document is that it requires well-formatted ASCII text. This is particularly important for marking up documents for the Web. Without engineering a good standard document, your HTML programming may be unduly burdensome. Conversion programs may not ease the burden completely, except for highly structured documents in which conversion is planned ahead of time.

SGML solves the digital multimedia document repurposing problems but awaits a few missing ingredients. It has not become a standard yet, although it has made some inroads, not the least of which is the Web. There are no SGML authoring programs available that are compelling you to part company with your favorite word processor. Developing DTDs is expensive, and the market is not yet flooded with shrink-wrapped DTDs.

Whatever your solution, the event of starting to use groupware is a good time to sit down and give these issues serious consideration. With a little foresight, you can be easily repurpose your text from a word processor to the Web to a polished multimedia CD and, nonetheless, still look good in an e-mail message and in a nicely printed report.

Chapter 21

TCP/IP GROUPWARE BRIEFS

MANAGE BY E-MAIL?

If you're the boss, you must be careful what you do with groupware. Watch what you say (write) because sarcasm and suggestions can be easily misunderstood. Sarcasm seems worse in electronic text than when spoken and may not be brushed off as easily. Suggestions may seem like commands online, and all your ideas—even the dumb ideas—offered for review may be put into action instead of being reviewed. Don't avoid unpleasant responsibilities that involve personal confrontation by sending e-mail instead of meeting in person. For example, don't fire anyone by e-mail. E-mail is another tool for communication with its own unique potential, but it's no substitute for good management. Review the second half of the training chapter, and make sure you are using groupware with care and common sense.

BROWSER + PLUG-IN + JAVA

The browser has been touted as the universal interface with the computer, but is it? When you can access any database application through a Web document, it makes sense. When groupware is programmed so that it works in an HTML format, it makes sense. When text is published in HTML format, it makes sense. When embedded programs (CGI scripts) create results in an HTML format, it makes sense. But that's not the whole story.

When a groupware developer takes a proprietary interface and uses a plug-in to get it into the browser, is the browser still a universal interface? Clearly, the answer is no. All the groupware vendor has done is tuck the proprietary interface into the frame of the browser. Users use the program the same way they do outside the browser. If a software vendor reprograms a group work program using Java so that it can be used in a browser, is the browser still a universal interface? Again, the answer is no. All Java does is allow the groupware to be used in the frame of the browser. The interface is still proprietary.

Today, there are as many legacy group work programs as there are new ones. If you port the legacy groupware programs to TCP/IP, they are exactly the same; they just run on a different network protocol than they were originally designed to run on. But if you tuck them into a browser with a plug-in or with Java, they are the same too. They do not really work in the HTML ambiance of the browser.

Therefore, if you are looking to TCP/IP to provide a universal interface in the Web browser, you might do well to make the interface a prime consideration in choosing groupware. Programs that are done in a Web document format will rate higher than programs that are not. If the universal interface doesn't matter to you, the only criterion is that a program be able to run on TCP/IP.

GRAPHICS ON THE WEB

Dupont shows its TV commercials (video clips) on its intranet, presumably to engender pride and good morale. The commercials are good, and they add an attractive feature to what might otherwise be routine text. Most organizations will not have TV commercials to add to their intranets, but good static color graphics can go a long way toward making any Web site on the Internet or on an intranet much more attractive. Don't skimp on the graphics. Attractive documents will get much more attention from employees.

Good graphics add more than just flash to a Web site. A judicious use of intuitive icons and other visual clues or themes makes your site easier to navigate. To add graphical functionality to your site, you will need some graphics software. Plenty of graphics software is available, and much of it is inexpensive. For example, Aldus SuperPaint is a reasonably powerful graphics software package for Windows and Mac, and it sells for around $50. Most graphics programs will let you save files to the *.GIF* or *.JPG* formats, the standard for Web documents. If your program does not have this capability, there are several good shareware conversion utilities that you can download from the Internet. One example is LView Pro; another is PaintShop Pro.

You can use icons from one of the graphics indices on the Web. Hundreds of sites provide an index of different buttons, icons, bullets, lines, and more that are free for your use. To download a graphic from the Web in a Netscape browser, you right click on the image with your mouse and choose *Save As* from the pop-up menu that appears (see Figure 21.1). But don't use an image from a site without the permission of the Web site owner.

STANDARDS-BASED AND PROPRIETARY PROTOCOLS

Much groupware that runs on TCP/IP uses a proprietary protocol; that is, it uses its own programming and interface instead of an

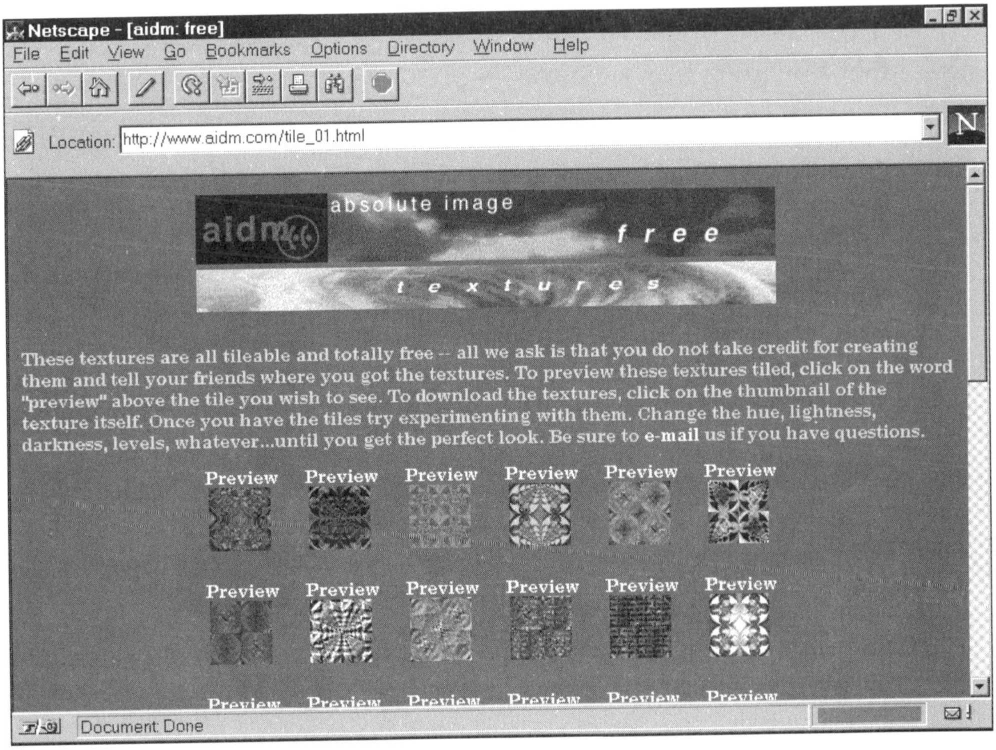

Figure 21.1: Some Web sites provide free graphics for Web documents.

established TCP/IP protocol. There are advantages and disadvantages to this. One prime advantage is that only through experimentation and innovation do new protocols materialize that become widely adopted. One disadvantage is that using an established TCP/IP protocol may be preferable to doing the same thing with a proprietary protocol.

Two programs illustrate this point: Netmanage IntraNet Forums Server and Allaire Forums. The IntraNet Forums Server uses NNTP, the well-established Usenet protocol for conferencing. It works efficiently and well and has a history of proven performance. Many people know how to use it. A news reader for NNTP is included in the Netscape browser. On the other hand, Allaire Forums uses the Web protocol (HTTP) and mimics Usenet. It is, in effect, a graft onto the HTTP protocol to achieve essentially the same functionality as the NNTP system. Thus, Allaire Forums cannot be used by a newsreader but requires a Web browser instead. The program itself is different from a newsreader and requires users to learn it. It seems that rather than reinvent the wheel, Allaire might have used NNTP.

In this particular case, Allaire presumably had good reason to create its conferencing software in such a manner. It is apparently the first of a group of anticipated group work programs it intends to offer, all of which will work through the Web using an HTML-like markup language. (Allaire Forums is also very similar to the NNTP system.) But without such a compelling rationale to do things differently, a groupware vendor should not invent a new program that provides the same services as an existing protocol with which many users have some familiarity and experience and for which clients already exist.

Thus, a standards-based approach to developing groupware has merit. This means that groupware developers, wherever possible, should take advantage of existing Internet protocols and standards to develop programming rather than invent something new, unless there is a compelling reason to do otherwise. You might note that much groupware that does not conform to existing TCP/IP protocols was originally developed for other network protocols before TCP/IP and the Internet became popular. Such groupware can work easily on TCP/IP when converted but embodies its own way of doing things, requiring users to learn yet another new interface.

VIRTUAL ORGANIZATIONS

Much has been said about virtual organizations. The common definition is a group of people who come together via a network for a common purpose; the group has no physical location. In other words, the organization exists only online, and the participants conduct their organizational affairs via online communications.

Does this really work? Yes and no. It works best when participants are being paid by someone. It's on shaky grounds when all work is being done on spec. It works well when the leadership is strong, but it works poorly when leadership is weak. It works well when participants can meet physically, at least occasionally. It works poorly if physical meetings are not practical and are not held. It works well for small groups, but it works poorly for large groups. It works well for people who know each other outside the online medium. It works poorly for people who have never met.

Like every new fad, virtual organizations are overrated. That is not to say that they can't work well in appropriate situations. Online media offers power and flexibility to get things done. As long as you keep your expectations within reason and use common sense, there is no reason a virtual organization can't accomplish great things. How does groupware fit in? Groupware provides the work structure online for getting work done. Thus, groupware, appropriately used, can help define a virtual group and provide the means to get things done too.

Suppose you are a business consultant in Kansas City and represent a small developer of oil drilling instrumentation. Your client in its research and development effort inadvertently invented an instrument that can monitor soil conditions for agricultural endeavors. Since agriculture is outside its expertise, your client asks you to assemble a team that can set a plan in motion to patent, manufacture, and market the device. You get together a team consisting of a patent attorney specializing in instrumentation in Boston, an agricultural instrumentation expert in San Jose, an instrument manufacturing consultant in Milwaukee, and an industrial marketing professional in Houston. All agree to work online with the common purpose of realizing the client's goal. Presumably, you choose these people because the people having such expertise in Kansas City are currently unavailable, are not fully qualified, cannot be identified, or do not exist. This team with proper leadership and consulting fees might be very successful. Keep in mind, though, that ideally it would be best for all these people to be together in one place, in one office. They could interact and cooperate more easily and more efficiently to get the job done. In other words, a virtual organization is invariably second best for most situations, all things being equal.

Therefore, creating a virtual organization just to have a virtual organization doesn't make sense. There must be a sound reason for making any organization virtual. In the Kansas City case, if it is true that comparable specialists are not available in Kansas City, the virtual work group is justified. It might be better than a group of half-qualified specialists from Kansas City. On the other hand, if comparable specialists are available in Kansas City, your risk in managing the project is less if you choose experts nearby with whom you can meet easily and routinely as the project may require. The general conclusion, therefore, is that the more often a virtual workgroup's members can meet in person, the greater the likelihood the group will be successful. To believe you can have a large geographically dispersed group of people who don't know each other and have never met be an effective workgroup just because they can interact and collaborate online is overly optimistic.

THE STATUS OF E-MAIL

Don't leave your employees' (or work group members') e-mail usage to chance. Make guidelines and policies. Are employees supposed to take e-mail seriously? Or is e-mail to be just an informal scribble-it-in-a-memo medium that is not used for important communications? Is e-mail to be archived and considered a legal record? Or is it to be discarded routinely so that it will not become a legal record? Is e-mail to be archived and used as an information resource for the organization (the organization's memory)? Or it is to be carelessly archived in a way that it will not be accessible? Is e-mail to be used by all employees? Or is it to be used by only those employees who can use it effectively? If you don't answer these questions and more, e-mail may turn out to be something you did not anticipate. Guidelines should not be oppressive, but they should cover the basics.

NETWORK COMPUTER

By 1997 the network computer (NC) will be well on its way to becoming a part of the intranet landscape. Network computers have been around for most of 1996, marketed by smaller corporations such as Network Computing Devices (NCD), which had sold 60,000 *Xploras* by midyear. In 1997, major corporations like IBM, Sun, and Apple will be providing NCs to both corporate and consumer customers. Oracle is developing NC programming, and Netscape will sell a version of the Netscape Navigator for NCs.

What is an NC? It is a powerful computer that runs on a TCP/IP network and can run TCP/IP programs. It has no floppy drive, no hard drive, and only limited memory—typically 4MB of RAM. It is inexpensive, but capable. It is designed to run like a PC but gets its computing resources from the Internet or an intranet. For instance, if you want to store digital files on your NC, you save them to the network server's hard disk. Your NC has no permanent memory. Programming will be delivered through an NC's browser in the form of CGI scripts and Java applications. The NC itself runs an operating system, a browser, an e-mail client, and perhaps one or two other programs.

Who will use NCs? Network computers are not designed to replace PCs necessarily, although they may do so in some cases. They are designed to bring onto the intranet employees who do not normally use computers. NCs, because they rely on a Web browser, are easy to use. They are comparatively inexpensive, and they will extend the power of computing more broadly across organizations. NCs are also expected to replace about 33 million dumb terminals still in use, not because NCs are dumb, but because they are inexpensive. NCs have received an extraordinary amount of bad press from PC-entrenched journalists. Don't let that dissuade you from giving full and objective consideration to NCs as a possible addition to your intranet.

Applix (http://www.applix.com) has a full-fledged spreadsheet and word processor that can be used via an intranet by an NC. Other software vendors are likely to develop programming to be delivered via a TCP/IP network and through a Web browser. In fact, that's what Java is all about. One of the advantages to providing software this way is that the software is easily kept current, and there are no installation or configurations problems. Everything is provided from the server.

Perhaps the most important thing to consider is not what NCs can do, but what they can't do. Inevitably, you will have NCs on your intranet. Once they are there, you will have to understand their limitation so that you can operate your intranet in such a manner that no users are excluded just because they use an NC.

One version of an NC does not even carry the name *computer*. In late 1996 Sony and Phillips will introduce set-top boxes featuring WebTV.

This is an inexpensive means of accessing the Internet while using a TV for a monitor. The set-top box, or whatever such devices will come to be called by the public, is essentially an NC and fully capable—if so enabled with software—of doing anything an NC can do. WebTV itself is an ISP through which the set-top boxes connect to the Internet. Whatever functions WebTV enables will be available through the Sony and Phillips set-top boxes. WebTV will also license other manufacturers. Initially, WebTV will enable a Web browser and an e-mail client. It is probably not stretching the imagination to envision that set-tops may play a role in the future of your intranet, even if it is just to accommodate occasional work at home by employees.

AUDIO CONFERENCING

The Netscape CoolTalk program contains an audio conferencing capability that functions much as a Web telephone does. In fact, CoolTalk contains an answering machine—like a real telephone answering machine—for people who are connected to an intranet or the Internet full time. It will answer calls from other CoolTalkers. CU-SeeMe also has audio conferencing capability. Unfortunately, audio conferencing technology has a long way to go before it becomes useful as groupware. You may have noticed that it is not covered seriously elsewhere in the book. Ironically, videoconferencing works better.

VIDEOCONFERENCING WITH CU-SEEME

Videoconferencing exists in a crude form with which you can experiment today. Cornell University offers CU-SeeMe videoconferencing software that White Pine Software (`http://www.wpine.com`) has enhanced. To experiment with this you will need a camcorder and a video board or a cam (video camera) that plugs into a serial port (available for as little as $90). Regardless of your bandwidth, videoconferencing is not high quality yet because of the inherent limitations of a packet network. Nonetheless, research is being done and techniques for increasing the frame rate are being invented. It won't be long before this will be a usable technology for group work (see Figure 21.2).

Meanwhile, it's fun to experiment. The picture quality, as poor as it is, does add something to the communication process. Rates of four to

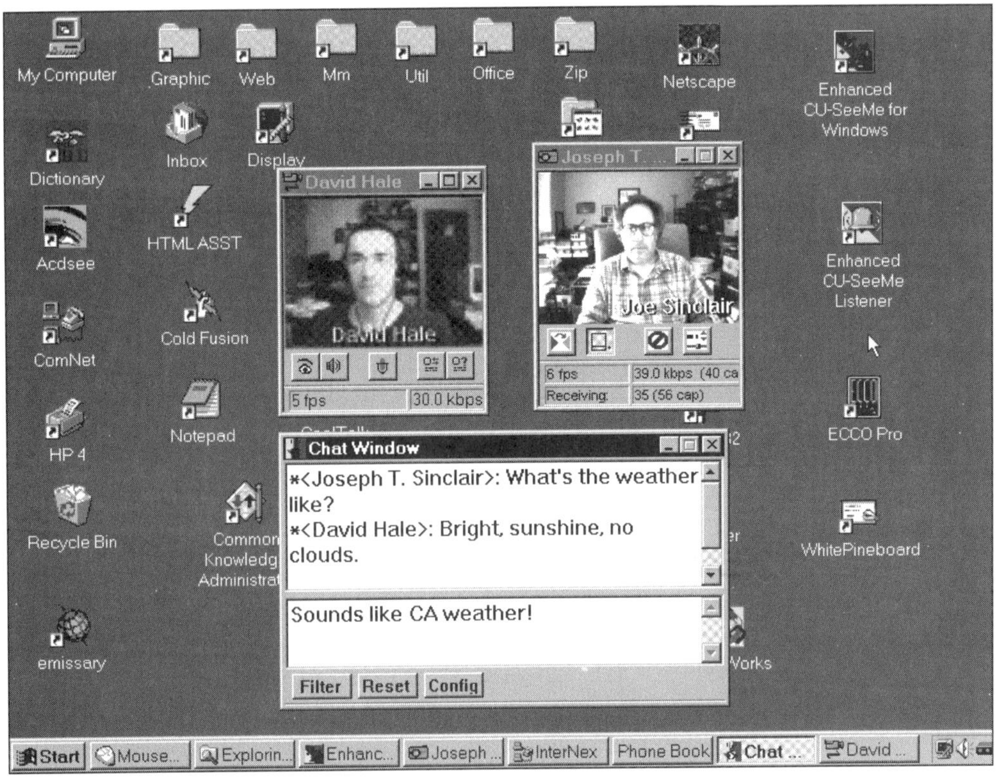

Figure 21.2: The authors having a videoconference session via CU-SeeMe, White Pine Software version.

seven frames per second are achievable in small windows of 160 × 120 pixels. Small as they are, the windows do convey visual information that becomes addictive. There's something about seeing the other person or persons, even in crude visual form, that adds value to the communication process. This is powerful technology. Give it a try, but don't expect to be able to use it for groupware yet.

Unfortunately, the audio portion of the CU-SeeMe videoconferencing works poorly. The White Pine text chat program works better than the audio. There is a white board you can use, too. One solution to the poor audio capability is to use the telephone instead of CU-SeeMe for audio. Get on the phone and talk, then start CU-SeeMe and get connected for video. These two technologies make a pleasant combination.

At a rate above 20 frames per second, this video/telephone combination will be usable for business. However, it will require an ISDN line, a better serial cam than is currently available, and an improvement in the TCP/IP videoconferencing technology. Coordinating conferences on the telephone as well as via the Internet will be burdensome. Regardless, this capability is just around the corner and will be usable. Capability for effective video plus audio conferencing via the Internet is further away.

THE DIFFERENCE BETWEEN ONLINE SERVICES AND ISPS

Online services such as America Online, Prodigy, and CompuServe are not the Internet, although they do provide Internet service. Online services are self-contained entities. They provide their own proprietary interfaces to their own proprietary information that resides on their own computer systems. You pay an online service a fee for connecting to its systems and using its information. Before the Web gave the Internet a graphical user interface, the online services enabled users to experience a virtual community with point-and-click navigation. Now, though, if all you want is access to the Internet, you may choose not to go through an online service. Although the online services now connect their members to the Internet, you still have to use their software. Unless you need access to one of their proprietary discussion groups or services, why not just connect straight into the Internet rather than go through a system and client that have been retrofitted to browse the Web? When you get an account with an ISP, you are merely using the ISP as a connection point—a place to plug into the Internet with your modem. You are not limited to the software that you can use. Any TCP/IP program will do. It gives you considerable flexibility in the software you can use and with which you can experiment for group work.

Chapter 22

TCP/IP CASE STUDIES

This chapter presents some examples of companies that are currently using TCP/IP programs and briefly relates how they are using them.

SCIENCE APPLICATIONS INTERNATIONAL CORPORATION

Science Applications International Corporation (SAIC) prides itself on being a leader in high technology. It is no surprise, then, that it has been using Internet tools like the Web since early in 1993, before most businesses had even heard of the technology. Of course, in those days there were even quite a few people at SAIC who did not know what the Web was, either. But a few trailblazers in the company pushed the Web into prominence by spearheading an intranet initiative. "In the beginning," says one of those pioneers, SAIC Web Manager Carol Rathburn, "it was a challenge to get some people to buy into the idea of the Web." She says that the key is education. Once they see the benefits, people (especially managers and executives) begin to focus on developing the intranet as much as possible. Today SAIC's intranet Web site is used to distribute employee information such as current stock data (a popular topic in an employee-owned company like SAIC), policies and procedures in the form of an online employee handbook, and other corporate information. In fact, Rathburn says that she has been approached by more than one person who doubted the need for such a system in the early days and who apologized for not being able to see the benefits.

An initiative is under way at SAIC to provide access to data on legacy mainframe systems. The long-term goal of the initiative is for the Web to provide a single point of access to all of SAIC's distributed applications. The legacy systems include financial and invoicing data, so the method of access must be secure. SAIC has a state of the art firewall in place and other security enhancements include password protection down to the field level in some documents.

The most popular section of the SAIC Web is the internal employment opportunities posting area. Employees have first claim on new positions in the company as soon as they become available and can apply on the spot using the Web and e-mail. Another initiative that Rathburn is excited about is the new intranet *company store*. SAIC has partnered with software vendors, including Netscape, to provide software for purchase over the intranet. All billing and record keeping is handled through the Web. "The employees really seem to like being able to come here to get what they need, and it helps us in managing licenses and tracking installations within the company."

It isn't just large corporations with many employees, however, who benefit from using TCP/IP technology. Small businesses with just several people can also see marked improvements in contacts, client base, and efficiency by using TCP/IP programs.

MIDWEST ANIMAL BLOOD SERVICES

When the Michigan winters force everyone inside for months at a time, the founder of Midwest Animal Blood Services (MABS) in Lansing is still making contacts on the outside. The company provides specialized life-saving blood services to veterinarians throughout the Midwest. Building a solid reputation and loyal customers is essential to keeping MABS competitive. One way that MABS has made contacts in the veterinary world is with its Web site. The Web presentation not only provides information for the highly trained professionals who use MABS services but also explains the information on a level that the average pet owner can understand. When a pet owner goes to see a vet, he or she may tell the vet about the MABS services, and a potential client has been reached.

At MABS, the Internet *is* the intranet. MABS uses an ISP for Web services and for e-mail to correspond regularly with other animal blood service companies around the country. MABS owner, Dr. Anne Hale, says that the kind of services the company provides requires a close working relationship, rather than a competitive one, with the other blood services. "We are providing cutting-edge life-saving services here that are in great demand. We tend to operate in an environment of shared information [with the other services]. Right now, we are the only [animal blood service] providing information over the Web." In the future, Dr. Hale expects to provide a knowledge base about animal blood transfusions for veterinarians around the world. In the office, the small staff uses the normal office suite programs on their LAN. Dr. Hale also maintains close contact with researchers at Michigan State University by connecting the office LAN to the MSU campus network by modem. Because the nature of the business forces the doctor to be on call 24 hours a day, she maintains her connectivity at home using a modem to access the ISP.

TEAMWORX

TeamWorx provides digital and investment services to companies that do business primarily online. Of the company's 25 employees, about half work remotely in other offices. TeamWorx keeps everyone plugged in with an intranet that remote personnel access via the Internet. According to Hal Casteel, they use their e-mail in an interesting way. All e-mail is translated into HTML by a CGI script named MHONARC. A search engine named SWISH indexes the e-mail. A file named *www.wais* in the *cgi-bin* folder serves as a gateway to use the search engine through a Web server. Thus, all the e-mail can be searched, displayed in a Web browser when found, and printed nicely typeset. This makes a useful repository of information (threaded e-mail messages) for TeamWorx personnel.

TeamWorx's Web server is GNNserver with the Illustra database. This Web system provides its employees with multiple virtual servers that they put to good use for internal multimedia publishing. In addition, they use the Illustra database extensively for Web publishing as well as for other chores. For Web publishing, TeamWorx has developed a means of providing bulk raw data to the Illustra database without inputting it through HTML forms. This provides for more efficient administration of the publishing process.

The company's intranet enables TeamWorx to fully integrate remote personnel, who otherwise would have to be in a central office, into all office processes.

THE UNIVERSITY OF TENNESSEE, DEPARTMENT OF STATISTICS

Professor Ramón Leon has always been an innovator. When he was at Bell Labs, he encouraged his team members to find the best technological tools to do their jobs and to invent them when they could not be found. Now Leon has taken his pioneering spirit into the classroom of the University of Tennessee where he is a statistics professor. Leon has refined an intranet system for use in teaching his courses. He uses e-mail discussions for the rapid exchange of information among the students in his classes, but that is just a small part of his virtual classroom.

Leon uses the Web for making available syllabi, course materials, external information, and other resources for his students. Students submit papers and other assignments by attaching them to e-mail messages using Eudora. Leon recently expanded the system so that all the professors in the department can use it. He set up an Apple Workgroup server that came bundled with the Apple Internet Server Solution. The server provides Web hosting services for each professor, AppleScript CGI services, and an FTP server for making files available to students. Leon uses Adobe SiteMill to manage the Web site.

THE AUTHORS

The authors of this book, one in the San Francisco Bay Area and one in Knoxville, Tennessee, make up a workgroup. Writing a book is a straightforward collaboration project. Both authors had MIME e-mail and exchanged Microsoft Word files and screen shot graphics (*.PCX*). The authors edited each other's chapters. The revision functions in Word were used, and some chapters traveled back and forth across the country to be revised several times by each author. Parts of chapters were also copied and pasted into e-mail messages on many occasions.

Certain parts of the book were stored in database tables (e.g., the software list) and mail merged into Word documents. Thus, the authors had occasion to send ASCII comma-delimited files (raw data) back and forth via e-mail too. A heavy traffic in e-mail, in addition to sending chapters, facilitated the exchange of ideas and the flow of detailed information. On one occasion, one author set up a temporary Web server to demonstrate to the other author a Web-database application that had no relevance to the book except that it demonstrated some concepts covered in the book.

Once each chapter was finished, it was sent to the publisher in Boston as a Word file attached to e-mail. The screen shot graphic files were delivered attached to e-mail, too. The chapters were written in a Word template supplied by the publisher. Thus, they were already typeset by the time they got to the publisher. There was e-mail traffic also between the publisher and the authors.

In addition to network traffic, there were many telephone calls between the authors and a few between the publisher and the authors. There was very little snail mail. In effect, the authors together with the publisher used the Internet as if it were their private intranet. Both the Internet and the telephone were important to writing this book. Snail mail was of no consequence.

Aside from writing the book, the authors had great fun testing some of the new groupware programs on the Internet such as CoolTalk and CU-SeeMe. Both authors downloaded several hundred megabytes of programs to review. They also drew heavily from the Web's huge repository of information about software. This is an unusual book in the overall scheme of things, however, because the Internet itself is an important element in the book. Nevertheless, that should not obscure the probability that were the book about flowers, physical therapy, or foreign films, the Internet would have likewise been a valuable source of information.

The authors have never met face to face except via CU-See-Me and, in fact, made their first contact over the Internet. Not too much should be made of this, however, as the telephone played a very important role in the collaboration. It seems likely that for the *Third Edition* of this book due out in late 1998, the authors will have switched from telephone to Web phone and perhaps even teleconferencing for nontext communication. Whether the authors will have met in person by then is difficult to predict.

SUMMARY

It doesn't matter whether you have one employee or a thousand—TCP/IP tools are available today that can improve the way you do business. Once you have determined that TCP/IP offers features that will benefit your business, take action. Start small—perhaps with e-mail—and work your way up. It's working well for other people, so why not for you?

Chapter 23

SUMMARY

Groupware is a big idea with many parts, some of which haven't been invented yet. Perhaps you will make a contribution with your ideas, and the authors hope the rendition of the current possibilities on the Internet for group work set forth in this book is helpful to you. The book provides plenty of building blocks as well as many specific group work applications.

But it is only a beginning. The landscape changes at a fast clip. The day of the objects is coming quickly, and it is appropriate to discuss object-oriented technology at the end of the book. Because it is so important for the future, it is necessary to provide an overview before the book is closed.

OBJECT-ORIENTED PROGRAMMING

Put yourself in the place of the software developer, the programmer. The idea behind object-oriented programming is that each programming function becomes an object. String some objects together and you have a full-fledged application (e.g., word processor). That sounds like modular programming, but unfortunately, it's more than that, making it a little difficult to understand. Each object is more than just a module of code. Each object includes data and communication capability. Each object is capable of doing something by itself. Because programming is created to do something and because anything starts with data, an object includes its own data (e.g., the data can be variables). Because objects must be able to work together with other objects, objects have communication capability. The organization of objects in an object-oriented programming language is important too. By arrangement into classes and subclasses, an object takes on more capability than is evident by looking solely at its code.

An object is an asset that is reusable. It is usable with other objects, even ones that someone else programs. It has an enduring quality to it. For instance, a printing utility can be an object. If you develop a printing utility as an object, it should work as a printing utility for other people's programs as well as the program you are developing. Moreover, it should work for future programs that you will develop as well as the one you are currently working on. In that sense, it becomes an asset. Other people can use it. You might license it to them. You can reuse it. How many times do you want to write a printing utility? Doing so is expensive work.

Once you have acquired enough assets by developing them yourself or licensing them from others, you can build a full-fledged application with them. Thus, objects become a means of rapid prototyping and rapid development for software developers. You don't have to reinvent the wheel every time you build a new program, and the building blocks (objects) fit neatly together because they are designed in the first place to fit in a structure and with a set of rules provided by an object-oriented standard.

DISTRIBUTED OBJECTS

If you can build a full-fledged program with objects, why not do it dynamically? That is, why not assemble and deliver to people just the needed objects to do whatever work they have to do? In other words, instead of using a huge oversized word processor (a year old) that will do everything from print a letter to publish an annotated legal brief, why not use one designed specifically for the task at hand and delivered and assembled dynamically via a network—a word processor that's always up to date using new objects as well as old? Thus, the idea of using objects to build full-fledged programs lends itself well to the idea of distributing such objects over a network to those who need them.

PROGRAMMING IDEA?

So far using objects sounds like a programming idea, a way to make programs faster and less expensively. In fact, that's how many people see it. Oddly enough, it didn't start that way. It started with the idea that software should simulate real-world processes. The real world is made up of physical objects that people use to do things. A natural way to build and use software is to simulate such physical objects. As object-oriented programming gets more sophisticated, more widely used, and more commonplace, it is likely that the idea of object technology will eventually get back to its origins, and people will come to understand it in terms of the relationship between software and people rather than as merely a software development and production technique.

OBJECT TECHNOLOGY

Part of the drive for object-oriented programming has to do with more efficient, faster, and less costly software development. Part of it has to do with developing reusable objects that become enduring assets. Part of it has to do with the intelligent distribution of programming over networks. And part of it has to do with the flexibility of assembling of objects in one place at one time to provide the programming to get a job done. But there's another side to object-oriented programming that's of special interest to those interested in groupware. If the other side of object technology is the relationship between software and people, then the relationship between software and *business* people performing business tasks is of special interest. Indeed, this idea is expressed eloquently in *Business Engineering with Object Technology* by David A. Taylor (John Wiley & Sons, New York, 1995), in which the author discusses *convergent engineering* to explain how to express business concepts directly in executable software objects.

The point to be made here is that on its face, object-oriented programming currently appears to be a fashionable software-centric idea, whereas it is really a human-centric idea. Object technology aspires to deliver to people the software necessary to assist them in doing the things that need to be done in the way it's natural for people to do such things. In other words, it bends software toward meeting the requirements of people rather than bending people toward meeting the requirements of the software.

Object-oriented programming and technology have important implications for groupware. If you can deliver objects to people where they need them when they need them via a network to provide the functionality they need for the tasks at hand, you have a powerful groupware system that supports and assists people to do their work.

JAVA

Java is an object-oriented programming language. What makes it of particular interest is that unlike other object-oriented languages, it was developed to run on a network. Today Java is a hot technology for the Web. The first wave of Java products have been Java *applets*. These tend to be cute little animation and other programs with limited usefulness. Nonetheless, practical Java applications exist too, and many more will become available shortly.

The way Java works is that the executables (programs) rather than running on the server computer are downloaded into the browser where they run on the client computer. Thus, the server computer does not have to provide the computing horsepower for all the functionality in the client/server system. Executables can be spread around where they can be put into action more efficiently. Because today's bandwidth is limited for many, the Java programs tend to be small so that they will not take forever to download; thus, the term *applet*. Java is not limited to applets, however, and there's no reason full-fledged programs cannot be written in Java even though they may take longer to download. On an intranet, presumably the download times will be shorter because of the greater bandwidth. Already, full-fledged programs have been written in Java, and it is just the beginning. Java brings the power of object technology to TCP/IP networks. Java is now distributing objects over the Web.

NETWORK COMPUTERS

Perhaps in light of object-oriented programming and distributed objects, network computers (NCs) make more sense. If you have your programming distributed to you over an intranet as you need it, why do you need a floppy drive, a hard disk, or a huge amount of RAM? All you need is an NC. It will be interesting to see over the next few years if and how distributed objects and NCs change the way people use computers.

OZ VIRTUAL

By the time you read this book, OZ Interactive (http://www.oz-inc.com) will be marketing OZ Virtual, a 3-D business conferencing program that runs on TCP/IP networks. It uses the latest Web technologies such as video, VRML, and Java and features avatars as well as visual environments. This is groupware programmed with Java that starts to look like the distributed objects discussed in this chapter.

THE QUEST FOR GROUPWARE

What is the best groupware? What is the best of the breed? In your quest to find the best groupware, you will undoubtedly consider a wide range of software from Ecco Pro to Lotus Notes. At best, the choices are likely to be confusing. At worst, they may be overwhelming. To keep things in perspective, ask yourself this question: "Is groupware groupware?" The answer may be no. In fact, groupware isn't very useful unless it can do some very specific things. On the other hand, human behavior is so complex that even in a well-defined business situation there is an infinite number of ways of doing things. Today you use one way. Tomorrow another. Add a few more people to the scene, and it may be that no groupware can possibly measure up to the task of supporting the complexity of human behavior and interaction in doing a simple task. The way anyone works or any group works is to grab some of the tools at hand and get the job done.

The tools at hand are never limited to software. They include staplers, copy machines, answering machines, the Postal Service, perhaps an assistant or secretary, airlines, attorneys, telephone directories, research services, temporary services, *Forbes Magazine*, fountain pens, and dictionaries. Why would one think that one groupware program can do it all? Perhaps the best groupware, after all, is just a software collection that is nothing but a bag of tricks. Perhaps the best groupware is the ad hoc handful of digital devices you pull out of the bag of tricks to get a specific job done. From this perspective, groupware is not groupware. The most any groupware can be is just another digital device in the bag of tricks.

Indeed, from this perspective, you may be able to develop a useful strategy. Today pick a tool or a handful of tools that seem to serve your purposes. For some this may mean Lotus Notes and OZ Virtual. For others it may mean Eudora, Majordomo, and WebSite. Learn to use the tools. Migrate toward an object-oriented approach to groupware in which objects can be distributed and assembled dynamically on an ad hoc basis to get a job done. It is this last idea that may prove to be the ideal groupware, but it isn't groupware at all. It's the system itself.

Appendix A

Adobe

PageMill
SiteMill
http://www.adobe.com
1585 Charleston Rd.
Mountain View, CA 94039
415-961-4400

Aimtech

Jamba
http://www.aimtech.com
Nashaua, New Hampshire
603-883-0220

Alaris

Videogram
http://www.alaris.com
510-770-5700

Allaire

Cold Fusion
http://www.allaire.com
7600 France Avenue
Edina, MN 55435
612-831-1808

Allen Systems Group

WebGalaxy
http://www.webgalaxy.net
750 11th Street South
Naples, FL 33940
800-475-7171

AmicusNetworks

ToolBelt
Community Builder
http://www.omicus.com
9390 Research Blvd., Suite 2-110
Austin, TX 78759
512-418-8828

Anawave Software

Hot Dog Pro
http://www.anawave.com
1300 Bristol N.
Newport Beach, CA 92660

Applix

Data
Spresdsheet
Real Time
Words
Help Desk
Graphics
Mail/Open Mail
http://www.applix.com
112 Turnpike Road
Westboro, MA 01581
508-870-0300

Architext Software

Excite
http://www.atext.com
2700 Garcia, Ste. 300
Mountain View, CA 94043
415-934-3611

askSam

Web Publisher
http://www.asksam.com
PO Box 1428
Perry, FL 32347
904-584-6590

Aspect Software Engineering

dbWeb
http://www.aspectse.com
808-539-3781

Attachmate

Emissary
OpenMind
http://www.attachmate.com
1129 San Antonio Rd.
Palo Alto, CA 94303
800-872-8649

Best-Seller

BestWeb Pro
BestWeb Intelligent Interface Builder
http://www.bestseller.com
3300 Cote-Vertu, Suite 303
Montreal, Quebec H4R 2B8
514-337-3000

Bitstream

True Doc
http://www.bitstream.com
215 First Street
Cambridge, MA 02142-1270
617-497-6222

Blue Sky Software

Robo Help
7486 La Jolla
LaJolla CA 92037
619-459-6365

Bluestone

Sapphire/Web for Win 95
http://www.bluestone.com
1000 Briggs Road
Mount Laurel, NJ 08054
609-727-4600

Brooklyn North Software Works

HTML Assistant Pro 3
http://www.brooknorth.com
Halifax, Nova Scotia

BulletProof

JDesigner Pro
http://www.bulletproof.com
15732 Los Gatos Blvd., Ste. 525
Los Gatos, CA 95032

Cadmus Interactive

E-Community System
http://www.cadmus-i.com
5203 South Royal Atlanta Drive
Tucker, GA 30084
770-621-6900

Caravelle

WebWatcher
http://www.caravelle.com
210 Colonnade Road S., Suite 301
Nepean, Ontario, Canada K2E 7L5
613-225-1172

CE Software

Web Arranger
Quick Mail
QM-Postman
http://www.cesoft.com
P.O. Box 65580
West Des Moines, IA 50265
515-221-1801

Connect

Connect-On-Line
http://www.connectinc.com
515 Ellis Street
Mountain View, CA 94043-2242
800-262-2638

Corel

Web.Data
Photo Paint
http://www.corel.com
1600 Carling Ave.
Ottawa, Ontario K1Z 8R7
800-455-3169

CP Software Group

InText Island
http://www.intext.com
120 Montgomery St., Ste. 450
San Francisco, CA 94104
415-391-5290

CrossWind Technologies

Synchronize
http://www.crosswind.com
1505 Ocean Street, Ste 1
Santa Cruz, CA 95060
408-469-1780

Cyber Networks

Brainstorm
http://www.cybernetworks.com
4631 Northwest 31st Avenue, Ste. 265
Fort Lauderdale, FL 33309
800-292-3741

DigitalStyle

WebSuite
htpp://www.digitalstyle.com
10875 Rancho Bernardo, Suite 110
San Diego, CA 92127
800-388-7895

DocuMagix

HotPage
http://www.documagix.com/
2880 Zanker Road
San Jose, CA 95134
408-434-1138

DSP Group

TrueSpeech
http://www.dspg.com
3120 Scott Blvd.
Santa Clara, CA 95054
408-986-4332

Durand Communications Network

MindWire
http://www.durand.com
147 Castilian Dr.
Sanat Barbara, CA 93117
805-961-8700

EBT

DynaBase
DynaText
DynaBase
http://www.ebt.com
One Richmond Square
Providence, RI 02906
401-421-9550

Empress

DataWeb
http://www.empress.com/
6401 Golden Triangle Drive
Greenbelt, MD 20770
301-220-1919

Everyware

Tango
Bolero
http://www.everyware.com
7145 West Credit Ave., Bldg. 1, Unit. 2
Mississauga, Ontario, Canada, L5N6J7
905-819-1173

Excalibar Technologies

RetrievalWare
http://www.excalib.com
800-788-7758

ExperTelligence

WebBase
http://www.expertelligence.com
805-962-2558

ForeFront Group

Web Whacker
RoundTable
http://www.ffg.com
1360 Post Oak Blvd., Ste.1660
Houston, TX 77056
713-961-1101

Frontier Technologies

SuperWeb Server
SuperTCP Suite
http://www.frontiertech.com
10210 N. Port Washington Rd.
Mequon, WI 53092
800-929-3054

FTP Software

X OnNet
KEYview
OnNet
Esplanade
OnTime
GroupWorks
http://www.ftp.com
100 Brickstone Square
Andover, MA 01810
508-685-4000

Fulcrum Technologies

Surfboard
Search Builder
Search Server
http://www.fultech.com
785 Carling Ave.
Ottawa K1S 5H4
613-238-1761

GNN

GNNserver
GNNpress
http://www.tools.gnn.com

Gradient

Web Crusader
http://www.gradient.com
2 Mount Royal Avenue
Washborough, MA 01753
508-624-9600

iband

Backstage
http://www.iband.com
2959 Winchester Blvd.
Campbell, CA 95008
408-374-4086

IBM

DB2
World Wide Connection
http://www.ibm.com
Route 100
Somers, NY 10589

ICL Enterprises

Embla
TeamWare
http://www.icl.com
11490 Commerce Park Drive
Reston, VA 22091
714-855-5505

Iconovex

AnchorPage
http://www.iconovex.com
7448 West 78th Street
Bloomington, MN 55439
800-943-0292

InContext Systems

InContext Spider
InContext 2
http://www.incontext.com
4650 N. Port Washington Road
Milwalkee, WI 53212
800-263-0127

Infinite Technologies

Connect2
11433 Cronridge Drive
Owings Mills, MD
410-363-1097

InfoAccess

HTML Transit
Guide Author
http://www.infoaccess.com
2800 156th Avenue SE
Bellevue, WA 98007
800-344-9737

Information Dimensions
Basis
http://www.idi.oclc.org
5080 Tuttle Crossing Blvd.
Dublin, OH 43016-3569

Informix
Illustra
WebDatablade
Universal Server
http://www.informix.com
4100 Bohannon Drive
Menlo Park, CA 94025
415-926-6300

Infrastructures For Information
VISion1-3
990 Hayman Place
Los Altos, CA 94024

Inmagic
DB/Text WebServer
http://www.inmagic.com
800 West Cummings Park
Woburn, MA 01801
617-938-4442

InterCon
InterServer Publisher
http://www.intercon.com/
950 Herdon Parkway
Herdon, VA 22070
703-709-5500

Interleaf
Cyberleaf
http://www.ileaf.com/
Prospect Place 9 Hillside Ave
Waltham, MA 02154
617-290-0710

Internet Factory
Commerce Builder
http://www.aristosoft.com
6654 Koll Center Parkway, Ste. 165
Pleasanton, CA 94566

JSB
MultiView
Internet Jazz
http://www.jsb.com
Whispering Pines Drive, Suite 115
Scotts Valley, CA 95066
408-438-8300

Level\5
Quest
http://www.l5r.com
1335 Gateway Drive, Suite 2005
Melbourne, FL 32901
407-729-6004

Lotus
InterNotes Web Publisher
Lotus Notes
http://www.lotus.com
55 Cambridge Parkway
Cambridge MA 02142

Macromedia
Director
Shockwave
http://www.macromedia.com
600 Townsend St.
San Francisco, CA 94103
415-252-2000

MicroMass Communications

IntelliWeb
http://www.micromass.com
1011 Schaub Dr., Ste. 200
Raleigh, NC 27606
919-851-3182

Microrim

R:WEB
http://www.microrim.com
15395 SE 30th Place
Bellevue, WA 98007
206-649-9500

Microsoft

Internet Information Server
SQL Server
Access
Access Internet Assistant
FrontPage
http://www.microsoft.com
One Microsoft Way
Redmond, WA 98052-6399

net.Genesis

netForm
http://www.netgen.com
68 Rogers Street
Cambridge, MA 02142
617-577-9800

NetCarta

Cyber Pilot Pro
http://www.netcarta.com
5617 Scotts Valley Drive, Suite 100
Scotts Valley, CA 95066
408-461-8920

NetManage

ECCO Pro
ECCO Share
Z-Mail
InPerson
IntraNet Server
IntraNet Forums Server
Chameleon
http://www.netmanage.com
10725 North DeAnza Blvd.
Cupertino, CA 95014
408-973-7171

NetPhonic Communications

Web-On-Call
http://www.netphonic.com
1580 West El Camino Real, Suite 8
Mountain View, CA 94040
415-962-1111

Netscape

servers
CoolTalk
Collabra
Navigator
http://www.netscape.com
501 East Middlefield Road
Mountain View, CA 94043
415-528-2555

NetScheme

NetScheme
http://www.netscheme.com
201 Boston Post Rd., Suite 400
Marlborough, MA 01752
508-480-0877

Network Computing Devices
Xplora NC
WinCenter
http://www.ned.com
101 Rowland Way, Ste. 300
Novato, CA 94945
415-898-8649

Next Software
WebObjects
http://www.next.com
900 Chesapeake Drive
Redwood City, CA 94063
800-879-6398

No Hands Software
Common Ground
http://www.commonground.com
1301 Shoreway Road, Suite 220
Belmont, CA 94002
415-802-5800

Nomad Development
WebDBC
http://www.ndev.com
81 Vine St., Ste. 203
Seattle, WA 98121
206-448-1956

O'Reilly & Associates
WebSite
PolyForm
WebBoard
http://www.website.ora.com
101 Morris St.
Sebastopol, CA 95472
707-829-0515

Object Design
Dbconnect
Object Store
Object Manager
Object Forms
Extended Object Management Suite
http://www.odi.com
25 Mall Road
Burlington, MA 01803-4194
617-674-5000

ON Technology
Common Knowledge
Meeting Maker XP
http://www.on.com
One Cambridge Center
Cambridge, MA 02142-1604
617-692-3106

Open Environment
Mambo
http://www.openenv.com
25 Travis Street
Boston, MA 02134
800-826-1047

Open Market
Web Server
Web Reporter
http://www.openmarket.com
335 Bryant St.
Palo Alto, CA 94301

Open Text
Livelink Internet
Internet Anywhere
http://www.opentext.com
180 Columbia Street West, Suite 2110
Waterloo, Ontario, Canada N2L 3L3
800-507-5777

Oracle
WebServer
Personal Oracle
Oracle 7
PowerBrowser
Power Objects
Universal Server
Designer 2000
http://www.oracle.com/
500 Oracle Parkway
Redwood Shores, CA 94065
415-506-7200

OZ Interactive
Oz Virtual
http://www.oz-inc.com
Reykjavik and San Francisco
213-733-4254

Paracel On-line Systems
Paracel Today
http://www/online.paracel.com
12770 Coit Road, Suite 450
Dallas, TX 75251
214-789-1990

ParcPlace Digitalk
Visual Wave
http://www.parcplace.com
999 E. Arques Avenue
Sunnyvale, CA 94086-4593
408-481-9090

Passage Systems
PassagePro
PassageHub
http://www.passage.com
10596 N. Tantau Ave.
Cupertino, CA 95014

Personal Library Software
PLWeb
http://www.pls.com
2400 Research Blvd., Suite 350
Rockville, MD 20850-3243
301-990-1155

Process Software
Purveyor
http://www.process.com
959 Concord Street
Framingham, MA 01701-4682
800-722-7770

QUALCOMM
Eudora
http://www.qualcomm.com
6455 Lusk Boulevard
San Diego, CA 92121-2779
619-658-5806

Quarterdeck
HiJaak Graphics Suite
Iware Internet Suite
WebAuthor
WebSTAR
WebTalk
TALKShow
http://www.quarterdeck.com
13160 Mindanao Way
Marina Del Rey, CA 90292
800-828-8088

Rad - Nct
WebShare
http://www.radnet.com
58 Charles Street
Cambridge, MA 02141

Rad Media
Power Media
http://www.radmedia.com
745 Emerson St.
Palo Alto, CA 94301
415-617-9430

Raima
Velocis Web Server Gateway
http://www.raima.com
1605 NW Sammamish Rd., Suite 200
Issaquah, WA 98027
206-557-0200

RealAudio
Real Audio
http://www.realaudio.com
616 First Ave., Suite 701
Seattle, WA 98104
800-230-5975

Revnet Systems
groupMaster
http://www.revnet.com
4835 University Sq., Suite 2
Huntsville, AL 35816
205-721-1420

Shelby Group
TILE & Tgate
http://www.shelby.com
4618 Maple Avenue
Bethesda, MD 20814
301-718-7840

Ski Soft
Web Publisher
http://www.skisoft.com
587 Tremont Street
Boston, MA 02118
617-262-2044

SoftArc
First Class
http://www.softarc.com
1902 Ridge Road
West Seneca, NY 14224
800-763-8272

SoftQuad
HotMetal PRO
Panorama Pro
http://www.sq.com
56 Aberfoyle Crescent
Toronto, Ontario M8X2W4
416-239-4801

Software Engines
Software Engine
http://www.engine.com
129 Washington Street
Hoboken, NJ 07030
201-963-7731

Software Publishing
WebShow
http://www.spco.com
111 N. Market Street
San Jose, CA 95113
800-336-8360

Software.com

Post.Office
http://www.software.com
805-882-2470

Spider Technologies

NetDynamics
http://www.netdynamics.com
1054 Elwell Court
Palo Alto, CA 94303
415-944-7400

Spry

Spry Web Server
Spry Safety Web Server
Internet Office
http://www.spry.com
3535 128th Ave. SE
Bellevue, WA 98006
206-957-8000

Sun Microsystems

Java
JDBC
http://www.sun.com
2550 Garcia Avenue
Mountain View, CA 94043
415-960-1300

Sybase

Web.sql
SQL Anywhere
SQL Server 11 for Windows NT
http://www.sybase.com
6475 Christie Avenue
Emeryvilloe, CA 94608
510-922-3500

Symantec

Delrina CommSuite 95
http://www.delrina.com
10201 Torre Ave.
Cupertino
800-441-7234

Telos

NetSeer
NetFlow
http://www.telos.com
460 Herndon Parkway
Herndon, VA 22070-5201
800-944-0018

Third Planet Publishing

Digiphone
http://www.planeteers.com
17770 Preston Road
Dallas, TX 75252
214-713-2607

Thuridion

Crew
http://www.thuridion.com
269 Mt. Hermon Road Suite 200
Scotts Valley, CA 95066-4029
408-439-9800

Tippecanoe Systems

Tecumseh
http://www.tippecanoe.com
5674 Stoneridge Drive, Suite 119
Pleasanton, CA 94588
510-416-8510

Trend Micro

E-mail Virus Wall
http://www.trendmicro.com
20245 Stevens Creek Blvd.
Cupertino, CA 95014
800-228-5651

Tympani Development

Net Attache
http://www.tympani.com
1307 South Mary Avenue, Suite 102
Sunnyvale, CA 94087
408-735-9555

United States Postal Service

Postal ECS
http://www/usps.gov
475 L'Enfant Plaza SW, Room 5610
Washington, DC 20260-2425
202-268-3435

VDOnet

VDO
http://www.vdolive.com
4009 Miranda Avenue, Suite 250
Palo Alto, CA 94304
415-864-7700

Verimation

Memo
50 Tice Blvd.
Woodcliff Lake, NJ 07675
800-967-6366

Verity

topicWeb Organizer
topicTeam
topicNewscast
Topic Agent Server
Topic Internet Server
Topic Enterprise Server
http://www.verity.com
1550 Plymouth Street
Mountain View, CA 94043
415-960-7600

Vocaltec

Internet Phone
http://vocaltec.com
35 Industrial Parkway
Northvale, NJ 07647
201-768-9400

Voxware

Tool/Vox RT
http://www.voxware.com
172 Tamarack Circle
Skillman, NJ 08558
609-497-1212

WebFlow

WebFlow
http://www.webflow.com
3160 De La Cruz Boulevard #206
Santa Clara, CA 95054
415-335-8640

Xing Technology

Xing MPEG Encoder
Xing MPEG Player
SteamWorks Player
Steamworks Server
Steamworks Transmitter
http://www.steamworks.com
1540 West Branch Street
Arroyo Grande, CA 93420
805-473-0145

Glossary

a-mail Electronic mail that uses audio instead of text to deliver its message.

Access Control List A list of user IDs and other relevant information used for controling access to computer information. Lotus Notes uses an ACL to manage access to databases, documents, and fields.

ACL See Access Control List.

ActiveX A set of technologies introduced by Microsoft that are used to create dynamic content for the Web. ActiveX is used to put user controls within a Web document, allow Web documents to access other programs on the server, and more.

American Standard Code for Information Interchange The code built-in to most personal computers used to represent characters for text as well as communication and control of some peripherals.

API See Application Program Interface.

Application Program Interface A language used by an application to communicate with another program that interacts with the application by sharing data.

ARPAnet The precursor to the Internet built in 1969 under the direction of the Defense Advanced Research Projects Administration.

ASCII See American Standard Code for Information Interchange.

attachment A binary file (e.g., Microsoft Word) sent with an email message. Internet email attachments are specially encoded so that messages are able to pass through the standard SMTP mail system which was designed to handle ASCII text only.

authentication A common security mechanism that requires a person attempting to access a computer system to identify themselves with a user ID and to know some privileged information associated with that user ID, such as a password.

authoring The process of document creation.

auto-responder A feature of an email server that automatically returns a standard message to email requests sent to the server. A business (XYZ) might set up an auto-responder to send out company information when a customer sent email to info@xyz.com.

bandwidth The capacity of a communications wire or computer channel to deliver information. The higher the bandwidth, the more information can be transmitted in a given time. Often expressed in bits per second.

binary file A computer file that holds binary numbers. Binary numbers use all 8 bits of a standard byte. In contrast, ASCII characters use only 7 of the bits to represent information. Especially significant when deciding how to transfer the file over a network.

Binary Large Object A field in a database used to store audio, video, or other multimedia objects in a database management system.

Blob See Binary Large Object.

bridge A connector between two segments of a LAN. Bridges are used to make network segments smaller and to thereby improve network performance.

browser A software tool used to access and view documents on the Web. Examples are Netscape's Navigator and Microsoft's Internet Explorer.

certificate An indentifying marker in a Lotus Notes user.id file which is unique to the issuing family of Notes servers. Allows the owner of the user.id file to be granted access to all servers with similar certificate histories.

CGI See Common Gateway Interface.

client The computer in a client/server system which requests services from the server. For example, a desktop PC running a Web browser is a client which requests files for download from a Web server.

comma delimited A method of laying out records, such as those in a database, so that each data field is separated with a comma. Useful for moving data from one database application to another.

Common Gateway Interface A standard for the creations of scripts which allow user interaction over the Web. CGI scripts run on a Web server and perform actions based upon input from a client or browser.

conversion Translating a text file from one format to another format. For example, converting a Word for Windows document to an HTML document.

cross-platform Software which is capable of running on multiple computer platforms. For example, Lotus Notes is available in Mac, PC, Unix, and OS/2 versions, each of which can communicate with the other.

daemon A program on Unix which performs similar to a server. Runs in the background at all times so that it can provide services upon demand.

digital signature A method of assuring that the origin of a message sent over a network is the authentic sender.

DNS

See Domain Name Service.

DocLinks Hypertext links between documents in Lotus Notes. Can connect documents in the same database, or in separate databases on different Notes servers.

domain name A word based TCP/IP address, such as www.jiminy.com. Designed to be easier to understand and remember than IP addresses.

Domain Name Service TCP/IP protocol used to translate domain name addressess (e.g., www.jiminy.org) into IP addresses (e.g. 122.132.24.13) that are useable by TCP/IP programs.

email Electronic mail. A system used for the transmission of correspondence (letters, memos, etc.) over a computer network.

encapsulation The process by which protocols attach information to a data packet before transmission over a network.

encryption A security method which encodes data before transmission over a network so that intercepted packets cannot be read without a decryption key.

Ethernet A connection method for local area networks which can carry multiple protocols at up to 100 Mbits per second. Can use twisted pair, coaxial cable, or optical fiber.

file server A computer on a LAN which users may connect to over the network in order to access and store files, run software, or access certain groupware files.

File Transfer Protocol FTP is the protocol used to transfer files from one computer to another over a TCP/IP network. Includes user commands for moving through directory structures of remote computers and moving or copying files.

firewall A way of preventing unauthorized access to intranet which is connected to the Internet. Typically works by disallowing some or all accesses by computers with external IP addresses.

flat-file A one-dimensional data file consisting of rows (records) and columns (fields).

folder A term used interchangeably with the word directory. A folder is a place to store files or subfolders (sub-directories). Many graphical interfaces use a representation of a traditional paper folder to represent folders or directories.

FTP See File Transfer Protocol.

gateway A computer that connects dissimilar networks to allow communication between them by converting the different protocols back an forth.

GIF See Graphics Interchange Format.

Gopher A protocol and software tool developed at the University of Minnesota designed to ease navigation of the Internet. Predates the Web. Many valuable Internet resources are still on Gopher systems, even though it lacks hypermedia and graphics.

Graphics Interchange Format A graphics file format which is one of the standard formats used by browsers on the Web.

groupware Software specially designed to help groups work together more effectively. Typically includes email, document sharing, workflow, calendaring and scheduling, and conferencing.

header The information attached to the beginning of a data packet by each protocol as it is passed from one protocol layer to another.

home page A Web document that serves as the primary starting point for a comprehensive Web site.

HTML See Hypertext Markup Language.

HTTP See Hypertext Transfer Protocol.

hyperlink A link in a hypertext document to another document or another part of the same document.

hypermedia Enables a hyperlink from any media to any other media.

hypertext Enables a hyperlink from a word or phrase to another word, phrase, or block of text.

Hypertext Markup Language The standard set of markups used to mark up documents for display by a Web browser.

Hypertext Transfer Protocol The protocol used to transfer files over the Web.

Integrated Services Digital Network A means of attaching a computer to a network at a much higher bandwidth than is possible with a modem but, nonetheless, over a regular telephone line.

interactivity The process of giving a computer user a choice thereby enabling him or her to interact with the digital presentation.

Internet Protocol The protocol in the TCP/IP family which is in charge of routing data packets from one computer to another over the network.

Internet Service Provider A service which provides businesses and private citizens with access to the Internet via modem, ISDN, or other connection methods for a fee.

InterNIC The agency charged with assigning domain names and IP addresses for the Internet.

intranet An internal or private TCP/IP network.

IP See Internet Protocol.

IP address The numeric identifier used by the TCP/IP suite of protocols to assign unique addresses to every computer on the network. Internet IP addresses are assigned by InterNIC.

ISDN See Integrated Services Digital Network.

ISP See Internet Service Provider.

Java A programming language developed by Sun Microsystems. Can be used to write applications and applets which run within a Web browser.

JavaScript A scripting language used to create enhanced interactivity in documents on the Web. Can be used alone, or in combination with Java applets.

Joint Photographic Experts Group A file format which is one of the standards used by Web browsers for the display of images within Web documents. Can achieve high compression rates for image files. Useful for transfer of photos over a network.

JPEG See Joint Photographic Experts Group.

LAN See Local Area Network.

Listserv One of the original mailing list programs. It's now a generic name for mailing list programs.

Local Area Network A computer network which allows computers within a relatively small geographic area (e.g., inside a building) to communicate.

Lotus Notes The industry standard for groupware products. Includes email, databases, replication, application development, and Web capabilities.

Mail Application Programming Interface A standard Microsoft communication protocol used for communication between 32-bit Windows programs.

mailing list A program which automatically forwards email messages sent ot it to everyone on a mailing list.

MAPI See Mail Application Programming Interface.

MIME See Multipurpose Internet Mail Extensions

Multipurpose Internet Mail Extensions Extension to mail protocol which enables an email message to carry a binary or text file(s).

network A group of computers connected together for the purposes of enabling communication among them.

network computer A computer without storage capability which receives its programming resources from a network.

Network News Transport Protocol The Internet communication protocol for Usenet. Can be used privately.

newsgroups Conferences on Usenet.

NNTP See Network News Transport Protocol.

o-mail Omni-mail, a combination of email, audio mail, and video mail.

object A portion of code with its own data which can communicate with other objects in an object-oriented programming environment.

object-oriented database A database which can store objects. For the purposes of this definition, objects can be either binary files or text files.

object-oriented programming A programming langauage which uses objects to construct an application.

ODBC See Open Database Connectivity.

online service One of the national online services such as Compuserve or America Online.

Open Database Connectivity A standard Microsoft programming interface which provides a language for Windows applications to access databases on a network.

open standards Programming standards that are published and open to all software developers to use.

packet A segment of digital information that moves across a packet-switched network.

packet piggybacking Running two network protocols simultaneously. Because TCP/IP can coexist with another network protocol, having two network protocols running at the same time is not unusual.

peer-to-peer A network without a server. Each computer on the network is a peer of the others.

platform The infrastructure for programming created by an operating system. The operating system or operating environment is said to be a platform.

plug-in A browser API which enables other programs to connect and provide additionally functionality to the browser.

Point of Presence An access phone number for an ISP.

Point-to-Point Protocol A protocol that enables dial-up access to the Internet and is more advanced than SLIP.

POP See Point of Presence.

PPP See Point-to-Point Protocol.

protocol A program providing specific communications capability over a network that has come to be an accepted standard.

real-time You see it as it happens.

relational database A method of database organization that builds a data structure by linking tables with common columns (fields).

replication The process of making an exact copy of a database including its data.

router A device that routes packets across a network.

Serial Line IP The dial-up protocol for the Internet that preceded PPP.

server A software server is a program that serves documents, graphics, email messages, and other files to clients that request such files.

SGML See Standard Generalized Markup Language.

shrink-wrapped Programs in a shrinkwrapped which are sold at retail.

Simple Mail Transfer Protocol An email protocol for TCP/IP networks.

SLIP See Serial Line IP.

SMTP See Simple Mail Transfer Protocol.

snail mail US Postal Service.

SQL See Structured Query Language.

Standard Generalized Markup Language A standard for setting the formatting for a text document.

streaming The process of playing a media file as it is downloaded such as Real Audio, an audio file which begins to play as soon as downloading begins after being accessed over a network by a browser..

Structured Query Language A standard language used to access and process the data in a database application.

subfolder A folder (directory) lower on the folder tree than another folder.

TAPI See Telephony Applications Programming Interface.

TCP/IP See Transmission Control Protocol/Internet Protocol.

Telephony Applications Programming Interface A standard Microsoft protocol which enables multiple Windows programs to use the same modem.

Telnet A terminal emulation protocol used on the Internet which enables one computer to use another computer.

template A programming device which provides structure for variable data.

text search A search through text documents or other text data which locates the key words inputted by the user.

thread A topic which is the subject of an exchange or posting of messages.

Transmission Control Protocol/Internet Protocol The network protocol for the Internet.

twisted pair The standard thin wiring (two wires twisted together) used for a phone line.

Uniform Resource Locator An address on the Internet.

Unix An operating system traditionally used for the Internet. It enables multitasking and multiple users.

URL See Uniform Resource Locator.

Usenet A massive conferencing system (bulletin board) on the Internet providing public access.

v-mail Video mail.

Value-Added Network A network service that provides something special above and beyond the average.

VAN See Value-Added Network.

Virtual Reality Modeling Language A programming enabling 3-D graphics on the Internet.

VRML See Virtual Reality Modeling Language.

WAN See Wide Area Network.

Web See World Wide Web.

Web server A software server that serves up Web documents.

Wide Area Network A network that spans an extended geographical area such as over multiple cities.

World Wide Web An Internet publishing system based on the HTTP protocol.

Bibliography

Business Engineering with Object Technology. David A. Taylor, John Wiley & Sons, New York, 1995.

Computer Telephony. Ed Tittel and Dawn Rader, AP Professional, Boston, 1996.

Creating Cool Web Databases. Joseph T. Sinclair and Carol McCullough, IDG Books, Foster City, 1997.

Designing Groupware. Geoffrey E. Bock and Dacid A. Marca, McGraw-Hill, NY, 1995.

Essential Client/Server Survival Guide. Robert Orfali, Dan Harkey, and Jeri Edwards, John Wiley & Sons, NY, 1994.

Getting Connected. Kevin Dowd, O'Reilly & Associates, Sebastopol, 1996.

Getting Started In A New Medium—Designing For The Web. Jennifer Niederst with Edie Freedman, O'Reilly & Associates, Sebastopol, CA, 1996.

How to Plan, Develop, and Implement Lotus Notes in Your Organization. Mike Falkner, John Wiley & Sons, NY, 1996

Hybrid HTML Design, A Multibrowser HTML Reference. Janine Warner, New Riders, Indianapolis, 1996.

Introduction to Groupware, Workflow, and Workgroup Computing. Setrag Khoshafian and Marek Buckiewicz, John Wiley & Sons, NY, 1995.

Managing Internet Information Services. Cricket Liu, Jerry Peek, Russ Jones, Bryan Buus, Adria Nye, O'Reilly & Associates, Sebastopol, CA, 1994.

Marketing on the Internet. Michael Mathiesen, Maximum Press, Gulf Breeze, FL, 1995.

Multimedia - Making It Work, Second Edition. Tay Vaughn, Osborne McGraw-Hill, Berkeley, 1994.

Network and Internet Security. Vijay Ahuja, AP Professional, Boston, 1996.

Object-Oriented Technology: A Manager's Guide. David A. Taylor, Addison-Wesley Publishing, NY, 1990.

Publish It on the Web. Bryan Pfaffenberger, AP Professional, Boston, 1996.

SGML Handbook. AP Professional, Boston, 1996.

SQL Self-Teaching Guide. Peter Stephenson and Glenn Hartwig, John Wiley & Sons, NY, 1992.

TCP/IP for Everyone. Peter Loshin, AP Professional, Boston, 1995.

TCP/IP Unleashed. Timothy Parker, Bret Curran, Salim M. Douba, James Edwards, Jason Garms, Chris Negus, Sams Publishing, Indianapolis, 1996.

The Essential Distributed Objects Survival Guide. Robert Orfali, Dan Harkey, and Jeri Edwards, John Wiley & Sons , NY, 1996.

The Internet Complete Reference, Second Editon. Harley Hahn, Osborne McGraw-Hill, Berkeley, 1996.

The World Wide Web Complete Reference. Rick Stout, Osborne McGraw-Hill, Berkeley, 1996.

Using Email Effectively. Linda Lamb and Jerry Peek, O'Reilly & Associates, Sebastopol, CA, 1995.

Using Novell GroupWise 4. Bill Bruck, Que, Indianapolis, 1994.

Web publisher's design guide for Windows. Mary Jo Fahey and Jeffrey W. Brown, Coriolis Group Books, Scottsdale, 1995.

Index

A

B

C

E

J

K

L

M

Q

W